Endorsements for the Second Edition

"As a CEO, executive coach, author, and adjunct professor of leadership at NYU and Columbia, I am obsessed with leadership books and have read, literally, hundreds of them over the past twenty-five years. And I can truthfully state that Gary DePaul's brilliant *Nine Practices of 21st Century Leadership* is one of the best and most important books on the topic I've ever read. Both scholarly and practical, this information-packed and inspirational guidebook will appeal to – and benefit – business professionals, academics, and students alike. Meticulously researched and masterfully written, DePaul references hundreds of different resources to help define, describe, and demystify what leadership is. And – of equal importance – what it is not. Through his innovative "Nine Practices" framework, as well as the numerous additional models, metaphors, processes, roadmaps, quotes, and sources he provides along the way, this book is a masterclass on the topic of leadership, and one that will help anyone, at any level, to become a more educated, effective, and inspiring leader."

Todd Cherches
CEO of BigBlueGumball
Author of *VisuaLeadership: Leveraging the Power of Visual Thinking in Leadership and in Life*

"In *Nine Practices of 21st Century Leadership*, Gary DePaul provides a masterfully comprehensive resource for leaders. Gary provides specific examples and recommended actions that will encourage leaders at all levels to try new practices and expand their leadership capabilities."

Colonel Kim Campbell, USAF, Retired
Managing Director, Victory Strategies
Co-author of *Aiming Higher: A Journey Through Military Aviation Leadership*

"Dr. Gary DePaul has provided a smart, concise, user-friendly manual for 21st Century Leadership. I gained valuable insights in these pages – both cautionary (for example, the traditional leadership assumptions) and endorsed (for example the principles of leadership).

"From learning about the brain and the systems it uses to make decisions (introducing us to the reality of unconscious bias) to the beliefs that guide the way we acknowledge others and work together, Gary provides a roadmap for effective leadership that centers on people and relationships.

"As a speaker, facilitator, and consultant in the field of Equity, Diversity, and Inclusion, I appreciate that the awareness and application of the information presented in these pages (and how it is presented) can help support a strong commitment to EDI.

"As Gary shares, 21st leadership focuses on the action, not the role. The way he has laid out and explained the nine practices (along with tools, techniques, resources, guidelines, "to-do's" and "a word of caution"!) allows for a practical and well-rounded understanding designed to make our actions not only more effective, but more *meaningful* - which is what creating inclusive and equitable spaces for our colleagues and teams is all about."

Annemarie Shrouder
Speaker, Facilitator, & Consultant in EDI

"Gary DePaul's *Nine Practices of 21st Century Leadership* is authentic and practical in its applicability of leadership principles. His deliberate approach provides profound insight into leadership practices past the well-worn theories found in other books. Gary brings depth to employing effective leadership practices within real world environments. He demonstrates how 21st century qualities for impactful leadership incorporates empathy, storytelling, and integrity. Gary debunks the leadership notion of command and control in favor for a human approach of engage and embrace. This is one, and possibly only, leadership book you'll need in your library."

Ajay M. Pangarkar, CTDP, FCPA, FCMA
CEO & Partner, CentralKnowledge.com and LRNOnline.com
Award-winning Performance Strategist and Author,
The Trainer's Balanced Scorecard

"If you are looking for a foundational reference to hone your leadership skills Dr. DePaul has created that reference. One of the biggest challenges for a leader is ensuring that members of the workforce are engaged, satisfied, and productive. The Nine Practices of 21st Century Leadership guides the readers to a clear understanding of creating the blueprint of taking care of their most precious resource, the only resource inside an organization that can increase in value. When the workforce is successful, the leader and the organization are successful."

Chris Cebollero
President/CEO of Cebollero & Associates
Author of *Ultimate Leadership: 10 Rules for Success*

Endorsements for the First Edition

"Gary DePaul's comprehensive *Nine Practices of 21st Century Leadership* makes sense of the vast sea of leadership books. Written with both managers and scholars in mind, DePaul's study situates—and demystifies—the language of leadership in systems thinking. In 15 well-organized and lucidly written chapters, the author builds a series of metaphors to explain the practices of expert managers—analyzing, detecting, guiding, nurturing and more. This book will change your thinking about leadership."

Edwin Battistella, PhD
Author of Sorry about That: The Language of Public Apology

"Gary has saved anyone with an interest in the topic of leadership a tremendous amount of legwork and created an incredible resource for leadership growth. The meta-analysis approach allows us to readily see patterns among leadership thought leaders and distills them into nine essential 21st Century leadership practices. Most importantly, the rich assortment of examples, practices, and recommended actions provided are a tremendous asset to our development and growth as leaders. A note of caution: be prepared to see yourself and your own leadership assumptions and practices challenged (in a good way)."

Rick Rummler, President
The Rummler Group
Co-author of White Space Revisited: Creating Value through Process

"In *Nine Practices of 21st Century Leadership*, Gary DePaul weaves together and builds on some of the best current writers and thinkers on leadership. The Nine Practices – leadership in action – are challenging, but Dr. DePaul makes them eminently approachable. Trying even a few of the practices can strengthen your leadership qualities, capabilities, and behaviors. There is insight and practical advice for all levels of an organization, from individual contributors to the CEO."

Don Kirkey, Ed.D.
Director, Leadership Development
Lowe's Companies, Inc.

"Transitioning from traditional to 21st Century Leadership is a must. This book gives you the tools to achieve such a goal by analyzing, diagnosing, directing, nurturing, exposing, facing, developing, and communicating the elements that enhance the mental and moral qualities, as well as the capabilities and behaviors. Practicing this leadership approach ultimately improves personal and team performance, especially when Command and Control is shifted from a traditional leader to a shared team function."

Joel Rodriguez, Ed.D.
Superintendent, Chapel Operations
US Air National Guard

"All too often people are put into supervisor, manager, or leader positions because they are excellent engineers, accountants, or sales people. Most are not prepared for those positions in any systematic way. This book provides a roadmap for developing leadership practices within seven suggested underlying principles. The grids for aligning practices with the suggested principles and beliefs will be of particular value to the newly promoted, inexperienced manager or leader."

Margo Murray, MBA, CPT, C-EI
President & Chief Operating Officer
MMHA The Managers' Mentors, Inc.

"Gary has done an excellent job of reframing leadership with his emphasis on practices versus traits or qualities. Gary's approach provides a deeper understanding of what constitutes leadership compared to what has been done in the past. The book will be an invaluable resource. Every learning and human resource professional can use this book to better ensure their programs focus on practices that contribute to sustainable gains in human capital."

Judith A. Hale, Ph.D., CPT
CEO, The Institute for Performance Improvement, L3C
Author of The Performance Consultant's Fieldbook and
Performance-Based Certification

"In *Nine Practices of 21st Century Leadership,* Gary DePaul provides a Performance Improvement view of leadership practices. Section I demystifies leadership. Section II introduces the nine practices of leadership from a performance improvement viewpoint. These include: focus on results, take a systematic approach, add value, and partner. Throughout, Gary draws on his experiences as a Performance Improvement professional. A good choice to add to your Performance Improvement library."

Dr. Roger M. Addison, CPT
Chief Performance Officer, Addison Consulting
Co-author of Performance Architecture

"*Nine Practices of 21st Century Leadership* removes the mystery and provides much needed shortcuts to deciphering the wide range of current leadership techniques and philosophies. It is a fantastic tool to help both new and successful leaders build and expand their repertoire and target the areas they want to explore further. A must read, and the foundation of every professional library, Dr. DePaul provides a fantastic starting point with lots of helpful tips and best practices."

Matt Peters, MBA, CPT
Director, Talent Management
Washington Metropolitan Area Transit Authority (WMATA)

"In my work with the TLS Continuum as discussed in our Achieving HR Excellence through Six Sigma, we discuss the need to convert managers into leaders as a critical requirement to implement the procedures we discuss. Gary DePaul's new book provides a precise roadmap for that journey which can be followed by anyone in a leadership role."

Daniel T. Bloom SPHR, Six Sigma Black Belt, SCRP
CEO, Daniel Bloom and Associates, Inc.
Author of Achieving HR Excellence through Six Sigma

"Gary DePaul does a masterful job of highlighting best practices for those interested in boosting their leadership skills. The chapter, Facing the Unknown Like Lions, is a great reminder of the importance of staying in the moment and listening to your mind and heart before taking action."

Roberta Matuson, The Talent Maximizer®
Matuson Consulting
Author of Talent Magnetism *and* Suddenly in Charge

"In his new book, Dr. DePaul provides a helpful combination of tactics, tools, and resources for leaders at every level. It's a handy, accessible, and easy-to-use guide for everyone interested in expanding his or her leadership capabilities."

Jim Hill, CEO
Proofpoint Systems

Nine Practices of 21st Century Leadership

Near the end of the 20th Century, the leadership concept radically evolved away from the traditional concept of accomplishing work through others. Unfortunately, too many professionals unconsciously still have faulty traditional assumptions that can get them, their teams, and their organizations in trouble.

The author has researched the evolution of leadership and summarizes seven contemporary principles, twenty-six underlying leadership beliefs, and nine crucial practices of 21st Century Leadership. While too many leadership books focus on qualities, DePaul explains specific behaviors for practicing leadership.

The second edition includes new research about leadership and leadership development. With the pandemic, organizations have had to rely more on effective leadership to build high-performing teams, often at a distance. Training departments have had to radically update how they develop employees at all levels, and executive coaches have transitioned to virtual client support. With all these environmental changes as well as new social pressures on organizations to embrace diversity, equity, and inclusion, organizations need to change how they lead and avoid allowing their culture to develop by chance.

Nine Practices of 21st Century Leadership

A Guide for Inspiring Creativity, Innovation, and Engagement, 2nd Edition

Gary A. DePaul, PhD, CPT

Second Edition Foreword by L. David Marquet
Author of *Turn the Ship Around!* and *Leadership Is Language*

First Edition Foreword by Edward G. Muzio
Author of *Iterate, Make Work Great,* and *Four Secrets to Liking Your Work*

Routledge
Taylor & Francis Group
A PRODUCTIVITY PRESS BOOK

First published 2023
by Routledge
605 Third Avenue, New York, NY 10158

and by Routledge
2 Park Square, Milton Park, Abingdon, Oxon, OX14 4RN

Routledge is an imprint of the Taylor & Francis Group, an informa business

ISBN: 978-1-032-22634-7 (hbk)
ISBN: 978-1-032-22633-0 (pbk)
ISBN: 978-1-003-27344-8 (ebk)

DOI: 10.4324/9781003273448

Typeset in Garamond
by KnowledgeWorks Global Ltd.

To the stewards and members of the
International Society for Performance Improvement
who continue to guide and inspire me.

Contents

Foreword, Second Edition xxi

Foreword, First Edition xxv

Preface, Second Edition.. xxix

Preface, First Edition.. xxxiii

SECTION I   DEMYSTIFYING 21ST CENTURY LEADERSHIP

1   Clarifying Why Leadership Is Confusing 3

Introduction...3

Reason 1: Leadership Is Like a Role but Different................................4

    Defining "Role"..4

    Leadership Differs from a Role..6

    Does "Leadership" Include a Set of Roles or Qualities?....................7

    Conclusion..7

Reason 2: Leadership Is More than a Set of Qualities............................8

    Many Authors Explain Leadership in Terms of Qualities....................8

    Leadership Qualities Are Necessary but Not Sufficient....................8

    Conclusion...10

Reason 3: Leadership Is Like a Skill but Different..............................10

    Leadership Is Like a Skill...10

    Leadership Is More than a Skill..12

    Conclusion...12

Reason 4: Some Leadership Theories Overlap with
Leadership Styles..12

    Leadership Theories Explain Leadership Behaviors.........................12

    Leadership Theories Referenced as Leadership Styles......................12

    Conclusion...12

Reason 5: Leadership Is Like Management, but Different..........................13

Introduction...13
Management Defined..14
Management Categories..14
    Organization Managers..15
    Process Managers...15
    Project Managers...15
    Managers of People..15
Three Performance Needs..16
Management and Leadership Can Accomplish the Same Tasks..........17
Leadership Differs from Management....................................17
Conclusion..17
Reason 6: The Meaning of Leadership Is Changing.............................19
Summary...20

2 Defining 21st Century Leadership...23
Introduction...23
Definition of 21st Century Leadership and Desired Results....................24
Desired Results...26
    Introduction..26
    Immediate Results...27
        Fulfilled Needs..27
        Removed or Reduced Performance Barriers.......................29
        Improved Performance...30
    Short and Long-Term Results..30
        Cultural Results...30
        Partnership Results...32
        Individual Growth Results..32
    Business Results...33
    Societal Results...35
    Conclusion...35
Maturing Mental and Moral Qualities, Capabilities, and Behaviors........35
    Maturing Mental Qualities..36
    Maturing Moral Qualities...36
    Maturing Capabilities...37
    Maturing Behaviors...37
Bidirectional..37
Seven Principles, Twenty-Six Beliefs, and Nine Practices....................38
Summary: What to Do...39

3 Revealing Traditional Leadership and Assumptions 41
Introduction...41
   Traditional Leadership Definition 41
   Traditional Leadership Includes Accidental Leaders 41
   The Extreme Case of Traditional Leadership.......................................42
   Why Anyone Would Practice Traditional Leadership 42
   Traditional Leadership Assumptions..43
Assumption 1: Leaders Need Authority...43
   Rationale 43
   Why the Leaders Need Authority Assumption Is Wrong....................45
Assumption 2: Leaders Are Heroes Who Leave a Legacy 45
Assumption 3: Intimacy Weakens Leadership 47
Assumption 4: Giving Away Power Weakens Leadership 48
Assumption 5: Only One Person—Typically a Manager—Functions
as the Leader..48
Assumption 6: The Leader Is the Smartest 49
Assumption 7: Team Members Are the Cause of Unproductivity...........50
Assumption 8: Team Members Cannot Be Trusted 51
Assumption 9: Team Members Are Less Important than Revenue,
Profit, Operational Costs, and Leaders..52
Assumption 10: Talking Is More Important than Listening....................53
Assumption 11: Recognition Is a Formal Process 54
Assumption 12: Leadership Requires Little or No Training....................54
Assumption 13: Leaders Know How Effective Their Leadership Is........55
Summary: What to Do 56

**4 Explaining 21st Century Leadership Principles
and Beliefs 57**
Introduction: Because of the Environment and Our Brains, We
Need Guiding Principles...58
Seven Leadership Principles and Beliefs..60
Principle 1: Believe in Others..60
   How Growth and Fixed Mindsets Affect Believing in Others 62
      Mindsets..62
      Fixed Mindset...62
      Growth Mindset 63
      People Can Shift Mindsets 64
      How Fixed and Growth Mindsets Affect Believing in Others 64

Belief 1: Intelligence Isn't Static and Can Be
Developed Continuously..64
Belief 2: Everyone Can Practice Leadership Regardless of Role..........65
Principle 2: Connect with Others...65
Psychological Safety...66
Ingroup and Outgroup..66
Belief 3: Being Vulnerable and Getting to Know Others
Builds Trust...68
Without Trust, It Is Difficult to Maintain Relationships...................69
Getting to Know Others Builds Trust...69
Belief 4: Sharing Your Mistakes Builds Credibility.............................70
Belief 5: Celebrations Build Community, Connect Events to
Values, Renew Commitment, Promote Social Support, and
Improve Everyone's Well-Being..70
Principle 3: Put Others First...71
Belief 6: Giving Credit for Accomplishments to Others Is More
Important than Taking Credit..71
Belief 7: Employees Serve Customers Before
Serving Management..72
Belief 8: When Outcomes Are Disappointing,
Accepting Responsibility but Never Blaming Is
Critical for Personal Accountability...73
Belief 9: Leadership Is Action That Focuses on Others and Not
the Actor..74
Belief 10: Volunteering Time, Energy, Resources,
Ego, and Previous Priorities to Help Others Inspires
Loyalty and Commitment..74
Principle 4: Give Up Control..76
Belief 11: Control Erodes Relationships...76
Belief 12: Leading Well Is about Empowering Others.........................77
Belief 13: By Making Yourself Dispensable, You Make
Yourself Indispensable...78
Belief 14: Command and Control Is a Shared Responsibility..............79
Principle 5: Encourage Growth..80
Belief 15: Helping Others Figure Out Their Development
Enhances Their Ability to Contribute..80
Belief 16: Encouraging People to Grow and Leave Their Role
Contributes to Organizational Growth...80

Belief 17: Allowing Teams to Make Mistakes Enables
Them to Be Open with Their Mistakes and Learn
from the Experience 81
Belief 18: If You Change the Conditions in Which Others
Operate, You Can Change Their Behaviors 82
Principle 6: Collaborate with Others 82
Belief 19: Organizational Charts Limit Thinking 82
Belief 20: Considering Problems from a Systemic Perspective
Minimizes Using Blame 84
Belief 21: Leadership Doesn't Reside with One Person 85
Belief 22: Influence Comes from All Directions 85
Belief 23: Leadership Practices Work the Same with
All Populations Including Peers, Customers,
Supervisors, and Subordinates 86
Principle 7: Develop Leadership Practices Continuously 86
Belief 24: To Become Fluent in Leadership, You Need to Practice
Leadership Regularly and Monitor Your Effectiveness 87
Knowledge 87
Conformational and Corrective Feedback 87
Belief 25: Knowing Everything about Leadership Isn't Enough 88
Belief 26: Leadership Involves Helping Others Learn Leadership 89
Summary 89

SECTION II IMPROVING PERFORMANCE WITH SYSTEMIC THINKING

5 Practice 1: Analyzing Like Detectives 95
Introduction: Importance and Benefits of Analyzing
Like Detectives 95
Characteristics of Analyzing Like Detectives 97
Rummler's Fundamental Laws of Organizational Systems 98
Law 1: Understanding Performance Requires Documenting
the Inputs, Processes, Outputs, and Customers That
Constitute a Business 99
Law 2: Organization Systems Adapt or Die 99
Law 3: When One Component of an Organization System
Optimizes, the Organization Often Suboptimizes 99
Law 4: Pulling Any Lever in the System Will Have an Effect on
Other Parts of the System 100

Law 5: An Organization Behaves as a System, Regardless of
Whether It Is Being Managed as a System 100
Law 6: If You Pit a Good Performer against a Bad System, the
System Will Win Almost Every Time 100
Conclusion 101
Anatomy of Performance and the Human Performance System 101
Introduction 101
Anatomy of Performance of Organizations (Organization Level) 102
The Human Performance System (Performer and Process Levels) 105
Identifying Trouble Spots in the Human Performance System 106
Conclusion 108
The Performance Chain Model and the Six Boxes® Model 108
Introduction 108
Performance Chain Overview 109
Six Boxes® Model Overview 110
Common Mistakes with Influencing Behaviors 111
Mistake 1: Attempt to Influence without Focusing on the
Valuable Accomplishments Needed to Support Desired
Business Results 111
Mistake 2: Attempt to Influence without Collaborating with
Other Departments 114
Mistake 3: Attempt to Influence with Only One Category 115
Mistake 4: Using Influence to Optimize a Subsystem While
Compromising the Whole System 115
Troubleshooting with the Six Boxes® Model 116
Conclusion 116
Leading Examples 116
Individual Contributor Leading Example: Investigating
Inventory Losses 116
Manager Leading Example: Investigating Opportunities through
Skip-Level Dialogues 120
Executive Leading Example: Mapping the Primary and
Support Processes 125
Background 125
Clint Analyzes the Organization 125
Results 126
Summary: What to Do 126
Summary 126
What to Do 128
Word of Caution 129

6 Practice 2: Diagnosing and Treating Like Doctors.................**131**

Introduction: Importance and Benefits of Diagnosing and
Treating Like Doctors...131

Characteristics of Diagnosing and Treating Like Doctors 133

Rummler's RIP...133

    Introduction..133

    Phase I (Analysis and Diagnostics): Desired Results
    Determined and Project Defined...134

    Phase II (Analysis and Diagnostics): Barriers Determined and
    Changes Specified 136

    Phase III (Treatment): Changes Designed,
    Developed, and Implemented 138

    Phase IV (Treatment): Results Evaluated and Maintained
    or Improved...142

    Conclusion...142

Leading Examples 142

    Introduction...142

    Individual Contributor Leading Example: Diagnosing and
    Treating Project Management 142

    Manager Leading Example: Diagnosing
    Ineffective Performers 143

    Executive Leading Example: Diagnosing Fighting Fires...................145

Summary: What to Do 146

    Summary 146

    What to Do...146

    Word of Caution 147

**7 Practice 3: Finding Key Behaviors Like Social
Psychologists** **151**

Introduction: Importance and Benefits of Finding Key Behaviors
Like Social Psychologists 151

    Mistakes That Occur When Not Using This Practice.........................152

        Reason 1: Difficulty Finding Key Behaviors.................................152

        Reason 2: Promoted Due to Technical Capabilities 152

        Reason 3: Choose Not to Develop Change
        Management Capabilities 153

Characteristics of Finding Key Behaviors Like
Social Psychologists 153

    Think Like Social Psychologists...153

Setting Goals and Measures 154

Systematic Approach for Finding Key Behaviors 157
  Grenny et al. on Finding Key Behaviors 157
  Duhigg on Finding Key Behaviors 158
Influencing and Adopting New Key Behaviors 159
  Grenny et al.'s Six Sources of Influence for Influencing
  Key Behaviors 159
  Duhigg and Influencing Key Behaviors 159
Leading Examples 161
  Individual Contributor Leading Example: Inspiring
  Multidirectional Collaboration 161
  Manager Leading Example: Changing the Selling Process 163
  Executive Leading Example: Eliminating Tribal Knowledge 164
Summary: What to Do 167
  Summary 167
  What to Do 167
  Word of Caution 167

SECTION III SUPPORTING CHANGE

8 Practice 4: Communicating Like Agents 173
Introduction: Importance and Benefits of Communicating
Like Agents 173
  Clarification: Differences among Practices Aligned
  to Communication 174
Characteristics of Communicating Like Agents 174
Tactics for Influencing Others to Take Action 176
  Point of Clarification between Teams and Groups 179
  Influence Tactics for Those Assigned to Manage Individual
  Contributors and Teams 180
  Tactics for All Formal Roles to Influence Others to Act 181
Marquet's Intent-Based Leadership (IBL) 181
  Begin with the End in Mind 181
  IBL 182
  Conclusion 184
Drexler/Sibbet Team Performance Model 184
Leading Examples 186
  Individual Contributor Leading Example: Knowledge
  Sharing across Teams 186

Manager Leading Example: Transitioning from Traditional
C2 to a Shared C2 187
Executive Leading Example: Blaming the VP 188
Summary: What to Do 189
Summary 189
What to Do 192
Word of Caution 194

9 Practice 5: Directing Like Guides 195
Introduction: Importance and Benefits of Directing Like Guides 195
Characteristics of Directing Like Guides 196
Assessing Abilities Using Situational Leadership® II 196
SLII® Example 198
Techniques for Building Capability 199
Bandura's Vicarious Learning 200
Cognitive Apprenticeship 200
Grenny et al.'s Tactics for Influencing Personal Ability 201
Leading Examples 202
Individual Contributor Leading Example: Helping an Aircraft
Maintainer Build Competence 202
Manager Leading Example: Transitioning from Academic to
Business Writing 203
Executive Leading Example: Transitioning a
Training Department 203
Summary: What to Do 204
Summary 204
What to Do 205
Word of Caution 207

10 Practice 6: Nurturing Like Gardeners 209
Introduction: Importance and Benefit of Nurturing Like Gardeners 209
Characteristics of Nurturing Like Gardeners 211
Grenny et al.'s Structural Ability Tactics 211
Make It Easy: Handshaw and Performance-Support Solutions 212
Leading Examples 214
Individual Contributor Leading Example: Using Job Aids for
Performance Support 214
Manager Leading Example: Establishing Department Standards 215
Executive Leading Example: Making Managers More Accessible
by Changing the Space 216

Summary: What to Do 217
    Summary 217
    What to Do 218
    Word of Caution 219

SECTION IV   ADDING VALUE

11   Practice 7: Facing the Unknown Like Lions 223
Introduction: Importance and Benefits of Facing the Unknown
Like Lions 223
Characteristics of Facing the Unknown Like Lions 224
Serious Listening 225
    Why Listening Is Undervalued, Underrated, and Challenging 225
    Graves' Five Levels of Listening 230
    Miscommunication 230
Obtaining Feedback 232
    Kouzes and Posner on Receiving Feedback 233
    Goldsmith's Feedforward Technique 233
Using 360° Feedback 234
    Word of Caution 235
Giving Feedback 236
Leading Examples 236
    Individual Contributor Leading Example: Hunter's
    Leadership Assessment 236
    Manager Leading Example: Identifying Annual Leadership
    Objectives Using 360° Feedback 237
    Executive Leading Example: Obtaining Executive Team
    Feedback for a General Manager 238
Summary: What to Do 239
    Summary 239
    What to Do 241
    Word of Caution 241

12   Practice 8: Developing Like Scouts 245
Introduction: Importance and Benefits of Developing Like Scouts 245
Characteristics of Developing Like Scouts 246
Robinson and Schroeder's Mechanisms for Innovation: Idea
Activators and Idea Mining 246
Kouzes and Posner's Tactics for Generating New Ideas 248
Leading Examples 249

    Individual Contributor Leading Example: Vendor
    Management Process..249
    Manager Leading Example: Starting a New Training Department.........249
    Executive Leading Example: College Competition Sponsorship.......250
    Summary: What to Do..250
        Summary...250
        What to Do..251
        Word of Caution...253

13 Practice 9: Communicating Like Broadcasters 255
    Introduction: Importance and Benefits of Communicating
    Like Broadcasters 255
    Characteristics of Communicating Like Broadcasters............................256
    Maxwell's Eight Guidelines for Connecting with Others......................256
    Leading Examples 256
        Individual Contributor Leading Example: Sharing
        Technical Expertise...256
        Manager Leading Example: Leadership Development
        Breakfast Club 258
        Executive Leading Example: Sharing Leadership at the
        Corporate Office..259
    Summary: What to Do..260
        Summary...260
        What to Do..260
        Word of Caution...260

SECTION V CONTINUING TO GROW

14 Maturing and Sustaining Your Leadership Practices 265
    Introduction...265
    The Leadership Development Process 266
        Step 1: Foundation 266
        Step 2: Feedback 267
        Step 3: Friction 268
            Step 3.A: Share Results...268
            Step 3.B: Apologize 268
            Step 3.C: Ask for Help..269
            Step 3.D: Get Started...270
        Step 4: Follow-Up...270
    The 21st Century Leadership Development Roadmap 270
    Stage I: I Know 273

Characteristics...273
What You Need to Advance to Stage II 276
Stage II: I Don't Know 277
Characteristics...277
What You Need to Advance to Stage III 277
Stage III: I Know That I Don't Know..278
Characteristics...278
What You Need to Advance to Stage IV 279
Stage IV: I Don't Know What I Don't Know................................279
Characteristics...279
What You Need to Maintain Stage IV 280
What to Do: Using the Roadmap to Sustain Your Journey 280

15 **Considering Organizational Implications................................281**
Introduction...281
Managing the Strategy Portfolio 283
The Competitive Advantage of Having Employees at All
Levels Practice Leadership 283
The Way Organizations Form, Monitor, and Refine
Their Strategies...284
Building Teams with Diversity and Inclusion 285
Rethinking Leadership Development 285
Advancing 21st Century Leadership 287

Afterword: The Fundamental Attribution Error 291

**Appendix I: 21st Century Leadership Definition, Principles,
Practices, and Results..295**

**Appendix II: 21st Century Leadership Principles, Beliefs, and
Practices Alignment 297**

**Appendix III: Traditional Leadership Assumptions and
Related Consequences 303**

Appendix IV: Nine Practices 307

Appendix V: Nine Practices 360° Feedback Diagnostic Tool..........311

Appendix VI: Related Quality Terms 317

Appendix VII: Intent-Based Leadership (IBL) Manifesto...............323

Endnotes **325**

Bibliography **341**

Index **351**

Acknowledgments **363**

Author **365**

Foreword, Second Edition

There is something wrong with work these days. And that means there is something wrong with leadership.

We call it "The Great Resignation." More and more people are calling it quits. Figures show Americans are leaving their jobs in record numbers. These people figure that the cost to their health, emotions, relationships, and lives that comes from work is just not worth their paycheck. Sure, it has been sparked in part by a massive re-evaluation of priorities that accompanied the COVID-19 pandemic. Still, at the same time, pundits claim we are experiencing a world characterized by more and more (and more) VUCA—short for Volatility, Uncertainty, Complexity, and Ambiguity. And the journals are full of calls for new ways of working and other cultural and business transformations.

Anyone in a leadership position ought to ask themselves what is going on.

According to a study published in MIT Sloan to understand why people are leaving their jobs [https://sloanreview.mit.edu/article/toxic-culture-is-driving-the-great-resignation] the number one reason provided was "toxic culture." This was cited almost as much as the next four reasons put together.

It is possible that the prevalence of toxic cultures has somehow multiplied as the virus did, turning once healthy work environments into unhealthy ones. Reacting to COVID induced a stress upon company leaders trying to balance caring for the team, the company, and the customers. The uncertainly at the outset of the virus was enormous with the prospect of a reemerging dark age not unfathomable.

The impact of stress on humans is well studied. Our prefrontal cortices are impaired. We become more selfish, inward-focused, and defensive. We over-bias toward playing not to lose. We don't think as well. We struggle to counter uncertainty with more controlling behaviors. For leaders, this means telling more, listening less, and having less patience for diverse and outlying opinions. This would be perceived as a less fun place to work, at the least.

But I do not think that is a powerful enough force to explain what we see. Something seems to have happened during the COVID-19 experience that brought the cost of toxic culture to light.

Here's the puzzle. None of the leaders I talk to is trying to create a toxic culture. They are doing the best they can. They do care about their people. They want good outcomes, but there is still something missing. For example, I consistently hear that they all want their people to take more ownership, make bolder decisions, do more thinking—the same things workers say! They want less (not more) stovepiping and meetings that matter because people aren't afraid of "presentation" and just say what they honestly think. None of them wants a toxic culture—or even an unhealthy one.

But if people are fed up with toxic cultures and leaders are trying to build healthy cultures, not toxic ones, then what is wrong?

My hypothesis is that the way we work and interact in the office is becoming more and more disconnected from how 21st-century organizations actually work. Essentially, we have a 20th or even a 19th century way of working and way of speaking laid over a modern workplace. A way of speaking and a way of behaving: that is important. The "way" is not a nebulous feeling or theory. It is manifested in our words and actions.

It is this fundamental disparity that people are feeling.

Our behaviors at work have not fundamentally changed since the Industrial Revolution. We organize using similar hierarchies, and we run meetings in a similar way. Robert's Rules of Order came out in 1876, and I still hear it cited. We speak similarly, and we ask questions using similar language. A modern person reading the description of factory work in 1850s England in Charles Dickens' Hard Times would recognize the relationships and interactions as similar to their own.

Sure, some things have improved, but the fundamental structures remain. Everything needs to change—right down to the way we run meetings and ask questions.

This book is the answer.

What I love about this book is that it is fundamentally about practices. Not about theories and not about mindsets but about practices. Leadership is an interactive sport that always involves others. It is manifested in our behaviors and, in short, our practices. The revision of these inherited Industrial Age practices will lead the way forward. We will act our way to new thinking.

This book will help you implement practices in three general areas that are critical for leaders: Improving performance, supporting change, and adding value. As he developed his book, Dr. DePaul drew upon a host of modern leadership thinkers, including many of my favorite thinkers and writers.

This is right. You will learn from Simon Sinek, John Maxwell, Liz Wiseman, Carl Binder, Ken Blanchard, Charles Duhigg, James Kouzes, and others in a coherent way. There is no one correct answer, leadership habit, or way to fit every situation and person. There are, however, patterns.

DePaul reveals many of these patterns. For example, there is a broad consensus that the traditional leader-follower structures do not fit the modern workplace. These are organizations where we "follow the leader" above us. The limitation of that archetype, among many, is that people are following people. These structures were designed to scale the physical labor that humans do. The focus was on doing (not thinking). But what replaces that? It is this: Structures that want to scale thinking.

In these new structures, people are encouraged to participate in the decision-making space as much as possible. This sense of agency and cognitive involvement invites ownership, engagement, and accountability. There is a sense of being valued which, in turn, encourages contribution, which then builds the sense of value.

Humans feel valuable when they can contribute. Hollow words from the boss which claim to "appreciate your work" don't make someone feel they have contributed when they know they were simply cogs in a machine where their bosses made all the important decisions.

The most underutilized resource we have on earth is the cognitive ability of humans that goes unheard, unused, and unappreciated. Start here, and you will start to unlock that resource in yourself and the others around you.

L. David Marquet
Englewood FL, Winter 2021

Foreword, First Edition

I know, I know, you're already an expert on leadership. On *bad* leadership, anyway.

We all are. Ask any ten of us, and you're guaranteed ten anecdotes of a person in power who is leading poorly. Our leaders fail to delegate, and they fail to take ownership. They fail to trust, and they fail to monitor details. They fail to envision the future, and they fail to see reality. They fail to learn from others, and they fail to act as role models. Whatever our leaders may actually be doing, we're all expert at noticing when and how they fail us.

But ask those same ten people how to help a poor leader recover, or how to help a good leader improve, and things get murky pretty fast. You'll likely hear ten different answers based on ten different sets of underlying assumptions, with the only commonality being a troubling lack of specificity. This *other* half of our leadership expertise—the part that's about *good* leadership—isn't quite as solid.

It's not our fault. Leadership isn't easy to define in the first place; the remarkable abundance of authors and publishers attempting to do so has, on the whole, further clouded the issue. Though many of their best efforts contain large nuggets of truth, their end points—and their journeys, and their assumptions, and even their starting points—vary widely.

To whom should we listen? To which theory shall we subscribe? Must a leader be an expert at guiding people through change? Must he or she know how to motivate and engage the masses? Must he or she be a visionary, seeing the future before the rest of us? Must he or she simply have the constitution to whip, prod, and cajole great masses of people into higher levels of productivity than they might achieve on their own? Is leadership born? Is it made? Is it the secret to our future success? Is it an obsolete notion from an age gone by?

Frustratingly, the answer seems to be yes *and* no on all accounts. One can find a source to support or refute nearly any imaginable notion about leadership. Each source has its particular viewpoint, each its loyal followers. But with so little exclusivity in the definition, so much variation in the parameters involved, and such fundamental disagreement over what we mean by the word, one wonders whether we share any practical understanding of how to become a capable leader at all. Are we forever doomed only to recognize and lament the failures of those who try?

I hope not. I've spent the better part of my career consulting internally and externally with a variety of organizations—many of them large, successful, and highly ambitious—on the twin topics of behavior and culture. In my firm, we focus on what real people actually do—what individual contributors do, what supervisors do, what managers do, and what executives do—to achieve high output at low stress. We employ a finely honed understanding of the behavioral patterns employed within the most successful organizations, pulled from decades of research regarding collaboration, communication, decision making, feedback systems, and (dreaded above all else) meetings. Our primary work is to describe, define, and import those practices into the entities we serve, helping our clients to make the behavioral patterns their own. So, we pay a lot of attention to what makes organizations succeed.

And as we do, client after client, year after year, one thing becomes ever clearer: The need for leadership at every level. Without executives taking the lead in their spheres, organizations become rudderless. Without managers taking the lead in their spheres, product delivery and company performance become slipshod. And without frontline supervisors taking the lead in their spheres, customer service and execution become substandard.

But with so many experts, so many ideas, and so little agreement, how do we find a language and definition for leadership that's practical and usable? How do we keep from getting lost in debate over which guru to follow and which theory to espouse?

Enter Gary DePaul, with a characteristically level-headed approach.

I first met Gary in early 2011. I was talking about culture with a group of leaders within the International Society for Performance Improvement, Gary among them. The society—the ISPI, as members call it—is a meeting of minds around the notion that organizational solutions should solve organizational problems. In the same way that doctors diagnose before they prescribe and engineers analyze before they design, ISPI practitioners take pains to fully understand the desired human performance, the current state, and the most important gaps *before* they begin to consider specific solutions.

From outside, it sounds so straightforward as to be redundant. But in a world where trainers want to train, facilitators want to facilitate, organizational redesign experts want to redesign organizations, and coaches want to coach, there's tremendous power in simultaneously recognizing the value in those disciplines (and many others), while reserving judgment about which one to use until the need is clearly understood. First, *begin with the present state*, then *define the need*, and then *design the solution*.

From our first encounter, Gary and I quickly recognized each other as kindred spirits in this kind of clear, analytical thinking. With his PhD in performance consulting and my degree in engineering, we speak and think similarly about organizational challenges. Both of us prefer models, research, and experimental results to unfounded (albeit slickly presented) hypotheses. Neither of us cares much for human resources (HR) or training programs *du jour*. We don't tie our work to "industry trends" or subscribe to the theory that only what's new is good (or, for that matter, that only what's old is good). Instead, Gary has proven himself a thinker and analyst of the highest order in the human performance space. And while it's a gross oversimplification of a substantial intellect, I think it's fair to say that at the core of Gary's analytical horsepower lies a simple two-part question constantly begging to be answered: What has been proven to work, and how might it meet this particular need?

All of which is why, when Gary first shared with me his plans to write a leadership book, I didn't immediately ask whether he was crazy. Instead, I found myself fascinated. This isn't a man who would wade unsystematically into a sea of discordant voices just to add his own. What need did he perceive?

I'd scarcely framed the question mentally as he was answering it: Despite the huge variety of disparate opinions, we enjoy no conclusive result. We share no collective understanding of what leadership is, no common language about how to develop it, and no clear picture of how doing so successfully will benefit us. If leadership in the 21st Century is so critical, we need more than disparate opinions about how to avoid failure. We need a map and a plan. We need a way forward that integrates the dissonant voices into a clear picture of what everyone can do to become a better leader— actually, specifically *DO*—here, now, and today. It's no longer enough to recognize leadership's absence; we need to encourage and engender its presence. And the way to do so, Gary explained, isn't to add another voice to the cacophony; it's to integrate the truths already presented.

Gary delivers comprehensively on his promise. First, he presents a crisp and enlightened look at various notions about leadership that are rampant in today's literature. This has the dual effect of cutting through the confusion and creating the basis for the rest of his book. *Begin with the present state.* Then, he presents a view of what leadership in the 21st Century should look like, based on a variety of research into human productivity. *Define the need.* Finally, from an assortment of sources, he extracts a straightforward (though not easy) list of nine plainly worded behavioral practices, which the reader can employ right away or use as a framework to assess other leaders. *Design the solution.*

His language is specific, his research thorough, and his advice actionable. For my money, Analyzing Like Detectives, the first of his nine practices, is worth the investment in the whole book. If more leaders employed this level of active attention to cause and effect in their workplaces, many organizations would improve nearly overnight. Of course, Analyzing Like Detectives is followed by eight additional and equally valuable practices— each with tools, research citations, quotations, and examples to bring everything to life.

If you're most clear about the leadership *failures* in your organization, you're not alone. If your conversations on the subject turn to comparative debates over expert opinions, you're not alone. If you feel like your organization would benefit from less *talk* about leadership and more *actual* leadership, you're not alone. You're also not doomed. With Gary's book, you're well on your way to a greater understanding of leadership and—more importantly—some concrete steps forward, starting today.

It's time for all of us to bolster the *other* half of our leadership expertise.

Ed Muzio
CEO, Group Harmonics
Austin, TX

Preface, Second Edition

Leadership Continues to Evolve

Since publishing the first edition, much has happened, including a political divide in the United States, the Stoneman Douglas High School mass shooting, the COVID-19 pandemic, the murder of George Floyd, and multiple weather disasters, costing billions in damages such as in 2017 ($519 billion) and 2021 ($329 billion).[1] One phenomenon, *The Great Resignation*, has raised concern about the reliability and effectiveness of the workforce.

The Great Resignation

Anthony Klotz, Associate Professor of Management at Texas A&M University's Mays Business School, predicted the phenomenon called *The Great Resignation*. After mass layoffs due to pandemic concerns and after the economy began recovering, the United States experienced high employment resignation rates at all career levels. The healthcare, hospitality, and technology industries were hit the hardest, but employers from all industries experienced the effect.[2]

The phenomenon may have started in 2020, but it is expected to continue. In November 2021, 4.5 million workers quit their job. In January 2022, the count was 4.2 million.[3] In a December 2021 Resume Builder commissioned a survey of 1,250 employed adults. Of those adults, 23% reported that they plan to find new jobs in 2022. Of employees planning to quit, the majority are from management:

- 26% middle management
- 23% non-management
- 17% upper-management

The reasons for quitting are numerous. Employees had told me they quit their jobs for better working conditions, preferred remote work when the organization required everyone to return to the office, and wanted early retirement.[4]

Economist Ulrike Malmendier suggests that the pandemic caused people to experience an existential change.[5] Many have reassessed their values and found that their jobs didn't align. For example, my veterinarian realized that he wasn't happy as a co-owner of his practice. He retired early and moved to the coast.

The Great Inertia

While the Great Resignation is alarming, there may be a deeper problem: People who quit but stay. These people aren't engaged at work or are disengaged. Some may dislike their work, but others cannot recall why they stay in their job. With the latter, the effort to leave for something better may not be worth it. As a result, they do nothing. When that happens, their performance suffers, yet they perform well enough to keep their jobs. As shown in Box P2.1, Doshi and McGregor call this state *inertia*.

A Possible Cause for Inertia

In bonus episode 126 of the *Unlabeled Leadership* podcast, Peri Chickering shares an observation: We tend to hire and promote people to management, not because of their leadership capabilities but their technical/functional skills. These skills reflect intellectual expertise rather than emotional expertise. When we overemphasize strengthening the intellectual muscle, the heart or emotional muscle suffers. Stated differently, the heart goes offline when the intellectual muscle gets over-exercised.[6]

When this happens, people who learn about leadership principles and better ways to lead fail to internalize these principles and leadership practices. As Hunter explains, getting people to move leadership principles from their head to their heart and then from their heart to form habits can become too distant of a journey.[7]

A Wake-Up Call for Executives to Embrace New Ways of Leading

Whether employees quit and then leave or stay, management needs to do more to help employees engage with their work and organization. In the first edition preface, I describe the engagement challenge and how management is often the source of the engagement problem.

BOX P2.1   INERTIA: THE MOST INDIRECT MOTIVE

With inertia, your motive for working is so distant from the work itself that you can no longer say where it comes from—you do what you do simply because you did it yesterday. This leads to the worst performance of all…An executive continues at his job not because he's engaged in it, but because he can't think of a good reason to leave.[8]

If you're in an organization with low turnover and employees are not engaged with their work, the reason could be inertia.

In their research, Doshi and McGregor discovered six motivators, three direct and three indirect. The direct motivators are correlated with high performance. The indirect ones are correlated with low performance. Inertia is the most ineffective motivator and is harmful to organizational performance.[9]

One notation about people motivated by inertia: Many are happy. When in unfavorable circumstances, people can synthesize their happiness. They may not favor their jobs, but they find ways to be happy. Dan Gilbert describes this phenomenon as synthetic happiness, which is different from natural happiness. According to Gilbert, synthetic happiness explains why, after a year, someone who is paraplegic is as happy as someone who wins $14 million in a lottery. In his talk, Gilbert describes several cases of people who experience difficult hardships but describes those experiences as the best thing that happened to them.[10] If someone can find happiness while being in imprisoned for a crime that they didn't commit, then someone who is unmotivated and unengaged in their job can find happiness as well.

When people are not engaged at their jobs but are happy, management can mistakenly assume they are engaged and doing well. However, when a traumatic experience such as the 2020 pandemic occurs, these employees may reassess their priorities and quit for a better work environment.

The Great Resignation is a wake-up call for management. From executives to frontline supervisors, managers need to do more. They need to practice 21st Century Leadership and embrace diversity, equity, inclusion, and belonging.

There is hope. More authors and experts seem to discourage traditional leadership and advocate for 21st Century Leadership. With hope, more managers will learn new leadership behaviors, internalize them, and form healthier habits.

What's New in The Second Edition

New Foreword

I asked David Marquet to write the second edition foreword. Since retiring from the Navy, David has been at the front of elevating leadership. From his leader-leader concept to Intent-Based Leadership, David and his team have helped tens of thousands rethink and practice 21st Century Leadership. He has partnered with and learned from hundreds of companies about implementing leadership practices.

Chapter Changes

In addition to minor corrections and grammatical improvements, I added additional author quotations. Table P2.1 outlines the chapter revisions.

Table P2.1 Chapter Revisions

Chapters	Description
1	• Expanded the distinction between *management* and *leadership*.
2	• Removed the concept of leadership as a performance-improvement profession. • Removed the description of the four performance-improvement principles. • Added a new figure to describe the relationship among behaviors, practices, beliefs, guiding principles, and qualities.
4	• Added an introduction to explain why guiding principles are crucial. • Added growth and fixed mindsets. • Added psychological safety. • Added ingroup and outgroup bias.
8	• Added Intent-Based Leadership • Added Marquet's Four Levels of Accountability Systems
10	• Expanded Performance-Support Solutions topic.
11	• Expanded the listening topic. • Expanded the feedback topic. • Added Goldsmith's Feedforward technique.
14	• Added the Leadership Development Process • Expanded Stage I of the 21st Century Leadership Development Roadmap.
Appendices	• Removed the appendix about professional associations. • Added Appendix VII: Intent-Based Leadership (IBL) Manifesto.
Bibliography	• Changed bibliography to APA 7th edition. • Updated references, especially URLs. • Added additional references.
About the Author	• Updated the author's biography.

Preface, First Edition

Most likely, you've noticed that there are thousands of leadership books. Walk into any airport newsstand, big-box bookstore, or conference bookstore—leadership books are everywhere. With all the available books, how can you make sense of it all? Can you read any leadership book and then become a successful leader? What value does each book really have for improving your leadership?

More importantly, with hundreds of leadership books published annually, are there indications that organizational roles—regardless of career level—leverage leadership to improve organizational performance? According to Gallup, most managers are ineffective at influencing employee engagement.

In 2013, Gallup published the 2012 State of the American Workplace Report. Based on the research of 49,928 business/work units and nearly 1.4 million employees, Gallup reports these findings[1]:

- In 2012, 30% of US employees were engaged in their work (refer to Table P1.1 for engagement definitions).[2]
- From 2000 to 2012, 26%–30% of US employees were engaged in their work, as depicted in Table P1.2.[3]
- Employee engagement is linked to business outcomes, as depicted in Table P1.3.[4]
- Actively disengaged employees cost the United States between $450 billion and $550 billion each year in lost productivity.[5]
- In the global report, Gallup states that managers are responsible for the low engagement because managers account for at least 70% of the variance in employee engagement.[6]

If managers aren't influencing employee engagement effectively, they aren't practicing leadership effectively. Moreover, with the hundreds of

Table P1.1   Engagement Levels and Descriptors[a]

Engagement Level	Descriptors
Engaged	Intellectually and emotionally connected with their organization and teams Work with passion Drive innovation and move the company forward
Not engaged	Don't feel connected with their organization Give their time to the work but without energy or passion
Disengaged	Intellectually and emotionally disconnected with their organization and teams Express their unhappiness at work Likely to jeopardize the performance of their teams

[a] Gallup, 2014, *State of the Global Workplace*, 17; Gallup, 2014, Great Jobs and Great Lives, 3; Sorenson and Garman, 2013, *How to Tackle US Employees' Stagnating Engagement*.

Table P1.2   2000–2012 US Engagement Ranges by Category[a]

Percentage Range	Employee Engagement Category
26–30	Engaged
50–56	Not engaged
15–20	Disengaged

[a] Sorenson and Garman, 2013, *How to Tackle US Employees' Stagnating Engagement*.

Table P1.3   Nine Performance Outcomes Linked to Employee Engagement by Category[a]

Category	Performance Outcome
Organizational performance	Profitability Shrinkage (theft) Customer ratings
Human resource metrics	Turnover (for high and low-turnover organizations) Absenteeism
Team performance	Productivity Quality (defects) Safety incidents Patient safety incidences

[a] Gallup, 2014, *State of the American Workplace*, 25.

leadership books published annually, why has engagement remained in the 26% to 30% range? Why are the majority of managers failing to practice leadership?

One reason is that leadership books have a limiting effect on leadership practice. While many leadership books offer insights, some have serious limitations. I classify these limitations in the following way: leadership lite, personal empirical approach, leadership and management blend, and leadership founded on traditional assumptions.

Leadership Lite

Leadership lite books tell a good story or explain concepts like *vision*, *honesty*, and *agility*, yet their main message is difficult to retain and even more challenging to apply. In other words, these books fail to help readers apply what they learn to practice leadership.

Personal Empirical Approach

Many authors take a personal empirical approach: They write about what they believe to be critical for successful leadership, but they base their perspectives on personal observations, the occasional opinion survey, case studies, and insights from their own leadership development. Even though these books can provide value, they don't ground their approach in the social sciences. This includes the fields of sociology, psychology, education, history, and communication studies.

Leadership and Management Blend

John C. Maxwell states, "There are very few leadership books; most deal with management."[7] While management books are important, their authors explain leadership from the perspective of roles with power or authority. When authors blend management with leadership, authors can mislead readers with the meaning of *leadership* and potentially hinder their leadership development. If you are seriously interested in leadership, remarkably few books can effectively explain how to practice leadership from the perspective of any formal role at any career level.

Leadership Founded on Traditional Assumptions

Similar to integrating management and leadership, several authors focus on traditional leadership or base their approach on traditional leadership assumptions. Traditional assumptions can mislead readers on how leadership should be practiced and hinder their leadership development. In Chapter 3, I define traditional leadership and describe 13 traditional leadership assumptions. In contrast, in Chapter 4, I describe the 21st Century Leadership principles and beliefs.

How This Book Is Different

Want to inspire creativity, innovation, and engagement? This book can help you practice leadership effectively from the perspective of your formal organizational role—regardless of your career level. In these pages, I avoid the trappings of leadership lite by focusing on leadership rather than management and exposing faulty traditional assumptions. As much as possible, I avoid relying on personal empirical evidence by basing my findings on an analysis that I describe in the next topic.

The Method Used in This Book

Most authors tend to explain leadership using one of the following methods:

- Describe leadership theories and styles.
- Explain the qualities needed to lead successfully, such as empathy, integrity, and coaching.
- Illustrate leadership through storytelling, parables, and fables.
- Interview well-known leaders about their leadership philosophy and qualities.
- Reflect on leadership experiences through memoirs.

While these methods can be effective, I use a different method that identifies practical leadership practices and related principles and beliefs. In this book, I report the findings from an analysis of 21st Century Leadership books. These findings may not be apparent when reading one or two books. Still, when comparing 15 books collectively, you discover patterns and insights for practicing 21st Century Leadership successfully, for building leadership fluency and helping professionals promote effective leadership within their organizations.

21st Century Leadership isn't a new concept. If you search online bookstores for that title, you will find several books with 21st Century Leadership somewhere in the title. When I reviewed these books, I noticed that most describe traditional leadership only or describe a blend of new and traditional approaches.

I began understanding 21st Century Leadership when I listened to James C. Hunter's audiobook, *The Servant Leadership Training Course.*[8] Since then, I have read other authors with a similar leadership perspective. From these books, I incorporated their approach into my own leadership practice.

For the analysis, I analyzed books about 21st Century Leadership. I list the books in the Bibliography. This isn't an exclusive list of 21st Century Leadership books, and the authors don't always write exclusively about 21st Century Leadership; at times, they still take a traditional leadership approach. These books provided enough data to complete my analysis of 21st Century Leadership and the nine practices. In addition to these books, I reference other sources that provide insight into leadership practices.

What This Book Is Not

This book isn't a substitute for the leadership books that I reference. Instead, think of this book as an analysis that combines the perspectives of different 21st Century Leadership authors to identify leadership patterns, insights, and guidance for building leadership fluency. Reading the books in the Bibliography would provide more depth to 21st Century Leadership.

This book isn't about storytelling, fables, or parables. However, I provide several real-life examples of applying 21st Century Leadership practices. I call these *leading examples,* and I designed them to illustrate the positive effects of performing leadership practices appropriately.

This book isn't about management, but it is about leadership and applying leadership practices at three organizational levels:

■ Individual contributor level
■ Manager level
■ Executive level

In Chapters 5 through 13, I provide three leading examples, with one at each level.

In summary, this book

- Is an analysis of 21st Century Leadership.
- Provides insights and examples for applying 21st Century Leadership practices.
- Helps you interpret the perspective of other leadership books.

Readers Who Should Care about This Book

Readers may find this book valuable for assisting with leadership growth, including those whose roles involve building their organizations' capabilities. The following subtopics detail the reader categories as I perceive them.

Individuals Entering the Workforce

You may be starting your career at a corporation, firm, government agency, nonprofit entity, one of the armed forces, or any organization. This can be exciting and scary. Your family, friends, and future employers may have described the experience, but until you start working, you won't know for sure. Sooner rather than later, you will want to know what to expect from management, what success looks like, and of course, how to avoid failure. This book will give you not only perspective but also concrete actions.

Experienced Individuals in the Workforce

Having been in the workforce, you have a reasonable understanding of how your organization and culture function. You have a better concept of what leadership means within your organization, and you have probably seen good and bad examples of leadership. You might want some insight into your experiences, how you can increase your contributions, and how you can find more meaning in your work.

Individuals in Management Including Officers, Executives, Directors, Managers, and Supervisors

Because of your role, others may recognize you for your leadership. You may have completed several leadership courses and read leadership books, but you want more clarity about what leadership is and how to apply this to your job. You may have learned about leadership competencies, but those might seem somewhat abstract and difficult to apply. When leading, do you really think about the competencies you are using? Regardless, you may have had a mix of success and mistakes in how you lead, and you want something that might help you become more fluent.

Executives and Managers Who Own Strategy

As you know, you build the organization's strategy to realize new business opportunities and resolve business gaps. One way to do this is by implementing initiatives that would give your organization a competitive advantage. In talking with professionals who work in this area, leadership is something that strategy owners discuss frequently. If you recognize that leadership can give your organization a competitive advantage, then this book is for you.

Executives and Managers Who Own Diversity

Several organizations invest in diversity. These organizations recognize that having diverse thinking leads to higher productivity, creativity, innovation, and ultimately improved performance. You know that highly diverse cultures have a competitive advantage. Pivotal to building this is having the right people to champion team diversity.

Executives and Managers Who Own Training

Your department plays a strategic and critical role within your organization by improving how employees lead and serve. You continue to add to and modify your leadership programs. However, if you are like the learning and development professionals who talk with me, you have mixed results. You want to discover better ways to improve your leadership performance.

Professors, Researchers, Thought Leaders, and Students of Management and Leadership

As a member of a management and leadership department at an academic institute, you search for ways to advance the leadership body of work. How authors think about leadership is changing subtly, but professionals mix traditional ways of leading with the new ways, resulting in limited success. By expanding and researching concepts from this book, you have the opportunity to provide leadership clarity that ultimately improves how others lead.

What Is Unique about This Book

Contrasting 21st Century Leadership Principles and Beliefs with Traditional Leadership Assumptions

In the last quarter of the 20th century, some authors and researchers developed new leadership principles and beliefs and described harmful traditional assumptions. In this book, I expose traditional assumptions that can cause harm and contrast them with 21st Century Leadership principles and beliefs. By revisiting leadership assumptions, you can avoid behaviors that lead to less than favorable outcomes and concentrate on using 21st Century Leadership principles and beliefs that accelerate your leadership capabilities.

Focusing on Results

Instead of focusing on the competency level (think of viewing trees) or focusing on the high level of storytelling (think of viewing the forest), I focus on desired results and the practices to achieve them (think of viewing an assembly line that produces products). My intent is for you to learn 21st Century Leadership practices to apply them as different situations arise.

Guiding Growth Activities with the 21st Century Leadership Development Roadmap

In addition to the nine practices, I want you to have a roadmap to guide you to develop your leadership practices. This is why I built the 21st Century Leadership Development Roadmap. I base the model on a continuum of traditional leadership to 21st Century Leadership. Chapter 14 describes what happens at each of the four stages and what you need to accomplish to reach the next stage.

How This Book Is Organized

I organized the book into the following sections:

Table P1.4   Chapters and Goals of Section 1: Demystifying 21st Century Leadership

Chapter	Title	Goal
1	*Clarifying Why Leadership Is Confusing*	Demystify the confusion about leadership and how leadership works
2	*Defining 21st Century Leadership*	Define 21st Century Leadership
3	*Revealing Traditional Leadership Assumptions*	Define traditional leadership and 13 traditional leadership assumptions
4	*Explaining 21st Century Leadership Principles and Beliefs*	Explain the underlying principles and beliefs of 21st Century Leadership

Section I: Demystifying 21st Century Leadership

Section I sets the foundation for Sections II through V. In Section I, I discuss why *leadership* is confusing, define *traditional leadership*, and define *21st Century Leadership*. Table P1.4 lists the chapters and goals.

Sections II through IV: Using the Nine Practices of 21st Century Leadership

In Sections II through IV, I explain the nine leadership practices. Table P1.5 lists the chapters by sections and defines the chapters' goals.

In Chapters 5 through 13, I use the following structure:

1. Explain the importance and benefit.
2. Describe characteristics.
3. Provide more context with guidelines, rules of practice, models, techniques, and tools.
4. Provide three leading examples.
5. Conclude with a summary and suggest what to do immediately, in the short and long term.

Section V: Continuing to Grow

The last section describes how you can monitor your development, tactics to sustain your development, and implications for organizations. Table P1.6 lists the chapters and titles with the goals.

Table P1.5 Sections, Chapters, and Goals of Sections II through IV: Using the Nine Practices of 21st Century Leadership

Section	Chapter	Title	Goal
II: Improving Performance with Systemic Thinking	5	*Analyzing Like Detectives*	Explain the nine practices of 21st Century Leadership
	6	*Diagnosing and Treating Like Doctors*	
	7	*Finding Key Behaviors Like Social Psychologists*	
III: Supporting Change	8	*Communicating Like Agents*	
	9	*Directing Like Guides*	
	10	*Nurturing Like Gardeners*	
IV: Adding Value	11	*Facing the Unknown Like Lions*	
	12	*Developing Like Scouts*	
	13	*Communicating Like Broadcasters*	

Table P1.6 Chapters and Goals of Section V: Continuing to Grow Chapters

Chapter	Title	Goal
14	*Maturing and Sustaining Your Leadership Practices*	Manage and monitor your leadership development
15	*Considering Organizational Implications*	Guide process owners to improve • Organizational strategy • Diversity strategies • Leadership development training programs Describe leadership research and development opportunities

Importance of 21st Century Leadership

The practice of 21st Century Leadership inspires creativity, innovation, and engagement in your team, department, organization, and community. It also is used to model appropriate behaviors, promote a safe working environment, and influence others to lead. As reflected in the Gallup research, organizations need more people practicing 21st Century Leadership and breaking away from the leader-follower structure that debilitates mental and moral development.

DEMYSTIFYING 21ST CENTURY LEADERSHIP

I see leadership primarily as a form of service.[1]

Maxwell

These data challenge further the myth that leadership is about position and power. And they support the notion that leadership is about the action you take.[2]

Kouzes and Posner

There is a transition occurring from the old paradigm in which leadership resided in a personal or role, to a new one in which leadership is a collective process that is spread throughout networks of people.[3]

Petrie

In the last quarter of the 20th Century, authors wrote about a way to practice leadership that departs radically from traditional thinking. These authors shifted the focus from labels, such as *leaders* and *followers*, to actions and relationships.

Rather than collecting followers and leaving a legacy, the authors argue that you need to avoid thinking about yourself and feeding your ego. Instead,

DOI: 10.4324/9781003273448-1

focus on helping others develop. Encourage them and acknowledge their accomplishments—all while practicing leadership quietly in the background.

These contemporary leadership authors broke from tradition by proclaiming that anyone can practice leadership, regardless of role or career level.

Oh, and by the way, professionals in roles with power have more difficulty practicing leadership than those without assigned authority over teammates.

In Section I, I set the foundation for the nine practices. I clarify why the leadership concept can be confusing and define 21st Century Leadership. I then reveal traditional leadership assumptions that are problematic and harmful to organizations. Lastly, I present the 21st Century Leadership principles and beliefs, which align with the nine practices.

Chapter 1

Clarifying Why Leadership Is Confusing

How is "what I know" getting in the way of "what I don't know?"
By simply asking this question, I was compelled to venture beyond
the realm of my own understanding.[1]

Wiseman

Introduction

You may find the *leadership* concept elusive. With thousands of books on
the subject, there is no well-defined and universally accepted explanation of
leadership. As Maxwell asserts, leadership is obscure (Box 1.1).

I've seen simple and complex leadership definitions; some describe
leadership as qualities. A few authors interview famous people who are
recognized leaders and, at best, summarize underlying themes, or at worst,
place the burden of defining leadership on the reader.

To understand leadership, first, you need to understand why the concept
is puzzling. In this chapter, I analyze the leadership concept and present six
reasons why leadership can be confusing (Box 1.2).

DOI: 10.4324/9781003273448-2

BOX 1.1 WHAT IS LEADERSHIP?

Everyone talks about it; few understand it. Most people want it; few achieve it. There are over fifty definitions and descriptions of it in my personal files. What is this intriguing subject we call leadership?[2]

Maxwell

BOX 1.2 SIX REASONS WHY LEADERSHIP IS CONFUSING

1. Leadership is like a role but different.
2. Leadership is more than a set of qualities.
3. Leadership is like a skill but different.
4. Some leadership theories overlap with leadership styles.
5. Leadership is like management but different.
6. The meaning of leadership is changing.

Reason 1: Leadership Is Like a Role but Different

Defining "Role"

Often, people describe leadership as a role. For example, you might hear someone say, "She has a leadership role in our agency" or "In our company, our executives have a clear leadership role." On Forbes.com, Rob Asghar describes the nine most demanding leadership roles.[3] Interestingly, Asghar lists nine formal roles—roles that you can find in organizational charts—including corporate chief executive officer (CEO), mayor, and editor for a daily newspaper. If these formal roles are also leadership roles, there must be a way to distinguish formal roles from leadership roles. To differentiate, consider this definition of a role.

The *Encyclopaedia Britannica* describes *role* in sociological terms. Roles are social positions. For people to recognize someone as having a role, the person must

■ Perform a set of recognized actions when recurrent situations occur.
■ Assume a set of qualities that are associated as part of the recognized actions.[4]

Table 1.1 Teacher Role with Example Actions and Qualities[a]

Action	Quality
Deliver lectures Assign homework Prepare exams	Dedicated Concerned Honest Responsible

[a] Encyclopaedia Britannica, (n.d.) *Role*.

The *Encyclopaedia Britannica* provides the example of a teacher's role, shown in Table 1.1. Teachers perform specific agreed-on actions and exhibit certain qualities.

Actions are the work performed by someone who assumes a role; *qualities* are the characteristics of a role. Table 1.2 defines *quality* and four terms synonymous with or, at least, similar to *quality*.

For *leader* to be a role, leaders must perform a set of agreed-on actions and possess a set of qualities. For example, Table 1.3 illustrates a sampling of possible actions and qualities.

A role is relatively stable. Many people can assume the same role with a reasonable and acceptable variance in role execution.[5]

Table 1.2 Definitions of Quality and Quality-Related Terms

Term	Lexico Definition
Quality	A distinctive attribute or characteristic possessed by someone or something[a]
Competency	The ability to do something successfully or efficiently[b]
Skill	The ability to do something well[c]
Trait	A distinguishing quality or characteristic, typically one belonging to a person[d]
Ability	Possession of the means or skill to do something[e]

[a] Lexico, n.d., *Quality*.
[b] Ibid, *Competency*.
[c] Ibid, *Skill*.
[d] Ibid, *Trait*.
[e] Ibid, *Ability*.

Table 1.3   Leadership Role with Examples of Simple Actions and Qualities

Action	Quality
Coaches someone Explains a vision Mentors someone	Agile Authentic Fair

Leadership Differs from a Role

After reviewing the definition of a role, you may notice that a role is more than just a set of actions and qualities. A role implies a social contract with those who assume a role. Thus, to accept a person as having a role, the person must behave in an agreed-on manner.

Organizations have formally defined roles, and human resource (HR) departments document roles using job descriptions, which are formal ways to describe roles. If you examine an organization's job descriptions, you may find titles such as those listed in Table 1.4.

While you probably won't find *leader* listed as a formal role, you might find a role that has *leader* in the title, such as *program leader*. Most likely, though, roles with *leader* in the title tend to describe supervisory tasks rather than tasks that relate to leadership.

Often, people in organizations hire professionals with the expectation that they will function as leaders, but they assign these new employees to formal roles other than something called *leader*.

In formal role job descriptions, you may find references to leadership, and HR may classify specific roles informally as leadership roles. Given this, leadership is something people do from the perspective of a formal role. Therefore, you may describe *leadership* using role terminology (having actions and qualities, as depicted in Tables 1.1 and 1.3), but leadership doesn't function the same way formal roles do. In this sense, leadership isn't a role.

Table 1.4   Formal Role Examples

Accountant	Manager	Project manager
Business analyst	Marketing specialist	Sales representative
Director	Partner	Supervisor
Engineer	Principal	Trainer
Physician	Programmer	Vice president

In Chapter 4, I argue that anyone can practice leadership regardless of role or level of assigned authority. Even if an organization's HR Department classifies certain positions as leadership roles and others as follower roles, this doesn't prevent those in non-leadership roles from practicing leadership. Maxwell, as well as Kouzes and Posner, explain that leadership isn't a role that can be assigned.[6] Interestingly enough, one organization where I worked requires its immediate managers to assess employees for their leadership practices—regardless of their career level. To prepare for the annual assessment, managers write business goals for their direct reports. The performance management system prepopulates leadership goals that managers cannot modify or remove; the organization's executive board expects all employees to function as leaders.

Does "Leadership" Include a Set of Roles or Qualities?

When reading leadership books, you may come across authors who describe leadership as a set of roles. An author, for example, may dedicate a chapter on being a visionary, another on being a change agent, and another on being a relationship builder. After examining the *Encyclopaedia Britannica's* definition of role (roles consist of actions and qualities), describing the authors' terms as roles doesn't seem accurate because they describe qualities but not actions. Instead of roles, terms like *visionary*, *change agent*, and *relationship builder* are leadership qualities. In these examples, leadership isn't a collection of multiple roles; instead, leadership is described as a set of qualities.

Authors who focus on qualities make a substantial contribution to the leadership field. Clarifying leadership qualities can be a powerful way to help readers learn about leadership. Keep in mind, though, that while qualities are a necessary component of leadership, so are actions. When describing leadership, focusing on qualities alone and providing examples of applying qualities doesn't explain leadership fully.

Conclusion

Leadership isn't a formal role. While leadership meets the two role characteristics (having repeatable actions and a set of qualities), we don't discuss leadership the same way we discuss formal organizational roles. Moreover, when several authors write about leadership, they neglect to define leadership actions and focus primarily on leadership qualities.

Reason 2: Leadership Is More than a Set of Qualities

Many Authors Explain Leadership in Terms of Qualities

In Reason 1, I state that roles consist of actions and qualities. Qualities include competencies, skills, traits, and abilities. Table 1.2 shows how these terms are closely related.

Authors tend to explain leadership in terms of qualities. If you review the table of contents in several leadership books, you may find chapters dedicated to qualities such as agility, integrity, and honesty. For example, Table 1.5 lists qualities from three leadership books.

In the first book, Gini and Green review several necessary qualities for effective leadership. Gini and Green pair each quality with a description of a famous person who demonstrates the quality. In the second book, Gonzalez explains how she coaches and teaches mindfulness to professionals. Leaders who experience mindfulness possess the nine qualities described in her book. In the third book, Molinaro describes the terms shown in Table 1.5. He explains a leadership contract: By choosing to lead, you commit to specific terms of the agreement.

Leadership Qualities Are Necessary but Not Sufficient

Although necessary, possessing a set of qualities is insufficient for defining a role. You also need actions or practices that are associated with leadership.

Table 1.5 Leadership Qualities Book Comparison

Leadership Book	Gini and Green, Ten Virtues of Outstanding Leaders[a]	Gonzalez, Mindful Leadership[b]	Molinaro, The Leadership Contract[c]
Qualities	Deep honesty Moral courage Moral vision Compassion and care Fairness Intellectual excellence Creative thinking Aesthetic sensitivity Good timing Deep selflessness	Be present Be aware Be calm Be focused Be clear Be equanimous Be positive Be compassionate Be impeccable	Leadership is: A decision An obligation Hard work Community

[a] Gini and Green, 2013, *Ten Virtues of Outstanding Leaders: Leadership and Character.*
[b] Gonzalez, 2012, *Mindful Leadership.*
[c] Molinaro, 2013, *The Leadership Contract.*

Table 1.6   Addison Process/Practice Definitions[a]

Term	Definition
Process	Series of actions to achieve results
Practice	Way of acting (action); manner; conduct; execution; habit; custom

[a] Addison, 2010, *How Can I Use HPT*, 10.

Underlying the practices are qualities. Hence, leadership has certain practices with a set of related qualities.

To understand better how this works, consider the relationship between *process* and *practice*. Roger Addison, author and performance-improvement consultant, defines *process* and *practice* in a particular way, as shown in Table 1.6.

Addison illustrates the terms with the following story:

Imagine that you are a process expert. Today, at a small grocery store, you observe Wendell and Shantel, two cashiers performing the store's point-of-sale (POS) process. You have a copy of the store's POS documentation, and you intend to use it to confirm that both cashiers complete the process steps appropriately with each customer.

After watching each cashier perform several transactions, you notice that both successfully and consistently complete the process steps defined in the POS documentation. Both do so within step-specifications, including expected durations.

While observing, you notice something unusual: Shantel's customer line is substantially longer than Wendell's. Even though both stations are identical, customers seem to prefer Shantel. This holds true even when customers seem to realize that they can complete their transactions sooner by standing in Wendell's shorter customer line.

Watching both cashiers, you discover a subtle difference. While both cashiers greet customers with a smile (required in the process), Shantel greets customers by name. In fact, Shantel seems to know her customers well. While scanning merchandise, Shantel does the following things that aren't documented in the POS process:

■ Asks customers questions about their day.
■ Asks if they like previous purchases.
■ Comments about items that they purchase (in a nonjudgmental or offensive way).

■ Mentions new products coming to the store.
■ Expresses how much she appreciates seeing them.

Both cashiers complete their sales by thanking each customer (required in the process), but Shantel does so in a way that seems to resonate better with customers.

Although both cashiers are sincere, pleasant, and efficient, Shantel *practices* the POS process differently than Wendell. They follow the same process but use different practices.

Professionals may perform the same process; some may practice the process and produce the desired outcome. However, others may practice the process differently (leveraging different tactics and a different blend of qualities) without deviating from the process but produce better outcomes.

Conclusion

Possessing certain leadership qualities is necessary for effective leadership. However, you must apply the qualities in a particular way to increase process effectiveness. You accomplish this through *practice*. A *practice* is a set of related actions that you apply to processes to achieve a more desired outcome.

When reading leadership books, consider how the authors explain leadership. Do they only describe a set of qualities? Do they illustrate how to practice the qualities in certain situations?

Reason 3: Leadership Is Like a Skill but Different

Leadership Is Like a Skill

Is leadership really a skill? In *The 21 Irrefutable Laws of Leadership*, Maxwell reveals that leadership isn't just a skill but a collection of skills that you can learn and develop.[7] If leadership includes a collection of skills, then you can develop leadership to different proficiency levels such as beginner, intermediate, or advanced. According to Kouzes and Posner, you need deliberate hours of practice to build leadership expertise.[8]

Hunter declares that there is a difference between leadership as knowledge and leadership as a skill. He recalls several professionals who know all about leadership, yet they don't know how to lead. In *The Servant*,

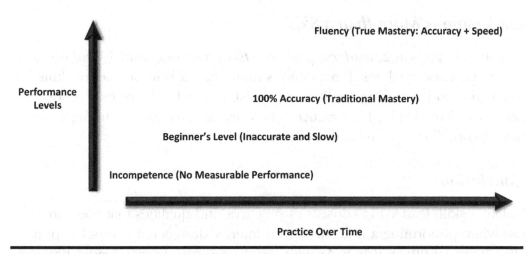

Figure 1.1   Binder's skill development levels. (Adapted from, 2003. With permission.)

he proclaims, "Like any skill, leadership has to be practiced regularly in order to develop the skills and facilitate true change."[9] Hunter suggests that your leadership skills may be ineffective or, worse, counter-effective without practice.

Binder describes skill fluency as performing a skill at 100% accuracy and at a useful pace or speed.[10] Figure 1.1 illustrates the maturity fluency levels.

At the lower levels, individuals perform slowly, with difficulty, with errors. After becoming fluent, though, they can:

- Retain leadership skills and knowledge long after formal training and without the need for annual retraining.
- Maintain the desired performance levels and concentrate on tasks for extended periods without allowing distractions to interrupt concentration.
- Perform more complex leadership skills in creative ways and with new situations.[11]

With the third outcome, you don't need to attend exclusively to the mechanics of a skill and can focus more on higher-level skill application. Thus, fluent individuals focus more on application, creativity, innovation, and problem-solving than skill mechanics.[12]

In this sense, leadership is more like a skill that you can develop rather than a naturally occurring competence. By practicing frequently and deliberately, you can improve your leadership effectiveness.

Leadership Is More than a Skill

As I state in Reason 2, *leadership is more than a set of qualities*; *skill* is one way to describe qualities. Leadership is more than a skill or a set of skills. In addition to possessing qualities (or skills), leadership involves a set of practices. Using leadership practices and qualities enables you to improve how you perform role-related processes.

Conclusion

Unlike a skill, leadership consists of practices and qualities that you can use when performing a role such as an interior designer, a counselor, or a chief financial officer (CFO). As with a skill, you can develop leadership and become fluent in both leadership practices and their related qualities. For more references on fluency, refer to *The Fluency Project* (http://fluency.org).

Reason 4: Some Leadership Theories Overlap with Leadership Styles

Leadership Theories Explain Leadership Behaviors

In graduate school, I learned about different leadership theories. Even though the theories provided a historical perspective about how leadership has changed, I didn't understand how leadership theories differ from styles.

In their independent work, Cherry, Nandan, and Zigarelli describe categories of leadership theories that I summarize in Table 1.7.[13] Cherry notes that the theories focus on differentiating leader and follower qualities; other theories focus on additional factors such as situations and skill levels.[14]

Leadership Theories Referenced as Leadership Styles

A few authors describe leadership theories as leadership styles. For example, Bogardus lists transactional and transformational theories as a leadership style.[15] This emphasizes the elusiveness of the leadership concept.

Conclusion

While leadership theories may provide some insight into leadership, they can also cause confusion. Some theories conflict with one another, and some

Table 1.7   Leadership Theories

Theory	Key Points
Great man theory	Individuals are born with leadership capabilities. Example traits: Courage and self-confidence.
Trait theory	Individuals are born with certain qualities that enable them to lead.
Contingency theory	Environmental factors determine the type of leader needed.
Situational theory	The leadership situation indicates which leadership style should be used.
Behavioral or skill theory	Individuals learn leadership through instruction and observation.
Participative theory or leader-member exchange theory	Leaders consider inputs from others to make decisions.
Transactional or managerial theory	Leaders use rewards and punishment to control behaviors.
Transformational theory	Leaders encourage and inspire their team by explaining the importance of their tasks.
Servant leadership theory	Leaders focus on meeting the needs of others.

overlap with styles. What is particularly unclear is how to use the theories collectively.

Reason 5: Leadership Is Like Management, but Different

Introduction

During a graduate leadership course, I had trouble distinguishing *leadership* from *management.* I thought *leadership* was what the CEO or a public figure did, and *management* had more to do with daily operations. When someone asked me how management and leadership differ, I might have muttered something like, "Leaders lead, and managers manage." After studying 21st Century Leadership books, I developed a distinction.

Management Defined

Established organizations have job descriptions that include various types of management positions. Each management description consists of desired qualities and specific, well-defined tasks.

Mary Parker Follett, a pioneer in the field of organizational design, defines *management* as "the art of getting things done through people."[16] For example, Elaine manages seven direct reports. She assigns work to them, monitors their progress, and provides support as needed. Elaine doesn't do the work herself but gets things done through her direct reports.

What's curious about Follett's definition is that some experts define *leadership* as inspiring people to accomplish goals (or some variation of this). Similar definitions explain why people have trouble differentiating *management* and *leadership*. In one video, the narrator defines *leadership* as "a process of social influence, which maximizes the efforts of others towards achieving a goal or a specific target. It is the art of motivating a group of people." The video continues by defining *management* as "the art of work done through people with the satisfaction of the public, employer, and the employees."[17] In another video, the speaker defines *management* as "the process of dealing with or controlling things or people" and *leadership* as "the action of leading a group towards a common goal." The speaker further explains that leaders and managers can be good or bad.[18] Neither video effectively distinguishes the difference. At best, they describe the traditional thinking about leadership and management. In Chapter 2, I define 21st Century Leadership in a way that discredits the idea that leadership can be bad.

Another curiosity is how some experts associate *management* as bad and leadership as good. For example, Sinek refers to management as "the manipulation of others for personal gain."[19] While management is neither good nor bad, understanding *management* helps clarify what leadership isn't. Try this: Using an Internet search engine, search for "leadership vs management" and examine the images.

Management Categories

I identified four management categories that involve accomplishing tasks through others: Managers of (1) organizations, (2) processes, (3) projects, and (4) people.[20]

Organization Managers

Managers are responsible for the structure of a group. They determine the division of labor among the group. Managers can be responsible for a company, a business unit or division, or a department. They often use organizational charts to determine the size and role responsibilities.

Process Managers

Managers are responsible for specific processes, parts of processes, or subprocesses. For example, a department head of training is responsible for acquiring, developing, and implementing a training process. A contact or call center manager is responsible for how customers contact the business to resolve issues.

Project Managers

Managers are responsible for ad hoc projects. This includes process improvement projects that use methodologies, such as Six Sigma, Lean Manufacturing, or Business Process Management (BPM), and Kaizen (continuous improvement).

Managers of People

Managers are responsible for the work of direct reports.

Professionals can work in one or more of these categories. For example, Alex, a department head, is responsible for managing the department (organization manager), including maintaining the organization chart structure. That same department head manages direct reports (manager of people) and is responsible for specific processes (process manager). In addition, Alex runs a few cross-functional projects (project manager).

In addition to managing organizations, processes, projects, and people, managers also are individual contributors. For example, Pascal supervises eight direct reports which respond to customer inquiries. In addition to supervising, Pascal handles customer escalations.

One more thing: Directing others to do the work is a monumental challenge for managers. Too often, managers choose to complete tasks that should be assigned to direct reports. Some do this because the effort to explain a task and coach direct reports takes longer than doing it themselves. Others find that individual contributor work to be more comfortable than the work of management. There's a tendency to prefer working within our comfort zone, which could be why some find the transition from individual contributor to manager difficult.

There is something that I call The Manager's Fallacy. This occurs when the effort to train a direct report to learn a task is greater than the effort for managers to do the task themselves. The fallacy is the failure to recognize that training direct reports to do these tasks gradually increases their value and reduces the overburdened managers' workload. Initially, training them may be more work, but it helps everyone.

A variation of the fallacy happens when managers assign the most difficult tasks to the most competent direct reports and the mundane, more straightforward tasks to the least competent employees. Over time, the competent employees feel bitter about having a heavier and more time-consuming workload while their less competent teammates have less work. Likewise, the less competent employees resent the manager for assigning the more exciting work to their teammates and leaving them with the less crucial work. Everyone needs to be appreciated and given a chance to contribute more substantially.

Three Performance Needs

The four manager types have three performance needs: (1) goals, (2) design, and (3) monitor and adapt.[21] Each sets goals for the work to clarify the desired outcomes. They then design how to work towards the set goals. Finally, they monitor progress and adjust efforts as circumstances and priorities change.

For example, the chief officers set the company goals by assessing competitors, available investments, how the company positions itself in the marketplace, and prospective products and services. To achieve company goals, the chief officers design the organization's structure, division of labor, and functional relationships among business units. Once the organization is operational, the chief officers monitor goal progress, organizational performance, resource usage, and business units' boundaries. For instance, the officers handle disputes about the division of labor (sometimes informally called turf wars). They also monitor marketplace changes and competitor accomplishments. They search for unexpected opportunities, regulation changes, and public opinion. As they discover changes, the chiefs assess if and how the company should adapt (deviate from the strategy).

Management and Leadership Can Accomplish the Same Tasks

Management is a category for a variety of formal organizational roles. These roles serve at least one of two functions. The first is to contribute toward monitoring and correcting an organization's primary or support processes and involves two high-level tasks:

1. Ensuring that the process continues to align with the process' design, process' goals, organizational design, and organizational goals.
2. Implementing process improvements to align better with process and organizational designs and goals.

The second management function is monitoring and correcting the behaviors of direct reports, indirect reports, and ad hoc teams to ensure that processes are executed as designed. Typical formal management titles include supervisor, manager, director, principal, partner, and vice president.

Leadership is a way to practice management activities. Table 1.8 provides examples of typical roles to demonstrate the differences between management and leadership.

In the examples, the management column describes what the manager does. The leadership column describes how the manager does (or practices) the action from a leadership perspective.

Leadership Differs from Management

Leadership practices are not managerial tasks, such as hiring, firing, promoting/demoting, micromanaging, or increasing/decreasing pay because those activities are managerial processes. Firing someone may not involve practicing leadership. I'm not implying that terminating an employee is wrong; it's often a necessary managerial process to protect the interests of teams and the organization, but this isn't a leadership task. Executives and managers only fire employees from an authoritative role.

Conclusion

Management and leadership are different. *Management* is a formal role, while *leadership* applies specific practices to strengthen their formal role's processes and tasks.

Table 1.8 Comparisons between Management and Leadership with Examples

Category	Management	Leadership
Relationship to formal roles	Category of formal organizational roles Example roles: Supervisor, manager, and vice president	From the perspective of a formal role, practices processes and tasks in a particular way
Function	Contributes to monitoring and correcting an organization's primary or supporting processes Monitors and correct behaviors of direct reports, indirect reports, or ad hoc teams	Matures individuals' mental and moral qualities, capabilities, and behaviors from the perspective of a formal role
Call-center supervisor example	Corrects a call-center agent who didn't comply with a process	Helps a call-center agent understand how the process contributes to the organization's goals and improves the customer experience Shares some real examples of how customers negatively reacted when an agent didn't follow the process and how customers positively reacted when agents followed the process
Project manager example	Corrects a team member who is behind schedule on a task	Collaborates with the team member who is behind on a task and involves others to help identify a reasonable way to correct the timeline and support the team member with the task
Chief executive officer	Creates a new organizational vision and strategy	Using input from several employee focus groups facilitates a meeting with the executive board to draft the vision and strategy Asks employee focus groups to continue to refine and finalize the vision and strategy and identify feasible ways that departments would apply the new vision and strategy to processes

> ### BOX 1.3 ANYONE CAN PRACTICE LEADERSHIP BUT NOT ALL EXECUTIVES PRACTICE LEADERSHIP
>
> Leadership is a choice. It is not a rank. I know many people at the senior-most levels of organizations who are absolutely not leaders. They are authorities, and we do what they say because they have authority over us, but we would not follow them. And I know many people who are at the bottom of organizations who have no authority and they are absolutely leaders, and this is because they have chosen to look after the person to the left of them, and they have chosen to look after the person to the right of them. This is what a leader is.[22]
>
> **Sinek**

Organizations authorize specific types of power to management roles; leadership practices don't have power or leverage power assigned to a role.

Regardless of title, anyone can practice leadership, so leadership practitioners aren't necessarily managers. In his TED talk, Sinek contrasts management and leadership (Box 1.3).

Chapter 2 defines 21st Century Leadership. Chapter 3 describes traditional leadership and 13 related assumptions that can be harmful if believed consciously or unconsciously. Chapter 4 continues clarifying 21st Century Leadership by explaining seven principles and 26-related beliefs.

Reason 6: The Meaning of Leadership Is Changing

Over time, the meaning of words can change. For example, Table 1.9 illustrates the definition of terms from previous centuries.

In contrast to the terms in Table 1.9, some words can change dramatically over a shorter duration. For example, Lexico defines *literal* as "Taking words in their usual or most basic sense without metaphor or allegory: *dreadful* in its literal sense, full of dread."[23] However, Lexico recognizes that you can use *literally* informally to "express strong feeling while not being literally true."[24] For example:

- Football pundit Jamie Redknapp once told us that Wayne Rooney was playing so well, he was "literally on fire."
- Deputy Prime Minister Nick Clegg said low-rate taxpayers were "literally living in a different galaxy."[25]

Table 1.9   Historic Terminology Definitions

Term	Century	Definition
Pedant	Sixteenth	Schoolmaster[a]
Bully	Sixteenth	Good fellow or darling (term of endearment)[b]
Nice	Fourteenth	Foolish or silly[c]
Abandon	Fourteenth	To subjugate or subdue someone or something[d]
Husband	Thirteenth	Homeowner[e]

[a] Dent, 2012, *What Is the Strangest Change in Meaning that Any Word Has Undergone.*
[b] Ibid.
[c] Ibid.
[d] Mirror.co.uk, 2014, *From Abandon to Nice.*
[e] Ibid.

As with the term *literal*, the meaning of *leadership* has changed during the fourth quarter of the 20th Century. One critical change, for example, is the shift from emphasizing the leader-follower relationship. Traditional leadership assumes that leaders must have followers who do what the leader wants to achieve a goal. Childhood games such as follow-the-leader emphasize the relationship between leader and follower by having followers mimic obediently what the leader does.[26] In contrast, Marquet, one of the 21st Century Leadership authors, writes about the need to give up the leader-follower structure and adapt a leader-lead structure.

Because of the substantive and fundamental change in the meaning of *leadership*, I clarify the leadership transformation in the next three chapters. In Chapter 2, I define 21st Century Leadership. In Chapter 3, I define traditional leadership and explain the problems with its assumptions. In Chapter 4, I contrast traditional assumptions by explaining 21st Century Leadership principles and beliefs.

Summary

I started this chapter by stating that *leadership* is elusive: Although a meaningful concept, *leadership* is difficult to analyze. In this chapter, I examined leadership structure and described *leadership* to be vague and open to multiple interpretations. Some interpretations can guide us to develop leadership positively, while others contribute to the elusiveness of *leadership.*

I described six reasons why the leadership concept is confusing. Terms that you frequently use, such as *leadership role, leadership skill,* and *leadership style,* can be ambiguous. What managers do might or might not be *leadership.* When you observe someone being *friendly* (in Appendix VI, No. 110 in the leadership-related quality terms), you may not know if someone exhibits leadership or something else.

Sections II through IV of this book are about leadership practices. As you read Sections II through IV, think about how I discuss leadership practices and their underlying qualities. Consider situations in which you could have applied the practices to achieve a better outcome.

Chapter 2

Defining 21st Century Leadership

Sometimes leadership is imagined to be something majestic and awe-inspiring. Grand visions, world-changing initiatives, transforming the lives of millions—all are noble possibilities, but real leadership is in the daily moments.[1]

Kouzes and Posner

Leadership, more than anything else, is about the way we think. It's a moment-to-moment discipline of our thoughts. It's about practicing personal accountability and choosing to make a positive contribution, no matter what our role or "level." A receptionist, an engineer, a sales person, a temp, a cashier: They all can be leaders.[2]

Miller

Introduction

This chapter defines 21st Century Leadership and elaborates on its components and results. From my analysis, I derived the definition, short- and long-term results, and societal results on how the authors describe and illustrate leadership. The *immediate results* primarily come from James C. Hunter's servant leadership perspective,[3] and the business results from Gallup's reports.[4]

DOI: 10.4324/9781003273448-3

In addition to explaining the 21st Century Leadership definition and results, I introduce seven leadership principles that align with the 26 leadership beliefs and the nine practices described in Chapter 4. In Chapter 3, I contrast 21st Century Leadership with traditional leadership by presenting 13 traditional assumptions that could impede desired individual, team, and organizational results.

Definition of 21st Century Leadership and Desired Results

21st Century Leadership is bidirectional and designed to mature mental and moral qualities, capabilities, and behaviors. To accomplish this, people apply nine leadership practices to how they perform their formal, organizational role. The 21st Century Leadership practices aren't strategic or visionary; they are tactical and practical. For example, Hunter asserts that *leadership* is character in action,[5] and Maxell describes *leadership* as a verb rather than a noun.[6] For Kouzes and Posner, "Leadership is not about who you are; it's about what you do."[7]

We practice leadership from the perspective of our formal roles. Every day, we have opportunities to make a difference in someone's life through leadership practices (Box 2.1).

Table 2.1 summarizes the 21st Century Leadership definition, principles, practices, and desired results. The acts of leading produce desired results: immediate, short- and long-term, business, and societal. Underlying the definition and practices are seven principles. Derived from the principles are 26 beliefs. In the following topics, I expand on the definition and related concepts.

BOX 2.1   21st CENTURY LEADERSHIP

■ Emphasizes collaborative conversations in which someone advocates a belief while others query details for clarity. Next, someone else advocates while others inquire.[8]

■ De-emphasizes roles such as *leader* and *follower.*

Table 2.1   21st Century Leadership Definition, Principles, Practices, and Results

Definition	• A bidirectional set of practices founded on guiding principles and beliefs	• Designed to mature mental and moral: • Qualities • Capabilities • Behaviors
Principles	• Believe in others • Connect with others • Put others first • Give up control	• Encourage growth • Collaborate with others • Develop leadership practices continuously
Practices	• Analyzing Like Detectives • Diagnosing and Treating Like Doctors • Finding Key Behaviors Like Social Psychologists • Communicating Like Agents	• Directing Like Guides • Nurturing Like Gardeners • Facing the Unknown Like Lions • Developing Like Scouts • Communicating Like Broadcasters
Immediate Results	• Fulfilled needs rather than wants	• Removed or reduced barriers • Improved performance
Short and Long-Term Results	• Improved work environment • Increased feelings of safety among teammates • Increased collaboration	• Strengthened relationships • Increased mental and moral capabilities, especially creativity, innovation, and learning
Business Results	• Increased employee engagement • Increased profitability • Decreased operational costs • Improved customer experience	• Decreased absenteeism and turnover • Reduced product theft, defects, and damages • Decreased safety incidents (amount and severity)
Societal Results	• Improved local and larger communities • Improved leadership communities of practice	• Increased volunteering activities • Increased stewardship practices

Desired Results

Introduction

To understand the intent of leadership, begin with the end in mind. Think about results as three types: Performance, business, and societal. I define *performance* as a set of activities that generates specific results. *Performance results* generate *business results*. Table 2.2 defines the different types of results.

For 21st Century Leadership practices, I classify performance results at two levels:

- Immediate results
- Short and long-term results

Practicing leadership can have an immediate effect on individual and team performance. Individuals and teams can realize short and long-term performance results through consistent practice. Over time, the practices can affect business and societal results.

21st Century Leadership authors write how leadership effectively achieves performance and business results, as described in this chapter.

Table 2.2   Results Definitions

Definition	Explanation
Result	An outcome from specific activities[a]
Performance result	In the context of an organization, tactical outcomes of the work produced by individuals and teams
Business result	In the context of an organization, strategic outcomes of performance results
Societal results	Outcomes from people's activities that benefit a group of individuals with similar interests within a community. Societal results can be at any of these levels: • Local • Regional • National • Global

[a] Adapted from Lexico, n.d., *Result*.

Immediate Results

When people apply the nine leadership practices within their formal role, those who are helped experience the following performance results:

- Met needs rather than wants
- Experience the removal or reduction of performance barriers
- Experience performance improvement

The results may overlap, and *experience performance improvement* may be a consequence of the first two results.

Fulfilled Needs

Imagine what your productivity would be like if you worked on projects as part of a team with a clear purpose and knew that the work would help the organization and benefit the organization's customers substantially. Picture in your mind that you had everything you need to be productive: Tools, templates, and process maps. Teams from other departments were ready to help, and you had no distractions. Simply stated, all your needs were met. The 21st Century Leadership practices can help individuals fulfill such needs.

As Hunter states, a *need* "is a legitimate physical or psychological requirement for the well-being of a human being."[9] The type of needs that Hunter refers to aren't necessarily the needs for food, clothing, and shelter. Instead, they are higher-level needs that commonly occur within a workplace. In *The Servant*, Hunter identifies such needs. Table 2.3 summarizes Hunter's needs as well as some performance needs.[10]

Fulfilled needs are enablers to optimize performance, while unfulfilled needs can become barriers to efficient and effective performance. For example, Blanchard comments that people "are social beings and have a need to belong and be accepted by people who are important to them."[11] Likewise, this is true for teams. Imagine the effect on your productivity if you had the impression that you weren't part of a functional team that worked well together. Imagine the effect of your teammates behaving as if they didn't accept you.

Hunter notes that you have different needs at any given time. For example, someone starting a new job would have different performance needs than someone who has successfully performed in the same role for

Table 2.3 Examples of Fulfilled Needs

Needs Identified by Hunter		Other Performance Needs
Feelings and Beliefs	*Structural Needs*	

Appreciated
Respected
Valued Communicated
  with
Encouraged
Treated with dignity
  Included
Listened to
Treated consistently
Treated honestly
Received authentic
  feedback
	Being held
	  accountable
	Established healthy
	  boundaries
	Defined rules
		Organizational, process, and
		  role information
		Resources such as tools and
		  templates
		Incentives including recognition
		Training on knowledge and
		  skills
		Capability support such as
		  disability accommodations
		Motivation such as believing
		  that work contributes to
		  something larger than oneself

ten years.[12] Not only do individual needs differ, but the type of needs may differ as well. Table 2.4 summarizes the categories of needs that West et al. identify for practitioners to use when determining needs based on different categories.[13]

Table 2.4 Categories of Needs

Category	Explanation
Normative	Gaps between norms and the current situation experienced by an individual, team, or organization; norms are what researchers or experts define as being normal or desirable
Expressed	Requirements that individuals, teams, or organizations believe that they don't have but would spend time, money, and resources to acquire
Felt	Requirements or gaps that individuals, teams, or organizations don't overtly express and are unable or unwilling to spend time, money, or resources to acquire
Comparative	Gaps between what others experience and benefit from and what individuals, teams, or organizations lack and could benefit from having
Anticipated or future	Requirements that are likely to occur at a later time

Categories of needs are useful for systematically identifying the needs of others and for determining actions to meet individual, team, or organizational needs.

In contrast to needs, Hunter describes *wants* as "a wish or desire without any regard for the physical or psychological requirements for the well-being of a human being."[14] *Wants* may not be best for us in either the short or long-term. Likewise, what we need might not be what we want. In other words, thinking abstractly about needs and wants may be straightforward, but sometimes when we apply this to our own lives, what we need and want may not be as apparent as we would like. At times, we need others to help us put our situation in perspective to determine our needs and wants (i.e., not identifying a want as a need) and help us make better choices. Freiberg and Freiberg, along with Hunter, convey that leadership is about helping others identify and fulfill their needs so that unmet needs don't act as barriers to performance.[15]

Removed or Reduced Performance Barriers

Imagine what your productivity would be like if you didn't have to deal with unnecessary approvals. Instead of ignoring your requests or withholding valuable information that you need for your work, people from other departments and teams gladly help you when asked. Also, imagine how productive you would be if your teammates supported one another and helped you when asked. Practicing 21st Century Leadership contributes to this state by removing or reducing performance barriers or what Wiseman calls *blockers*.[16]

The first immediate performance result, fulfilled needs, is one example of how those practicing leadership can remove barriers. Another example involves blockers; blockers can be anyone or anything that hinders performance, including individuals, processes, artificial boundaries, cultural norms, budgets, organizational structures and ownership, or rules. The practices help others remove, reduce, or even bypass blockers.

A system barrier example is archaic processes. A financial application may require supervisor approval. While the approval step may have been necessary several years ago, the original need for the approval may have become obsolete, and employees seeking supervisor approval may unnecessarily waste valuable time trying to find someone who has approval authority. Modifying the system to allow any employee to function as the approver could eliminate this barrier.

In *Multipliers*, Wiseman comments that managers can be barriers to performance by being too involved or taking over their employees' work. Managers who appropriately restrain themselves exemplify a way to remove the managerial barrier. As Wiseman writes, "It is a small victory to create space for others to contribute. But it is a huge victory to maintain that space and resist the temptation to jump back in and consume it yourself."[17] Managers may agree with Wiseman's statement, but often, they unknowingly succumb to the temptation.

Leadership includes helping others by removing or reducing barriers or even identifying alternative ways to work, which avoids barriers. In Sections II through IV, I identify specific leadership practices and resources that you can use to help others remove, reduce, or avoid performance barriers.

Improved Performance

Because leadership practices result in fulfilled needs and removed barriers, individual and team performance improves. When we practice leadership, we enable individuals and teams to deliver products or services faster, cheaper, and of a higher quality.

Short and Long-Term Results

Consistently practicing leadership and achieving immediate performance results lead to short- and long-term results. These apply at either the individual level or the team level. The team level includes cross-functional teams and teams within a larger group such as a department or a business unit. Of the five short and long-term results that I identify, the first two align with culture, the next two align with partnerships, and the last align with individual growth.

Cultural Results

Imagine waking up and wanting to go to work. Envision yourself enjoying the work because of the people you work with and because you believe that your work makes a difference for the organization and customers. Also, picture being valued by your teammates, and imagine that your teammates openly share their thoughts and values. They sincerely listen to your ideas and support your work. Conflicts are resolved or addressed in a way that the team has overall positive feelings about the original disagreement even when one teammate disagrees with the resolution.

21st Century Leadership practices help shape and build a positive culture by improving the work environment and increasing feelings of safety among the team. In *Leaders Eat Last*, Sinek writes passionately about how leadership practitioners can set the culture they want.[18] He argues that people aren't the problem or the cause of dysfunction. Instead, the problems are with the environment in which people work.[19] Rummler describes the environmental problem: "Put a good performer against a bad system, and the system will win almost every time."[20] Sinek further comments on the vast number of inadequate systems or work environments existing today that somehow bring out the worst in performers.[21]

If you work in bad systems and don't feel safe when working, Sinek argues that you suffer from work-life imbalance.[22] This works both ways. At Southwest Airlines, when people have problems in their personal life—such as when a flight attendant's son had the first of two bone marrow transplants—the problems affect their work. However, Southwest finds ways to support its people in difficult times. In addition, the airline discourages employees from compartmentalizing their work life and personal life because doing so doesn't work. Southwest benefits and society benefits when employees achieve genuine work-life balance.[23] For Sinek, work-life balance has nothing to do with time but has everything to do with safety. When you feel safe at home and at work, you experience a work-life balance.

Practicing 21st Century Leadership changes environments so that performers can feel safe working within their teams and become more productive. The nine practices can rebuild a team's mental and moral behaviors and provide the direction to achieve this. Sinek describes how those in charge at the organizational level can set the culture so that it functions efficiently and effectively or not (Box 2.2).

BOX 2.2 THOSE IN CHARGE SET BEHAVIORAL STANDARDS—GOOD AND BAD

Hypocrites, liars, and self-interested leaders create cultures filled with hypocrites, liars and self-interested employees. The leaders of the companies who tell the truth, in contrast, will create a culture of people who tell the truth. It's not rocket science. We follow the leader.[24]

Sinek

Whether at the micro or macro level, leadership practitioners can change the work environment and increase feelings of safety among teammates; the influence can affect other teams and, ultimately, the organization.

Partnership Results

Imagine working in cross-functional teams or departments where everyone works together and supports one another. Teammates would recognize people's strengths and talents. They would even recognize their personal preferences (such as someone being more productive in the morning than at the end of the day or a teammate who prefers a telephone conversation to a lengthy email). Also, imagine that teammates respect each other's diversity and unique viewpoints they bring to the team.

Applying the nine practices results in more collaboration and strengthened relationships. Hunter, Sinek, and Maxwell write about the importance of building relationships.[25] For example, Hunter states, "the key then to leadership is accomplishing the tasks at hand while building relationships."[26] Building and strengthening relationships is a critical outcome of leadership practices. Non-leadership practices can accomplish tasks through others but may compromise the relationship in the process. For example, managers can threaten direct reports with unfavorable performance reviews or termination if they don't accomplish the tasks. This may effectively achieve the goal, but consider how this could negatively affect the manager-direct report relationship. Leadership practices don't rely on coercion to accomplish work because of negative consequences, and leadership practices aren't about causing casualties in the workplace. Like all performance-improvement disciplines, leadership practitioners determine the desired performance and business results and then apply leadership practices so that no harm is caused but ensures that the team achieves the desired business and performance results.

Individual Growth Results

Imagine being a part of a learning organization or a team that values doing what is best for the organization rather than taking potentially costly shortcuts. Imagine experiencing a team meeting that resulted in discovering new ways of working smarter, cheaper, and better than the old ways! After a few weeks, you realize how much you've learned and developed. Practicing 21st Century Leadership results in individuals' increased mental and moral capabilities.

Applying the nine practices from the perspective of a formal role results in helping others increase their mental and moral capabilities or what Hunter calls *character*[27] (and I expand on this in the next topic, Maturing Mental and Moral Qualities, Capabilities, and Behaviors). In particular, the leadership practices promote learning, creative thinking, and opportunities for teams to innovate.

Business Results

Because 21st Century Leadership improves performance, it also improves business results. In their books, Collins[28], Wiseman[29], Kouzes and Posner[30], and Sinek[31] share stories about leadership practitioners who had extraordinary business results. Abrashoff's book, *It's Your Ship*, is a personal testimonial of his leadership practices that produced extraordinary business results. When individuals practice 21st Century Leadership, they, their teams, and their organizations produce the performance and business results that I describe in Table 2.1.

If 21st Century Leadership practices result in an increase in employee engagement, then Gallup provides evidence that indicates that 21st Century Leadership practices contribute to the other business results described in Table 2.1.

As mentioned in the Preface, Gallup reported that employee engagement scores strongly predict business results.[32] Putting this in perspective, consider these Gallup findings from the report:

- In 2012, Gallup reported that the employee engagement percentages of the US working population (with full-time jobs) were:
  - Engaged: 30% (30 million)
  - Not engaged: 52% (52 million)
  - Actively disengaged: 18% (18 million).[33]
- Actively disengaged employees cost US organizations an estimated $450–$550 billion annually.[34]
- According to Jim Clifton, Gallup's Chairman and Chief Executive Officer (CEO), the engaged employees (30 million) generate the most innovative ideas, add most of the organizations' new customers, and "have the most entrepreneurial energy."[35]
- Gallup concludes that "managers are primarily responsible for their employees' engagement levels."[36] Clifton argues that when you hire the wrong person for a managerial position, "nothing fixes that bad decision. Not compensation, not benefits—nothing."[37]

Clifton labels these wrong hires as *managers from hell*.[38] Although Clifton might seem harsh, the report supports his judgment by characterizing how bad these managers are. In contrast to bad managers, the report describes good managerial behaviors. For example: "Gallup has found that managers who focus on their employees' strengths can practically eliminate active disengagement and double the average of U.S. workers who are engaged nationwide."[39] If businesses wrongly place people in managerial roles who don't focus on their employees' strengths, then Clifton is on to something.

Gallup illustrates their claim that employee engagement is a strong predictor for business results by examining business/work units that have engaged employees compared to those with actively disengaged employees. Gallup examined the median differences between top-quartile and bottom-quartile units, depicted in Table 2.5.

21st Century Leadership practices contribute to the business results described in Table 2.1 and Table 2.5. The Gallup report, Collin's research, Wiseman's research, and real stories reported by the authors in my study make a strong case for practicing 21st Century Leadership. However, no study exists to my knowledge that proves that this leadership

Table 2.5   Business Results of Top-Quartile Employee-Engagement Business/Work Units Compared with Bottom Quartile[a]

Percentage Difference	Business Result Category
10% Higher	Customer ratings
22% Higher	Profitability
21% Higher	Productivity
25% Lower	Turnover (high-turnover organizations)
65% Lower	Turnover (low-turnover organizations)
37% Lower	Absenteeism
28% Less	Shrinkage (such as theft)
48% Fewer	Safety incidents
41% Fewer	Patient safety incidents
41% Fewer	Quality (defects)

[a] Gallup, 2014, *State of the American Workplace*, 25; percentage indicators (higher, lower, less, and fewer) found in Gallup, 2014, *Engagement at Work*, 1.

approach conclusively causes these favorable business results. Given this acknowledgment, the indirect evidence is worth considering.

Societal Results

Kaufman wrote an intriguing article in the *Performance Improvement Journal*, "Becoming Your Own Leader." Kaufman makes a pragmatic case for aligning our actions with improving the world because "adding value to our shared society is practical, realistic, and vital."[40] Practicing 21st Century Leadership contributes toward Kaufman's call to contribute to society.

Leadership practices not only lead to favorable performance and business results, but the practices also lead to favorable societal results. By maturing individuals' mental and moral qualities, capabilities, and behaviors, they can apply their developed character to improve how they work, interact with family and friends, and participate in local communities such as clubs, religious organizations, associations, societies, and government. Likewise, what happens in our personal lives affects our work. Thus, maturing our character benefits ourselves, teams, organizations, and nonwork relations such as with our families and society.

Conclusion

If performance equals activity plus results, to lead, you need to know the results you want to achieve to accurately plan your journey. Knowing the results at the different levels helps guide your leadership journey and enables you to evaluate your leadership progress and how well your team is progressing.

Maturing Mental and Moral Qualities, Capabilities, and Behaviors

While 21st Century Leadership practices contribute to improving individual and team performances that ultimately improve business results, the fundamental intent of leadership is to mature mental and moral qualities, capabilities, and behaviors. Helping others meet their needs and overcome barriers and obstacles is a means to achieving this intent.

Consider the terms in Table 2.6. In the 21st Century Leadership definition, I could have stated that this 21st Century Leadership influences others

Table 2.6 Definition of Terms Related to Leadership[a]

Term	Definition
Mature	Become fully grown or developed; having reached an advanced stage of mental or emotional development
Develop	Grow or cause to grow and become more mature, advanced, or elaborate
Build	Construct something by putting parts or material together over time
Influence	The capacity to have an effect on the character, development, or the behavior of someone or something, or the effect itself
Character	Mental and moral qualities distinctive to an individual
Moral	Concerned with the principles of right and wrong behavior
Quality	A distinctive attribute or characteristic possessed by someone or something
Capability	Power or ability to do something
Behavior	The way one acts or conducts oneself, especially toward others

[a] Lexico, n.d., *Mature*; ibid, *Develop*; ibid, *Build*; ibid, *Influence*; ibid, *Character*; ibid, *Moral*; ibid, *Capability*; ibid, *Behavior*.

to build their character. However, using *influence, build,* and *character* oversimplifies the meaning of leading and overshadows the moral element that some might find discomforting.

Maturing Mental Qualities

Maturing mental qualities involves building the techniques or specific ways to execute tasks associated with concepts such as programming, risk management, people management, marketing, merchandising, accounting, customer service, facility maintenance, data processing, and product development.

Maturing Moral Qualities

Maturing moral qualities involves building the commitment, criteria, and priorities to make the best choices that benefit society, customers, the organization, or a team without necessarily benefiting yourself. Hunter calls this "doing the right thing" and doing what is right even when you don't feel like doing what is right.[41] Moral qualities also involve putting the needs of others ahead of your own. Hunter might describe it like this: Stop your *me-thinking* and focus on the needs of others.

Maturing Capabilities

Maturing capabilities involves building a desire to learn continuously, learn from failures, and learn how to learn. Learning is critical for being the best you can be. In the context of leadership, Maxwell explains that successful leaders are learners; he describes learning as an ongoing process resulting from self-discipline and perseverance.[42] Kouzes and Posner assert that leaders need a passion for learning.[43] They and Wiseman state that you need to learn from failures and mistakes.[44] Blanchard and Ridge consider mistakes and things that go wrong as *learning moments*.[45]

Maturing Behaviors

Maturing behaviors involves applying mental and moral qualities to your work and daily actions. Having mental and moral qualities is necessary, but these qualities are insufficient without applying them through action. As Hunter describes, "All the good intentions in the world don't mean a thing if they don't line up with our actions."[46]

Bidirectional

When leading, everyone, those leading and those being led, builds character. Bill Daniels, CEO and co-founder of American Consulting & Training, mentioned to me that someone recently approached him for mentoring. Bill said that mentees appreciate how much time and energy he puts into the relationship and how much they learn. Mentees don't realize that through the mentees' experiences, Bill also learns, and through the process, he improves on how he practices consulting.[47] Marquet describes this as mentor-mentor: "I learned as much from them as they did from me. Hence, we were practicing a mentor-mentor program."[48] Maxwell describes this experience as well, "The truth is that empowerment is powerful—not only for the person being developed but also for the mentor. Enlarging others makes you larger."[49]

Through the leadership experience and by applying the practices in different situations, practitioners develop a deeper understanding of

BOX 2.3   LEADERSHIP IS BIDIRECTIONAL

Influence flows back and forth between leaders and collaborators. This means that influence does not always originate with the executive officers of Southwest Airlines. As John Gardner [leadership author] suggests, leaders both shape and are shaped. The result is mutual influence. The implication is that anyone, at any level within a company, has the opportunity to influence the system.[50]

Freiberg and Freiberg

leadership principles and beliefs. They strengthen their mental and moral qualities. As noted in Chapter 1, practitioners become more fluent as they learn from their leadership experiences.

In *Nuts!*, Freiberg and Freiberg present a different perspective on how leadership is bidirectional. At Southwest Airlines, employees can act as leaders and collaborators. In some situations, they lead, and in other situations, they follow. Regardless of the situation, people in the roles mutually influence one another (Box 2.3).

Seven Principles, Twenty-Six Beliefs, and Nine Practices

In my research, I identified seven leadership principles. From the principles, I derived 26 leadership beliefs. The principles and beliefs align with the nine practices.

Figure 2.1 illustrates how these concepts align. When someone leads, you observe their behaviors. Like an iceberg, you can see the ice above the surface (the behaviors), but you cannot see the part of the iceberg that floats below the surface. What is hidden are the underlying practices, knowledge and skill capabilities, beliefs, principles, and qualities. Similarly, when I observe someone running, I cannot see why the person runs. At best, I can only infer or guess why someone chooses to run.

Appendix II illustrates how the principles, beliefs, and practices align. In Chapter 4, I explain the seven principles and the 26 beliefs. In Sections II through IV (Chapters 5 through 13), I explain the nine practices.

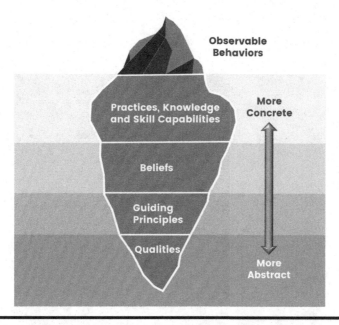

Figure 2.1   Iceberg image illustrating the difficulty of identifying the underlying practices, knowledge, skills, beliefs, principles, and qualities that align with observable behaviors.

Summary: What to Do

This chapter defined 21st Century Leadership and leadership results. I explained that this leadership approach is bidirectional, meaning that by internalizing and applying the nine practices, leadership practitioners help others mature their mental and moral qualities, capabilities, and behaviors. In other words, they help people build character. I ended the chapter by showing how the definition, principles, beliefs, and practices support leadership behaviors.

One technique for developing 21st Century Leadership capabilities is to learn more about performance improvement. In the Bibliography, I recommend performance-improvement books.

Chapter 3

Revealing Traditional Leadership and Assumptions

> We make assumptions about the world around us based on
> sometimes incomplete or false information...our behavior is
> affected by our assumptions or our perceived truths.[1]
>
> **Sinek**

Introduction

Traditional Leadership Definition

Traditional leadership is the practice of leading followers—usually a team or
an organization—to achieve a set of goals that relate to producing products
and services. This approach strongly emphasizes the leader's role rather than
the follower's. Leaders tend to command and control followers' actions and
expect them to comply with orders. Traditional leadership tends to be top-
down in which leaders typically have an authoritative position (such as a
manager) that gives the power needed to lead followers.

Traditional Leadership Includes Accidental Leaders

In organizations, those in superior positions often promote others to
managerial roles because of how well they performed as individual
contributors. When superiors expect these individuals to perform well as

DOI: 10.4324/9781003273448-4

managers—especially without providing formal training or only minimal coaching—and when these newly appointed supervisors have no interest in training in leadership, they become accidental leaders.

As Kouzes and Posner explain, people watch how managers perform in their role and with their leadership practices, whether they know it or not. Managers have the most influence on how direct reports perceive the organization, moral behavior, and career development.[2] Direct reports watch their managers resolve problems, handle stress, accept or distribute blame, and promote or demote feelings of safety among the team. When superiors don't prepare new managers to balance their power with leadership practice, and when the new managers show disinterest in developing their leadership, direct reports may become disengaged and less effective in their role and potentially leave the team or organization.

The Extreme Case of Traditional Leadership

When traditional leadership is at its worse, followers serve leaders. Often, traditional leaders don't express this openly, and they might even claim that they serve their followers. However, traditional leaders' behaviors indicate that they are more inclined to serve themselves than their followers.

Traditional leaders set the vision, direction, and commands. They use influence—often with coercion—to ensure follower obedience. They perceive themselves as the smartest person on the team and unconsciously may believe themselves to be a kind of hero who fixes problems that followers are incapable of resolving. They also perceive followers as the cause of unproductivity and conclude that followers cannot be fully trusted.

Why Anyone Would Practice Traditional Leadership

There may be a substantial number of traditional leaders simply because traditional leadership is easy to practice, and, as Marquet notes, it is tremendously rewarding.[3] Anyone can leverage the power that organizations assign to them. Anyone can avoid developing their leadership capabilities or even fall into the trap of deluding themselves into thinking that they are an effective leader. All the pitfalls I mentioned in Chapter 1 make contemporary leadership elusive and make it easy for traditional leaders to rationalize their disinterest in developing their leadership practices.

Traditional Leadership Assumptions

Assumptions are things that you accept to be true without the need for proof.[4] In terms of leadership, some people are unaware of some of their leadership assumptions. Maybe they never explored them or, over time, they simply acquired them. Like most habits, assumptions influence our behaviors without realizing what is happening. In a way, assumptions can be similar to underlying irrational beliefs. As described in rational emotive behavior therapy, they affect your perceptions, feelings, and behaviors and how you practice leadership.[5]

From my analysis, I identify 13 traditional leadership assumptions. Some of these are interrelated. Others may strengthen the beliefs of complementary assumptions. While some people are aware that they work from these assumptions, others may not realize that the assumptions influence their thinking, feelings, and behavior.

From the perspective of 21st Century Leadership, these assumptions are misleading and cause more harm than good. With each assumption, you may experience enough positive, immediate results to reinforce believing in them. However, actions based on these assumptions cause short- and long-term harm. Ironically, traditional leaders often fail to connect their actions with the harm that they cause.

Table 3.1 lists the traditional assumptions by category. In Appendix III, I provide a detailed summary that includes related consequences.

When I refer to *leaders*, I am referring to traditional leadership. When I refer to *teams* or *team members*, I am using these in the context of traditional leaders having followers. I use *team members* instead of *teammates* because managers as leaders distinguish themselves from the teammate level. In 21st Century Leadership, the focus is on the action and not the role. In Appendix III, I list the short-term results on the team when leaders act from these assumptions. For all assumptions, Table 3.2 displays the long-term result examples.

Assumption 1: Leaders Need Authority

Rationale

Organizations assign formal roles with varying degrees of authority. Human resources (HR) and information technology (IT) departments manage formal roles and the related authority. HR maintains the job descriptions that list

Table 3.1   Traditional Leadership Assumptions by Category

Category	Assumption
Characterizing leadership	1. Leaders need authority 2. Leaders are heroes who leave a legacy 3. Intimacy weakens leadership 4. Giving away power weakens leadership
Characterizing team members	5. Only one person—typically a manager—functions as the leader 6. The leader is the smartest 7. Team members are the cause of unproductivity 8. Team members cannot be trusted 9. Team members are less important than revenue, profits, operational expenses, and leaders
Working in teams	10. Talking is more important than listening 11. Recognition is a formal process
Becoming a leader	12. Leadership requires little or no training 13. Leaders know how effective their leadership is

high-level authority. For example, a programmer may be authorized to work with subject-matter experts when building code. A department head may be authorized to create the strategy for a department. IT assigns system access levels to formal roles. For example, a system may authorize a vice president (VP) to initiate a hiring request or approve annual performance ratings that the VP's direct reports completed for their reports.

To lead others, traditional leaders believe that they need their organizations to assign them authority, especially those with direct reports. This includes the power to hire, fire, increase pay, demote, promote, and award bonuses. Only by having the authorization to leverage this type of power can you influence subordinates and others to listen and obey.

Table 3.2   Example Long-Term Results of Traditional Leadership Assumptions

Increase in…	Decrease in…
• Stress • Feelings of being unsafe at work • Distrust toward the organization, manager, and team • Turnover	• Engagement • Tenure • Productivity and performance • Favorable business results

Why the Leaders Need Authority Assumption Is Wrong

This assumption is wrong for two reasons. First, some mistakenly believe that leadership requires position power to be effective. Believing that management is the same as leadership and that leadership uses formal power is wrong. Maxwell calls this mistake "the greatest misunderstanding about leadership."[6] In Chapter 1, I discussed how *leadership* and *management* aren't the same. In Chapter 4, I expand on this when discussing Belief 2, Everyone Can Practice Leadership Regardless of Role.

Second, thinking that formal power is appropriate for leadership is wrong. Freiberg and Freiberg, Kouzes and Posner, Hunter, and Wiseman argue against this assumption.[7] Maxwell acknowledges that power gives those who wield it an incredible advantage: When all else fails, those with military rank can "throw people in the brig," and in business, a manager can use pay adjustments, bonuses, demotions, and termination to ensure cooperation.[8] Sinek seems to agree: Traditional leaders who use incentives and punishments can obtain the desired behaviors effectively.[9] However, Sinek notes that this can only work initially, and power has a negative long-term effect (Box 3.1).

In his next book, Sinek comments that just as parents cannot buy a child's love, organizations cannot buy employee loyalty.[10] In Chapter 4, I expand on the problems with power when describing the 21st Century Leadership Belief, *Control Erodes Relationships*.

Assumption 2: Leaders Are Heroes Who Leave a Legacy

In the western part of the United States and during the 19th century, American cinema depicts heroes who would save towns from outlaws. Not even the local government and sheriffs could protect the town as these

---

BOX 3.1 ON USING INCENTIVES AND PUNISHMENTS TO INFLUENCE BEHAVIORS

Over time, such tactics cost more money and increase stress for employee and employer alike, and eventually will become the main reason people show up for work every day.[11]

Sinek

BOX 3.2   THE LEADER AS HERO MYTH

Intellectually, most of us would agree that no one person—no matter how great—does it alone. Yet we have been conditioned to think of leadership in terms of the heroic figure who comes to the rescue of people who are either too dumb or too weak to help themselves.[15]

Freiberg and Freiberg

---

heroes could. Like the old West heroes, leaders behave as if they are the heroes, and their teams are incapable of solving problems without leaders. The leader alone steps into the situation, issues orders, salvages the situation, and, similarly to a western movie, walks off into the sunset.

In addition to being the hero, some leaders talk about leaving their legacy within an organization. Through their accomplishments, they believe that the organization and its employees will recognize a legacy left behind after leaders move on to another organization or retire. Freiberg and Freiberg describe the assumption (Box 3.2).

Leadership isn't heroism. As Maxwell describes it, "There are still leaders who hold up the Lone Ranger as their model for leadership...There are no Lone Ranger leaders. Think about it: If you're alone, you're not leading anybody, are you?"[12] When Kouzes and Posner describe what leadership isn't, they include being a hero (Box 3.3).

Leadership isn't about being the hero but helping everyday heroes. In the *Star Wars* movie, leadership aligns less with Luke Skywalker and more with Ben Obi-Wan Kenobi or Yoda.[13] In *The Hero with a Thousand Faces*, Campbell describes common themes found in mythology and religion about the hero and the hero's journey.[14] In the hero's journey, the hero encounters a protective figure who provides aid to help the hero when facing

---

BOX 3.3   WHAT LEADERSHIP IS NOT ABOUT

We've focused on everyday leaders because leadership is not about position or title. It's not about organizational power or authority. It's not about fame or wealth. It's not about the family you are born into. It's not about being a CEO, president, general, or prime minister. And it's definitely not about being a hero.[16]

Kouzes and Posner

challenges.[17] With 21st Century Leadership, those practicing leadership do so in the background. Like the protective figure, these leadership practitioners aid others, enabling them to face their challenges and overcome barriers. Practicing leadership this way doesn't include heroically rescuing teams or taking credit for a team's accomplishments.

In 21st Century Leadership, those practicing leadership don't consider the possibility of leaving a legacy. A focus on leaving a legacy is a focus on oneself. In contrast, leadership focuses on others and helping them mature their mental and moral qualities, capabilities, and behaviors. Ideally, when an effective leadership practitioner leaves an organization, those who remain continue to excel.

Assumption 3: Intimacy Weakens Leadership

Intimacy means close familiarity or friendship.[18] *Weakness* involves lacking the power to perform.[19] In *The Leadership Challenge*, Kouzes and Posner discuss the managerial myth that leaders cannot be friends with team members.[20] Early in my career, I also heard or read that leaders want to avoid compromising their command by being friends with direct reports. The don't-be-friends advice is to avoid favoritism toward friends in your care or prevent friendships from compromising your ability to discipline.

There are two problems with the Intimacy Weakens Leadership assumption: First, Kouzes and Posner cite a study that contradicts the myth. In the study, when compared with groups of acquaintances, groups of friends completed three times the projects, 20% more effectively, and they were two-and-a-half times more satisfied with their role.[21] Maxwell is right: "For leaders to be effective, they need to connect with people."[22] To connect, he means developing a close familiarity.

The second problem with this assumption is that there is no conflict of interest. If leaders really want what is best for their teams, wouldn't they want the same for those with whom they are friendly with or have close familiarity? Regardless of being a team member or a friend, leadership practices should help fulfill the legitimate requirements for their well-being rather than meeting their wants that don't consider consequences.

At Southwest Airlines, Freiberg and Freiberg write, "Employees who wear masks and avoid the kind of intimacy that many consider a sign of vulnerability and weakness don't last very long."[23] In a healthy environment using 21st Century Leadership, leadership practices seem similar to friendship practices—wanting what is best for others.

> ## BOX 3.4 LEADERSHIP EGO DISCOURAGES CREATIVITY
>
> If the people in charge are very egotistical, then they want to take credit for everything that happens, and they want to feel like they are in control of everything that happens. And that means, consciously or unconsciously, they will discourage creativity in other people.[24]
>
> **John Cleese**

Assumption 4: Giving Away Power Weakens Leadership

Maxwell writes, "The number one enemy is the fear of losing what we have. Weak leaders worry that if they help subordinates, they become dispensable."[25] Hence, empowering team members helps them accomplish their work. If they accomplish their work without the traditional leader controlling the process and output, then observers of the team may question the leader's usefulness. Therefore, for self-preservation, leaders need to appear in control and take credit for the output. Discussing creativity with an audience, John Cleese describes this fear (Box 3.4).

Sinek cites a study's findings in which teams with a directive leader initially outperform teams with empowering leaders, but the teams with empowering leaders have a higher performance over time due to "higher levels of team-learning, coordination, empowerment, and mental model development."[26]

Maxwell states that "the only way to make yourself indispensable is to make yourself dispensable," which increases your value to your team, peers, and the organization.[27] Maxwell also notes that leaders who refuse to empower become barriers to team members and the organization.[28] Through empowerment, though, your team benefits and becomes more productive, and the team and you increase your organizational value.

Assumption 5: Only One Person—Typically a Manager—Functions as the Leader

With traditional leadership, there is one leader and many followers. When connecting this assumption with the first assumption (Leaders Need Authority), individual contributors follow one leader—their manager—and indirectly their manager's manager. Organizations assign individual contributors to report typically to one manager rather than many. That manager is responsible for performance reviews, managing a team, and the actions of their direct reports. When individual contributors start acting as a leader, the manager perceives this as a threat to his power and insubordination. By not allowing others to lead, managers functioning as leaders decrease creativity, innovation, and employee engagement.

In 21st Century Leadership, there is no conflict with having multiple people practicing leadership in the same team. Anyone can lead, and those with authority should encourage and nurture others to lead. Allowing team members to lead doesn't diminish organizational assigned authority. No matter how strong a team member leads, the team member will never assume managerial duties such as conducting performance reviews. Chapter 4 expands on the multiple-leader concept, which Marquet calls the leader-leader structure.[29]

Assumption 6: The Leader Is the Smartest

A central theme in *Multipliers*, Wiseman notes that those in authority, called *diminishers*, believe that intelligence is rare within the workforce but that they are among those who have this intelligence. They obsess about their intelligence and about proving that they are smarter than those in lower positions and among their peers.[30] They believe that their team could never solve problems without them.[31] In their role, diminishers set out to prove repeatedly that those around them are failures and need to be controlled. Through their actions, diminishers destroy the confidence and competence of others. Wiseman also labels diminishers as *idea killers* and *energy destroyers*.[32]

Jennings writes, "Any boss who has to be the smartest person in the room hijacks the dialog, signaling 'correct' comments and conclusions that stifle good ideas."[33] In their ongoing fight to be the smartest, diminishers have a powerfully negative effect on others' capabilities. Kouzes and Posner comment that team members who follow a diminisher cannot perform at their best when the diminisher makes "them feel weak, dependent, or alienated," causing them to want to resign.[34] According to Wiseman, those diminished often "stay and wait, hoping things will turn around."[35] Sinek seems to agree. He states, "Even when we know that feeling insecure at work hurts our performance and our health, sometimes even killing us, we

BOX 3.5   SELF-FULFILLING PROPHECIES

Research on the phenomenon of self-fulfilling prophecies provides ample evidence that people act in ways that are consistent with others' expectations of them...When you expect people to fail, they probably will. If you expect them to succeed, they probably will.[36]

Kouzes and Posner

stay in jobs we hate."[37] Sinek references a study that "one in three employees seriously considered leaving their jobs," but only 1.5% voluntarily leave.[38] After being diminished, their lower self-confidence and self-esteem may affect their ability to interview for jobs.

When leaders assume that those around them are unintelligent, they perceive them as behaving that way. Kouzes and Posner describe this as self-fulfilling prophecies (Box 3.5).

In Chapter 4, I describe how 21st Century Leadership practitioners assume that people aren't only intelligent, but they can also increase their intelligence. Abrashoff has it right: "If we stopped pinning labels on people and stopped treating them as if they were stupid, they would perform better."[39] Sinek takes a different approach: Instead of focusing on how smart others are or aren't, you need to focus on how well they work together.[40] Reinforcing working together rather than finding who is smart or not is better for improving performance.

Assumption 7: Team Members Are the Cause of Unproductivity

Because team members are the ones who do the work, leaders believe that team members cause unproductivity. Collins describes these leaders as looking out a window to find someone to blame for poor results but looking at a mirror to give themselves credit for great results.[41] The more teams fail to meet quality, time, and cost standards, the more the leaders blame the blame for the results and struggle to control the team. This leads to micromanaging, more stress, and more harmful performance and business results. Wiseman states that leaders who micromanage fail to leverage their teams' "full complement of talent, intelligence, and resourcefulness." Later, they wonder why their teams "aren't more productive and are always letting them down."[42]

Years ago, I read a book on qigong in which Cohen describes the art and science of Chinese healing. In the book, Cohen addresses the medical establishments' criticism of alternative medicine. Cohen writes, "So, when a physician points his finger at qigong or other alternative treatments and says, 'It's only placebo,' look where the other three fingers are pointing."[43] Likewise, when a traditional leader points the finger at their team and blames them for being unproductive, look at where their other three fingers are pointing.

Assumption 8: Team Members Cannot Be Trusted

Of course, if teams cause unproductivity, how can leaders trust their teams? At an organization's office, Sinek presents an example of exempt employees, such as engineers and accountants, being treated differently from nonexempt factory workers. As a factory worker complains to a leader, "You trust them to decide when to get a soda or a cup of coffee or take a break; you make me wait for a bell."[44]

Kouzes and Posner write that those without trust fail to become leaders. By being unable to rely on team members' word or depend on them to produce deliverables without the leaders' help, these leaders "either end up doing all the work themselves or supervising work so closely that they become overcontrolling."[45]

When leaders mistrust teams, they micromanage, blame team members for mistakes, and use their authority to punish by:

- Giving poor performance reviews
- Withholding annual salary increases
- Forcing them to work longer hours
- Placing them on action plans
- Terminating them

Consequently, team members fear these punishments and either hide mistakes or blame others for problems. As Sinek states, "In organizations in which there is no safety provided, people are more likely to hide mistakes or problems, if not addressed, often add up and appear later when they become too big to contain."[46]

With 21st Century Leadership, building trust among team members, including all role levels within the team, is essential to inspire creativity and innovation. Doing so leads to improved performance and business results. Teams and departments need trust to build a healthy work environment, process deliverables, and grow the business. Moreover, you need trust to improve how your organization contributes to society and improves communities.

Assumption 9: Team Members Are Less Important than Revenue, Profit, Operational Costs, and Leaders

In a recent Internet search of images representing *leadership*, I discovered one image that stood out from the rest. During the search, I found several images characterizing the leader and the followers. Some showed the leader on a pedestal with the followers facing the leader. The leader tended to be one color, such as red, while the followers were another color, such as white. The particular image that I discovered showed chess pieces in a line. At the front was a blue-colored king, representing the leader. Behind the king were white pawns, representing followers (Box 3.6).

During economic difficulties, organizations need to manage their revenue and expenses, and several organizations use workforce reductions as a preferred way to do this. In most organizations—especially the larger ones—most of their operating cost comes from salaries. Knowing that top executives can replace teams and departments after a financial crisis, executives readily eliminate part of their workforce to protect the organization and leaders. When financial problems are terrible, top-level leaders even terminate lower-level leaders.

BOX 3.6   CHESS ANALOGY: SACRIFICING FOLLOWERS TO BENEFIT LEADERS

If you play chess, you know that the goal is to checkmate the opposing king while protecting your own. Players frequently sacrifice pawns not only to protect their king but also to force their opponents to make mistakes that expose their king. By analogy, team members or pawns are justifiably expendable in situations that either benefit or protect leaders or kings.

Organizations and those in authority sacrifice employees needlessly. They do so to manage profit and Wall Street expectations. Instead, thinking systemically, owners and executives could identify solutions that might involve executive sacrifices. Imagine a publicly traded company experiencing economic pressures in which executives decide unanimously that for one year, they will take a 20% pay cut and give up their annual bonus to avoid reducing the workforce. Consider the executives' message about employee value to their employees and customers. Imagine that the executives challenge their employees to help sustain the executive sacrifice by finding new ways to generate revenue, better serve customers, or cut operational costs. Imagine how this could inspire teams!

Assumption 10: Talking Is More Important than Listening

Have you ever had a conversation with someone who interrupts you repeatedly and doesn't appear to be listening to what you are trying to communicate? Like how some believe that they practice leadership when they don't, traditional leaders believe they listen when they don't. Leaders tend to talk or broadcast their ideas without seriously considering what others think. Even when talking, leaders often fail to confirm that what they say is understood. As Jennings writes in *Reinventors*, "If there's one thing I discovered that separates good communicators from poor ones, it is that the best start by taking responsibility not for what they say but for making sure what they say is understood."[47] Jennings later writes that these communicators become so focused on their agendas and objectives that they filter out what others want to discuss.[48] Abrashoff describes leaders' lack of listening to this way: "Like most organizations, the Navy seemed to put managers in a transmitting mode, which minimized their receptivity."[49] Hunter eloquently writes about selective listening (Box 3.7).

BOX 3.7   SELECTIVE LISTENING

We may even believe that we are good listeners, but what we are often doing is listening selectively, making judgments about what is being said, and thinking of ways to end the conversation or redirect the conversation in ways more pleasing to ourselves.[50]

Hunter

In Chapters 4 and 11, I discuss how some of the 21st Century Leadership authors advise readers on improving their listening and communication skills.

Assumption 11: Recognition Is a Formal Process

Many executives and managers express their dislike for recognition. Repeatedly, they would say something like, "organizations shouldn't have to recognize employees" or "everyone already knows how well they are doing." One manager said that he didn't recognize employees because they might expect him to do this all the time, and he didn't want that expectation.

Part of these leaders' challenge is that they don't recognize employees without spending money or following some prescribed, formal process. Moreover, they don't understand recognition's value in building teams and reinforcing values.

In contrast, those who practice 21st Century Leadership know that recognition can happen informally and effectively in just about all of their interactions. They know that recognition isn't about buying things or giving financial rewards. I expand on recognition in Chapter 4 and share some of the most insightful thoughts on recognition by Kouzes and Posner. Their chapters on recognition are by far the most concise and best that I've read on the subject.[51]

Assumption 12: Leadership Requires Little or No Training

While executives and managers repeatedly expressed to me their dislike for recognizing employees, that is nothing compared with their disregard for leadership development. With few exceptions, most did whatever they could to avoid leadership training and training in general. Some would schedule attending required leadership training just to cancel the day before or the day of, arguing they had a problem that only they could resolve or they had a team that they needed to rescue. Ironically, those who avoid leadership development seem to be the ones who need the most development, yet they behave as if they require little or no training to be effective at leading others.

As I noted in the Preface and Chapter 2, Gallup reports that employee engagement has remained below 30% from 2000 to 2012.[52] Gallup concludes that "managers are primarily responsible for their employees' engagement levels."[53] Knowing that managers are responsible for low engagement, they should want to learn as much as possible about leadership to improve engagement, but many don't. Perhaps these leaders prefer to delude themselves by thinking that how they lead is adequate rather than learning how to improve themselves.

Assumption 13: Leaders Know How Effective Their Leadership Is

Apparently, many leaders believe that they know how effective they are at leadership. Based on personal empirical evidence, leaders behave this way by:

■ Not using 360° feedback tools.
■ Not asking for feedback informally.
■ Asking for informal feedback in such a way that those being asked may feel uncomfortable with providing honest and constructive comments.

While working in corporations, I can recall only three people who conducted 360° feedback requests voluntarily. One person was a manager, and the other two were individual contributors. None of the organizations that I worked at required 360° feedback assessments. The closest feedback has been employee opinion surveys, which doesn't seem to provide the feedback leaders need to improve their leadership practices.

Even when honest feedback is given informally, I've listened to leaders apply their defense mechanisms systematically—rationalization, denial, projection, and deflection—to avoid facing the obvious truth: They need to improve their leadership practices. After receiving low employee opinion survey results, one VP actually stated at an all-hands meeting that her employees own their engagement and are responsible for improving. A director reporting to the same VP commented to me that if employees don't want to get on board and act engaged, he would gladly help them leave.

To improve your leadership practices, you need feedback to validate what you're doing well and correct behaviors that interfere with leading. As Kouzes and Posner ask, "How can you really expect to match your words and your actions if you don't get information about how aligned they are?"[54]

Summary: What to Do

Traditional leaders may be unaware of believing some assumptions or unaware that these assumptions influence them. When reading about 21st Century Leadership practices, some may agree with the concepts, but their traditional assumptions prevent them from internalizing and applying these practices. In this chapter, I defined traditional leadership and presented 13 traditional leadership assumptions. In Appendix III, I summarize each assumption and its related consequences.

Consider exposing your assumptions by obtaining honest feedback about your leadership practices. I explore this in Chapter 11, *Facing the Unknown Like Lions*. Also, consider having someone administer the 360° feedback diagnostic tool that you can find in Appendix V.

Chapter 4

Explaining 21st Century Leadership Principles and Beliefs

If leaders and collaborators are not clear about what values form the basis of their relationships, those principles for which they truly stand, then how can they ever expect to lay the foundation for leadership, let alone have the capacity to effect change?[1]

Freiberg and Freiberg

We willfully ignore how profoundly the environment influences our behavior. In fact, the environment is a relentless triggering mechanism that, in an instant, can change us from saint to sinner, optimist to pessimist, model citizen to thug—and make us lose sight of who we're trying to be.[2]

Goldsmith

The most pernicious environments are the ones that compel us to compromise our sense of right and wrong. In the ultracompetitive environment of the workplace, it can happen to the most solid citizens.[3]

Goldsmith

DOI: 10.4324/9781003273448-5

Introduction: Because of the Environment and Our Brains, We Need Guiding Principles

Think about this expression:

Life is hard.

Is it really? Instead of *hard*, consider *perilous*: Full of danger or risk.[4] Is the statement really about life?

Life isn't hard or perilous. Life is a condition that includes growth, reproduction, and change before death.[5] When we exclaim that life is hard, we probably are referring to our circumstances. More accurately, we describe their environment: The surroundings or conditions in which we operate or function through time.[6]

Over time, we strive for what we think is best for us. Yet, the outcomes that we seek are elusive. People don't behave the way we anticipate. Actions we take don't have the desired effect, which can be frustrating.

The environment may be the primary source of peril, but there is something else–ourselves. Specifically, the source is our brains. Our brains cannot process everything that occurs in our environment. To function, the brain filters out less useful information and focuses on what's important. Because of its limited energy, the brain has ways to conserve resources. For example, we have two systems for thinking and decision-making. System 1 is quick, automatic, and reflexive. When asked what five times five is, reflexively, we respond 25. System 2 requires more effort and time. We use it with more complex circumstances. When asked what the square root of 4,355 is, we need more resources to answer the question. In *Neuroscience for Organizational Change*, Hilary Scarlett describes the systems (Box 4.1).

Our brains prefer the quick and easy System 1. When we cannot rely on System 1, we resort to shortcuts. Some of these shortcuts are heuristics, and others are biases. Using them saves time and effort, but there is a downside. Scarlett warns that using them can lead to flawed decisions. They distort how we view the environment and the people we interact with. Some biases protect our egos and self-perception. Scarlett writes, "They come into play in every conversation, every meeting, every decision we make."[7] Heuristics and biases obscure hazards and filter out crucial information. They can be perilous!

BOX 4.1 THINKING WITH SYSTEM 1 AND 2

System 1 will 'call up' System 2 when more considered thinking is needed. We tend to be much more aware of thinking and decisions made by System 2 because these take effort and are conscious. The systems use different parts of the brain: System 1, for example, uses the amygdala which, amongst many roles, process emotions, whereas System 2 uses the lateral prefrontal cortex (LPFC). The LPFC is involved in many higher cognitive processes such as working memory, goals, planning and self-control.[8]

Scarlett

Even though heuristics and biases can be perilous, they are necessary for functionality. In Lift, Quinn and Quinn summarize the need and the problem succinctly (Box 4.2).

Because of environmental perils and the over-used heuristics and biases of the brain, people need guiding principles. Principles can help shift us from normal to leadership states, as described by Quinn and Quinn (Box 4.3).

The more we study and internalize guiding principles, the more likely we are to overcome perils caused in our environment and heuristics and biases caused by our brains. The environment and the brain may be perilous, but principles can make a positive difference.

BOX 4.2 BELIEVING IN OTHERS

We need to respond automatically in order to keep from being overwhelmed by all of life's experiences. The problem is that many of our responses are inconsistent with values that we claim to hold... in our everyday lives, average citizens ignore people in need, break their word, speak poorly of others, or fail to exercise self-restraint... whatever our values may be, we live up to them less than we think we do.[9]

Quinn and Quinn

BOX 4.3   NORMAL STATE VS. THE FUNDAMENTAL STATE OF LEADERSHIP

Normal State:

1. Seek comfort.
2. React to situations automatically.
3. Focus on our own wants.
4. Believe that there is little we can do to improve.

Fundamental State of Leadership (psychological state):

1. Purpose-centered (the results we want are not weighted down by needless expectations).
2. Internally directed (our personal values guide our actions).
3. Other-focused (we feel empathy for the feelings and needs of others).
4. Externally open (we believe that we can improve at whatever it is we are trying to do.[10]

Quinn and Quinn

Seven Leadership Principles and Beliefs

This chapter describes seven leadership principles that align with the 21st Century Leadership definition. Table 4.1 describes the seven principles and 26 beliefs, which align with one or more principles. The principles and beliefs set a foundation for the nine practices, and in Appendix II, I illustrate the alignment among the principles, beliefs, and practices.

I derived the principles and beliefs from my leadership analysis. Each belief has references or quotations from leadership authors.

Principle 1: Believe in Others

Believing in others means having faith that people can solve problems, find opportunities, and deliver solutions. By believing in others, you become more capable of connecting with them, empowering them, and encouraging them to develop (Box 4.4).

Table 4.1   Twenty-Six 21st Century Leadership Beliefs

Principle	Beliefs
Believe in others	1. Intelligence is not static and can be developed continuously 2. Everyone can practice leadership regardless of role
Connect with others	3. Being vulnerable and getting to know others builds trust and relationships 4. Sharing your mistakes builds credibility 5. Celebrations build community, connect events to values, renew commitment, promote social support, and improve everyone's well-being
Put others first	6. Giving credit for accomplishments to others is more important than taking credit 7. Employees serve customers before serving management 8. When outcomes are disappointing, accepting responsibility but never blaming (others or bad luck) is critical for personal accountability 9. Leadership is action that focuses on others and not the actor 10. Sacrificing or volunteering time, energy, resources, ego, and previous priorities to help others inspires loyalty and commitment
Give up control	11. Control erodes relationships 12. Leading well is about empowering others 13. By making yourself dispensable, you make yourself indispensable 14. Command and control is a shared responsibility
Encourage growth	15. Helping others figure out their development enhances their ability to contribute 16. Encouraging people to grow and leave their role contributes to organizational growth 17. Allowing teams to make mistakes enables them to be open with their mistakes and learn from the experience 18. If you change the conditions in which others operate, you can change their behaviors
Collaborate with others	19. Organizational charts limit thinking 20. Considering problems from a systemic perspective minimizes using blame 21. Leadership doesn't reside with one person 22. Influence comes from all directions 23. Leadership practices work the same with all populations, including peers, customers, supervisors, and subordinates
Develop leadership practices continuously	24. To become fluent in leadership, practice leadership regularly and monitor your effectiveness 25. Knowing everything about leadership is not enough 26. Leadership involves helping others practice leadership

> ### BOX 4.4   BELIEVING IN OTHERS
>
> When people believe in you, they help you blossom; they help you become a bigger, stronger, more capable person.[11]
>
> **Freiberg and Freiberg**

When positioning others ahead of your own needs or giving time and energy to helping them, the personal investment is worthwhile if you believe in their capability to mature their mental and moral qualities.

How Growth and Fixed Mindsets Affect Believing in Others

In 2016, Dweck published her acclaimed book, *Mindset*, in which she contrasts fixed and growth mindsets.[12] Perceiving people from one mindset affects your capacity to believe in others. Because these mindsets are prevalent throughout organizations, learning about them is crucial for two reasons. First, you need to recognize behaviors related to them to interact more effectively. Second, you can help others and yourself trend towards the growth mindset. As Scarlett writes, "One of the great things about mindset is how easily it can be changed...Just teaching people about the concept and the difference the two mindsets make, creates a difference to performance."[13]

Having a growth mindset enables you to believe in others. The following is a brief explanation of these mindsets.[14]

Mindsets

Mindsets are a set of conscious or unconscious beliefs that affect how you think about your abilities, how you behave, and how you affect those around you.

Fixed Mindset

With a *fixed mindset*, you think and act to some extent as if you cannot further develop your IQ, EQ, traits, skills, abilities, and competencies. Believing that these are fixed in adulthood leads to thoughts such as:

- "I can't draw."
- "Michael Jordan is a gifted athlete."

- "I'm not as smart as people believe."
- "Failing is harmful."

Fixed mindset behaviors include avoiding tasks outside of your comfort zone, laughing when others appear foolish, and even spreading rumors to make a team member look bad. People with a fixed mindset may do the following:

- Allow others to fail.
- Cheat and deceive.
- Claim credit for achievements but blames others for mistakes.
- Gossip about other team members.
- Reserve knowledge and keep secrets.

Growth Mindset

In contrast, with a *growth mindset,* you think and act to some extent as if you can develop and improve your IQ, EQ, traits, abilities, and competencies. Believing that adults can continue to grow leads to thoughts such as:

- "Taking an art class can help me learn to draw."
- "Michael Jordan's dedication to practice and learning led to his remarkable achievements."
- "I still can improve how smart I am."
- "Failing is a fantastic way to learn and improve."

Growth mindset behaviors might include working diligently to solve a problem, asking your manager for stretch assignments, seeking peers for help, and giving team members credit for their contributions. People with a fixed mindset may do the following:

- Believe in the organization's purpose.
- Collaborate, share information, and value teaming.
- Commit to working for the organization.
- Experience a thrill when resolving issues or improves skills.
- Feel empowered to innovate and be creative.
- Give credit to others but own their mistakes.

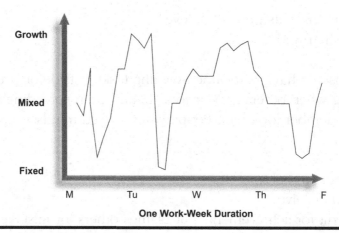

Figure 4.1   Dynamic mindset spectrum example.

People Can Shift Mindsets

During a given week, your mindset can often shift, as Figure 4.1 illustrates. When circumstances and environments change, your mindset may change as well.

How Fixed and Growth Mindsets Affect Believing in Others

People who think predominantly from a fixed mindset are less likely to believe in others. They conclude that people are unlikely to improve and develop. As Scarlett writes, "managers with a fixed mindset…are less likely to notice improvements because they are stuck with their initial impressions."[15]

People who think predominantly from a growth mindset are more likely to believe in others. They acknowledge that people can improve and develop, and they work to help them do so. Scarlett writes, "managers with a growth mindset are more likely to notice an improvement in their employees because they are aware that people can learn."[16]

Belief 1: Intelligence Isn't Static and Can Be Developed Continuously

At the beginning of *Multipliers*, Wiseman shares a powerful story about a tank commander. Under one officer, the tank commander failed and questioned his own capabilities. Under another officer, the same tank

> **BOX 4.5   WHAT BELIEVING IN OTHERS CAN DO**
>
> Find the undeveloped potential in the people with whom you work. Take a moment to see them not as they are, but as they can be. When you do, our bet is that two things will happen. First, they will act and perform according to the image you have of them, and second, your faith in the potential of the human spirit will be restored.[17]
>
> **Freiberg and Freiberg**

commander flourished.[18] Why the difference? Before the tank commander failed, the officer behaved as if competing against the tank commander and *publicly mocked* the tank commander when he made mistakes. When moved under a more supportive superior, the tank commander excelled. Wiseman notes, "Some leaders make us better and smarter. They bring out our intelligence."[19] In Wiseman's story, the superior officer revitalized and validated the tank commander's capabilities. Freiberg and Freiberg write about how believing in the potential of others can change their behavior (Box 4.5).

Belief 2: Everyone Can Practice Leadership Regardless of Role

Regardless of role, anyone can incorporate leadership practices into their daily activities. Authority isn't a prerequisite, and it may interfere with leading when you use power mistakenly to coerce compliance. Leadership practices apply to all roles because they are tactical, day-to-day actions used to help others and are independent of a role's authority. Whether a chief executive officer (CEO) is applying the practices to build an organizational vision or an employee is helping a colleague resolve a problem, anyone at any organizational level can leverage leadership practices.

Kouzes and Posner, Blanchard and Ridge, and Miller write about how anyone can learn and apply leadership universally.[20] Kouzes and Posner, as well as Maxwell, describe leadership as a set of learnable skills.[21]

Principle 2: Connect with Others

You cannot practice leadership without involving others. Even in traditional leadership, leaders need to connect with followers at some level. How traditional leaders and those who practice 21st Century Leadership connect with others differs.

Connecting with others involves building relationships, and building relationships involves building trust. When you have trust and strong relationships, you have more opportunities to mature individuals' mental and moral qualities, and in the process, build your own character. As Maxwell states, "the deeper the relationship, the stronger the potential for leadership."[22]

Psychological Safety

Another way to build trust is with psychological safety. When you remove the fear of being embarrassed, ridiculed, or punished from human interaction and replace fear with feeling valued, respected, and free to contribute and learn, you have psychological safety.[23] In her research, Edmondson observed that there is a fundamental truth about organizational life: We cannot know when someone is withholding their thoughts or tell by looking at employees when they are overwhelmed with problems or don't know how to complete a task. If we observe someone being silent or hear an employee saying that everything's okay, we can either accept what they say or guess their intent.[24] Instead of guessing, we can encourage others to share their thoughts.

To build psychological safety, we share what's happened in our lives, especially our mistakes and imperfections. By being vulnerable, we create a path for others to express their vulnerability.

Vulnerability builds trust. Being vulnerable is like saying, "I'll share my shortfalls with you, and I trust that you won't use them against me."

Ingroup and Outgroup

Imagine the following: You attend the first meeting of a cross-functional team. As you walk in, you notice that everyone is wearing a black suit like you except for one in a brown suit. The brown suit person is the only female and looks Arabic while everyone else is white. During the meeting and future ones, the person in the brown suit is treated as an outsider. She is often ignored, and her opinion is discounted.

Within seconds of meeting someone new, we quickly can identify with someone or not (Box 4.6). Ingroups are people who strongly

> ## BOX 4.6 INGROUPS AND OUTGROUPS
>
> Within fractions of a second of meeting people, our brains automatically categorize them—ingroup or outgroup...
>
> Outgroup faces activate the amygdala, the part of the brain that activates our fear response (Hart et al, 2000). We are less empathetic and do not try as hard to understand people from an outgroup.
>
> Linville and Jones (1980) showed that people tend to process information about outgroup members in extreme, black and white, simplistic ways (hence prejudice), whereas we process ideas about people who are like us in more nuanced and complex ways....We process thoughts about people we are close to in the same way as thoughts about ourselves.[25]
>
> **Scarlett**

identify with one another, and outgroups are people who you do not identify with.[26]

The brown suit story is based on a story told by Judith Hale in one of my *Unlabeled Leadership* podcasts.[27] The example clearly illustrates who's in and out. However, ingroups and outgroups can be subtle. Managers can create ingroups and outgroups within a team based on how they treat teammates. If you manage a team and do any of the following, you may have inadvertently created an ingroup and outgroup.

■ Spend more personal time with some teammates.
■ In team meetings, engage with some more than others.
■ Give opportunities to some but not others.
■ Listen and act on ideas more from some teammates than others.
■ Share more information with some teammates than others.

When we connect with some teammates more than others, we create ingroups, and the outgroup teammates notice. When they notice, they become more distant—a circumstance that hurts team performance.

Fortunately, training professionals about ingroups and outgroups can help mitigate the bias and minimize the bias from occurring. Through training, they begin to discover and identify ingroups and outgroups. After a training event, Scarlett shared what one participant said (Box 4.7).

BOX 4.7   SCARLETT'S INGROUP AND OUTGROUP TRAINING HELPS

One of the points that resonated very strongly during the training was the notion of 'ingroups'. I would have liked to say I was a naturally inclusive manager and certainly didn't think I had an 'ingroup'. And yet the training helped us to think about this from the point of the view of the team. Thinking from that point of view made me realize that it was entirely possible that they would see an 'ingroup' in the team—there are people who work geographically closer to me...I tested this with the team and was disappointed to see that my hunch was correct—they did indeed feel a slight sense of an 'ingroup'. The learning was about how easy it is to create a situation like this, by simply failing to look at the team dynamics from the perspective of the team members.[28]

Thoughts from a Manager

Belief 3: Being Vulnerable and Getting to Know Others Builds Trust

Sinek believes that building trust only requires being truthful.[29] This includes:

- Acknowledging mistakes rather than ignoring or downplaying them.
- Crediting others for their contributions rather than taking credit unfairly.
- Admitting when things are going wrong, such as knowing that a project is behind schedule, letting others know, and explaining why.

Being truthful also involves personal disclosures. Kouzes and Posner write about how building trust involves sharing about yourself (Box 4.8).

Doing so requires you to risk that others won't use the information to somehow harm you. Someone has to begin risking themselves, and Kouzes and Posner believe that those practicing leadership need to open up, "show vulnerability, and let go of control. Leaders go first."[30] Once you start showing vulnerability, trusting begins, and it continues to build. However, Kouzes and Posner caution that, while groups can build trust contagiously, they can likewise build distrust contagiously.[31]

> ### BOX 4.8   SHARING ABOUT YOURSELF BUILDS TRUST
>
> To become fully trusted, you must be open to and with others. This means disclosing things about yourself in order to build the basis for a relationship. This means telling others the same things you'd like to know about them—talking about your hopes and dreams, your family and friends, your interests and your pursuits.[32]
>
> **Kouzes and Posner**

Without Trust, It Is Difficult to Maintain Relationships

Kouzes and Posner, as well as Hunter, believe that you cannot maintain positive relationships without trust.[33] When you don't trust, those you work with distrust. When they distrust, they work together ineffectively, act more in their self-interest, and may even work against others—even causing harm.

As Sinek writes, "The more abstract people become, the more capable we are of doing them harm."[34]

Getting to Know Others Builds Trust

Sinek links getting to know others with building bonds of trust. "The more familiar we are with each other, the stronger our bonds."[35] This familiarity isn't limited to personal information. As Kouzes and Posner note, you implicitly communicate that you trust others when sharing professional and personal information with teammates and colleagues.[36] Professional information examples include:

- Information about company changes (business acumen).
- Learned techniques and resources that can help others with their work.
- Stories of how you benefited and learned that others could also benefit by hearing.

Storytelling can be powerful for letting others get to know you and contribute to building trust. At one company, a new executive took over the department. On his first day, the executive held an impromptu meeting that afternoon with all direct and indirect employees. In the meeting, he shared a personal story and explained how the experience shaped who he was and how he approached work. Afterward, a few talked about the meeting and quickly expressed their appreciation toward the new executive simply because he shared his story.

Belief 4: Sharing Your Mistakes Builds Credibility

When you hide mistakes and others suspect this, you lose credibility. When you share mistakes, you gain credibility. Maxwell notes that people can be forgiving when you allow yourself to admit when mistakes happen.[37] This may have something to do with how sharing mistakes exhibits honesty and moral growth. By telling others about mistakes, you model that acknowledging errors is acceptable and that you don't need to carry a façade that you're perfect. Our word becomes more believable to others.

This also applies to admitting when you lack knowledge. As Sinek notes, acknowledging knowledge gaps and mistakes encourages others to step in to help as well as adopt similar behaviors of sharing their own limitations and missteps.[38]

Belief 5: Celebrations Build Community, Connect Events to Values, Renew Commitment, Promote Social Support, and Improve Everyone's Well-Being

Connecting with others isn't just about a one-on-one relationship with teammates: It's about connecting with groups at various levels. This includes a team, a department consisting of teams, a business unit consisting of departments, and an organization consisting of business units. Celebrations are a way to build community.

Celebrations have substantial benefits for a team. Kouzes and Posner found that celebrations improve a team's daily performance and long-term health.[39] When teams regularly celebrate, they perceive their manager's leadership effectiveness to be nearly one-third greater than managers who have teams that celebrate less.[40] Teams that celebrate more experience lower burnout.[41]

Celebrations serve a critical function. They enable teammates to pause and reflect on what they are doing. Celebrations remind us of a team's purpose and values, encouraging us to appreciate our teammates. Celebrations provide an opportunity to have fun and remind everyone that work can be fun. Kouzes and Posner write, "Having fun sustains productivity, creating what researchers refer to as 'subjective well-being.'"[42] Celebrations can reenergize feelings of trust and remind you that you cannot

> ### BOX 4.9   IMPORTANCE OF CELEBRATIONS
>
> Celebrations infuse life with passion and purpose...They bond people together and connect us to shared values and myths...When everything is going well, these occasions allow us to revel in our glory. When times are tough, ceremonies draw us together, kindling hope and faith that better times lie ahead.[44]
>
> **Kouzes and Posner**

complete extraordinary accomplishments without the help of others.[43] Kouzes and Posner write about the importance of celebrations (Box 4.9).

Celebrations don't need to be complex or elaborate. They can be as simple as coming together to discuss tasks and talk about how teammates have supported one another. They can recognize personal milestones such as birthdays, work anniversaries, or team milestones. They can be farewells to those leaving the team or welcoming moments for new teammates. Celebrations build community, and Freiberg and Freiberg note that building community starts by "honoring the sacredness of each person who comes to work for the company."[45]

Principle 3: Put Others First

In *Good to Great*, Collins describes executives who practice 21st Century Leadership as Level 5 leaders. People at Level 5 integrate "extreme personal humility with intense professional will." While doing so, they "channel their ego away from themselves and into the larger goal of building a great company."[46] They put others first. While believing and connecting with others are essential for leadership, adding this principle begins to establish the purpose of 21st Century Leadership. As Maxwell comments, "The heart of leadership is putting others ahead of yourself."[47]

Belief 6: Giving Credit for Accomplishments to Others Is More Important than Taking Credit

Those practicing 21st Century Leadership help others succeed. Part of this involves recognizing others for their accomplishments. In organizations,

---

BOX 4.10   FAILING TO APPRECIATE

When polled, employees reveal that their number one complaint is that they aren't recognized for their notable performances. Apparently people hand out praise as if it were being rationed, usually only for outstanding work. Make a small improvement, and it's highly unlikely that anyone will say or do anything.[48]

Grenny et al.

---

people are bad at practicing this. Grenny et al. write about our incapability to recognize employees (Box 4.10).

In Collin's research, he found people at Level 5 are remarkably humble. They tended to credit accomplishments to others (Box 4.11).

Belief 7: Employees Serve Customers Before Serving Management

With traditional leadership, the focus is on the leader: Followers serve the leader. Leaders attract followers (or an organization assigns followers to the leader), and the leaders need to figure out how to get followers to obey their commands. Imagine a service organization where individual contributors look to managers for what they should be doing. Managers look to directors, directors look to lower-level executives, and so on. While looking toward the top of the organizational hierarchy for directives, individual contributors don't look to customers for directives. Thus, followers cannot engage customers fully.

Hunter, as well as Blanchard and Ridge, write about a different way of behaving: Everyone faces toward customers.[49] Using the 21st Century Leadership approach, consider the same organization. Instead of looking

---

BOX 4.11   HUMILITY AND CREDITING OTHERS

Level 5 leaders look out the window to apportion credit to factors outside themselves when things go well (and if they cannot find a specific person or event to give credit to, they credit good luck).[50]

Collins

---

to the manager for directives, individual contributors look to customers to identify customer needs and help customers meet them. Managers look to individual contributors to determine how they can enable individual contributors to better serve customers. This could include, for example, giving more approval authority to individual contributors so that they can serve customers faster and avoid having to obtain approval from a manager. Directors and the rest of the hierarchy look to those closest to customers to identify ways to improve capabilities for serving customers.

Belief 8: When Outcomes Are Disappointing, Accepting Responsibility but Never Blaming Is Critical for Personal Accountability

Collins describes those at Level 5 as claiming and owning responsibility when things go wrong. Even when problems seem out of control, such as a downturn in the economy, they never rationalize what happened as *bad luck*.[51] Those practicing 21st Century Leadership don't allow themselves to think of themselves as victims. Miller explains that influencing personal accountability involves asking questions that begin with *what* or *how*; they avoid asking questions that start with *who, when,* or *why*.[52] When things go wrong, they might ask questions that promote personal accountability (Box 4.12).

By asking yourself better questions, you avoid blaming, procrastinating, and acting like a victim; you change your perception of situations and become personally accountable.

BOX 4.12   TYPES OF QUESTIONS THAT PROMOTE PERSONAL ACCOUNTABILITY

- How can I adapt to the changing environment?
- What can I do to improve the situation?
- How can I let go of what I can't control?
- How can I set a better example?
- How can I support others?
- How can I achieve with the resources I already have?[53]

Miller

BOX 4.13   LEADERSHIP FOCUS OF ADVANCING OTHERS

But contrary to conventional thinking, I believe the bottom line in leadership isn't how far we advance ourselves but how far we advance others. That is achieved by serving others and adding value to their lives.[54]

Maxwell

Belief 9: Leadership Is Action That Focuses on Others and Not the Actor

21st Century Leadership is about serving others and not oneself. Except for leadership development, actions associated with the leadership practices focus on helping others. Even when developing and learning, the intent is to leverage new knowledge and skills to benefit others more than oneself. Maxwell believes that this is the bottom line in leadership (Box 4.13).

Belief 10: Volunteering Time, Energy, Resources, Ego, and Previous Priorities to Help Others Inspires Loyalty and Commitment

One aspect of putting others first involves making a personal sacrifice. This belief distinguishes 21st Century Leadership from traditional leadership. With 21st Century Leadership, practitioners sacrifice for the benefit of others. With traditional leadership, leaders sacrifice followers for their own benefit.

When 21st Century Leadership authors write about how you should sacrifice to benefit others, the authors didn't mean a *sacrifice* in the religious sense: "offer or kill as a religious sacrifice."[55] Neither did they mean *sacrifice* as used in chess: "Deliberately allow one's opponent to win (a pawn or piece)."[56] Rather, the authors use the term to mean, "give up (something important or valued) for the sake of other considerations."[57] For these authors, *sacrifice* describes how those practicing leadership give up valued things to help others.[58] The title of Sinek's 2014 book, *Leaders Eat Last*, exemplifies the importance of this belief (Box 4.14).

Sinek further explains that you understand what it means when those who practice leadership give up valuable commodities such as time and energy. The act of sacrifice is a way to demonstrate how much you value others. In return, people become loyal and committed to practicing leadership.[59]

BOX 4.14 SACRIFICING TO HELP OTHERS

Leaders are the ones who are willing to give up something of their own for us. Their time, their energy, their money, maybe even the food off their plate. When it matters, leaders choose to eat last.[60]

Sinek

Table 4.2 categorizes types of sacrifices and provides three examples. Each set of examples includes one from the perspective of an individual contributor (IC), a manager (Mgr), and an executive (Exec).

Table 4.2 Examples of Sacrifice from Different Career Levels

Category	Examples
Time and energy	An IC helps a teammate to use a new tool. Afterward, the IC stays later than expected to complete her own work that is due the next day. Walk the floor where teams work and ask how they are doing. Invite teammates to a coffee break to answer questions about the organization.
Personal resources	An IC donates three of her vacation days to a grieving peer so that the peer could spend more time recovering from the loss of his spouse. Using his own money, a Mgr buys each teammate a custom mug that displays the team's primary project name. The mug also has each teammate's name and primary contribution. An executive team unanimously decides to take a one-time annual 20% pay cut instead of laying off employees.
Ego	An IC argued with a peer that he knew a procedure but didn't. Later, he realized his mistake and apologized to the peer. A Mgr apologized to the team for embarrassing an IC in front of the team during the previous team meeting. An Exec learns that her new policy did more harm to employees. She ended the policy, apologized to the department in a memo and during a department meeting, and she promised to obtain more input before implementing departmental policies.
Previous priorities	An IC volunteers to change shifts with a peer who has a family emergency, even though the change would disrupt the IC's plans. A Mgr cancels a luncheon with a friend to coach an IC having troubles with a teammate. Someone interrupts an Exec who is meeting with some ICs to inform the Exec that a client has arrived early. The Exec sends a Mgr to meet with the client and continues meeting with the ICs.

> ### BOX 4.15   BENEFITS OF GIVING CONTROL
>
> The more energy is transferred from the top of the organization to those who are actually doing the job, those who know more about what's going on on a daily basis, the more powerful the organization and the more powerful the leader.[61]
>
> **Sinek**

Principle 4: Give Up Control

Complementing Putting Others First is Giving Up Control. Power is intended to be transferred from those higher in an organization to those closer to performing the work. Power transfer enables teams to achieve organizational goals and help customers more efficiently and effectively. Sinek notes that, in the discipline of physics, scientists define power as the "transfer of energy."[62] Sinek also writes about how the organizations benefit when those at the top give up control (Box 4.15).

Power is meant to be shared and not hoarded by a few. Those who hoard power use it ineffectively. Instead, empowering others by sharing control helps teams achieve the extraordinary.

Belief 11: Control Erodes Relationships

Managers with direct reports have more challenges in practicing 21st Century Leadership than individual contributors. Executives and managers assign work to direct reports. When assigning work, managers might be more comfortable using power than leadership practices.

When a manager assigns work, for example, without explaining why or allowing discussion about the assignment, the manager uses control implicitly: Do the work or else. The manager doesn't allow for a choice, which implies that not complying with the assignment leads to negative consequences. If direct reports delay completing the assignment or don't perform to quality, the manager may take one of three actions identified by Grenny et al.: nag, guilt, or threaten.[63] The authors warn: "The more we push others to comply, the less it works."[64] Granted, using control to coerce others to perform can be effective for a while. Over time, though, either the manager ends up firing direct reports for their performance, or the direct

BOX 4.16   IMPORTANCE OF AUTONOMY AND CHOICE

When you swap coercive methods with personal choices, you open up the possibility of influencing even the most addictive and highly entrenched behaviors by gaining access to one of the most powerful human motivations, the power of the committed heart.[65]

Grenny et al.

reports leave on their own. They are more likely to stay but only accomplish the minimum to avoid trouble.

Wiseman describes those who stay but are underutilized as *the walking dead*. She writes, "On the outside, these zombies go through the motions, but on the inside they have given up. They *quit and stay*."[66] When direct reports become zombies, you can bet that the manager's use of power has eroded the relationship. Hunter explains: "You can get a few seasons out of power, even accomplish some things, but over time power can be very damaging to relationships."[67]

Whether you realize that you are doing so or not, the problem with using control is that you aren't giving direct reports or anyone else a real choice. As Grenny et al. write, "...a change of heart can't be imposed; it can only be chosen."[68] Instead of using power and the traditional leadership way of coercing, give direct reports a choice. In doing so, teams can accomplish the extraordinary. Grenny et al. also write about the shift from power to choice (Box 4.16).

In Chapter 9, *Directing Like Guides*, I describe the fifth of the nine practices. This practice involves providing a personal choice that enables others to take up the cause willingly and passionately. In *Influencer*, Grenny et al. capture this masterfully in their chapter, "Help Them Love What They Hate."[69]

Belief 12: Leading Well Is about Empowering Others

Empowering others makes them more capable. Empowerment can be in the form of knowledge, resources, and authority. For example, empowerment could be showing someone a faster way to use an application. A supervisor could authorize teammates to make certain decisions when working with customers so that the teammates wouldn't need to find the supervisor for approval.

BOX 4.17 BENEFITS OF EMPOWERING OTHERS

A key element of this set up is to push decision making closer to where the work actually gets done. When capable workers respond successfully—and they will—many will graduate to other types of decisions that relate to the operations of their work sections or their department's connectivity with another department...This is important to organizational progress and productivity since every good decision that can be made "above the water line" allows senior management more time to consider other decisions below the water line...The ability to push power down will continue to be important as the workplace becomes increasingly dynamic.[70]

Hill

Empowerment helps improve performance by enabling others to perform better. As Kouzes and Posner note, you would prefer your teammates to "feel strong, capable, and efficacious" with empowerment rather than "feel weak, incompetent, and insignificant," in which the latter leads to underperformance.[71]

Empowerment decreases dependencies. Sinek writes, "When a leader has the humility to distribute power across the organization, the strength of the company becomes less dependent on one person and is thus better able to survive."[72] In *Giving Away Power*, Hill writes about how authorizing decision-making to lower levels benefits those at lower levels and those at higher levels (Box 4.17).

Belief 13: By Making Yourself Dispensable, You Make Yourself Indispensable

People respect those who transfer power to others. As I discussed in Chapter 3, traditional leaders fear giving power away would make them weaker and dispensable. Their thinking is that if those they give power to become more successful, others may perceive them as dispensable. The opposite is true: The more you help others improve and excel, the more those you empower perceive you to be indispensable. Sinek describes how empowering others can make you indispensable and rewarding for doing so (Box 4.18).

> ### BOX 4.18 EMPOWERING OTHERS MAKES YOU MORE INDISPENSABLE
>
> The more we give of ourselves to see others succeed, the greater our value to the group and the more respect they offer us. The more respect and recognition we receive, the higher our status in the group and the more incentive we have to continue to give to the group.[73]
>
> **Sinek**

Belief 14: Command and Control Is a Shared Responsibility

In *Understanding Command and Control*, Alberts and Hayes write about how the concepts of command and control (C2) have changed. They write, "Traditional approaches to Command and Control aren't up to the challenge. Simply stated, they lack the agility required in the 21st Century."[74] Table 4.3 describes the functions of C2.

When you transition from traditional leadership to 21st Century Leadership, you shift from one person responsible for C2 to many being responsible. Alberts and Hayes state, "Command and Control applies to endeavors undertaken by collections of individuals and organizations of vastly different characteristics and sizes for many different purposes."[75]

One effect of shifting C2 to more than one person is that teams take ownership and responsibility. Kouzes and Posner describe how Ward, a military officer, shifted C2 to those who reported to him. Instead of direct

Table 4.3 Functions of Command and Control

Definition	Functions
Command	1. The establishment and communication of the initial set of conditions 2. The continuous assessment of the situation 3. Changes to intent[a]
Control	1. Determine whether current and or planned efforts are on track 2. If adjustments are required, adjust if they are within the command guidelines[b]

[a] Alberts and Hayes, 2011, *Understanding Command and Control*, 57.
[b] Ibid., 59.

reports reporting their problems and waiting for Ward to issue a command, Ward would push the problem back to the officer to have the team figure out a solution.[76]

Principle 5: Encourage Growth

Part of the 21st Century Leadership definition is "design to mature mental and moral qualities, capabilities, and behaviors." This leadership approach encourages growth in a way that benefits those who experience the change, their organizations, and society.

Belief 15: Helping Others Figure Out Their Development Enhances Their Ability to Contribute

To accomplish the extraordinary, you need to develop those around you. As the people you work with develop, their contributions become more effective. This, in turn, produces better results and helps the organization's reputation. As Hill notes, "Few things are better for an organization than being known as the developer of great talent."[77] Freiberg and Freiberg also write about helping others to contribute (Box 4.19).

Belief 16: Encouraging People to Grow and Leave Their Role Contributes to Organizational Growth

Wiseman expresses that you should help others mature their mental and moral qualities, capabilities, and behaviors. Still, to take this to a higher level, you should encourage them to leave their current role. When they

---

BOX 4.19   BELIEVING IN OTHERS

Find the undeveloped potential in the people with whom you work. Take a moment to see them not as they are, but as they can be. When you do, our bet is that two things will happen. First, they will act and perform according to the image you have of them, and second, your faith in the potential of the human spirit will be restored.[78]

Freiberg and Freiberg

decide to leave, Wiseman writes that you should "celebrate their departures and shout their success to everyone."[79] By doing so, you help grow the organization.

When practicing 21st Century Leadership, you think of others first. You want those around you to mature their mental and moral qualities. At some point, a person's role starts to limit their development: The work becomes easier to accomplish, less challenging, and starts to lose interest. As a manager of such individuals, you benefit by spending less time developing these stars. Unfortunately, wanting them to stay in the role is selfish and not in their best interest. Instead, you should help them find a role that would be more challenging. The role should help them continue to grow and develop.

Teams that encourage growing and leaving improve their reputation within the workforce. Alumni may work in different organizations and speak highly of the team. Alumni may refer qualified candidates to their former team, and the workforce may perceive your organization as a preferred employer. Thus, helping others grow and leave helps the organization as well.

Belief 17: Allowing Teams to Make Mistakes Enables Them to Be Open with Their Mistakes and Learn from the Experience

Many organizations are unforgiving when teams make mistakes or fail, but they wonder why teams aren't creative or innovative. For creativity and innovation to flourish, 21st Century Leadership practitioners need to make four changes with their teams. First, they need to recognize overtly that with creativity and innovation, mistakes and failures happen. This is part of the process. Second, they need to stop focusing on outcomes regardless of whether they are positive or negative. Third, teams need to learn from the outcomes without blaming when negative results occur. Fourth, they need to reinforce activities and processes that promote creativity and innovation.

Wiseman writes that "If you want your organization to take risks, you have to separate the experiment from the outcome."[80] Grenny et al. provide a Kaizen example in which an organization recognized a team with the organization's highest reward for following the Kaizen principles. A team of waitresses who served tea during lunch at one of the plants determined the optimum amount to serve. They eliminated wasted tea leaves by half. While the cost savings were small compared with other projects, "it captured what the judges thought was the best implementation of Kaizen principles. They rewarded the process."[81]

Belief 18: If You Change the Conditions in Which Others Operate, You Can Change Their Behaviors

In the book, *Influencer*, Grenny et al. developed a model that can radically influence people's behavior. The authors discovered that influencers do not need to change every negative behavior to improve performance. Instead, those who practice leadership need only focus on one, two, or even three vital behaviors or "actions that lead to important results."[82] These vital behaviors are enough to trigger a range of behavioral changes that benefit individuals, teams, organizations, and society. Vital behaviors are critical in determining whether an organization's culture is functional or dysfunctional. The only problem is that leadership practitioners are terrible at changing vital and even nonvital behaviors. Regardless, change the vital behaviors, and other behaviors will also change. In Chapter 7, *Finding Key Behaviors Like Social Psychologists*, I discuss vital behaviors in more detail.

Principle 6: Collaborate with Others

If teams and organizations want to achieve extraordinary results through creativity and innovation while improving employee engagement, teams must collaborate. Kouzes and Posner, Sinek, and Freiberg and Freiberg write about how necessary collaboration is for sharing ideas, building commitment, and sustaining outstanding performance.[83]

Belief 19: Organizational Charts Limit Thinking

Rummler and Brache describe two purposes of organizational charts:

1. Identify how roles are grouped "for operating efficacy and human resource development."
2. Identify role-reporting relationships.[84]

What organizational charts don't tell you is how the business works, why the business works that way, and what the business is.[85]

One problem occurs when "it's the organization chart, not the business, that's being managed."[86] Figure 4.2 illustrates the problem using a simplified organizational chart.

Suppose someone asked Director 1 what she does. She might respond that she manages call centers. Each call center, though, has a manager who

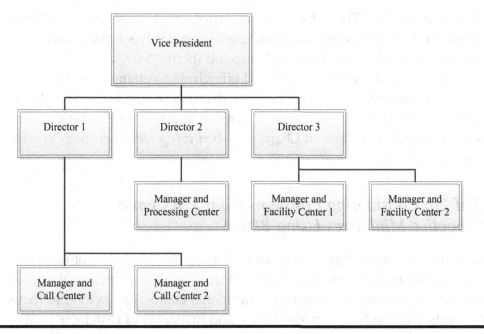

Figure 4.2   Simplified organizational chart.

happens to be competent. Rummler and Brache take the position that this isn't the primary role of a manager of managers (Box 4.20).

Too many organizations manage their business using organizational charts and inadvertently ignore the white space. They manage the vertical organizational boxes rather than how people execute the horizontal processes—processes that are hidden because they aren't represented on an organizational chart. As a result, organizations tend to

- Hold power at the upper levels.
- Manage down rather than across.
- Risk becoming micromanagers who cause competent employees to become overly dependent on them.

BOX 4.20   PRIMARY ROLE OF MANAGER OF MANAGERS

A primary contribution of a manager (of the second level or above) is to manage interfaces. The boxes already have managers; the senior manager adds value by managing the white space between the boxes.[87]

Rummler and Brache

Wiseman writes, "These hierarchical structures make it easier for Tyrants to reign. And in their reign, these managers can easily suppress and constrain the thinking of the people around them."[88]

To correct organizations to respond effectively to changes in the environment, Rummler and Brache state that this should begin by taking a systems view of the organization.[89] Anyone at any level can begin doing this, and I expand on how in Chapter 5, *Analyzing Like Detectives*, the first of the nine practices.

Belief 20: Considering Problems from a Systemic Perspective Minimizes Using Blame

One of the challenges that organizations have is the development of silos or teams that isolate themselves from other teams. While unintentional, this is a by-product of managing through organizational charts. Teams tend to focus only on their immediate responsibilities, and managers of managers focus on ensuring that those below them perform to expectations. In other words, they tend to manage down the organizational chart rather than manage the work across the processes. This could be due to several reasons, including limitations to the physical structure, unclear expectations, or lack of incentives.

A consequence of focusing more on managing silos is that management may optimize the silos at the expense of the overall business process or other silos. Organizations inadvertently build inefficiencies. (In Chapter 5, I expand on this concept.) When things go wrong, management defends their silos and blames others. This blaming can happen at the macro-level between business units or at the micro-level within teams where teammates build personal silos.

Wiseman recognizes this problem and writes about addressing it (Box 4.21).

BOX 4.21   SHIFTING SILO OPTIMIZATION TO SYSTEM OPTIMIZATION

When people are given ownership for only a piece of something larger, they tend to optimize that portion, limiting their thinking to this immediate domain. When people are given ownership for the whole, they stretch their thinking and challenge themselves to go beyond their scope.[90]

Wiseman

Typically, the point in which the problem occurs isn't the sole cause. Throughout the business, teams more than likely contribute to the problem by doing something or not doing something that benefited the silo but harmed either other silos' productivity or the value stream as a whole. To stop the blaming, teams need to think beyond the silo scope of work and systematically examine the business and problems. By doing so, teams can work together to optimize the value stream by compromising individual silo productivity to better the business.

Belief 21: Leadership Doesn't Reside with One Person

Southwest Airlines has a powerful collaboration model in which everyone, regardless of title, practices both collaboration and leadership. As Freiberg and Freiberg state, "leadership is something leaders and their collaborators do together."[91] Imagine a team meeting at Southwest. A manager might lead with a challenge. After that, teammates switch rapidly from leading to collaborating. Someone may lead with an idea, and others would collaborate. Freiberg and Freiberg write about this as well (Box 4.22).

Belief 22: Influence Comes from All Directions

Freiberg and Freiberg write that influence doesn't always start at the organization's executive level.[93] Often, changes may come from one team to benefit other teams or the whole organization. They cite how Southwest pilots influenced "ground operations to support the Cutting Edge Team," saving hours on the ground time between flights.[94]

BOX 4.22 SUSTAINING COMMITMENT THROUGH SHARED PURPOSE, VISION, AND VALUES

Leadership is getting people to want to do what you want them to do because they share your purpose, vision, and values. When the interests of leaders and collaborators overlap, the result is long-term, sustained commitment. When people are committed, they are bound emotionally or intellectually to a purpose or course of action.[92]

Freiberg and Freiberg

Employees can influence top-level executives. At one global organization where I worked, the executives informed employees that a workforce reduction was coming, and we knew that the organization was ready to close within several months. As an individual contributor working in the technology business unit, I suggested to my manager a way to handle the upcoming workforce reduction. The next day, my manager called me and said that the chief information officer (CIO) had decided to implement my suggestion for our business unit. As a result, the organization released employees at all levels more dignifiedly.

Belief 23: Leadership Practices Work the Same with All Populations Including Peers, Customers, Supervisors, and Subordinates

21st Century Leadership works with all populations universally. In *The Servant*, Hunter shares the CEOS acronym: Customers, employees, owners, and suppliers.[95] With these, organizations need to build relationships. What better way to do so than to practice leadership.

If this is universal, think about how some supervisors behave toward buying customers compared with direct reports: They may treat customers with dignity but less so with employees. Sometimes, the reverse is also true. If you practice leadership with all populations, you can help more than just those on your teams.

Principle 7: Develop Leadership Practices Continuously

In *Helping People Win at Work*, Blanchard and Ridge share Noel Tichy's belief "that learning, teaching, and leading are intricately intertwined…"[96] To practice leadership effectively, you need to learn about leadership and practice leadership continuously. In their research, Kouzes and Posner found a strong correlation between learning and leadership effectiveness, and they cite other studies that identified the correlation.[97]

You need to develop your leadership practices in a particular way: You need to know the reasoning behind leadership practices and dedicate time to practice with conformational and corrective feedback. Without both of these, your leadership effectiveness is limited.

Belief 24: To Become Fluent in Leadership, You Need to Practice Leadership Regularly and Monitor Your Effectiveness

Practicing leadership deliberately is the key to becoming fluent. To accomplish this, you need two things: Underlying knowledge and conformational and corrective feedback.

Knowledge

Imitating others who practice leadership is important but not enough. Knowing the nine practices is important but not enough. You also need to comprehend the underlying knowledge of the practices and associate that knowledge as you perform the practices. As Wiseman writes, "If someone wants to lead like a Multiplier, he or she can't simply mimic the practices of the Multiplier. An aspiring Multiplier must start by thinking like a Multiplier."[98] As with medical education, following procedures is critical, and you need to know the reasoning behind the procedures. When (and not if) something goes wrong, you can use that underlying reasoning to assess the situation quickly and take corrective actions.

Conformational and Corrective Feedback

Some think that they get *leadership*. They read books, go to seminars, want to change, and for example, declare themselves officially to be humble servant leaders who practice from the heart. They then go about their daily tasks without changing but believe they have changed. Hunter explains the problem from a reader's perspective (Box 4.23).

BOX 4.23   KNOWING ABOUT LEADERSHIP IS NOT ENOUGH TO PRACTICE LEADERSHIP

I have ten crazy, command-and-control Gestapo-like supervisors in my building, so I told them to read your book. They liked your book. They agreed with your book. But they are still crazy! How do you get them to change? If everyone agrees, why isn't every leader behaving in the way they know they should behave?[99]

Hunter

The problem is that you need practice with feedback to identify what Grenny et al. call our *blind spots*.[100] In other words, you are incapable of knowing how effective your leadership practices are without authentic information about your behaviors in relation to how your behaviors affect others. As Grenny et al. describe the importance of feedback, imagine two comparably skilled people learning tennis.[101] Both novices practice for the same amount of time. One has a coach who provides feedback, while the other has a coach who doesn't provide feedback. Can you imagine which novice plays better after a week of practice? Of course, the novice with feedback is substantially better.

Feedback is critical for practicing leadership. In Chapter 11, *Facing the Unknown Like Lions*, I discuss obtaining data to adjust and improve leadership practices.

Belief 25: Knowing Everything about Leadership Isn't Enough

Hunter makes a powerful distinction between knowing about leadership and knowing leadership (Box 4.24).

After reading Box 4.24, consider what Hunter does to support leadership development. He facilitates leadership seminars and writes books. I don't think that Hunter implies that leadership seminars and books are unnecessary. Instead, they are insufficient for developing leadership practices. To make his point, Hunter asks readers if they know of anyone who learned to swim merely by reading a book.[102]

I know two executives who are knowledgeable about leadership. They are well connected with leadership authors and facilitators, including those I identify in this book. While they tell their colleagues how they are humble

---

BOX 4.24 KNOWING ABOUT LEADERSHIP IS DIFFERENT FROM KNOWING LEADERSHIP

Only a very small percentage of people actually make sustainable changes after attend leadership seminars or reading books. There is a world of difference between knowing about something and knowing it. You can learn about leadership reading books and attending seminars, but you will never know leadership doing those things.[103]

Hunter

> ### BOX 4.25   LEADER–LEADER STRUCTURE
>
> Instead of more "leadership" resulting in more "followership," I practiced less leadership, resulting in more leadership at every level of the command.[104]
>
> **Marquet**

leaders in their organization, neither practice 21st Century Leadership. The two executives are friendly people and often lecture about leadership, but they ineffectively lead the teams under their care. As Hunter might state, they know of leadership but don't know leadership.

Belief 26: Leadership Involves Helping Others Learn Leadership

A critical element of 21st Century Leadership is helping others lead. Marquet argues that if you practice leadership correctly, the practice enables others to practice leadership (Box 4.25).

Maxwell furthers this point by stating that when leaders develop others to lead, the organization experiences explosive growth.[105] Helping others grow and lead is a powerful way to inspire creativity, innovation, and engagement!

Summary

In this chapter, I continued to distinguish 21st Century Leadership from traditional leadership by describing the principles and beliefs of 21st Century Leadership. As with all the performance-improvement disciplines, 21st Century Leadership has underlying principles and beliefs that support the practices that I identify in Sections II through IV. The principles and beliefs help explain what this leadership approach represents and how individuals, teams, organizations, and society could benefit through its successful adaption.

IMPROVING PERFORMANCE WITH SYSTEMIC THINKING

> To lead others well, we must help them to reach their potential.
> That means being on their side, encouraging them, giving them
> power, and helping them to succeed. That's not traditionally what
> we're taught about leadership.[1]
>
> **Maxwell**

Introduction to Sections II through IV: The Nine Practices

In Section I, I define 21st Century Leadership, reveal harmful traditional
leadership assumptions, and explain 21st Century Leadership principles and
beliefs. Sections II through IV describe how to apply the principles and
beliefs with nine practices. I present the practices in three sections:

- Section II: Improving Performance with Systemic Thinking
  (Practices 1–3)
- Section III: Supporting Change (Practices 4–6)
- Section IV: Adding Value (Practices 7–9)

DOI: 10.4324/9781003273448-6

Each chapter introduces a practice and has the following standard structure:

1. Importance and benefits
2. Characteristics
3. Guidelines, rules of practice, models, techniques, and tools
4. Three leading examples
5. Summary table
6. What to do immediately, in the short term, and in the long term
7. Word of caution

Each chapter introduces a practice and provides enough information for you to begin applying the practice to your daily routine. You may find some practices familiar and easier to apply, but you may discover other practices to be more challenging. While you can start using all of the practices after reading about them, you most likely will need additional resources and support to develop fluency. Reading this book alone isn't enough. At the end of each chapter, the *What to Do* topic describes further resources and how to further your development with the practice. For myself, I continue to study the principles, beliefs, and nine practices, and I still have a great deal to learn.

Each chapter ends with a *Word of Caution* topic. This topic warns how you can misapply the practices in a way that supports traditional leadership thinking. Specifically, traditional assumptions (not trusting others, wanting to be a hero, and the leader is the smartest) might influence them to apply a practice alone and without involving teammates. Remember that leadership is collaborative and that the practices are a means to build collaboration. Practicing 21st Century Leadership is about helping others grow and mature. The benefits from practicing leadership collaboratively not only lead to more creativity, innovation, and engagement but working collaboratively also leads to better solutions and work environments.

The nine practices also are meant to be shared with others. 21st Century Leadership is about helping others grow and mature their mental and moral qualities, capabilities, and behaviors. Sharing your knowledge about 21st Century Leadership and the nine practices is a way to build character in others...and yourself.

Introduction to Section II: Improving Performance with Systemic Thinking

> We spend too much of our time "fixing" people who are not broken, and not enough time fixing organization systems that are broken.[2]
>
> **Rummler and Brache**

In a Skillsoft live event, Marquet states that leadership isn't about doing stuff; leadership is about getting people to think.[3] Complementing this concept, the research findings of McKinsey & Company identified four key behaviors typically displayed by high-quality leadership teams and closely correlated with leadership success.[4] The four key behaviors are

■ Solve problems effectively.
■ Seek different perspectives.
■ Operate with a strong results orientation.
■ Be supportive.

In Section II, the first three practices align to performance-improvement behaviors. The practices involve getting people to think about problems and to use analytical and diagnostic tools.

Section II are the foundational practices for 21st Century Leadership:

■ Analyzing Like Detectives
■ Diagnosing and Treating Like Doctors
■ Finding Key Behaviors Like Social Psychologists

Practitioners can apply these practices independently and in conjunction with other practices. For example, when practicing *Facing the Unknown Like Lions*, the seventh practice, leveraging one or more foundational practices improves your results.

How Foundational Practices Help: Fixing Bad Systems, Ending Unwarranted Blame, and Eliminating Faulty Solutions

In *Serious Performance Consultants*, Rummler explains why, after several years of practice, he's still a performance consultant. He explains that, for him, performance consulting is value-added work at two levels. First, many organizations, which Rummler characterizes as having *bad systems*, need help in becoming more effective. Second, Rummler writes how upset he becomes when those in charge mistakenly accuse employees of being the source of organizational problems. As a result, organizations waste operational dollars and employee time by addressing symptoms rather than the problematic system. Rummler explains what he typically experiences: The bad system sets up employees to fail. Those at the executive and management levels allow this to happen because they are either incompetent or irresponsible in maintaining a safe and productive work environment. Moreover, when executives and managers become aware that they manage a bad system, no one accepts responsibility for its current state.[5] Sinek complements Rummler's perspective: He explains that those in charge do not understand that people aren't the problem, but the organization's environment is. If you get the environment right, then everything starts to improve.[6]

21st Century Leadership practices address the problem with bad systems. Section II describes three practices that help people working in bad systems. Whether addressing the micro or the macro level, these practices improve the performance of teams, departments, business units, and the whole organization.

The first three practices leverage systemic thinking. *Systemic thinking* involves considering the whole system and the subsystems and using that knowledge to analyze problems. Systemic thinking also involves identifying various behavioral influences and determining how the influences interrelate and affect behavior. In Chapter 5, I discuss systemic thinking. Chapter 6 explains how to systematically address presenting problems and how to handle when executives, managers, or sponsors request that you implement single-channel solutions. Chapter 7 discusses using systemic thinking to find key behaviors and introduces Grenny et al.'s Six Sources of Influence™ used to overdetermine change. I also introduce Duhigg's approach to changing habits and routines.

Chapter 5

Practice 1: Analyzing Like Detectives

I asked everyone, "Is there a better way to do what you do?" Time after time, the answer was yes, and many of the answers were revelations to me.[1]

Abrashoff

Too many times we attack the symptoms, not the cause.[2]

Maxwell

Introduction: Importance and Benefits of Analyzing Like Detectives

Want to help others improve how they investigate, ask critical questions that provide insights into their organization, and rethink how best to resolve challenges? *Analyzing Like Detectives* can help you and those you work with incorporate these behaviors.

If 21st Century Leadership is designed to mature mental and moral qualities, capabilities, and behaviors, then enabling others to make better decisions is an essential function of leadership. Marquet describes leadership as a means to get everyone thinking (Box 5.1).

DOI: 10.4324/9781003273448-7

**BOX 5.1   LEADERSHIP IS ABOUT
GETTING EVERYONE THINKING**

Leadership is not about getting people to do stuff. It's about getting people to think...I believe that what's going to win in the 21st Century...and in the future is organizations that allow everyone in their organization to think. Get everybody thinking—not doing.[3]

Marquet

Analyzing Like Detectives is a valuable practice for:

■ Discovering new data to help decision-makers.
■ Promoting creative thinking about problems and opportunities
■ Improving the collaboration process among teams.

In most organizations, people at all career levels struggle with analyzing problems and opportunities. This could be due to time constraints, frequent interruptions that interfere with critical thinking, or not having any systematic analytical techniques. Instead, they accept quickly developed explanations based on limited, biased, or inaccurate data. The data influence them to accept unfounded and false conclusions, and in turn, cause them to make faulty decisions. As Sinek writes, "We make assumptions about the world around us based on sometimes incomplete or false information...our behavior is affected by our assumptions or our perceived truths."[4]

Others may want quick and straightforward explanations based only on the initial facts. They mistakenly interpret symptoms as problems, blame those closest to the symptoms, and waste valuable time and money on a solution that, at best, fixes the problem temporarily and, at worst, causes more problems. To avoid this and help others improve their decision-making, you need to use and teach performance-improvement practices that include systemic thinking. That is, you need to *analyze like detectives.*

Of the nine practices, leadership practitioners are most likely not to recognize or practice *Analyzing Like Detectives.* Most limit their leadership scope to only two to five practices. Because of this, I put more effort and detail into this chapter. Those who want to practice 21st Century Leadership seriously will find *Analyzing Like Detectives* and the following two practices as important as the other practices for maturing mental and moral qualities, capabilities, and behaviors in others.

In this chapter, I discuss the characteristics of *Analyzing Like Detectives*. I then introduce the analytical models developed and used by Geary A. Rummler and the Performance Design Lab. Complementing these models, I introduce Carl Binder's Six Boxes® Model. As with all nine practices, I provide three examples of how you can begin to apply this practice as part of your 21st Century Leadership.

Characteristics of Analyzing Like Detectives

Like detectives searching for clues to solve a crime, leadership practitioners use systemic thinking to interpret organizational incidents. Systemic thinking involves:

- Considering the whole system and the subsystems and using that knowledge to analyze problems.
- Identifying current-state behavioral influences, categorizing influences in meaningful ways, recognizing how influences interrelate, and determining more effective influences for changing key behaviors.

Both are critical means for leadership practitioners to achieve the immediate team results of 21st Century Leadership that I identified in Chapter 2:

- Fulfilled needs rather than results
- Removed or reduced barriers
- Improved work performance

In crime novels and cinema, detectives skillfully invalidate what some perceive as an obvious conclusion, arrive at a contrary conclusion, and identify the criminals. By finding hidden evidence and following leads, a detective may conclude that an apparent suicide is actually a homicide, identify who murdered the victim, and use forensic evidence to convict the murderer. Like detectives investigating a crime, leadership practitioners inquire systematically to discover and examine seemingly unrelated facts of an event. This type of inquiry helps determine the truth or interpret what occurred and why (Box 5.2).

**BOX 5.2   CHARACTERISTICS OF
ANALYZING LIKE DETECTIVES**

■ Resist initial conclusions based solely on the presenting problem and conclusions reached by those who don't investigate.

■ Examine the facts of the current-state situation while filtering out opinions.

■ Follow multiple leads even knowing that some leads yield no relevance. Leads help confirm what you know, eliminate possible explanations, and provide new evidence.

■ Search and discover evidence that may not be obvious to those involved.

■ Use forensic tools to methodically examine evidence for patterns that may not be apparent to the casual observer.

Rummler's Fundamental Laws of Organizational Systems

In *Improving Performance*, Rummler and Brache describe six fundamental laws of organizational systems.[5] These laws illustrate the need for systemic thinking (Box 5.3).

**BOX 5.3   SIX FUNDAMENTAL LAWS OF
ORGANIZATIONAL SYSTEMS**

1. Understanding performance requires documenting the inputs, processes, outputs, and customers that constitute a business.
2. Organization systems adapt or die.
3. When one component of an organization system optimizes, the organization often suboptimizes.
4. Pulling any lever in the system will have an effect on other parts of the system.
5. An organization behaves as a system, regardless of whether it is being managed as a system.
6. If you pit a good performer against a bad system, the system will win almost every time.[6]

Rummler and Brache

Law 1: Understanding Performance Requires Documenting the Inputs, Processes, Outputs, and Customers That Constitute a Business

When starting a new job, departments might provide organizational charts to explain how the organization is structured and list employees' names and roles. New employees most likely won't receive high-level process maps explaining what the organization does and how departments accomplish their work.

Documenting how the business should work and comparing the documentation with the current state is an effective way to find opportunities and problems. This is true, especially when paying particular attention to where one group's output becomes the input of another group. Rummler and Brache note that the greatest opportunity for improving performance happens when examining these handoffs.[7]

Law 2: Organization Systems Adapt or Die

Rummler and Brache state that adaptation isn't a single event. Instead, adaptation is an ongoing process.[8] Organizations that wait for something to happen and then react adapt ineffectively. At one organization where I worked, we called this firefighting, which cost about $15 million from the bottom line. Reacting to single events instead of continuously adapting increases operational costs and unnecessarily wastes everyone's time. If those in charge and leadership practitioners shifted their thinking about adaptation from events to a process and if they used systems thinking to identify changing forces within and outside the organization, they would anticipate and respond to change proactively. This company that did the firefighting managed to shift from thinking of adaptation as an event to a process, and they reduced their operational cost by doing so.

Law 3: When One Component of an Organization System Optimizes, the Organization Often Suboptimizes

As Wiseman notes, department heads often optimize their own subsystem without considering the larger system. Doing so may unnecessarily limit how their departments integrate with other departments so that the workflow is seamless and unbroken.[9] For example, Rummler and Brache provide an example of a sales department that becomes so efficient at generating sales that the organization cannot produce products fast enough for new and existing customers.[10] This causes customers to become angry and hurts the organization's reputation and potential sales.

Organizations with departments that focus only on optimizing their subsystem tend to cause silo thinking—thinking about one's own department without considering or even caring about the other departments.[11] This type of thinking causes unnecessary conflict between departments. It prevents departments from working together to resolve interdepartmental issues such as preventing product damages, decreasing defects, and ensuring a consistent and positive customer experience. Silo thinking is the antithesis of systemic thinking.

Law 4: Pulling Any Lever in the System Will Have an Effect on Other Parts of the System

Decreasing the thickness of an appliance's casing saved thousands in raw material costs but generated hundreds of thousands in damages. New safety procedures decreased injuries at a processing facility, but they caused production to slow down so much that customers didn't receive their orders on time. Converting in-person sales training to web-based training decreased training delivery costs dramatically, but sales teams couldn't learn without in-person support. These examples represent silo thinking, which I later characterize as single-box solutions that frequently occur in organizations.

Law 5: An Organization Behaves as a System, Regardless of Whether It Is Being Managed as a System

Organizations that only manage vertically with organizational charts manage the organization inefficiently. To manage as a system, organizations need to manage the vertical organizational charts and the horizontal processes.

Law 6: If You Pit a Good Performer against a Bad System, the System Will Win Almost Every Time

As I discuss in Section II, organizations that are bad systems tend to turn good performers into mediocre performers. Reflecting on the previous five fundamental laws, organizations that aren't managed as systems, in which silo thinking is the norm, tend to restrict positive performance.

Not only do good performers fail to perform because of the system, sometimes those in charge cause the problem. In *Multipliers*, Wiseman provides several examples of how diminishers make extraordinary performance impossible. As a colleague once told me about his dysfunctional department, "Until I experienced this, I would have never believed that one VP could demoralize a department into producing only mediocre results."

Conclusion

In organizations with bad systems, you will most likely find silo thinking along with silo departments. You will also find quick reactions to presenting problems that turn out to be symptoms of a more significant problem, and by reacting quickly to solve the problem, the solution causes problems in other departments. To help organizations evolve bad systems into good systems, organizations need people to practice 21st Century Leadership. Thinking systemically in the way detectives analyze crime scenes is a step in the right direction.

Anatomy of Performance and the Human Performance System

Introduction

You may have seen images of Arthur Conan Doyle's fictional detective character, Sherlock Holmes, with his magnifying glass. The magnifying glass enables you to view evidence that isn't apparent without one. Also, the stronger the magnification, the more hidden details you can reveal. Leadership can become more effective when using frameworks and diagnostic tools similar to using a magnifying glass. Rummler provides us with this type of framework entitled the Anatomy of Performance (AOP). This framework provides the systemic perspective needed to analyze problems or incidents. As depicted in Table 5.1, the framework consists of three levels: organization, process, and performer.

Each level provides a unique perspective about the organization and can provide insight into what and where actual problems—rather than symptoms—exist.

Table 5.1 Three Levels of Performance

Level	Explanation	Characteristics
Organization	The relationship between capital markets (investors) and consumer markets (customers) within the perspective of needed resources, competitors, and the overall business environment	Less visible than performer level Strategy and metrics for the organization to meet investor and customer expectations Implied in mission and vision statements
Process	How organizations produce outputs that meet the expectations of the capital and consumer markets (investors and customers)	• Least visible • Process maps
Performer	Individuals who perform and manage the primary and supportive processes	Most visible Job descriptions Organizational charts

Anatomy of Performance of Organizations (Organization Level)

On the outside, people look different. When examining X-ray charts, people appear to have the same skeletal system but with few differences, such as size. The same is true with organizations. Rummler writes, "Although organizations are very different on the outside (big or small, public or private, products or services), inside they all have a common anatomy."[12] The AOP, depicted in Figure 5.1, illustrates the common parts of any business.

Before explaining the model, note that I use *business* to represent more than the private sector. Silber and Kearny explain that *business* includes government, nonprofits, educational systems, financial organizations, hospitals, and the like (Box 5.4).[13]

As with any business, the organization itself consists of the three organizational levels: Organization, process, and performer. The supersystem consists of the business, capital and consumer markets, resources, competition, and the business environment. Any of these can trigger problems within the organization (Box 5.5).

To practice Analyzing as Detectives, Rummler states that you need to use the AOP framework from two points of view. First, you need to know how any organization should work. Specifically, you need to know how the parts

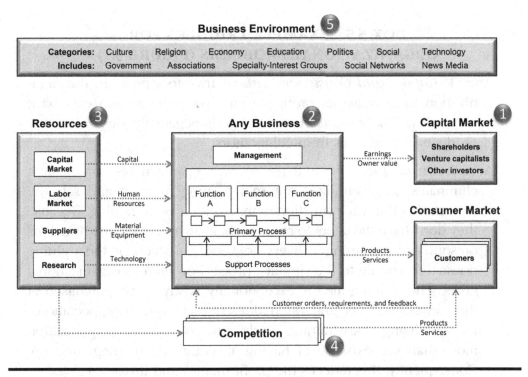

Figure 5.1   The AOP at the organization level. (Adapted from Rummler, G. A., *Serious Performance Consulting,* **17. ©2007. Geary A. Rummler and the Performance Design Lab. Used with permission.)**

of any business work together, the economic principles, and the language of business.[14] Second, you need to know how your business works. This helps with diagnostics, described in Chapter 6, and clarifies nonproblems (problems that seem important to those in the business but don't affect the primary process) and real problems (those that affect the primary process

---

BOX 5.4   BUSINESS DEFINITION

A business is any organization that:

1. Offers a product or service to customers and receives an income,
2. Has expenses it must meet to create its product or service and that tries to ensure at least enough income to meet its expenses, and
3. Has a strategy, processes, and people to make all this happen.[15]

Sibler and Kearny

BOX 5.5 EXAMPLE TRIGGERS FOR ORGANIZATIONAL PROBLEMS (FIGURE 5.1)

Area 1. *Capital and Consumer Markets*: Investors pressure the organization to increase its profit margin. The organization cuts back on quality. This impacts customer needs negatively. Customers buy products and services from competitors.

Area 2. *Any Business*: To cut expenses, the organization's management eliminates the centralized, internal training function and sets the expectation that each function manages their own training. Because they don't have the talent to manage their own training, the functions outsource the training delivery to vendors. Much of the training doesn't contribute to the primary process or align to organizational goals. The training also is exceptionally costly when purchased at the functional level and often doesn't meet quality expectations. Decentralizing the training ends up costing the organization more than the expense of having a centralized training function. Consequently, this reduces the profit margin and investor value.

Area 3. *Resources*: Suppliers decrease the material quality to save operational cost. This decreases the quality of the organization's products, impacts customers negatively, and causes customers to purchase from competitors.

Area 4. *Competition*: A competitor leverages open-source technology (such as smartphone technology) and decreases operational expenses. The organization has already signed a long-term agreement with a vendor to use an older technology. The capital market responds by increasing investments in the competitor and decreasing investments in the organization.

Area 5. *Business Environment*: The organization has been outsourcing its call center outside the country to take advantage of substantial tax breaks. Specialty interest groups, social networks, and the news media change public opinion about tax breaks for these types of outsourcing. Government responds by removing the tax breaks and taxing organizations that outsource outside the country. The capital market reacts by decreasing investments in the organization.

negatively).[16] Moreover, this helps identify unrealized opportunities for better alignment at the three performance levels. Lastly, you build your credibility and respect by knowing how your business works at the macro-level. A surprising number of people at all career levels don't know their own business, nor have they considered how this knowledge could help them.

The Human Performance System (Performer and Process Levels)

While the AOP is a macro-view at the organization level, the Human Performance System (HPS) is a micro view at the performer and process levels. HPS illustrates the relationship among a performer, a process, and behavioral influences. HPS also identifies ways to address problems and opportunities at the micro-level (Box 5.6).

The function of performers is to perform or manage the primary process or the support processes. The HPS, depicted in Figure 5.2, illustrates the relationship between a performer, a process, and influences. As with the AOP for organizations, the HPS applies to performers working or managing processes.

The five components work like this: Joe, a performer, (1) deals with various inputs (2) that need processing. He has a variety of inputs, including order forms, telephone calls, people stopping at his desk, and incoming emails. For each input, Joe creates the desired output (3), such as a processed order form and an answered email. For each output, there are consequences (4) that Joe interprets as being either positive or negative. Some consequences occur immediately, such as a thank-you email, while others take longer. Finally, Joe's supervisor, peers, mentor, or executives can provide feedback (5). While the feedback is best given frequently, timely, and accurately, some feedback takes a while. For example, Anne, a customer,

BOX 5.6 FINDING TROUBLE SPOTS USING HPS

Just as the AOP framework [at the organization level] acts as a template for identifying and understanding the components impacting organization performance, the HPS framework...can be used as a template for troubleshooting poor individual performance and designing an effective performance environment for an individual.[17]

Rummler

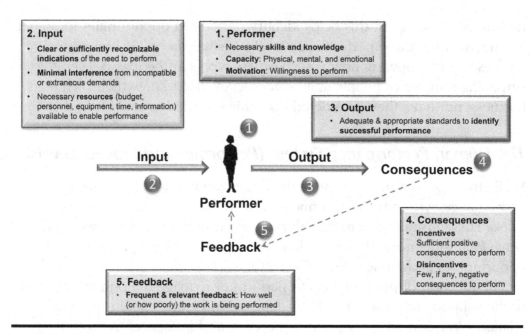

Figure 5.2   The HPS. (Adapted from Rummler, G. A., *Serious Performance Consulting*, 23. ©2007. Geary A. Rummler and the Performance Design Lab. Used with permission.)

appreciates how Joe handled her problem. She contacts Stewart, a customer-service executive, to express her appreciation for Joe and his company. Stewart thanks Joe for his service and shares the experience with other employees to demonstrate how performers apply the organization's values.[18]

Identifying Trouble Spots in the Human Performance System

At any of the five components of the HPS, problems can occur. However, Rummler observes that when problems occur, managers typically blame performers (Box 5.7).

BOX 5.7   BLAMING PERFORMERS FOR TROUBLE

...The performer is the component in the HPS that is most visible and recognizable to managers. When managers don't get desired job results, they tend to focus on that component almost exclusively... The performer is almost always going to be the default cause of poor performance in the eyes of the unenlightened management.[19]

Rummler

Although managers may blame the performer as the cause of a presenting problem, the performer component is the least likely source of trouble. Rummler observed two tendencies with trouble spots in the HPS:

1. Some components are more likely to have deficiencies than other components.
2. More than one component has deficiencies.[20]

As depicted in Figure 5.3, Rummler lists the components in the order of most likely to have deficiencies to least likely: (1) output, (2) input, (3) consequences, (4) feedback, and (5) performer.[21]

With each component, Rummler provides questions to guide you through your analysis of HPS. From these questions, you can discover that the underlying or *root* problems are sourced to other parts of the AOP levels: process and organization. Rummler states, "The cause of these HPS deficiencies may be traced ultimately to other factors in the organization, but the trail starts with the individual HPS."[22] Note that the two most likely

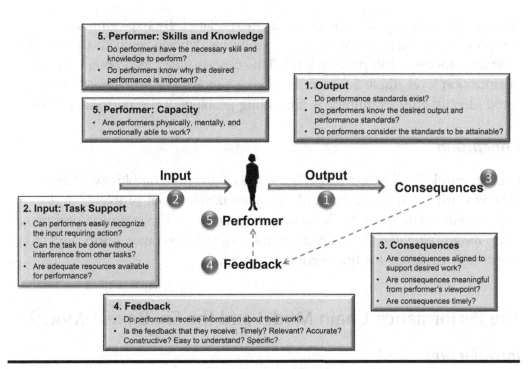

Figure 5.3   Troubleshooting the HPS. (Adapted from Rummler, G. A., *Serious Performance Consulting*, 25. ©2007. Geary A. Rummler and the Performance Design Lab. Used with permission.)

Table 5.2 Five Examples of Root Problems at the Three Performance Levels

Performer	Process	Organization
No procedural documentation Conflicting expectations No feedback Too many competing tasks Negative consequences for completing a task correctly	Performer goals no longer align to process goals Performer design no longer aligns to process design The process isn't managed and monitored effectively The functional department changed task priorities and no longer aligned with process-level priorities Process requirements aren't communicated clearly	Goals at the three levels are misaligned Changes to organizational functional structures (such as department structures) now make it more challenging to process products and services Workforce reduction causes processing delays due to a lack of performers The organization isn't effectively managed and monitored Management adapts to new customer needs and expectations inconsistently

components to have deficiencies are process-related. By exploring these components, you may discover more significant deficiencies with the primary business process at the process level. This can also lead to problems at the organization level. Table 5.2 identifies five example root problems that you could identify after examining a presenting problem at the performer level.

Conclusion

Using Rummler's AOP is a powerful way to learn the complexity of any business and a way to begin thinking systemically about problems and opportunities. The framework provides a way for you to examine problems using *magnifying glasses* of different magnitude (stated metaphorically) to reveal new evidence for how problems occur.

The Performance Chain Model and the Six Boxes® Model

Introduction

While Rummler's AOP and HPS are effective models to help you analyze the whole system and subsystems, the Performance Chain Model and the Six Boxes® Model are powerful tools for promoting systemic thinking from a different perspective and enabling you to use a shared framework for analyzing behavioral influences. As I stated earlier, part of systemic thinking involves

- Identifying current-state behavioral influences.
- Categorizing influences in meaningful ways.
- Recognizing how influences interrelate.
- Determining more effective influences for changing key behaviors.

Starting in the mid-1980s and for about 30 years, Binder developed and tested the Performance Chain Model and Six Boxes® Model with dozens of organizations and in hundreds of projects and applications. Since the beginning of the 21st century, Binder and the Performance Thinking Network have helped thousands of professionals across multiple industries apply and integrate the models to improve their performance and business results.[23] Because of how they refined the models, anyone can apply them. Binder writes, "we believe that it offers a model of human behavior influence that is accessible to anyone…in an organization, from the executive suite to the individual contributor."[24]

Performance Chain Overview

Figure 5.2 shows that inputs function as a trigger behavior. In Figure 5.4, the Performance Chain Model illustrates a critical way of thinking about

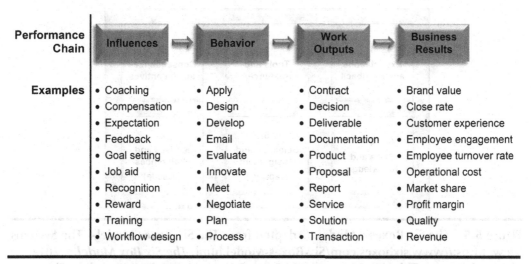

Figure 5.4 Performance chain with examples. (Adapted from *The Performance Chain—Connecting People to Results*, https://www.sixboxes.com/Performance-Chain.html. ©2012 The Performance Thinking Network. With permission.)

behavior triggers: influences. Grenny et al. define *influence* as the "ability to create changes in human behavior."[25] Influences can shape work to be effective or ineffective. Influences are interrelated and can complement or conflict with one another. While the Performance Chain Model introduces the importance of influences and provides perspective, the model doesn't provide a systematic approach for your detective work. In other words, you need a way to analyze the different influence types and to identify trouble spots. Binder and the Performance Thinking Network created the Six Boxes® Model to accomplish this.

Six Boxes® Model Overview

Binder writes that the Six Boxes® Model is "a comprehensive set of categories for identifying and organizing behavior influences to ensure desired behavior."[26] Instead of trying to guess all the possible influences for a behavior, the Six Boxes® Model provides six necessary influence categories that affect any behavior.

In Figure 5.5, the first three boxes (top row) are environmental influences that organizations manage directly. For example, at a large manufacturing plant, a facility team adds visual and audio facility maps to particular walls to help performers reach their destination within a facility without getting lost.

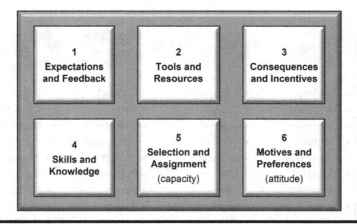

Figure 5.5 The Six Boxes® Model. (Adapted from The Six Boxes Model—The Systems View, https://www.sixboxes.com/Six-Boxes-Model.html. *The Six Box Model,* ©2012 The Performance Thinking Network. Six Boxes® is a registered trademark of The Performance Thinking Network. With permission.)

The remaining boxes (bottom row) are individual influences that organizations can manage indirectly. For example, to improve knowledge and skills for using a new software application, Bob, a trainer, provides training for the different teams and includes simulation practice that matches how specific roles would use the software.

Table 5.3 provides influence category examples to clarify the types of influences for each category. Note that the examples illustrate the depth of each category and aren't listed to address any specific key behaviors.

Leadership practitioners use the Six Boxes® Model to think about performance systematically and systemically. This involves the following:

■ Examining a set of influences represented in the six categories on a particular behavior and analyzing the interrelationships among the influences.[27] Some influences complement one another while others conflict.

■ Adding, removing, and modifying influences to improve the likelihood of the desired behaviors. This includes removing or minimalizing conflicting influences.

In the next topic, I explain how influences can conflict as I present common mistakes people make when influencing behaviors.

Common Mistakes with Influencing Behaviors

People seldom leverage influences effectively when designing and managing at the three performance levels (organization, process, and performer). Binder identifies four common mistakes made by those who design and manage (Box 5.8).

Mistake 1: Attempt to Influence without Focusing on the Valuable Accomplishments Needed to Support Desired Business Results

When designing or managing at any of the three levels, many fail to use a systematic approach for influencing behavior. They fail to use a defined and valid approach for selecting and using influences that lead to valuable accomplishments that achieve desired business results while strengthening relationships. When people don't analyze influences critically, influences among the different categories seldom align properly or only align partially.[28]

Table 5.3 Example Influences by Category

1. Expectations and Feedback	2. Tools and Resources	3. Consequences and Incentives
Expectations Performers know the standards and expectations, including: • How work contributes to achieving a business goal • What work output standards are • How to prioritize work • What metrics are used to measure work output quality, timeliness, and costs **Feedback** Performers receive feedback that is: • Immediate and frequent • Positive and constructive	Performers have access to tools, templates, and job aids (such as metrics, standard operating procedures, and reference materials) that are: • Designed to support performance • Current, accurate, and complete • Useful for monitoring quality Performers use a work facility designed to: • Support work • Remove distractors that can interfere with work • Enable access to tools, templates, and job aids • Remove work barriers (such as providing a ladder to access higher-level shelves)	**Consequences** The organization provides clear consequences for achieving or not achieving desired work outputs, including: • Informal and formal feedback (such as from managers, quality assurance teams, and peers) • Social support from peers and the team (such as recognition for achieving desired work output or coaching and encouragement for not achieving desired work output) **Incentives** The organization provides incentives that encourage desired work quality and discourage undesired work quality, including: • Financial (such as salary, bonuses, and benefits) • Non-financial (such as rewards, recognition, and flexible work arrangements)

4. Skills and Knowledge	5. Selection and Assignment (Capacity)	6. Motives and Preferences (Attitude)
Performers attend training or receive coaching designed to: • Improve the quality and speed of current work responsibilities • Prepare performers for future work changes (such as a new customer relationship management database) • Prepare performers for a new career or formal role Performers practice existing and new skills designed to: • Improve skill proficiency toward fluency	Ensure performers can work effectively by: • Accommodating performers as needed (such as providing a larger monitor and voice-recognition software for someone with a visual disability) • Scheduling work and breaks that minimizes fatigue • Using universal design equipment (such as using ramps instead of steps that are accessible by people with or without a wheelchair or adding wall guards for hand dryers in bathrooms so that people who have visual challenges won't bump into hand dryers)[a]	Ensure performers recognize how the team and organization value their work by: • Explaining how work-output aligns to process and organizational goals • Verifying with performers that work standards are fair • Obtaining performer input for strategy design and feasibility (at all levels) • Identifying ways to improve working conditions that can contribute to productivity Share success stories so that performers can learn vicariously through the achievements of others

[a] UniversalDesign.com, (n.d.), ADA Wall Guard.

BOX 5.8 FOUR COMMON MISTAKES WHEN DESIGNING AND MANAGING PERFORMANCE LEVELS

1. Attempt to influence without focusing on the valuable accomplishments needed to support desired business results.[29]
2. Attempt to influence without collaborating with other departments.[30]
3. Attempt to influence with only one category.[31]
4. Using influence to optimize a subsystem while compromising the whole system.[32]

Binder

At the performer level, Gilbert comments that unenlightened traditional leaders associate leadership with being a football coach stereotype that relies heavily on verbal persuasion to get things done (Box 5.9).

Gilbert later describes a successful football coach who uses influences from all six categories, shown in Figure 5.5, in the following order: 4, 1, 2, 3, 5, and then 6.[33] Using a variety of complementary influences, the coach would train a player, provide "frequent and detailed reports" on his development to enable continued development toward fluency, and then provide incentives such as awards or dinners. In reflection of leaders who rely more on Boxes 5 and 6, Gilbert writes, "It makes me suspicious that most of our managers who use football coaching as their management model played on mediocre or losing teams."[34]

In contrast to the influence examples in Table 5.3, Table 5.4 illustrates influence examples that promote incompetence.[35] Table 5.4 also illustrates

BOX 5.9 TRADITIONAL LEADERS AND THE BAD FOOTBALL COACH ANALOGY FOR LEADERSHIP

[The leader as football coach] consists of careful selection of "talent" and "leadership," which usually means pep talks and tough stances that threaten punishment. Capacity [Box 5 in Figure 5.5] and motives [Box 6 in Figure 5.5] are the chief variables [influences] for which they work. And such posturing gets heavily reinforced by other managers—if only because this is the behavior we have come to equate with management.[36]

Gilbert

Table 5.4 Creating Incompetence Applied to the Categories

1. Expectations and Feedback	2. Tools and Resources	3. Consequences and Incentives
Hide from employees what is expected of them Give employees little or no guidance about how to perform well Give employees misleading information about how well they are doing Don't let employees know how well they are doing	Design the tools of work without ever consulting employees who use them Don't document processes, or document them but don't share with employees Avoid creating job aids to help navigate poorly designed application user interfaces	Ensure that poor performers are paid as well as good performers Ensure that good performance gets punished in some way Don't make use of nonmonetary incentives Provide incentives that encourage the wrong behavior and discourage key behaviors

4. Skills and Knowledge	5. Selection and Assignment (Capacity)	6. Motives and Preferences (Attitude)
Leave training to chance Put training in the hands of supervisors who aren't trained instructors Make training unnecessarily difficult Make training that is irrelevant to employee needs	Schedule work for times when employees aren't at their sharpest Select employees for tasks that they would have difficulty performing due to physical limitations Don't provide response aids (example: magnification of difficult visual stimuli)	Design the job so that it has no career future Avoid arranging working conditions that employees would find more favorable Give pep talks rather than incentives to promote performance in punishing situations

Source: Adapted from Gilbert, *Human Competence*, Copyright ©2007 International Society for Performance Improvement. Used with Permission.

examples of "what management can do to make behavior ineffective."[37] Sadly, these descriptions are based on real examples.

Mistake 2: Attempt to Influence without Collaborating with Other Departments

Because departments tend to work in silos, they often fail to work collaboratively to influence behavior. This can cause problems. Binder

**BOX 5.10   THE PROBLEM WITH INFLUENCING
WITH TRAINING ALONE**

Many companies spend large sums on training and development, yet they do not prepare employees' daily work environments and management to support changes in behavior taught in the training programs.[38]

Binder

writes, "Examples include process improvement that is out of alignment with training and development, management goals and targets unsupported by compensation plans, new tools lacking explicit management expectations to use the tools."[39] Without alignment, implementation efforts can increase operational costs and fail to sustain the desired change.[40]

Mistake 3: Attempt to Influence with Only One Category

Grenny et al. surveyed several people to identify the number of influences they used to change behaviors. They write, "To our astonishment, most of the leaders had used only one or two [influence] methods. Not to our astonishment, most of their change efforts had failed."[41] Binder provides another typical example of using training as the only source of influence (Box 5.10).

Examples like this illustrate that leadership practitioners need to leverage influences from most, if not all, the categories to make sustainable changes.[42] The more categories that are leveraged in collaboration with other departments, the more likely changes can be sustained.

Mistake 4: Using Influence to Optimize a Subsystem While Compromising the Whole System

If a department excels at influencing and optimizing its subsystem, it could compromise the whole system. For example, if the sales department becomes too efficient, operations may not produce the products and services to quality standards or on time.[43] This can lead to customer complaints, substantial operational costs, customer loss, and hurt the organization's brand and reputation.

Troubleshooting with the Six Boxes® Model

When deciphering why performance is below expectations or productivity is low, the inexperienced traditional leader tends to blame employees. In doing so, they typically are incorrect (as noted in the *Identifying Trouble Spots in the Human Performance System* topic).

The Six Boxes® Model is sequenced to identify trouble spots starting with Box 1, then Box 2, followed by Box 3, and so forth. Gilbert cautions that this sequence doesn't reflect a hierarchy of importance. Gilbert writes, "Motives are surely just as important to performance as good data, for example. But the attempt to correct motive deficiencies [Box 6 in Figure 5.5] will seldom pay off as well as an attempt to correct data deficiencies [Box 1 in Figure 5.5]."[44]

Table 5.5 provides questions that you can ask to identify influences (or the lack of) for each category to find evidence of trouble spots related to problems. Use these questions followed by probing questions.

Conclusion

Leadership practitioners can use the Six Boxes® Model to add value by providing perspective, improving their team's environment, and influencing their departments. Managers and executives can use the model to identify trouble spots with horizontal and vertical work. Individual contributors also can use the model to strengthen their productivity and effectiveness.

Leading Examples

To help explain *Analyzing Like Detectives*, I provide examples at three different career levels. While I intend to keep these short, I provide a more extensive manager example to emphasize how the Six Boxes® Model can effectively improve performance.

Individual Contributor Leading Example: Investigating Inventory Losses

Matt, a trainer at a regional hardware chain, wanted to find out why cable shrinkage costs the company almost a million US dollars annually. Shrinkage is the reduction in earnings due to waste or theft.[45] On a shrinkage report, the company reported that of the 10 products with the highest shrinkage, five were cables.

Table 5.5   Example Troubleshooting Questions by Category

1. Expectations and Feedback	2. Tools and Resources	3. Consequences and Incentives
Expectations Do performance standards exist? Do performers: • Know the desired work output quality, quantity, duration, and cost? • Consider the standards to be attainable? • Know how work output contributes to business results? Can performers easily recognize the input requiring action? Can performers complete work without interference from other work? **Feedback** Who provides feedback to performers? How is feedback given? How frequent? Are there standards for providing feedback to performers?	Are resources such as tools, templates, and job aids (such as metrics, standard operating procedures, and reference materials): • Available to performers? • Accurate, current, and complete? • Useful for performers? How do you know that resources are effective for helping performers with their work? How does the work environment • Help performers accomplish work? • Prevent distractors from interfering with work? • Provide access to tools, templates, and job aids? • Remove work barriers?	**Consequences** Do consequences support desired work? Are consequences meaningful from the performers' viewpoint? Are consequences timely? **Incentives** What are the financial incentives for performers? How are financial incentives used to support performers' work? What are the non-financial incentives for performers? How are non-financial incentives used to support performers' work?

4. Skills and Knowledge	5. Selection and Assignment (Capacity)	6. Motives and Preferences (Attitude)
Do performers have the necessary skill and knowledge to perform? What training do performers receive? How is training determined for performers? How do you know that training is effective for improving skills and knowledge?	Are performers physically, mentally, and emotionally able to work? How are performers assigned work? How do you know if performers have too much or too little work? If workers lack the capability, how do you accommodate them? What is your process for selecting candidates for jobs? How do you know if candidates are capable of performing?	How do you know if performers are committed to performing work? What do you do to ensure performers are committed to performing work? What is the tenure and turnover for jobs? How do your tenure and turnover compare with industry standards? How do you identify performer preferences? How do you accommodate preferences?

Matt visited a few stores to learn more about the problem and interviewed four employees: Jeff, Stan, Karen, and Max. Matt also shadowed them while they cut cable and accepted customer returns. Matt learned more when talking about the shrinkage problem with Ed and Tammy, two store managers. Using the Six Boxes® Model, Matt categorized behavioral influences. Table 5.6 illustrates some examples of what Matt found. Table 5.7 provides some example recommendations for decreasing shrinkage.

Table 5.6   Example Findings for Cable Shrinkage

1. Expectations and Feedback	2. Tools and Resources	3. Consequences and Incentives
Cutting Cable No standards for cutting extra cable Managers either ignore or encourage cutting extra cable **Customer Cable Returns** No standards for accepting or rejecting customer cable returns No customer expectations for what can and cannot be returned Managers either ignore or encourage accepting all returns	No written policy for cutting cable or for accepting or rejecting customer returns No signage to set customer expectations for cutting cable or for acceptable returns No posted job aids for cutting cable that explains cutting policy or return policy Some suppliers provide footage count on the cable while others don't Don't have tools to assist returns (such as weighing prepackaged cable to determine if any has been removed)	No negative consequence for cutting additional cable No negative consequences for customers who return partially used cable

4. Skills and Knowledge	5. Selection and Assignment (Capacity)	6. Motives and Preferences (Attitude)
Training doesn't address allowing the cutting of extra cable Training doesn't address handling cable returns	Employees are unaware of the annual financial loss of almost a million dollars due to cutting extra cable or accepting deceitful returns Employees may not feel confident in handling customers who have deceitful cable returns	Employees often want to cut extra cable to please customers and to be friendly with customers Employees at the return desk want to avoid declining customer returns and having to explain the reason for the decline

Matt shared the results with Joel, Operations Vice President (VP), Eileen, a corporate operations director, and Allison, a supplier-relations director. Joel, Eileen, and Allison were surprised at what Matt discovered and recognized the value of the recommendations. Matt and the directors implemented most of the recommendations.

Table 5.7   Example Recommendations for Decreasing Cable Shrinkage

1. Expectations and Feedback	2. Tools and Resources	3. Consequences and Incentives
Set the standards for cutting or not cutting extra cable and for accepting or rejecting cable returns Obtain manager agreement and support and provide feedback for complying with the standards	Create written policy to address cable issue Create signage to alert customers and staff about cutting and return standards Negotiate with all suppliers to mark footage on cables to enable cutting accuracy Provide tools to help employees to determine if returns are acceptable or not	State clearly the consequences for complying or not complying with standards for cutting and returns

4. Skills and Knowledge	5. Selection and Assignment (Capacity)	6. Motives and Preferences (Attitude)
Update training to include standards Provide ample practice for discussing with customers the cutting policy and for addressing customer objections Provide ample practice for discussing why a customer's return isn't accepted without embarrassing or upsetting the customer; include practice for addressing customer objections and for defusing any escalated customer anger	Enable employees to find ways to please customers and be friendly with them while complying with cutting and return standards	Ensure that employees are aware of the annual financial cost to the company when cutting extra cable or accepting deceitful customer returns so that employees are enabled to make better choices

Manager Leading Example: Investigating Opportunities through Skip-Level Dialogues

Art Stadlin, a technology director at a mid-sized national corporation, wanted to conduct skip-level meetings with indirect reports.[46] Skip-level meetings are conversations between a director and individual contributors who report to the director's managers. While managers regularly meet with their direct reports, directors seldom have opportunities to meet with indirect reports. Using the Six Boxes® Model as a way to structure these skip-level meetings, Art set the following goals for the meeting:

1. Get to know indirect reports better.
2. Identify themes of trouble spots within the departments.
3. Take action to fulfill needs and remove barriers to minimize or remove trouble spots.

With the buy-in from his managers, Art performed the following steps:

1. Announce to the indirect reports that he will schedule a skip-level meeting with each indirect report and explain the goals.
2. Starting with the indirect reports of one manager, schedule the private skip-level meetings.
3. During the meetings, clarify confidentiality and the process for collecting themes. Have indirect reports prioritize the themes.
4. After the meetings, meet with the manager to debrief the themes he found. Then, collaborate with the manager to identify actions needed to address the themes. Ensure that the themes are specific and time-bound.
5. The manager meets with his direct reports to discuss the themes and validate the feasibility and accuracy of the action items.
6. Monitor the manager's progress with completing the action items.
7. Evaluate the process with the indirect reports. Challenge them to identify ways to improve the process and make the meetings more valuable.
8. Repeat the process with the next manager's direct reports.
9. Meet quarterly with managers to validate the process and review action items.

Table 5.8 lists the questions that Art asked indirect reports. Art asked the questions in the order of the six categories. Table 5.9 lists theme examples

Table 5.8   Skip-Level Questions by Category

1. Expectations and Feedback	2. Tools and Resources	3. Consequences and Incentives
How do you get your work assignments? How do you know what is expected of you and how you need to improve? How well does the feedback you receive from your manager meet your needs? How do you know if you are doing a good job?	What might the company do to make it easier for you to get your job done? Thinking about the last time you escalated an issue, how did that go? How available is your manager when you need to see them? How well do people in other organizations cooperate and collaborate with you?	To what extent does the company's compensation system stimulate your performance, and why? Thinking about the rewards and incentive programs we have here, which would you keep and which would you discard, and why? What ideas do you have for rewards or incentive programs that would peak your interest? How are you treated when you make a mistake?

4. Skills and Knowledge	5. Selection and Assignment (Capacity)	6. Motives and Preferences (Attitude)
What skills and knowledge gaps do you need to address to perform your job better? To what extent has the company supported your desires for job-related education and training?	Do you believe you are in the right job for you? Why do you say that? What ideas do you have for enriching your assignment? Is your manager giving you the work assignments you prefer? Why do you say that?	When you get up in the morning, what does that inner voice say to motivate you to come to work and do great things? What part does teamwork play in your motivations for work? What fears might you have that hold you back?

that Art discovered using this process. Table 5.10 lists some example action steps that include status and due-date columns.

From surveys, indirect reports responded favorably and expressed that they wanted to continue the skip-level process. While the process wasn't perfect and generated more work, Art continued refining the process and improving the experience. What helped with the success of the process was how Art engaged both managers and indirect reports for improving the work environment.

Table 5.9 Example Themes by Category

1. Expectations and Feedback	2. Tools and Resources	3. Consequences and Incentives
Software release planning: Changes in due dates are made without proper communications; causes surprises; forces people to be reactive; disrupts workflow in test; impedes test planning; causes confusion over priorities. **Assignments:** Need to clarify as it relates to contributing to test automation. Need clarity and specifics on assignments in general. **Manager relations:** Manager relates well to the team and in one-on-one meetings. Pays attention to administrative details. Manager often thanks his teammates. **Manager feedback:** Desire feedback from manager to be more specific and less general. "Telling me that I'm doing well doesn't give me anything to build on."	**Time reporting:** Need categories in PlanView that foster higher integrity in allocating hours. **Test automation tools:** Could existing computers in inventory be dedicated to automation? **Test environments:** Developers have their own hardware, but tests are virtual; need both on hardware or both virtual; inconsistency generates useless work. **Workspace:** Take out half the ceiling light bulbs to save energy and reduce screen glare; would like faster laptops. Meetings: "We have way too many project meetings, and they are getting in the way of real work."	**Rising to the top:** "My boss told me I need to 'do more.' What does that mean? I need specifics." "I feel helpless to control how my performance links to my compensation." **Recognition:** Several people expressed the need to be recognized more often for their accomplishments. "I want to feel wanted." "I want the recognition that will differentiate me from my peers." **Incentives:** Desire incentives tied to a schedule, quality, or team accomplishment. **Career path:** Basically, everyone in the group said they like doing their test assignment; they would like to better understand how to grow within the test function.

4. Skills and Knowledge	5. Selection and Assignment (Capacity)	6. Motives and Preferences (Attitude)
Application knowledge: Need to know how applications system is constructed; spend elbow-to-elbow time with architects (not easy to do). **Business knowledge:** Need to understand how the business uses the application; spend elbow-to-elbow time with end-users using the application. **Training:** Some people mentioned the need for external training and/or external certification in the testing discipline.	**Work schedule:** Often haphazard because of process issues. **Job assignment:** Everyone said they were in the best assignment for them. **Career path:** Some concerns that the company has no system to track careers. "I have no confidence that if I work to gain the skills required for a target role, that role will even exist by the time I'm ready to move."	**Quality assurance team:** Everyone mentioned that they really like their current teammates. "We have a strong team." "We have mutual respect in this team." **Beaten down:** Repeating the same mistakes (goes beyond this team). "Why aren't we learning?" **Attitude:** Disparaging remarks from leadership have degraded pride in testing work. "Why are we always trying to prove ourselves? There is no trust, no faith."

Table 5.10   Example Action Items and Follow-Up

No.	Box	Description of Action and Desired Result	Status	Target or Completion Date
1	1	Prepare better for each software release by having the test plan written, reviewed, and approved by the team before testing begins. Solicit input from the team on in-scope and out-of-scope items.	Solicited input and prepared Release 7.2 test plan before testing started. Sending out for review and approval today.	**Completed** for Release 7.2 and will continue this action item for future releases
2	2	Manager/teammate availability: All test teammates use cube whiteboards to post availability. Post when out on vacation. Post-meeting schedule and anticipated return to the desk. Manager will post an out-of-office when there is a call off sick.	All teammates have whiteboards and are using this process.	**Complete**
3	1	Provide better feedback on performance in monthly one-on-one meetings. Review the quarterly leadership talent assessments with each individual.	Gathering feedback to finalize first-quarter performance review before sharing results. Regular one-on-one meetings are already taking place.	**Target** 7/31/08
4	4	Implement a regular lunch-and-learn program to provide team training. Solicit input from teammates on training topics and presenters.	Test automation capabilities and next steps will be the first lunch-and-learn topic.	**Target** 8/30/08

Executive Leading Example: Mapping the Primary and Support Processes

After working for a few years in the retail industry, I met several executives who have shared powerful leadership stories. Clint, a relatively new senior executive, told me the following story of how his detective work uncovered a misalignment between the three performance levels.

Background

From the 1980s until the 2008 US recession, a Fortune 500 retail chain expanded rapidly by opening hundreds of stores annually. Along with rapid growth came growing pains felt at the corporate office. To support the multiple stores and the primary process, departments started addressing their own immediate problems independently rather than collaborating cross-functionally. This led to silo thinking. While addressing problems, department executives changed role expectations and hired new roles to fill process gaps. They purchased databases to manage their work, but they didn't connect to other department databases. This caused employees to enter data manually. Some departments duplicated work, causing unnecessary increases in operational costs. By the end of 2008, sales decreased due to the recession, and rising operational costs caused a substantial decrease in profits.

Clint Analyzes the Organization

Clint started looking at the AOP of his organization. He recognized that departments were unprepared for the rapid growth. Clint wasn't surprised to discover that most departments focused on resolving their own subsystem problems while ignoring how their changes affected the organization holistically. After meeting with several department heads, Clint discovered the following:

■ During the rapid growth, the goals and designs at the organization level, process level, and performer level became misaligned.
■ The high-revenue years hid the misalignment problems and enabled departments to spend more operational costs to resolve their own issues independent of other departments.
■ With the recession, the executive board became aware that they couldn't sustain annual increases in operational costs and annual decreases in revenue.

Clint persuaded Adam, the Chief Executive Officer (CEO), and the executive board to work with some external consultants to create high-level maps to explain the primary and support processes. Once completed, the consultants, department heads, and executives would examine the goal and design for the organization and process levels.

Results

After completing the mapping, Clint, the department heads, and the consultants identified a list of inefficiencies from ineffective and costly process flows, departmental structures, and technology support. With the problems listed, Adam and the executive board started to revise organizational goals and design. This led to restructuring departments, role assignments (job redesign), and costly technology changes.

While competitors solved their profit problems by closing stores and reducing their workforce, Clint's company worked with investors to allow more operational costs and time to reinvent the company. During the restructuring, investors generated fewer profits and, at times, lost patience. After about five years of restructuring with minor setbacks, the recovery and improved performance results led to a considerable investors' return on investment. After the five years, the stock value more than doubled, dividend payments increased by more than 60%, and earnings per share were higher than they had been in at least the previous ten years.

Summary: What to Do

Summary

Anyone can drive change, but extraordinary change requires leadership practices. *Analyzing Like Detectives* is the foundational practice for accomplishing change such as project innovation, team collaboration, creative product development, or even aligning cultural routines to support organizational goals. Such accomplishments become real as you leverage the other practices with *Analyzing Like Detectives.*

Analyzing Like Detectives enables you to view organizations with different lenses, from the macro-perspective (viewing the supersystem) to the micro perspective (viewing the HPS). Figure 5.6 summarizes this practice.

	Analyzing Like Detectives Practice
Characteristics	• Resist initial conclusions based solely upon the presenting problem and conclusions reached by those who don't investigate. • Examine the facts of the current-state situation while filtering out opinion. • Follow multiple leads even knowing that some leads yield no relevance. Leads help confirm what you know, eliminate possible explanations, and provide new evidence. • Search and discover evidence that may not be obvious to those involved. • Use forensic tools, examine methodically evidence for patterns that may not be apparent to the casual observer.
Principles, Guidelines, and Rules of Practice	*Related 21st Century Leadership Principles* • Put others first • Encourage Growth • Collaborate with Others *Rummler and Brache's Six Fundamental Laws of Organizational Systems* 1. Understanding Performance requires documenting the inputs, processes, outputs, and customers that constitute a business. 2. Organization systems adapt or die. 3. When one component of an organization system optimizes, the organization often suboptimizes. 4. Pulling any lever in the system will have an effect on other parts of the system. 5. An organization behaves as a system, regardless of whether it is being managed as a system. 6. If you pit a good performer against a bad system, the system will win almost every time. *Rummler and Brache's Three Levels of Performance* 1. Organization 2. Process 3. Performer *Binder's Four Common Mistakes When Designing and Managing Performance Levels* 1. Attempt to influence without focusing on the valuable accomplishments needed to support desired business results 2. Attempt to influence without collaborating with other departments 3. Attempt to influence with only one category 4. Using influence to optimize a subsystem while compromising the whole system
Models, Techniques, and Tools	*Rummler's AOP for Organizations* Use this to: • Learn about any business structure at the super-system level. • Organize how to learn about your organization's business. • Identify potential trouble areas. *Rummler's HPS and Troubleshooting the HPS* Use this to: • Help others to consider problem sources other than the performer. • Troubleshoot in the order where they most likely are sourced: (1) Output, (2) Input, (3) Consequences, (4) Feedback, and (5) Performer. *Binder's Performance Chain* Use this to explain how powerful influences can be used to obtain desired results. *The Six Boxes® Model* Use this to: • Categorize and identify current-state behavioral influences as well as their interrelationship. • Identify trouble spots of performance problems.

Figure 5.6   Practice summary: Analyzing Like Detectives.

What to Do

Table 5.11 lists recommendations for applying this practice immediately, in the short term, and in the long term.

Table 5.11   Recommended Actions for Applying Analyzing Like Detectives

Immediate
Learn about Your Business Discuss with your manager about adding business acumen as a developmental goal with the intent that you would meet informally with various career levels in different departments. Invite members of other departments to your team meetings to discuss what their departments do. Using the AOP of organizations as a guide, begin mapping your organization's macro system. Identify, for example, how your organization obtains capital. Use internal resources, the organization's annual plan, and external websites to find these details.
Short Term
Share with Others Share with others what you learned about *Analyzing Like Detectives*. Helping others understand these practices builds buy-in and helps you learn the practice. **Learn about Business** In *Serious Performance Consulting*, Rummler recommends reading *The Ten-Day MBA* by Silbiger.[a] Silbiger discusses marketing, ethics, accounting, organizational behavior, and several additional topics that can help provide additional organizational perspective when *Analyzing Like Detectives*. Part of learning about business is deliberately attending to organizational politics. To strengthen your knowledge about organizational politics, read *Survival of the Savvy*. The authors describe two political styles commonly found in any organization and how to develop a vital balance by having readers adopt their Power of Savvy political style.[b] **Study Performance Consulting** Read Rummler's books on performance consulting. In *Serious Performance Consulting*, Rummler provides a more in-depth perspective and several templates and tools. Explore the Performance Design Lab (performancedesignlab.com) website for resources. They have several free articles, presentations, and blogs available for downloading. Explore the Performance Thinking Network (sixboxes.com) website for resources. They have a resource library full of free articles, presentations, videos, and white papers.

Table 5.11 *(Continued)* **Recommended Actions for Applying Analyzing Like Detectives**

In *The Idea-Driven Organization*, read Chapter 3 entitled, "Aligning the Organization to Be Idea Driven: Strategy, Structure, and Goals." In this chapter, the authors describe vertical and horizontal alignment and misalignment and how most organizational structures can create barriers to process design.[c] ***Practice Using the Models*** Continue to use the AOP for organizations to map your organization's macro system. Practice using the HPS and Six Boxes® Model. Analyze the work you do and how your team works to find opportunities for improvement. Rather than doing this alone, collaborate with others or a team. Have peers validate what you found and allow them to add their perspectives. These are excellent tools for getting people to talk and learn from one another.
Long Term
Study Performance Consulting Read other performance consulting books, including Performance Architecture, Human Competence, Improving Performance, and Organizational Intelligence. You can find these in the Bibliography. Attend the International Society for Performance Improvement (ISPI) annual conference or chapter event. I found both valuable for support and developing systemic and think about performance-improvement techniques. Attend sessions and workshops on performance consulting. In addition to the ISPI annual conference, the Performance Design Lab (performancedesignlab.com) and the Performance Thinking Network (sixboxes.com) offer workshops and services to help you and your organization. Explore the garyadepaul.com website for more resources and links to additional resources on performance improvement.

[a] Rummler, 2007, *Serious Consulting*, 120; Silbiger, 2012, The *Ten-Day MBA*.
[b] Brandon and Seldman, 2004, *Survival of the Savvy*, 24–59.
[c] Robinson and Schroeder, 2014, *The Idea-Driven*.

Word of Caution

Before contacting organization and process owners, attend to your organization's politics. Let your manager know what you are doing and ensure that your manager and chain of command won't be threatened by meeting with their peers. At one organization where I worked, the senior VP ordered all managers and individual contributors not to talk or communicate with executives from other departments without prior approval. I hope your organization isn't that restrictive.

Because leadership is collaborative, *Analyzing Like Detectives* is collaborative as well. The intent isn't for you to analyze in isolation so that you suddenly appear to have some great insight into why things are wrong. Your objective isn't to draw attention to yourself but to engage others in the analysis practice so that the team learns the practice and discovers the findings together. This may involve sharing the three tools, explaining them, and having others collect evidence. The trick is to build the evidence collaboratively without dictating it to others. Leverage the *Communicating Like Agents* and *Directing Like Guides* practices to inspire the partnership needed to *analyze like detectives*.

Chapter 6

Practice 2: Diagnosing and Treating Like Doctors

When faced with a result that doesn't go according to plan, a series of perfectly effective short-term tactics are used until the desired outcome is achieved. But how structurally sound are those solutions?[1]

Sinek

Introduction: Importance and Benefits of Diagnosing and Treating Like Doctors

Want to help others become better decision-makers? Practicing *Diagnosing and Treating Like Doctors* and helping others learn this practice contribute toward their critical thinking and decision-making abilities. When others apply this practice, they mature their mental and moral qualities, capabilities, and behaviors.

Chapter 5 explained how *Analyzing Like Detectives* is a valuable practice for discovering new data to help decision-makers. Likewise, *Diagnosing and Treating Like Doctors* is a valuable practice for discovering root problems and creating comprehensive treatment plans to close result gaps. Diagnostics ultimately empowers decision-makers and helps them avoid reacting to symptoms and treating symptoms mistakenly instead of root problems.

DOI: 10.4324/9781003273448-8

BOX 6.1 EXAMPLES OF DECISION-MAKERS REACTING TO SYMPTOMS

1. Ted, a technology vice president (VP), learns that programmers spend 25% of their development time correcting coding mistakes and causing project delays. Ted hires a vendor to teach a software refresher course and requires all programmers to attend.
2. When safety incidents happen more than expected, Loren, a field supervisor, emails and lectures about the importance of safety. Loren believes that she has resolved the problem.
3. At a call center, several customers complain about long wait times before being able to talk to call-center agents. Mark, a call-center VP, directs managers to hire more agents.

In teams, departments, business units, and the organization level, people often react to symptoms by selecting and implementing treatments based on experience and guesswork (Box 6.1).

These examples illustrate reacting to problems and deciding on an intervention without knowing if the presenting problems are symptoms or root problems. Without investigating and using a diagnostic process, the intervention may not work. If it does, the intervention may temporarily resolve the problem but may unnecessarily increase operational costs. By applying the *Diagnosing and Treating Like Doctors* practice, you can help decision-makers.

When decision-makers react to presenting problems or symptoms, they may ask you to implement their treatment, or you may find out about the decision some other way. When this happens, you have the opportunity to help. In the programming example, you might not persuade Ted to reconsider the training for all programmers (although you could calculate the lost productivity time and show how costly the training is in terms of time). However, you might be able to persuade Ted to allow you to determine specific training topics so that training would be more useful. You might call this a training analysis. While doing so, you may identify additional ways to minimize coding mistakes. If Ted permits you to conduct the analysis, you can use Rummler's Results Improvement Process (RIP) to analyze, diagnose, and treat the root problem.

In this chapter, I discuss the characteristics of *Diagnosing and Treating Like Doctors*. I then present Rummler's RIP to analyze, diagnose, and treat performance problems and opportunities. Because many professionals attempt to resolve problems without using a systematic diagnostic approach, you can leverage RIP to help your peers, team, department, and organization look beyond symptoms and think about problems or opportunities systemically and systematically. After describing RIP, I provide leading examples and discuss how to use this practice.

Characteristics of Diagnosing and Treating Like Doctors

In their practices, doctors use diagnostics and analysis to determine treatment plans.

- Analyses involve examining components of a system or subsystem.
- Diagnostics involves synthesizing.

Doctors diagnose by comparing the patient's current state to a healthy human anatomical model. For example, doctors examine a patient's x-ray of a bone and then mentally compare the image to a healthy bone structure.[2] When examining an x-ray of LaShandra's arm, Sam concludes that his patient fractured her humerus bone. Sam recognizes the difference between a healthy humerus bone (desired state) and the one on LaShandra's x-ray (current state).

Like doctors, leadership practitioners know how a healthy business performs at the three levels (organization, process, and performer) and compare the desired state of performance with the current state by using three models: the Anatomy of Performance (AOP), the Human Performance System (HPS), and the Six Boxes® Model.[3] With AOP, for example, leadership practitioners consider seven key alignment points as depicted in Table 6.1. If an organization doesn't align with all seven points, the organization could have a critical issue. Box 6.2 summarizes the characteristics of *Diagnosing and Treating Like Doctors*.

Rummler's RIP

Introduction

In *Serious Performance Consulting*, Rummler presents RIP, a four-phase methodology for analyzing and diagnosing performance challenges,

Table 6.1   Healthy Organizations Have Seven Key AOP Alignment Points[a]

No.	AOP Component	Align(s)
1	Customer needs (consumer market)	To investor needs (capital market)
2	Organizational goals	To the reality of the supersystem
3	Primary process	To customer expectations and organizational goals
4	Support processes	To primary process
5	Functions, jobs, and roles	To perform the required tasks of the processes
6	Human Performance System components	With each other, vertically within the function and horizontally across the organization
7	Management monitors and maintains alignment	

[a] Rummler, 2007, *Serious Performance Consulting*, 33.

recommending solutions, and treating with interventions.[4] Rummler remarks that for more than 35 years, he practiced applying RIP successfully and that RIP evolved from a collaborative effort with Dale Brethower and Tom Gilbert.[5]

Leadership practitioners can scale RIP to work with any project size. The improvement can focus at the performer level, process level, or organizational level.[6]

In the description of each phase, I present how you can apply RIP formally. Depending on the scope and people involved, you can modify RIP to make it more informal and scale the phases to best suit your situation.

Phase I (Analysis and Diagnostics): Desired Results Determined and Project Defined

You have three objectives in the first phase:

1. Confirm that an issue or opportunity links to identified result gaps at the performer, process, or organization level.
2. If a link exists, create a project plan and proposal to obtain approval to continue to Phase II.
3. Create hypotheses for why result gaps exist (tested in Phase II).[7]

BOX 6.2   CHARACTERISTICS OF DIAGNOSING AND TREATING LIKE DOCTORS

■ While analysis is used to discover insights into the current state of performance, diagnostics is a type of synthesis used to compare the current state with the desired state. The comparison is then used to identify result gaps and barriers that prevent achieving the desired state.

■ Rummler's RIP is a way to analyze and diagnose at the three performance levels: Performer, process, and organization.

■ 21st Century Leadership practitioners use RIP to help others examine work incidents critically and act responsibly when addressing problems and opportunities.

■ RIP is scalable for resolving issues at each performance level, and you can apply RIP formally with written work plans, charters, and proposals for work or apply it informally.

■ Because performance is complex, prescribing only one treatment is most likely not enough to close result gaps. As Rummler states, there is no silver bullet for resolving result gaps.[8]

■ Like doctors, prescribing treatment plans isn't enough. Doctors set goals and measures to determine if treatment plans are effective. While administering treatment, doctors adjust their plans based on measurement results.

■ After completing the treatment plan, leadership practitioners need to determine how the process adds value to the organization and stakeholders.

■ Caution: The purpose of *Diagnosing and Treating Like Doctors* isn't to enable heroic behaviors. Heroics solve problems ineffectively, promote working in isolation, and harm collaborative cultures. The practice is intended to be used collaboratively with others while leveraging RIP to close result gaps.

To accomplish these objectives, you'll want to leverage the tools I described in Chapter 5. The tools enable you to analyze and diagnose enough to form hypotheses for gaps between the current and the desired states. Table 6.2 provides examples of result gaps at the three performance levels. Table 6.3 lists data-gathering techniques identified by Jonassen et al.[9]

Table 6.2 Examples of Result Gaps between the Current and Desired States

Performance Level	Example
Performer	For three quarters, a performer's sales remained the same but should have increased by 30%
	For the month, a call-center team's average handle time was 7:35 min but should have been under 3:00 min
	For the quarter, a performer's error-per-claim increased 22% but should have remained the same
	For the week, a performer produced 15% waste but should have produced only 5% waste
Process	For the previous three quarters, technology projects exceeded budget by 35% but should have been at or below budget
	For the quarter, product returns in the southeast region were at 35% but should have been at 7.5%
	During the summer, hiring costs increased 40% but should have decreased by 5%
	For the year, a manufacturing facility had 20 safety incidents but should have had none
Organization	On the annual employee opinion survey, engagement was at 20% but should have been at 60%
	For the quarter, the profit margin was at 10% but should have been at 25%
	For the past six months, frontline employee turnover was at 40% but should have been at 15%
	For year-to-date, new customers increased by 4% but should have increased by 20%

During Phases I and II, use the data-gathering techniques to complete the AOP, the HPS, and the Six Boxes® Model. In the leading example (executive level), refer to Table 6.5 for an example of a hypothesis table.

Phase II (Analysis and Diagnostics): Barriers Determined and Changes Specified

Phase II is about conducting a detailed analysis to create a more accurate diagnosis. Specifically, you look for misalignments (see Table 6.1) and determine the misalignments' impact. In Chapter 5, refer to Figure 5.2 and Table 5.3 for what good performance should look like. Figure 6.1 provides example activities that you could perform during Phase II.

Table 6.3   Data-Gathering Techniques and Function[a]

Technique	Function
Documentation analysis	Use documents for orientation and confirmation of findings. Use in conjunction with other data-gathering techniques.[b]
Observation: Unobtrusive and participative	Use observation to determine how performers accomplish tasks in the actual or simulated setting. Use unobtrusive to observe tasks without intruding. Use participative to seek cognitive clarification for why performers behave in specific ways while accomplishing tasks.[c]
Individual interviews	Use interviews to obtain the perspective and advice of exemplar performers and subject-matter experts.[d]
Survey questionnaires	Use surveys to discover attitudes and opinions about the current and the desired states, especially about identified problems and opportunities. Use in conjunction with other data-gathering techniques.[e]
Structured group interviews: Delphi Technique	Use interviews to synthesize consensus among experts or exemplar performers about the ideas, current and desired states, and future needs.[f]
Unstructured group interviews: Focus groups and brainstorming	Use interviews to generate ideas, hypotheses, and solutions to problems.[g]

[a] Jonassen et al., 1998, *Handbook of Task Analysis Procedures*, 371–401.
[b] Ibid., 375.
[c] Ibid., 378–379.
[d] Ibid., 385.
[e] Ibid., 390.
[f] Ibid., 397.
[g] Ibid., 401.

- Use AOP, Human Performance System, and Six Boxes® Model to analyze the current state at the three performance levels.
- For each performance level, analyze the current state for:
  - How management monitors and corrects problems
  - Roles and responsibilities
  - Compare the current state to the desired state.
- Determine what has the greatest performance variability (such as among managers, shifts, stores, tasks, and services).
- Identify and analyze exemplary performers.

Figure 6.1   Phase II: Example activities.

From your findings, you identify barriers that interfere with achieving the desired results and recommend a treatment plan to remove barriers to close result gaps.[10]

Phase III (Treatment): Changes Designed, Developed, and Implemented

Phase III involves defining the treatment plan and implementing the interventions intended to close performance gaps. For treatment plans, doctors know that the human body consists of multiple and interdependent systems. Because of this complexity, more than one treatment is usually necessary to resolve complex problems successfully. For example, in the medical field, a treatment plan for diabetes requires more than medication. The plan may include

- Stopping tobacco usage
- Eating specific foods
- Becoming more active
- Monitoring your blood glucose levels

Like human anatomy, the anatomy of performance involves interdependent systems, and one treatment isn't enough in most cases. Figure 6.2 lists example interventions that you could use in combination to close performance gaps. In the individual contributor leading example in Chapter 5, Table 5.7 listed examples of treatments that Matt recommends for resolving cable shrinkage.

Part of the design is identifying metrics to measure your progress in closing result gaps. Departments in organizations gather multiple metrics. The challenge that most have is identifying the needed metrics, identifying who has the data, and obtaining access to the data. To help identify metrics, refer to Table 6.4.

Over years of practice, I have found that you can obtain metrics if you ask. For some reason, people seem uncomfortable asking for data.

• Updated feedback systems (dashboards, gauges, structured feedback) • Job aids • Training • Standards	• Symbolic rewards • Technology support • Redesign physical space • Coaching • Tools and templates • Regular communications	• Real-time corrective and conformational feedback • Clarified expectations including posted metrics • Structured peer support • Redesign jobs

Figure 6.2   Example treatments.

Table 6.4 Balanced Scorecard Matrix

Category	Organization Level	Process Level	Performer Level
Financial	Profit and profit margin Earnings per share/price to earnings ratio Profitability • Return on investment (ROI) (assets/sales/equity) • Margin (operating/net/gross) Cash flow Costs • Direct/indirect • Variable/fixed Solvency • Current and debt-to-equity ratios • Asset turnover	Cost of goods sold (COGS) Salary and general administration (SG&A) Hire/replacement costs	Sales per salesperson Dollars collected/recovered
Customer	Size of market segment Share of market New customers Current customer renewal Complaints Net profit/customer	Cycle time Order fulfillment Returns Complaints	Complaints Customer approach/avoidance Customer requests for a specific performer

(Continued)

Table 6.4 *(Continued)* **Balanced Scorecard Matrix**

Category	Organization Level	Process Level	Performer Level
Product Service Image	Company image • Knowledgeable/innovative • Proactive/helpful • Speedy service Relationship between company and customer • Convenient/responsive • Guarantee/after-sale service Product/service • Novelty • Functionality • Returns	Product/service • Quality/timeliness/volume • Safety (number of accidents/ number of days without injury) • Order fulfillment (% complete/cycle time/number of defects) Image • Convenient/responsive • Knowledgeable (number of questions answered/number of inquiries handled without escalation)	Number of complaints Number of greetings or welcomes given/number of customers approached/number of thanks given Helpful (number of complaints resolved/problems resolved)
Process	COGS New products/services to market Number of process improvements (reduce COGS, cycle time, just in time)	Research and development/ production/distribution/post-sales/infrastructure • Quality • Cycle time/process time • Value-added activities • Coordination • Cost Work in process (WIP) Inventory Rework/waste	Value chain core competencies identified and tracked Productivity • Customers/accounts per employee • Items produced/resolved per hour • Rework/waste

| Internal | Salary and general administration (SG&A)
Information technology: Cost of ownership
Turnover/retention
Regulatory compliance | IT: Mean time between failures (MTBF)
Recruitment and hiring: Cycle time/costs
Human resources processes exist:
• Job design
• Career development
• Knowledge management
• Organizational learning
Performance goals exist, are communicated, and feedback mechanisms exist
An auditing process exists and is used
All major internal processes designed for effectiveness and mapped (e.g., IT, procurement, finance, and strategic planning) | Feedback is given/received regularly
Job satisfaction |

Source: Adapted from Principles & Practices of Performance Improvement Institute Participant Guide (Copyright © 2007). International Society for Performance Improvement, http://www.ispi.org/content.aspx?id=176. Used with Permission.

Phase IV (Treatment): Results Evaluated and Maintained or Improved

Phase IV involves working with management to monitor and evaluate the treatment-plan results. As with doctors, you monitor and adjust the treatment plan to ensure that the treatment resolves the problem successfully. At a predetermined point after implementation and monitoring, you evaluate the project's value for the organization, department, or team.

Conclusion

In the medical field, doctors who prescribe treatment plans without analyzing and diagnosing violate their ethical code and can be charged with malpractice. In organizations, people prescribe interventions without diagnosing them frequently. 21st Century Leadership practitioners can decrease malpractice and influence others to do so as well. The vital practice of using diagnosis can be a catalyst for how people work together, better align cultural norms with organizational goals, and promote a more enjoyable work environment.

Leading Examples

Introduction

For this practice, I provide two types of diagnostic examples. The individual contributor example illustrates how Susan handles a patient's self-diagnosis and treatment request. The manager and executive examples don't have a requested treatment but illustrate how someone can apply RIP to a problem. I intend to illustrate applying the practice and scaling RIP to address different complexity ranges.

Individual Contributor Leading Example: Diagnosing and Treating Project Management

After Susan's second month of employment, Kate, the senior VP of operations (Susan's boss's boss), asked Susan to train her direct reports on the basics of project management. Kate also wanted Susan to train all the directors and managers and several individual contributors who manage the operations business unit projects. When Susan asked why everyone needed project management training, Kate replied that no one in operations knew how to manage projects effectively or had received formal training.

About six months before Susan started working for the company, the chief operating officer (COO) hired Kate. Kate quickly discovered that most projects didn't have standard work plans, and none had charters. All of the larger projects had issues with the four things that project managers are supposed to monitor and control:

■ Quality issues
■ Unexpected delays
■ Unplanned costs
■ Unnecessary scope increases (what some call "scope creep")

While discussing Kate's concerns, Susan learned that training was nonnegotiable and must be completed by the end of the quarter. Susan agreed to design, develop, and deliver the training, and she negotiated time to conduct a training analysis. In other words, Susan negotiated time for her to diagnose.

Using the AOP and the Six Boxes® Model, Susan identified critical issues at each performance level. For example, at the process level, Susan found out that operations didn't have any project management standards, and projects sometimes disrupted continuity of service. Susan discovered that Kate was correct at the performer level: Susan couldn't find anyone with formal project management training.

While delivering the training, Susan also implemented project management standards, templates, and job aids. She provided coaching and support for operators functioning as project managers, their managers, and executives. Following the implementation, Kate's VPs hired some certified project managers, offered some advanced training, and supported the new process.

Susan learned from this experience that she sometimes has no choice but to implement a patient's treatment, especially if the patient is her boss's boss. However, she believes that there are ways to conduct analysis and diagnoses and expand and improve the treatment plan based on her findings.

Manager Leading Example: Diagnosing Ineffective Performers

Jordon's first day at the firm didn't begin as expected. The director who hired him had left the company, and Jordan now reported to Roberto, the director's VP. On the morning of his first day, Roberto informed Jordon of the reporting change and that Roberto had assigned Lisa, Greg, and Angie to report to Jordon. Roberto explained that Jordon's new reports were lazy and unmotivated. On occasion, Roberto saw the employees viewing nonwork websites, balancing their checkbooks, and bothering other employees trying to work. One of the reasons that Roberto wanted Jordon at the firm was that Jordon had experience firing employees.

Jordon decided to use the Human Performance System informally to identify any misalignments between the current and desired states. After talking with Lisa, Greg, and Angie, some of their peers, and other managers, Jordon learned the following:

■ Most of the critical work went to a few exemplar performers who had too much work already assigned to them.
■ Lisa, Greg, and Angie produced quality work but weren't trusted enough to get assigned the critical work.
■ Lisa, Greg, and Angie didn't have enough work to keep them busy.

Jordon put together a treatment plan:

1. Arrange to have some critical work moved from exemplar performers to his team. In return, Jordon will assure the other managers that his team will deliver on time and to quality.
2. Explain to his team the department's perception of them and explain that Jordon intends to change that perception with their help.
3. Offer the team a choice to continue maintaining things as they are or to take on a heavier workload as a team.
4. If they accept the heavier workload, Jordon promises to ensure that the team understands what is expected and will provide feedback and support while they accomplish the work.

Lisa, Greg, and Angie were aware of some of the perception problems. More importantly, they wanted meaningful work and to contribute more to the firm's success.

Before implementing the rest of the treatment plan, Jordon identified goals and metrics around project management and departmental perception. He shared these with his team and briefed Roberto on what he had found and how he planned to resolve the gaps.

In the following months, the team successfully completed deliverables on time and to quality. Jordon confirmed that peers, managers, and directors noticed a difference. Roberto was surprised at the results and admitted that the department's workload went to exemplar performers unfairly. After four years, Jordon was transferred to another department. Lisa had left the firm for a higher-level position, a director had promoted Greg to a manager, and Angie remained in the same role but was considered one of the exemplar performers.

Executive Leading Example: Diagnosing Fighting Fires

Brian started at his new company as the VP of client account management. His department was responsible for maintaining client relations after implementation, selling additional services to clients, and renewing client contracts. After a brief orientation, Brian spent most of his time handling escalated complaints and making decisions for client requests. Six months later, Brian began to understand why his predecessor had left the company. He felt exhausted and didn't enjoy his work. Brian knew that there had to be a better way to shift his time from reacting to problems to focusing on strategizing and leadership, but he had no idea how to change his focus.

A couple of months later, over lunch, Brian shared some of his frustrations with Fred, the COO. Fred commented that Brian understood the symptoms and some of the problems, but Fred didn't think Brian knew what excellent performance looked like. Fred suggested that he review the Baldrige National Quality Program. This foundation used performance-based criteria for judging quality in organizations.[11] Fred wasn't suggesting that Brian should use the award criteria to strive for excellence and an award. Instead, Fred intended for Brian to use the criteria to discover and prioritize the most significant gaps between his department's current performance quality and standards for performance excellence.

After reviewing the Baldrige criteria, Brian found several gaps for his department and the primary process (from implementation to support). For example, with Criterion 4.2, Knowledge Management, Information, and Information Technology, Brian realized that the organization didn't have any central databases that stored information about the company's products and services.[12] Brian created a list of hypotheses for further exploration. Table 6.5 illustrates the knowledge-management hypothesis.

For the knowledge management concern, Brian collaborated with other VPs to further define the knowledge-management gap and how the gap interfered with the company's performance. While pursuing gaps within his department, Brian obtained Fred's approval to sponsor a

Table 6.5 Knowledge-Management Hypothesis Example

Hypothesis	Explanation	Phase II Next Steps
The company doesn't have centralized databases for updated information about products and services.	Account managers rely on paper product manuals, emails, and electronic files on their hard drives to find information. About two-thirds of the client problems result from implementation specialists, account managers, or operational agents giving clients outdated or inaccurate information.	1. Confirm with the VPs of implementations and operations that the company doesn't have knowledge-management databases. 2. If so, work with the other VPs to determine how not having knowledge-management databases is a barrier to achieving company metrics.

knowledge-management solution that could potentially eliminate more than 50% of client problems and improve the client experience. The company formed a team to create a set of knowledge-management solutions and to monitor and maintain the company's knowledge.

Summary: What to Do

Summary

As I stated in Chapter 5, anyone can drive change, and extraordinary change requires leadership practices. *Diagnosing and Treating Like Doctors* is the foundational practice for identifying result gaps and barriers to achieving the desired state. The practice provides teams with a systematic way to accomplish the desired state using Rummler's RIP. By leveraging RIP, teams can improve how they critically address problems, innovate, and use creative thinking. The practice is a powerful way to mature mental and moral qualities, capabilities, and behavior. Figure 6.3 summarizes this practice.

What to Do

Table 6.6 lists recommendations for applying this practice immediately, in the short term, and in the long term.

	Diagnosing and Treating Like Doctors Practice
Characteristics	• Diagnostics is a type of syntheses that compares the current state to the desired state to identify results gaps and barriers that prevent achieving the desired state. • Rummler's Results Improvement Process (RIP) is a way to analyze and diagnose at the performance levels: Performer, Process, and Organization. • 21st Century Leadership practitioners use RIP to help others examine critically work incidents and act responsibly when addressing problems and opportunities. • RIP is scalable for resolving issues at all performance levels. You can apply RIP formally or informally. • Because performance is complex, prescribing only one treatment most likely is not be enough to close result gaps. • Like doctors, prescribing treatment plans isn't enough. While administering treatment, leadership practitioners adjust the plan as indicated by measurement results. • After completing the treatment plan, leadership practitioners need to determine how the process adds value to the organization and stakeholders. • Caution: The purpose of *Diagnosing and Treating Like Doctors* isn't to enable heroic behaviors. Heroics solve problems ineffectively, promote working in isolation, and harm collaborative cultures. The purpose is to collaborate with others while leveraging RIP to close result gaps.
Principles, Guidelines, and Rules of Practice	**Related 21st Century Leadership Principles** • Collaborate with Others • Put others first • Encourage Change **Rummler's RIP** 1. Analysis and diagnostics: Desired results determined and project defined 2. Analysis and diagnostics: Barriers determined and changes specified 3. Treatment: Changes designed, developed, and implemented 4. Treatment: Results evaluated and maintained or improved
Models, Techniques, and Tools	**Rummler's Seven Key AOP Alignment Points** Use this to compare the current state to the desired state and identify critical organization issues. **Jonassen et al's Data Gathering Techniques** Use this to collect data to determine the current state of an organization's performance levels. Techniques include: • Document analysis • Observation: unobtrusive and participative • Individual interviews • Survey questionnaires • Structured group interviews: Delphi Technique • Unstructured group interviews: focus group and brainstorming

Figure 6.3   Practice summary: Diagnosing and Treating Like Doctors.

Word of Caution

As with *Analyzing Like Detectives*, practicing *Diagnosing and Treating Like Doctors* is a group effort. The practice intent is for you and your team to work collectively to analyze, diagnose, and prescribe treatments to close result gaps while building the team's abilities to do this with or without

Table 6.6 Recommended Actions for Applying Diagnosing and Treating Like Doctors

Immediate
Learn about Your Business and Criteria for the Desired State As with Chapter 5, continue to use AOP to learn about your business. Referring to Table 6.1, consider the desired state in terms of alignment and compare it with the current state. Refer to Figure 5.2 and Table 5.3 to build your capability of identifying the desired state. Share the practice with others on your own team. Collaborate with others using the AOP, the HPS, and the Six Boxes® Model to analyze and diagnose your own team's performance. Work with them on feasible treatment plans that are feasible. Refer to the *Baldrige Performance Excellence Program* and Brown's guide for interpreting the Baldrige criteria.[a] ***Identify Performance Metrics*** Refer to Table 6.4: Balanced Scorecard Metrics menu. Using the table, start investigating who in your organization keeps this type of data. Start networking with them, and discover what they need to share data with you. ***Learn More about Data-Gathering Techniques*** Search the web to learn more about data-gathering techniques. If available, read the techniques described in the Handbook of Task Analysis Procedures.
Short Term
Share with Others Share with others what you learned about *Diagnosing and Treating Like Doctors* practice. Helping others understand these practices builds buy-in and helps you learn the practice. ***Learn More about Rummler's RIP*** In *Serious Performance Consulting*, Rummler provides a case study in Part 1 and several tools and templates in Part 2. ***Learn about Diagnosing Organizational Politics*** In *Survival of the Savvy*, the authors describe political styles, including their Power of Savvy political style. In Chapter 17, "A Leadership Wake Up Call," they have a topic entitled, "Diagnosing Your Organization's Political Health." Once you learn the preferred political style and potential organizational problem areas, you should be able to effectively diagnose your organization's political tendencies.[b]

Table 6.6 *(Continued)* **Recommended Actions for Applying Diagnosing and Treating Like Doctors**

Long Term
Study Performance Consulting Read the following books. You can find these in the Bibliography. Performance consulting books focusing on current and desired state comparisons: • *Performance Consulting* • *Strategic Business Partner* • *Handbook of Human Performance Technology* Evaluation books to help with setting and measuring goals for closing result gaps: • *Performance-Based Evaluation* Attend the International Society for Performance Improvement (ISPI) annual conference or chapter event. Both are valuable for developing my abilities to analyze and diagnose problems.

[a] NIST, n.d., Baldrige Performance Excellence Program; NIST, n.d., Baldrige Criteria for Performance Excellence; Brown, 2013, Baldrige Award Winning Quality.
[b] Brandon and Seldman, 2004, *Survival of the Savvy.*

you. The hallmark of leadership is for others to continue leading and collaborating after you have moved on.

Ultimately, leadership is about maturing others' mental and moral qualities, capabilities, and behaviors. When performed collaboratively, this practice helps others build character and produces better results than if you applied the practice alone. As John Foster states, you have a 20th Century hangover that causes you to believe that you must perform by yourself and be the hero who has all the solutions; if you don't work alone, you fail in your job.[13] If you want a healthy work environment, if you want to help others build character, and if you want better results, collaborate with this practice and encourage others to take the lead in diagnostic and treatment work.

Chapter 7

Practice 3: Finding Key Behaviors Like Social Psychologists

The goal of a leader is to give no orders…Leaders are to provide direction and intent and allow others to figure out what to do and how to get there…If people only comply, we can't expect people to take responsibility for their actions.[1]

Sinek

Find the genetic code for control and rewrite it.[2]

Marquet

Introduction: Importance and Benefits of Finding Key Behaviors Like Social Psychologists

Want to inspire creativity, innovation, and engagement? All you need to do is influence the right behaviors, and you can transform your team, department, or organization. Even individual contributors can help a controlling boss transition from acting as a traditional leader to practicing 21st Century Leadership. In Chapters 5 and 6, I discussed how to close performance and result gaps using the Anatomy of Performance (AOP), the Human Performance System (HPS), and the Six Boxes® Model.

DOI: 10.4324/9781003273448-9

- What would you use if you wanted to find key behavioral gaps?
- If AOP, HPS, and the Six Boxes® Model are effective, why would you want to focus on key behaviors?

To answer these questions, you need to think like a social psychologist.

Mistakes That Occur When Not Using This Practice

With any result gap, you might find several behaviors that need to change. Trying to change all of them isn't feasible or necessary. Focusing on the wrong ones can be disastrous. To achieve powerful and sustained results, you need to influence the key behaviors. Unfortunately, though, most change initiatives fail to influence these key behaviors. From a review of the last 30 years of change literature, Grenny et al. determined that less than one in eight change efforts achieve the desired results.[3] If you are like many, you've experienced how executives or department heads try to initiate changes, but instead, only produce items such as mugs, posters, or toys with a change initiative message given to employees. Most of these items soon end up in a landfill. Here are three reasons why change initiatives fail.

Reason 1: Difficulty Finding Key Behaviors

Many people don't have a systematic approach for finding faulty key behaviors and determining needed key behaviors to replace the current ones.

Reason 2: Promoted Due to Technical Capabilities

Organizations tend to promote people to the manager and executive levels because of their technical expertise rather than their ability to manage change. Don Kirkey, a leadership-development expert, explains that managers, especially executives, need to think critically and systemically. They need to manage behavioral changes. Unfortunately, too many managers and executives focus on technical work rather than learning about leadership and change management. When managers and executives try managing change without developing their change-management capabilities, they tend to fail or, at best, partially succeed.[4]

Reason 3: Choose Not to Develop Change Management Capabilities

Even though organizations hold management accountable for managing change, few offer change-management training. When they attend training, few programs instruct influence techniques. Grenny et al. write, "At best, we chip away at the edges of influence—maybe we attend a seminar or two—but we don't routinely study the topic, and we are not good at helping others to change."[5]

Finding Key Behaviors Like Social Psychologists helps anyone become more accomplished with change management.

This chapter discusses the characteristics of *Finding Key Behaviors Like Social Psychologists*. I explain Grenny et al.'s three keys to influence. I then describe two systematic approaches for finding current and desired key behaviors. Next, I highlight some tactics for influencing the adoption of new key behaviors. Finally, I provide leading examples and discuss using this practice.

Characteristics of Finding Key Behaviors Like Social Psychologists

Think Like Social Psychologists

Consider these accomplishments:

- A year after Paul O'Neill became Chief Executive Officer (CEO) of Alcoa, the company's profits achieved a record high.[6]
- For more than 30 years, Mimi Silbert and Delancey Street have transformed more than 16,000 felons and addicts into law-abiding citizens.[7]
- At one time, Rhode Island Hospital had a reputation for causing unnecessary and harmful medical mistakes resulting in patient deaths and permanent bodily harm; after 2009, the hospital eliminated these types of errors.[8]

In each example, people influenced their organizations to eliminate one or two key behaviors and replace them with key behaviors that are more functional. These new behaviors caused a cascading effect that influenced people to change several additional behaviors that improved results and promoted safer work environments.

Professionals in applied social psychology are effective at finding key behaviors. With their combined expertise in human behavior and research methodologies, they can solve small-group and real-world organizational problems.[9] Their knowledge of how people interact in social environments such as an office or a factory floor makes social psychologists ideal for finding key behaviors that can generate the results described in the previous examples. With the help of Duhigg and Grenny et al., we can learn how to apply the *Finding Key Behaviors Like Social Psychologists* practice. This will help us identify the right behaviors to change using multiple sources of influence.

You can practice the *Finding Key Behaviors Like Social Psychologists* while leveraging some of the guidelines for *Analyzing Like Detectives*, depicted in Table 5.11. I summarize the characteristics of *Finding Key Behaviors Like Social Psychologists* (Box 7.1).

Setting Goals and Measures

In *Influencer*, the first of Grenny et al.'s three keys for influencing behavioral change is to clarify the results you want to achieve. This includes plans for vigorously measuring your progress.[10] As I discussed in Chapter 6, part of Rummler's Results Improvement Process (RIP) is to define goals and set metrics. If you're serious about managing change, your goals need to be specific and measurable for two reasons: You need to clearly articulate to others what to expect after they accomplish the change. You need measures to know how well you are accomplishing the change. Table 7.1 illustrates examples of vague and clear goal statements. With vague statements, the goals seem more aspirational and challenging to implement. Clear goal statements don't give details on how you would achieve results, but the statements provide compelling and value-driven descriptions.[11]

Grenny et al. caution us that measures can be complex, and measurement itself can influence behavior negatively.[12] This can happen when you measure the results without measuring the teams using the new behaviors to obtain the results. For example, Rick, a manager, implemented a project management tracking database. He measured how often teams accessed the database and reported the results to his peers. Over time, team database usage increased significantly. Unfortunately, Rick later found out that

BOX 7.1 CHARACTERISTICS OF FINDING KEY BEHAVIORS LIKE SOCIAL PSYCHOLOGISTS

■ Grenny et al. use three phases for influencing key behaviors:
1. Set goals and measures.
2. Find needed key behaviors (and any that people currently use but produce negative results).
3. Leverage multiple techniques to influence new key behaviors.[13]

■ Rather than using one or two preferred techniques to influence many behaviors, use several techniques to influence the one or two key behaviors.

  ■ Pareto principle: 80% of your results come from 20% of your effort. If there are 10 behaviors that you want to change, you only need to change the two most important behaviors to obtain the change.[14] Duhigg calls these *keystone habits*, and Grenny et al. call high-priority behaviors *vital behaviors*.[15] For the purposes of this book, I label these as *key behaviors*.

  ■ Most people attempt to influence behavior using one preferred technique. Grenny et al. states that this is like "hiking the Himalayas with only a bag lunch...Bringing a simple solution to a complex behavioral challenge almost never works.[16] Frequently, they rely on one ineffective technique such as verbal persuasion (that is, using implied or explicit threats from an authoritative role, begging, or nagging) or training.[17] Grenny et al. conclude that to change complex key behaviors that are rooted deeply in a culture, you need to overdetermine success. You do this by using a combination of influence techniques and leveraging techniques from all Six Sources of Influence™, which is 10 times more successful at sustaining substantial change.[18]

■ Finding key behaviors consists of two phases:
  ■ Phase 1: Find current key behaviors that produce undesired results, or determine that there are no negative key behaviors that need replacing.
  ■ Phase 2: Determine desired key behaviors that can achieve goals.

■ After influencing new key behaviors, people tend to change other behaviors as well. Duhigg calls this *chain reaction*.[19]

■ Key behaviors are types of habits. This is critical for understanding why people continue to apply these key behaviors: They are habit-forming. When these types of habits exist in a culture, people don't think about performing the behavior consciously. Duhigg writes, "When a habit emerges, the brain stops fully participating in decision making. It stops working so hard, or diverts focus to other tasks. So unless you deliberately fight a habit...the pattern will unfold automatically."[20]

■ The system of habits is called the habit loop, which consists of cues, habits, rewards, and cravings that drive the habit loop.[21]

■ Habits are powerful in that they form and occur without our permission, but when we discover their existence, we can reshape them by "fiddling with the parts."[22]

■ The golden rule for changing a habit loop: Keep the same cues and rewards, but change the habit or routine.[23]

employees accessed the database and navigated randomly to different pages without entering real project data. While increasing the perception that they used the database, they continued managing projects as they did before Rick implemented the new database. Rick learned the hard way that he needed to measure time using the database and the teams' behaviors for managing projects. Thus, Grenny et al. explain that measuring vital behaviors are as important as measuring results.[24]

Table 7.1 Goal Statement Comparison

Vague Goal Statements	Clear Goal Statements
We will improve the team's interactions. We will improve employee morale. We will empower our employees.	By the end of the next quarter, team members will work with at least one other team member to complete project tasks. Compared with last year's employee engagement score of 32%, we will increase this year's employee engagement score to 50%. In six months, hiring managers will only need the approval to hire candidates from the human resource business partner and will no longer require three levels of additional approval within the chain of command.

This also applies to rewards. Recognizing people and teams for using new routines is more important than recognizing them for results; the former reinforces the right behaviors but focusing on results alone may encourage people to take costly shortcuts just to achieve the results.

Thus, you should recognize people who use the new routine rather than emphasizing results recognition.[25] If the new routines are the right ones, results will improve.

Systematic Approach for Finding Key Behaviors

Finding key behaviors can be challenging, but Grenney et al. and Duhigg provide some insight into this. Both have techniques for identifying the key to changing how a team, department, or organization operates.

Grenny et al. on Finding Key Behaviors

In *Influencer*, Grenny et al. provide four tactics for finding key behaviors. Table 7.2 summarizes these tactics. When searching for desired key behaviors, in some instances, you simply need to add new key behaviors.

Table 7.2   Tactics for Finding Key Behaviors

Tactic	Explanation
Find the obvious	Determine the obvious behaviors that people should be doing but seldom do (common sense that commonly isn't practiced). Research what experts believe behaviors should be.
Find crucial moments	Find failure modes. Expose triggers.
Learn from exemplar performers	Find those who succeed when others don't. Have standard performers observe exemplar performers. Have exemplar performers observe standard performers. Diagnose the current and desired key behaviors.
Find behaviors that enforce the code of silence	Find behaviors in which those in charge punish people who discuss the behaviors openly. "Unhealthy behaviors continue for years within organizations because confronting them openly just isn't done."[a] Collect stories that reveal cultural norms.

[a] Grenny et al., 2013, *Influencer*, 57.

BOX 7.2   HABITS THAT CAN RESHAPE BUSINESSES

Some habits have the power to start a chain reaction, changing other habits as they move through an organization. Some habits, in other words, matter more than others in remaking businesses and lives. These are keystone habits.[26]

Duhigg

In other instances, you may need to replace existing key behaviors that cause poor performance.

Duhigg on Finding Key Behaviors

Duhigg uses the term *keystone habits* instead of key behaviors. He describes how this type of habit can reshape businesses (Box 7.2).

For Duhigg, finding key behaviors involves finding moments that matter or inflection points, which are similar to crucial moments. These could be when a customer becomes overwhelmed, or a peer becomes frustrated.[27]

For habits in general, the difficult part is identifying all the parts of the habit loop. As depicted in Table 7.3, the habit loop consists of cues, the routine, rewards, and cravings.

Cues are the triggers for initiating the routine. The routine is the pattern of behaviors that you perform, and the *rewards* are what you gain at the end of the routine. *Craving* is an association between cues and rewards; this drives the habit loop.[28]

Table 7.3   Habit Loop Components

Component	Example
Cue	Smartphone beeps with a text message
Routine	Read the message and sometimes respond
Reward	Information and interacting with family, friends, colleagues, and peers
Craving	Wanting a distraction and feeling connected

Influencing and Adopting New Key Behaviors

Grenny et al. and Duhigg offer solutions for influencing key behaviors. Both offer well-documented research to support their approaches.

Grenny et al.'s Six Sources of Influence for Influencing Key Behaviors

Grenny et al. categorize influence types as personal, social, and structural, which are developed from psychology, sociology, and organizational theory.[29] Each type has two classifications: Motivation and ability. Table 7.4 lists Grenny et al.'s influences from their Six Sources of Influence in the first column and my interpretation for how each source aligns to Binder's Six Boxes® Model. Table 7.5 briefly describes nine influence tactics of the 26 that I identify from the *Influencer* book. In Part 2 of *Influencer*, Grenny et al. describe each source, explain the related tactics, and provide detailed examples.

Duhigg and Influencing Key Behaviors

To change a habit, Duhigg discusses the golden rule of habit change: Keep the same cues, deliver the same rewards, but change the routine.[30] For

Table 7.4 Alignment between the Influence Sources and Six Boxes® Model

Influence Sources	Six Boxes® Model
Personal motivation: Help them love what they hate	**Box 6**: Motives and preferences (attitude)
Personal ability: Help them do what they can't	**Box 4**: Skills and knowledge
Social motivation: Provide encouragement	**Box 6**: Motives and preferences (attitude)
Social ability: Provide assistance	**Box 2**: Tools and resources
Structural motivation: Change the economy	**Box 3**: Consequences and incentives
Structural ability: Change the space	**Box 2**: Tools and resources

**Table 7.5   Nine Examples of the 26 Influence Tactics That Align to the Six Boxes®
Model**

Box 2. Tools and Resources
Maximize peer support: Assign peers to help each other with task support, feedback, coaching, and modeling behaviors. Follow up with peers on how well they are supporting others.[a] *Change the space to make the right decisions more accessible and the wrong decisions harder*: For example, to encourage teams to interact and collaborate, move their workspaces closer together.[b] *Make it a game*: Make unpleasant, repetitive, but necessary tasks rewarding by enabling people to keep score or earn badges for achieving new performance levels.[c]
Box 3. Consequences and Incentives
Use small incentives (less is more): The symbolic significance of the incentive is more important than the monetary value.[d] *Reward for using process versus results*: Rewarding results might encourage people to use the wrong behavior to achieve the desired results but cause more harm.[e]
Box 4. Skills and Knowledge
Provide immediate feedback against a clear standard: When training others on confronting an inappropriate behavior, for example, have them practice while providing immediate feedback based on an explicit standard.[f] *To achieve mastery, set smaller process goals and provide positive feedback*: Top performers set goals to improve specific behaviors rather than focus on specific achievements.[g]
Box 6. Motives and Preferences (Attitude)
Allow authentic choice: For those in authority positions, giving others a real choice can radically improve results.[h] As Duhigg writes, "…simply giving employees a sense of agency…can radically increase how much energy and focus they bring to their jobs."[i] *Make the undiscussable, discussable*: A culture of silence sustains unhealthy norms and the status quo. At one organization, an executive encourages employees to speak their minds at all-hands meetings. No one does. At previous all-hands meetings, when Ed asked questions about the department's direction or managerial practices, Ed's manager disciplined him.[j]

[a] Grenny et al., 2013, *Influencer*, 205–206.
[b] Ibid., 275–284.
[c] Ibid., 108–110.
[d] Ibid., 225–230.
[e] Ibid., 231–235.
[f] Ibid., 128–130.
[g] Ibid., 130–133.
[h] Ibid., 84–90.
[i] Duhigg, 2014, *The Power of Habit*, 151.
[j] Ibid., 173–178.

example, instead of breaking to eat a snack, take a short walk with some peers. As long as the new routine satisfies the underlying reward and can be triggered by the old cues, the new routine can overtake the old routine.

Duhigg also offers three additional comments about changing key behaviors and habits in general:

1. To change a routine, having a sense of autonomy to make the change can help substantially.[31]
2. With some habits, you need the belief that you can change the routine.[32]
3. Having a moment of crisis or perceiving a crisis within a team or organization may cultivate the readiness to make a change. As Duhigg writes, "You never want a serious crisis to go to waste. This crisis provides the opportunity for us to do things that you could not do before."[33]

Leading Examples

Individual Contributor Leading Example: Inspiring Multidirectional Collaboration

Cara worked at a global firm for about a year in the technology business unit. Her team supported a network of about 25 desktop support technologists located in regional and local offices. The trainers were located primarily in the United States but with a few in Canada and Europe. Bob, one of the senior technologists on Cara's team, facilitated a bi-monthly conference call with technologists responsible for software training. Cara listened to these calls and occasionally facilitated when Bob wasn't available. One thing that bothered Cara was that the calls were one-directional. Bob, or whoever ran the call from Cara's team, would summarize the status of corporate projects and activities, but no one from the regional and local offices shared information. After reflecting on this for a couple of months, Cara concluded that the corporate office could leverage the trainers' expertise by getting them to share any innovations or problems that they encountered. The trainers occasionally offered feedback about training materials and job aids produced by the corporate office. Still, Cara had a feeling that the trainers created their own training solutions for their own office that better met the needs of employees.

Bob left the firm about a year later to pursue another role, and Dean, Cara's manager, assigned Cara to facilitate the trainer network calls. Cara was determined to increase the trainers' interaction on the calls. She set a goal to have at least one trainer share one innovative idea that could benefit others for each call.

During the following call, Cara asked the trainers if they would help her change the call's format. She recognized that the corporate office didn't always meet their needs and that the trainers may have created training solutions to meet employee needs. Cara asked if they could share their ideas so that other offices or even the enterprise could benefit. She also wanted to avoid each office duplicating efforts for the same type of problem, as the network would be more productive if they shared in the work. After some hesitation, some of the trainers talked openly about their concern that the corporate office wouldn't approve of what they did, and they didn't want to get into trouble for acting on their own. After others expressed this, Cara recognized that the trainers were breaking their code of silence; Bob and other call facilitators from the corporate offices had criticized them when they did try to talk about their local office solutions. Cara encouraged the trainers to express their ideas openly and explained that she would prefer to partner with them. Cara shared her goal for collaboration and asked if they could start the next call by sharing ideas.

During the next few calls, one trainer shared a job aid to help the accountants navigate a database. Another talked about a one-hour introductory course that she had created for their enterprise resource planning (ERP) system. As the trainers began to share what they had done, others wanted copies of the training files. Some asked if anyone had solutions for handling a specific problem, and others volunteered to help or had already created solutions. After about four calls, the trainers spoke about 85% of the time, and Cara spoke about 15%.

After about six months, the trainers contributed training materials to a shared server, and Cara coordinated development efforts that benefited the network. For one large global implementation, Cara received Dean's approval to invite about seven trainers to the corporate office to develop software training for a new proprietary system. Without the trainers sharing information, the corporate office wouldn't have considered leveraging the network for training development.

In this example, Cara leveraged the following influence types to help agents change.

1. *Personal motivation:* Cara gave the agents an authentic choice and a compelling reason for sharing their work.

2. *Social motivation*: Cara made the undiscussable, discussable. The trainers broke their code of silence and took a risk to share their work.
3. *Social ability*: By having the trainers share their expertise, Cara found a way to improve peer support and create a network of expertise beyond the conference calls. Trainers worked with each other between calls to create and share deliverables.
4. *Structural ability*: Cara used a shared server to host training deliverables created by the trainers so that anyone could access the resources.

Manager Leading Example: Changing the Selling Process

Changing routines can be accomplished quickly with a generous return on investment, especially when you have a crisis. At Beth's company, Yolanda, the vice president (VP) of sales, expressed her concern about the sales force. To achieve the company's strategy, the sales force needed to sell more of the new flagship product and less of the traditional products that would become obsolete and unprofitable for the company to maintain. The salesforce continued with their old behaviors of pushing the traditional products, and sales of the new product had been around 20%–25% of their quarterly sales goal. Interestingly, the company paid the same commission for the traditional products as with the new one, but the new one required a more complex setup and more of the sales representative's time. Given that these two factors wouldn't change, Yolanda asked Beth to train the field representatives in two states to sell the new product. In the two states, the competition had outperformed with their version of the new product and had taken the market share from Beth's company.

Instead of using the tools I shared in Chapters 5 and 6, Beth chose a different approach. She found out that Chris was the only sales representative who sold the new product successfully and accounted for most of the sales for the company's new product. Beth contacted Chris and learned how he used an innovative sales approach that others could leverage for their sales. Chris agreed to describe his approach during a conference call with the other sales representatives from the two states. Beth briefed Yolanda that Beth's team would conduct a training webinar to help the sales force in the two states.

Beth's team designed, developed, and moderated the meeting. During the training, Yolanda emphasized that selling the new device was vital for company survival. If the sales force was up for the challenge, they could radically change the company's direction. Chris then explained how he benefited from using his sales approach and discussed how the new product met customer needs better. Chris described his process, answered some questions, and provided a few tips that reduced installation issues. In one hour, Beth's team used three of the six influences: Personal motivation, personal ability, and social motivation. After the meeting, Yolanda wanted to repeat the training for the rest of the sales representatives, and Beth's team completed three sessions within two weeks.

Although some were skeptical that the training would make a difference, the following quarter saw more than a 75% increase in sales compared with the average of the three quarters before the training. In the next quarter, sales improved by more than 80%.

Executive Leading Example: Eliminating Tribal Knowledge

Recently, Samantha accepted a position as the VP of Call Center Services. The call center had three locations and received calls from clients, the organizations that subscribe to services that benefit employees, and customers who are the clients' employees. As part of her orientation, Samantha spent most of her first three weeks sitting with agents listening to calls. In each session, Samantha would wear headphones to hear the customer and agent talking while watching how the agent used the computer systems, paper manuals, and reference materials to answer questions.

From her observations, Samantha found three themes. The agents

1. Relied on their own memory to resolve problems frequently.
2. Referred to outdated manuals.
3. Interrupted more experienced agents with questions.

Samantha also discovered that most of the time, the experienced agents accurately answered questions but occasionally gave misleading or wrong responses. Samantha became concerned that when an agent shared bad information, the agents who heard it would share that with other agents. As a result, agents didn't provide quality information consistently. Samantha defined *quality information* to mean data that is accurate, current, and complete. The agents and management knew that they had a consistency issue with data and joked that if customers asked ten agents the same question, they would receive ten different solutions. Some of the managers knew about agents providing bad information. Managers labeled the sharing of information that was accurate, partially accurate, or wrong as *tribal knowledge.* Managers were frustrated because they couldn't figure out how to stop agents from relying on tribal knowledge.

In addition to quality concerns, Samantha thought that the average handle time or call duration was too long. Agents either wasted time waiting to talk to another agent or supervisor for help, or they spent too much time searching for answers. Some agents tried to shorten this time by creating job aids, and Samantha found some to be good but others to have inaccuracies.

Based on her experience running other call centers, Samantha knew she needed to stop agents from asking experienced agents for help, causing their handle time to increase. She needed to enable agents to find quality information quickly.

Samantha estimated that 80% of the calls received represented about 20% of the possible problem types. Samantha reasoned that if she had her newest agents resolve the 80% of the common problems and escalate the remaining 20% to her most experienced agents (to be known as the escalation team), she could improve the quality and average handle time. Table 7.6 illustrates Samantha's two-goal statements with the metrics needed to indicate achieving her goals. Table 7.6 also lists some of Samantha's objectives to achieving the goal statements.

Table 7.6 Samantha's Goals and Metric Examples

Goal Statements with Measures	Objectives
1. Within 12 months, frontline agents provide customers and clients with quality information for 80% of the problems (excluding calls transferred to the escalation agents) 2. Within 12 months, frontline agents reduce their average handle time by 25%	1. Within two months, identify and document standard resolutions for problems representing 80% of the calls that frontline agents can resolve. 2. Within four months, build and maintain a knowledge management database to store standard resolutions; a team will update the standard resolutions to be 100% accurate, current, and complete. 3. After training existing agents to use the knowledge management database, remove all paper manuals and documents from agents' cubicles. 4. After training, agents no longer interrupt other agents with questions and access the standard resolutions in the knowledge management database.

Within six months, Samantha had a team that identified standard resolutions and entered them into a searchable knowledge management database. At the beginning of training, Samantha explained the importance of this change and how using the database would provide a better customer experience and improve the agents' work experience. She explained that the change would be difficult, but she promised to give them enough time to practice using the database before taking calls. She asked them to commit to trying the new way of working. The training team then demonstrated using the database and provided several practice sessions. They used gamification to score how well they did against themselves and made the training more of an enjoyable game than typical training.

At the appointed time and with agreement from most agents, supervisors removed the paper manuals and documents. For the first two weeks, trainers and supervisors walked the floor as coaches. When an agent needed help, a coach would guide the agent to navigate the answer rather than saying the answer. Samantha also asked agents who were asked for help to provide navigational help rather than give the answer. Although this would take more time, Samantha explained that the interruptions should decrease substantially, and she was right.

Before 12 months, agents had successfully adapted to using the electronic database. The quality assurance team reported that quality responses had exceeded 80%, and the average call handle time had decreased by 40%. In addition, agent turnover had decreased, and the average agent tenure (months as an agent) had increased substantially. Although the agents met the goals, the database wasn't perfect. They experienced some growing pains, but regardless, the agents and customers' experience improved substantially.

Samantha leveraged the following types of influences to help agents make the change.

1. *Personal motivation*: Samantha asked agents if they would take on the challenge. She explained how doing so would help the company and give customers and agents a much better experience.
2. *Personal ability*: The training team provided practice sessions for using the database and used gamification to make the learning more rewarding.
3. *Social ability*: Instead of providing the answer, agents would help other agents navigate the appropriate standard resolution.

4. *Structural motivation*: By improving how they resolved problems accurately and in less time, customers appreciated the agents more than in the past. Supervisors would thank agents for their success, and agents would be rewarded when they found answers faster and challenged themselves successfully by decreasing their average handle time.

5. *Structural ability*: Samantha changed how agents accessed information. Supervisors removed paper manuals and documents.

Summary: What to Do

Summary

To analyze and diagnose effectively, you need to identify the current-state key behaviors and the desired state key behaviors. *Finding Key Behaviors Like Social Psychologists* helps you and your team accomplish this. Duhigg and Grenny et al. provide practical tactics and insights into how key behaviors work. Both note that you cannot change all behaviors but need to focus on the few key behaviors that will result in 80% of your effort (Pareto principle). Whether calling them vital behaviors or keystone habits, key behaviors influence people to change other behaviors as well. Key behaviors can shape cultures radically, help people become more productive, be intrinsically rewarding, and be enjoyable. Figure 7.1 summarizes this practice.

What to Do

Table 7.7 lists recommendations for applying this practice immediately, in the short term, and in the long term.

Word of Caution

As with the first two practices, *Finding Key Behaviors Like Social Psychologists* is meant to be practiced in collaboration with others. Helping those you work with learn this practice results in better and more accurate solutions and helps them develop their own mental and moral qualities, capabilities, and behaviors.

This chapter introduced the concept of managing key behaviors through goal setting, measurement, finding needed key behaviors, and influencing key behaviors. I underscored the complexity of Grenny et al.'s vital behavior concept and Duhigg's keystone habits. As with the other nine practices, I recommend reading more on the subject by providing resources in the *What to Do* topic. However, I strongly recommend closely examining the works of these two authors and exploring their websites for more information.

	Finding Key Behaviors Like Social Psychologists Practice

Characteristics	• Grenny et al use three phases for influencing key behaviors: (1) set goals and measures; (2) find needed key behaviors (and any that are used currently but produce negative results); (3) leverage multiple techniques to influence new key behaviors.[a]
	
	• Rather than using one or two preferred techniques to influence many behaviors, use several techniques to influence the one or two key behaviors.
	
	  • Poreto Principle: 80% of your results come from 20% of your effort. If there are ten behaviors that you want to change, you only need to change the two most important behaviors to obtain the change.[b] Duhigg calls these *keystone habits*, and Grenny et al call high-priority behaviors *vital behaviors*.[c] For purposes of this book, I call these key behaviors.
	
	  • Most people attempt to influence behavior using one preferred technique, Grenny et al states that this is like "hiking the Himalayas with only a bag lunch…Bringing a simple solution to a complex behavioral challenge almost never works.[d] Frequently, they rely on one ineffective technique such as verbal persuasion (that is, using implied or explicit threats from an authoritative role, begging, or nagging or training.[e] Grenny et al conclude that to change complex key behaviors rooted deeply in a culture; you need to over-determine success by using a combination of influence techniques and leverage techniques from all Six Sources of Influence™ are ten times more successful at sustaining substantial change.[f]
	
	• Finding key behaviors consist of two phases:
	
	  • Phase One: Find current key behaviors that produce undesired results, or determine that there are no key behaviors that need replacing.
	
	  • Phase Two: Determine desired key behaviors that can achieve goals.
	
	• After influencing others to the new key behaviors, people tend to change other behaviors as well. Duhigg calls this *chain reaction*.[g]
	
	• Key behaviors are types of habits. This fact is a critical insight into the sustained and repeated usage, especially harmful key behaviors. When these types of habits exist in a culture, people don't think about performing the behavior consciously. Duhigg writes, "When a habit emerges, the brain stops fully participating in decision making. It stops working so hard, or diverts focus to other tasks. So unless you deliberately fight a habit…the pattern will unfold automatically."[h]
	
	• The system of habits is called the *habit loop*, which consists of cues, habits, rewards, and cravings that drive the habit loop.[i]
	
	• Habits are powerful in that they form and occur without our permission, but when we discover their existence, we can reshape them by "fiddling with the parts."[j]
	
	• The golden rule for changing a habit loop: Keep the same cues and rewards, but change the habit or routine.[k]

Figure 7.1 Practice summary: Finding Key Behaviors Like Social Psychologists. (*Continued*)

Principles, Guidelines, and Rules of Practice	*Related 21st Century Leadership Principles* • Believe in Others • Put Others First • Give Up Control • Encourage Change • Collaborate with Others • Develop Leadership Practices Continuously *Duhigg: Golden Rule of Habit Change* Keep the same cues and deliver the old reward but change the habit or routine. *Grenny et al's three keys to influence change* 1. Set goals and measures for what you want to change. 2. Find the one to three key behaviors (current and desired states). 3. Use multiple sources of influences to help others change.
Models, Techniques, and Tools	*Grenny et al and Six Sources of Influence*™ 1. Personal Motivation 2. Personal Ability 3. Social Motivation 4. Social Ability 5. Structural Motivation 6. Structural Ability

[a] Grenny et al., 2013, *Influencer*, 13-14.
[b] Ibid., 44.
[c] Ibid., 6; Duhigg, 2014, *The Power of Habit*, 100.
[d] Grenny et al., 2013, *Influencer*, 67-68.
[e] Ibid., 67-68.
[f] Ibid., 28, 14; Grenny et al., 2008, *How to 10x Your Influence*, 2.
[g] Duhigg, 2014, *The Power of Habit*, 109.
[h] Ibid., 20.
[i] Ibid., 47-50.
[j] Ibid, 25-27.
[k] Ibid, 62.

Figure 7.1 (*Continued*) **Practice summary: Finding Key Behaviors Like Social Psychologists.**

Table 7.7 Recommended Actions for Applying Finding Key Behaviors Like Social Psychologists

Immediate
Find Key Behaviors Start using the tactics in this chapter to work with others to set goals and measures, identify current and desired state key behaviors, and determine how to influence key behavior changes. ***Learn More about Habits, Routines, and Behaviors*** On the Crucial Learning YouTube channel, watch some of the videos (https://www.youtube.com/cruciallearning). To learn more about the influences sources, watch the *All Washed Up!* video.[a] For more about habits, watch Fitzpatrick's *Change Habits* video.[b] For more on the motivational influences, watch Wallace's *Behaviour Change* video.[c]

Table 7.7 (*Continued*) **Recommended Actions for Applying Finding Key Behaviors Like Social Psychologists**

Build Your Expert Network   One strategy for finding key behaviors is to find out what experts say. Start by building your expert network. You can find experts at professional associations, universities, and services organizations. Below are a few services I've used. Your organization may already have subscriptions to similar services.   • Aberdeen Group   • APQC   • Josh Bersin Academy   • Corporate Executive Board   • Human Capital Institute   • Human Capital Media   • Process Excellence Network   • Skillsoft Books   • Strategy + Business
Short Term
Share with Others   Share with others what you learn about *Finding Key Behaviors Like Social Psychologists*. Helping others understand these practices builds buy-in and helps you learn the practice.   **Learn More about Habits, Routines, and Behaviors**   Read *The Power of Habit* and *Influencer*. I cannot capture the depth and power of these books in this chapter. You can find these in the Bibliography.   Read *Survival of the Savvy*. In Chapter 7, the authors have a topic entitled "Read the System and Unwritten Rules" that can help expose key behaviors. Throughout the book, the authors provide tactics that can help you identify types of solutions for influencing desired key behaviors.[d]
Long Term
Learn More about Habits, Routines, and Behaviors   Finding safe ways to break the code of silence can radically improve any team, department, or organization. To learn more, read *Crucial Conversations* and *Crucial Accountability*. You can find these in the Bibliography.

[a] Crucial Learning, 2009, *All Washed Up!*
[b] Fitzpatrick, 2013, *Change Habits.*
[c] THINK BIG, 2014, *BDI Behaviour Change Behavioural Dynamics Institute.*
[d] Brandon & Seldman, 2004, *Survival of the Savvy.*

SUPPORTING CHANGE

It's hard to initiate behavioral change, even harder to stay the course, hardest of all to make the change stick. I'd go so far as to say that adult behavioral change is the most difficult thing for sentient human beings to accomplish.[1]

Structure is how we overcome depletion. In an almost magical way, structure slows down how fast our discipline and self-control disappear...If we provide ourselves with enough structure, we don't need discipline. The structure provides it for us.[2]

Goldsmith

Change is difficult, but you can influence people to change.

I began Chapter 4 by explaining that people have difficulty changing because of the environment and how our brain works. Adapting to guiding principles can help strengthen our discipline and self-control, but people need more. You can provide more by leveraging the following three practices:

- *Communicating Like Agents* (Chapter 8) enables you to help others want to act in positive ways.[3]
- *Developing Like Guides* (Chapter 9) involves building competence and abilities in others, making keeping commitments easier.[4]
- *Nurturing Like Gardeners* (Chapter 10) is also about making commitments easier by changing the environment, removing barriers, and providing resources such as tools, templates, and job aids. Our environments tend to hinder more than help. Removing some of the hindrances makes it easier for people to behave in desirable ways.

DOI: 10.4324/9781003273448-10

In these chapters, you'll learn structures to give people structure. Structures strengthen two things:

1. Discipline: The ability to achieve desirable behaviors that enable us to complete our goals.
2. Self-control: The ability to avoid undesirable behaviors that keep us from completing our goals.[5]

With the challenges of our environments and how our brains work, everyone needs help developing discipline and self-control.

Chapter 8

Practice 4: Communicating Like Agents

I love what C. Northcotte Parkinson said about communication: "The void created by the failure to communicate is soon filled with poison, drivel, and misrepresentation."[1]

Blanchard and Ridge

With unclear expectations, you don't have the right to hold others accountable to violations they may not even be aware of.[2]

Patterson et al.

Introduction: Importance and Benefits of Communicating Like Agents

Do you enjoy working with highly motivated people but actually work with unmotivated people? Do you have trouble influencing others to want to act? If so, then *Communicating Like Agents* can help. Seriously considering how you communicate and represent others can profoundly change how you practice your role and interact with others. *Communicating Like Agents* contributes to building a safe environment for individuals, teams, departments, and organizations to openly communicate, and it contributes to creativity, innovation, and engagement.

DOI: 10.4324/9781003273448-11

From a leadership perspective, many people don't know what or how to communicate and haven't thought much about using communication techniques. They develop their thoughts and feelings based on trial-and-error practice or by watching others. When they communicate, they tend to use ineffective techniques such as verbal persuasion—telling people what to do and using threats, complaints, or begging to motivate. Doing so risks demotivating others and decreasing the likelihood of creativity, innovation, and engagement. In contrast, practicing *Communicating Like Agents* as part of your formal role helps you convey ideas and feelings purposely and effectively that, in turn, influence how others behave. When you influence without coercing and ensuring that those you influence have the autonomy to act or not act, you show direction and do so without harming the relationship. Coercive techniques such as threats, complaining, and begging can potentially harm relationships and deter their full engagement. Practicing *Communicating Like Agents* influences others to want to act effectively and morally.

In this chapter, I discuss the characteristics of *Communicating Like Agents*. I then discuss the tactics for influencing others to take action; I present them from two formal role perspectives: those whose organizations assign them to manage individuals and teams and individual contributors. I then introduce the Drexler/Sibbet Team Performance Model® that you can use to diagnose gaps between an existing team and the model team and as a guide for building clarity and commitment. Finally, I provide leading examples and discuss using this practice.

Clarification: Differences among Practices Aligned to Communication

Three of the nine practices encompass communication. Each addresses communication from different perspectives, as depicted in Table 8.1.

Characteristics of Communicating Like Agents

Within any team, department, or organization, effective communication is critical for achieving goals and performance outcomes. From clarifying what is happening within the organization to agreeing on clear expectations, 21st Century Leadership practitioners communicate to convey ideas and feelings that are critical for accomplishing work and promoting collaboration.

Table 8.1 Three Practices and Related Communication Perspective

Practice	Communication Perspective
Communicating Like Agents	Conveying ideas and feelings while representing stakeholders (such as communicating what a team is doing to other teams and communicating organizational messages to a group)
Facing the Unknown Like Lions	Listening and using empathy to receive ideas and feelings (such as accepting feedback from peers and comprehending improvement ideas from a direct report)
Communicating Like Broadcasters	Transmitting knowledge and skills to help others develop (such as facilitating a professional development event at a local chapter and presenting research findings and recommendations at an international conference)

When communicating, we act like agents. I'm not referring to secret agents as in spy movies but rather people who represent and act on behalf of others. When you communicate, you represent yourself and direct reports (if you have direct reports), peers, your direct manager, and entities such as your team, department, business unit, and the organization. For example, Bill, a customer, called Sandra at a call center. When Sandra didn't meet Bill's needs, Bill blamed the company—not Sandra. Why? Sandra acted as an agent of the company.

I summarize the characteristics of *Communicating Like Agents* (Box 8.1).

BOX 8.1 CHARACTERISTICS OF COMMUNICATING LIKE AGENTS

▪ When conveying thoughts and feelings, agents do so while representing and respecting the viewpoint of stakeholders (direct reports, peers, immediate manager, and executives) and entities (your team, department, business unit, and the organization).

▪ Agents provide clarity of the values and goals of stakeholders and entities as well as how stakeholders and entities align to organizational values and goals.

▪ The purpose of *Communicating Like Agents* is to share the command-and-control function and engage in collaboration, which ultimately builds confidence for others to act. To achieve this, I describe specific tactics in this chapter including co-creating plans, allowing authentic choice, and creating safety for thinking.

Tactics for Influencing Others to Take Action

To perform extraordinarily well, people need to meet two requirements: They need the appropriate amount of motivation and ability to perform. Goldsmith shares an example of why people find change difficult (Box 8.2). Table 8.2 describes how some leadership authors label these two requirements and what influences motivation.

Communicating Like Agents is the practice of influencing motivation, while *Directing Like Guides* and *Nurturing Like Gardeners* are practices for improving ability or increasing capability. How you practice *Communicating Like Agents* depends somewhat on your formal role. As explained in Chapter 2, people practice leadership from the perspective of their formal role. For example, chief executive officers (CEOs) are responsible for building an organization's vision. How CEOs practice leadership in building the vision is different from how individual contributors practice leadership in building the vision. CEOs may recruit employees to help shape the vision, and individual contributors may contribute by ensuring that teammates recognize how their work contributes to the vision's realization.

Authority is a factor and differentiates how some formal roles practice *Communicating Like Agents*. Managers of teams share authority, such as command and control, and teammates without authority influence the manager and teammates to clarify and collaborate. Hence, managers of teams practice *Communicating Like Agents* with one set of tactics while teammates practice from another set. Both attempt to achieve the same result: enabling teams to mature their mental and moral qualities, capabilities, and behaviors, consequently leading to extraordinary team performance.

BOX 8.2   EXAMPLE ABOUT WHY CHANGE IS CHALLENGING

There's a difference between motivation and understanding and ability. For example, we may be *motivated* to lose weight but we lack the nutritional *understanding* and cooking *ability* to design and stick with an effective diet. Or flip it over: we have understanding and ability but lack motivation.[3]

Goldsmith

Table 8.2 Labels Used by Authors to Describe the Two Requirements for Extraordinary Performance

Author	Motivation	Ability	Motivation Description
Marquet	Clarity	Competence	*Clarity* is helping others to understand thoroughly the organization, organizational goals, and how work aligns to these goals.[a]
Sinek	Why	How	*Why* is a belief that explains a team's purpose.[b]
Grenny et al.	Personal motivation Social motivation Structural motivation	Personal ability Social ability Structural ability	*Personal motivation* involves allowing for authentic choice and making the task meaningful.[c] *Social motivation* involves making sacrifices (your time, money, ego, previous priorities, and giving up self-centered values), engaging with opinion leaders, and creating group accountability.[d] *Structural motivation* involves using rewards but only after making the task intrinsically satisfying and obtaining social support. Rewards should be small incentives and reward key behaviors rather than results.[e]
Blanchard et al.	Commitment	Competence	*Commitment* is the amount of motivation and self-confidence someone has for accomplishing a specific task. If someone is low on commitment but has the ability, then you provide a supportive role.[f]

(Continued)

Table 8.2 (*Continued*) **Labels Used by Authors to Describe the Two Requirements for Extraordinary Performance**

Author	Motivation	Ability	Motivation Description
Wiseman	Liberators Challengers Debate makers	Investors	*Liberators* enable others to act by restraining themselves. They listen more and talk less, level the playing field, and insist on learning from mistakes.[g] *Challengers* present challenges, express the need, and create a starting point. They allow others to work on problems and help reframe problems if the team starts having difficulties. They co-create plans and solutions with their teams. They ask leading questions and challenge assumptions.[h] *Debate makers* frame the issue, create safety for big thinking, demand rigor, and clarify the decision-making process. They ask teammates to share their thoughts, ask hard questions, ask for data to justify their thinking, and communicate decisions and rationale.[i]

[a] Marquet, 2012, *Turn the Ship Around!*, 161.
[b] Sinek, 2009, *Start with Why*, 67.
[c] Grenny et al., 2013, *Influencer*, 111.
[d] Ibid., 182–183.
[e] Ibid., 245.
[f] Blanchard et al., 2001, *The 3 Keys to Empowerment*, 24, 26.
[g] Wiseman, 2010, *Multipliers*, 95.
[h] Ibid., 130.
[i] Ibid., 158.

BOX 8.3 LEADERSHIP TEAMS DEFINED

A leadership team is a small group of people who are collectively responsible for achieving a common objective for their organization.[4]

Lencioni

Point of Clarification between Teams and Groups

You may think that you are a member of a team, but you may be a member of a group rather than a team. A *team* is a type of group consisting of members that work together to produce products and services. Lencioni describes *leadership team* similarly (Box 8.3). According to The Grove, teams have a shared purpose for working together, have a high interdependency when accomplishing work, and are accountable for team results[5] (Box 8.4). A surgery team is an example of a highly interdependent team in which the surgeon cannot successfully complete an invasive procedure without anesthesiologists, nurses, physician assistants, and other specialists.[6]

The Grove also notes that the distinction between groups and teams is vital for determining the effort needed to build clarity and commitment. Obtaining shared clarity and commitment with a team is critical for achieving high performance and the extraordinary.[7] For a group with little interdependence, you may focus on clarity and commitment more at the individual level than at the group level.

BOX 8.4 GROUPS AND TEAMS DIFFER

The level of interdependence isn't nearly so great for some groups that call themselves teams...And many work "teams" are fully capable of performing its separate tasks with a minimum of interaction. So ask yourself, "How critical is each member to the overall success of the group?" If the answer is, "Members are each separately responsible for their fair share," then you probably aren't a strongly interdependent team. However, if you conclude that the loss of any member's contribution could undercut the whole effort, then you are definitely a team.[8]

The Grove

Influence Tactics for Those Assigned to Manage Individual Contributors and Teams

If an organization gives you the authority to manage direct reports or a team, the organization expects those whom you manage to produce specific results. You have the authority to determine how you accomplish the results and your leadership approach:

- Traditional leadership: You leverage command and control exclusively over the team and use authority to get your team to accomplish work.
- 21st Century Leadership: Practitioners leverage the *Communicating Like Agents* practice to:
  - Share command and control with your team.
  - Collaborate with your team to clarify the purpose.
  - Cocreate with the team.

With each member more involved and functioning at a higher capacity, the team can accomplish the extraordinary. I list tactics that can help those assigned as managers of individuals and teams to influence others to act (Box 8.5).

BOX 8.5 INFLUENCE TACTICS FOR THOSE ASSIGNED TO MANAGE INDIVIDUAL CONTRIBUTORS AND TEAMS

- Push authority to direct reports allowing them more decision authority and autonomy.[9]
- Share command and control (C2) and set expectations for what sharing C2 means.[10]
- Enable and involve others authentically in decision making and problem solving rather than making decisions and solving problems for them.[11]
- Make the code of silence (unhealthy norms that the culture is conditioned not to talk about for fear of punishment) discussable.[12]
- Allow others to contribute by practicing self-restraint and listening more than talking.[13]
- Sacrifice your time, ego, and traditional values that benefit management but not the team.[14]
- Explain decisions and rationales.[15]
- Influence accountability for key behaviors and create an environment in which everyone holds everyone accountable.[16]
- Reward others for doing their best work rather than for results alone.[17]

**BOX 8.6   TACTICS FOR ALL FORMAL ROLES
TO INFLUENCE OTHERS TO ACT**

- Obtain a shared understanding of clear expectations.[18]
- Cocreate plans with others.[19]
- Present challenges, help others discover needs, and share needs for the team to discuss.[20]
- Allow authentic choice rather than use coercive techniques.[21]
- Share meaningful stories to convey ideas and emotions and to promote vicarious learning.[22]
- Sacrifice your time, ego, and priorities to help others.[23]
- Create safety for thinking (share your views after hearing from others, encourage others to take opposing views, and encourage all points of view).[24]
- Obtain buy-in with influential individual contributors, managers, and executives.[25]
- Acknowledge and learn from mistakes.[26]
- Thank others and groups for their contributions.[27]
- Share with your direct manager the *Communicating Like Agents* practice and encourage your direct manager to implement some of the manager tactics.

Tactics for All Formal Roles to Influence Others to Act

As with team managers, teammates can influence others to act. I list tactics that individual contributors can use to influence their teams (Box 8.6).

Marquet's Intent-Based Leadership (IBL)

Begin with the End in Mind

Imagine a workplace where everyone:

- Engages
- Contributes their full intellectual capacity
- Is healthier and happier because they have more control over their work
- Leads[28]

David Marquet served as the Commanding officer of the nuclear submarine, the *Santa Fe*. During his service, Marquet developed IBL and has since refined the methodology through analysis of how organizations applied IBL.[29]

Marquet explains that when you successfully implement IBL, your organization should experience the following:

- Empowerment
- Engagement
- Ownership
- Having people think
- Allowing people to speak up
- Creating Psychological Safety
- Coaching instead of commanding[30]

Ultimately, IBL creates an environment where people can be at their best.[31] What you want to eliminate is a workplace where people are told what to do and are dependent upon management to act. Otherwise, you have an environment that has minimal desired performance or worse (Box 8.7)!

IBL

IBL is Marquet's leadership system that shifts authority to those with the information. Often, employees with the information work with customers—the frontline—or are handling operational or developmental problems.[32]

BOX 8.7 GROUPS AND TEAMS DIFFER

Here is the incredible lesson: People will do exactly what they are told. If the environment in your workplace recognizes people at the top as leaders and everyone else as followers, that is generally how your teams will function. In caustic environments where mistakes are used to determine who keeps their job and who doesn't, people will do everything to avoid making a mistake. This means that usually they do only what they are told, because then they would not be making a mistake, they would just be doing what they were told. It leads to a bias toward inactivity.[33]

When we give people instructions, we create dependence. When we give people intent, we create independence.[34]

Marquet

IBL has two key terms: Emancipation and accountability. Emancipation is the next step from empowerment. Marquet explains that management needs to empower employees "to undo all those top-down, do-what-you're-told, be-a-team-player messages that result from our leader-follower model."[35] However, empowerment is still part of a top-down structure and needs replacement. Empowerment infers that management can give power to employees. Emancipation indicates that employees have the power already, and management doesn't need to give them power. When they use their power, they can leverage their talents to be creative and innovate. As Marquet writes that you don't need to empower emancipated teams. There is no need. "Indeed, you no longer have the ability to empower them because they are not relying on you as their source of power."[36] Once they are an emancipated team and no longer follow a prescribed way to work, "they will be motivated to come up with ingenious ways to best accomplish the goal."[37]

With emancipation, employees operate at Marquet's fourth level of his Four Levels of Accountability Systems (Box 8.8).

In traditional organizations, management assumes that employees cannot hold themselves accountable; management does. In IBL, people hold

BOX 8.8   FOUR LEVELS OF ACCOUNTABILITY SYSTEMS

Level 1: People are not told what they are accountable for and therefore don't do their jobs. This is chaos.

Level 2: People are told what they are accountable for but don't do their jobs because of overwork or focus on the wrong things. This is the most inefficient because there is overhead for telling and monitoring but the work isn't getting done.

Level 3: People know what they are responsible for and do their jobs. There are systems to hold people accountable. It is a compliant system, where people feel like they are being forced into doing their jobs. This is where most organizations strive to be, but this is top-down.

Level 4: People are not told what they are accountable for because they've figured it out on their own, and so they do their jobs anyway. The monitoring system is discarded and the team monitors themselves. This is where we were able to get to after throwing out the monitoring systems. This is a highly energized system, where people are engaged in defining their work and doing it.[38]

Marquet

themselves accountable for their work and performance; management helps you do this. Marquet calls this Accountability Partners, which can be bosses but typically are peers and subordinates.[39]

Conclusion

IBL takes time to learn and to disseminate, but it is possible. Marquet developed IBL on the *Santa Fe*, and he details the results in his book, *Turn the Ship Around!* Since then, Marquet has trained hundreds of organizations to learn and implement IBL.

Drexler/Sibbet Team Performance Model

Whether you manage a team or are a teammate, you can leverage the Drexler/Sibbet Team Performance Model to influence your team's performance. Based on the theory of process by Arthur M. Young, research by Jack Gibb, and more than ten years of Drexler and Sibbet's research, the model addresses predictable issues and concerns that occur while creating and sustaining a team. As depicted in Figure 8.1 and Table 8.3, the model

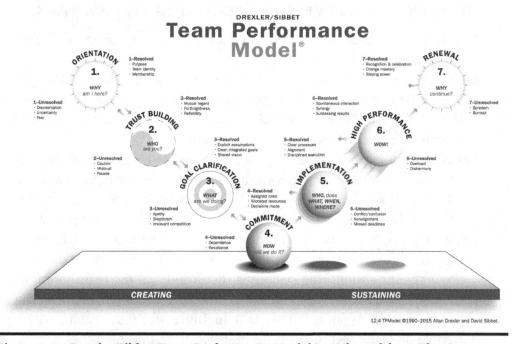

Figure 8.1   Drexler/Sibbet Team Performance Model®. (Adapted from The Grove, *Team Leader Guide*, 24–25, Copyright © 2008. Used with Permission.)

Table 8.3 Drexler/Sibbet Team Performance Model Stage Summary

No.	Stage Title	Description	Examples of Why Teams Fail
1	Orientation: Why am I here?	When teams are forming, everybody wonders why they are here, their potential fit, and whether others will accept them. People need some kind of answer to continue.	Unclear purpose, goals, and priorities.
2	Trust building: Who are you?	People want to know whom they will work with—their expectations, agendas, and competencies. Sharing builds trust and a free exchange among teammates.	Teammates mistrust the manager or each other.
3	Goal clarification: What are we doing?	The more concrete work of the team begins with clarity about the team goals, basic assumptions, and vision. Terms and definitions come to the fore. What are the priorities?	Inadequate teaming ability. (examples: putting personal goals before team goals; failing to address conflicts constructively)
4	Commitment: How will we work?	At some point, discussions need to end, and decisions must be made about how resources, time, and staff—all the bottom-line constraints—will be managed. Agreed roles are critical.	Fail to involve stakeholders at an appropriate level and fails to obtain stakeholder commitment.
5	Implementation: Who does what, when, and where?	Teams turn the corner when they begin sequencing work and deciding who does what, when, and where. Timing and scheduling dominate this stage.	Ignores interpersonal dynamics and commitments in favor of rushing to implement.
6	High performance: Wow!	When methods are mastered, a team can change its goals and respond flexibly to the environment. The team can say "WOW!" and surpass expectations.	Management fails to trust team performance and overcontrols tasks.

(Continued)

Table 8.3 (*Continued*) **Drexler/Sibbet Team Performance Model Stage Summary**

No.	Stage Title	Description	Examples of Why Teams Fail
7	Renewal	Teams are dynamic. People get tired; members change. People wonder, why continue? It's time to harvest learning and prepare for a new action cycle.	Fails to dedicate time on renewal and address burnout.

Source: Adapted from The Grove, *Team Leader Guide*, 24–25, 36, Copyright © 2008. Used with permission.

consists of seven stages representing the seven primary issues that teams must resolve to achieve high performance. Symptoms for whether or not a team accomplishes a stage successfully are listed in the model as *Resolved* or *Unresolved*. While the model provides a roadmap for what is needed to create and sustain a team, The Grove has documented 86 best practices to support resolving each stage. Example titles include:

■ Charter clarification
■ Sharing backgrounds
■ SPOT analysis
■ Agreeing on decision making
■ Progress charting
■ Team-based problem solving
■ Celebrations

Leading Examples

Individual Contributor Leading Example: Knowledge Sharing across Teams

Clarissa, Michele, and Carl were merchandising specialists who worked in a department of about 100 professionals. Although they were in different teams, they frequently met for lunch to improve their work and their team's product sales.

After getting together a few times, they realized how much they learned from each other by talking about tactics that did or didn't work for their unique products. Thinking that others could benefit, Clarissa, Michele, and Carl began a monthly support group that consisted of their peers but without management.

In these sessions, they expanded the scope of their discussions to talk about how they could contribute collectively toward the department's goals. They talked about the role of merchandising specialist and how they could contribute more to their teams. They revitalized their purpose and started sharing their view of the role with their direct managers.

After attending these social discussions, Clarissa, Michele, and Carl found that they enjoyed their work more and developed a sense that they were part of something bigger than supporting a set of products. Others expressed similar results and stated that they developed more clarity about what their department did and how it contributed to the business.

Manager Leading Example: Transitioning from Traditional C2 to a Shared C2

Pam, a chaplain assistant in one of the armed forces, was recently assigned to a new section, new location, and promoted. In her previous assignment, Pam worked in a highly structured C2 unit. While Pam was an expert in her field, she learned to follow orders and wait for her superior officer to make decisions.

After reviewing her records and talking with her, James, Pam's new superior officer, found her capable but suspected that she had worked in a traditional C2 structure. James needed to orient Pam to a shared C2 structure and ensure that they had the same expectations.

During their first meeting, James shared the section's vision and mission with Pam. Instead of explaining to Pam what the section's vision and mission meant to him, James asked Pam to talk about what these meant to her and how they differed from her previous section's vision and mission. James appreciated and learned from her perspective, and together they discussed the implications for how their duties supported the vision and mission.

Next, they reviewed Pam's new job description, and James provided examples of how previous chaplain assistants performed their duties. James did this so that Pam could visualize her journey into the new role and help her understand how critical her duties were for serving the section's vision and mission. James then discussed the implications for decision-making at her level, and together, they came to an agreement on what Pam should expect. For example, when unexpected situations arose involving suicide prevention, crisis intervention, and counseling referrals, James and Pam agreed that she would be accountable for the decisions made about these types of situations. James confirmed that Pam could make these decisions, and Pam recognized that she needed to act swiftly during a crisis and didn't have time to wait for her superiors to decide for her. Thus, during crises, Pam would use her expertise to make vital decisions to support persons in need.

James helped Pam appreciate how her new role would contribute to the section's vision and mission and appreciate her newly found and necessary autonomy to make decisions at her career level. As she worked in her role, Pam adapted to her new responsibilities and searched proactively for any indications of potential crises. In a short period, Pam had addressed crises related to workplace stress and had prevented a possible suicide attempt. Pam accomplished crisis resolutions without contacting James for permission to act. Instead, Pam debriefed these incidents with James after resolving the crises successfully and completed referrals to other professionals like mental health and physicians.

Executive Leading Example: Blaming the VP

Ursula, a Vice President (VP) of Implementations, made a tough decision that caused some departments a noticeable amount of rework. Ursula's options were clear, though: Either the organization changed now, resulting in rework, or the organization would remain the same but suffer long-term consequences. This decision wasn't what troubled Ursula. What troubled her was what she learned about Emily, one of Ursula's managers. The two had talked about the decision; Emily was against it, but Ursula made the final decision and asked Emily to carry the news to the different department directors to implement. Reluctantly, Emily agreed to deliver the message. What bothered Ursula was how Emily had delivered the news: Emily had blamed Ursula for the decision in each conversation with a director and acknowledged that she disagreed with Ursula's decision. Ironically, the directors understood Ursula's reasoning and took the news well. Emily's attitude bothered the directors more, and some of the directors let Ursula know.

Ursula talked about what happened with Emily and explained what she had learned from the directors. Ursula clarified that while she didn't like making the decision, she knew that the decision was best for the company. As an executive officer, Ursula had to consider all stakeholders that she represented and take action; sometimes, she had to make less favorable choices for some stakeholders. Ursula asked Emily to consider thinking of herself as an executive officer and an agent of the organization. Being an agent means that she represents her subordinates, peers, and even her boss, Ursula. Ursula explained that this meant that when Emily agreed to deliver a message, she represented Ursula and her department. Rather than blaming Ursula as the villain, Emily should have owned the decision and delivered the message as if she had made it herself. When Emily blamed Ursula, the directors perceived Emily as disloyal and acting unnecessarily.

Ursula and Emily had more conversations about what it meant to be an agent of the company with delivering bad news to others and being accountable. Emily realized that she occasionally would have to deliver difficult news, and blaming someone else could undermine that person, the department, and the management team. Emily could recall several times when those she reported to blamed their superiors for bringing bad news and how poorly the manager had delivered the message reflected on them. Emily didn't want to be like that and vowed to fairly represent those above her and support their difficult decisions, especially when she disagreed with them. If Emily disagreed with another of Ursula's decisions, both felt comfortable for Emily to let Ursula know in private while supporting the decision in public. Ursula agreed to explain to Emily the rationale for the decision and the benefit to the company. Ursula agreed to listen to Emily's objections and understand Emily's thinking.

Since then, Emily has practiced consciously being an agent for her diverse stakeholders. Occasionally, she has had to deliver unpleasant messages, but she accepts ownership of the messages and does her best to carry out the task. While doing so, Emily feels that she has become more mature morally and a better steward for her company, her department, her stakeholders, and of course, for Ursula.

Summary: What to Do

Summary

Communicating Like Agents is about influencing others to want to take action. In other words, this practice involves motivating and obtaining commitment. Part of this practice involves representing different stakeholders when communicating with others. Figure 8.2 summarizes this practice.

Characteristics	***Communicating Like Agents Practice*** • When conveying thoughts and feelings, agents do so while representing and respecting the viewpoints of your stakeholders (direct reports, peers, immediate manager, and executives) and entities (your team, department, business unit and the organization). • Agents provide clarity of the values and goals of stakeholders and entities as well as how stakeholders and entities align to organizational values and goals. • The purpose of *Communicating Like Agents* is to share the command-and-control function and engage in collaboration, which builds confidence ultimately for others to act. To achieve this, I describe specific tactics in this chapter including co-creating plans, allowing authentic choice, and creating safety for thinking.
Principles, Guidelines, and Rules of Practice	***Related 21st Century Leadership Principles*** • Believe in Others • Connect with Others • Put Others First • Give Up Control • Encourage Growth • Collaborate with Others ***Influence Tactics for Those Assigned to Manage Individual Contributors and Teams*** • Push authority to direct reports allowing them more decision authority and autonomy.[a] • Share command and control (C2) and set expectations for what sharing C2 means.[b] • Enable and involve others authentically in decision making and problem solving rather than making decisions and solving problems for them.[c] • Make the code of silence (unhealthy norms that the culture is conditioned not to talk about for fear of punishment) discussable.[d] • Allow others to contribute by practicing self-restraint and listening more than talking.[e] • Sacrifice your time, ego, and traditional values that benefit management but not the team.[f] • Explain decisions and rationales.[g] • Influence accountability for key behaviors and create an environment in which everyone holds everyone accountable.[h] • Reward others for doing their best work rather than for results alone.[i] **Tactics for all formal roles to Influence Others to Act** • Obtain a shared understanding of clear expectations.[j] • Co-create plans with others.[k] • Present challenges, help others discover needs, and share needs for the team to discuss.[l] • Allow authentic choice rather than use coercive techniques.[m] • Share meaningful stories to convey ideas and emotions and to promote vicarious learning.[n] • Sacrifice your time, ego, and priorities to help others.[o] • Create safety for thinking (share your views after hearing from others, encourage others to take opposing views, and encourage all points of view).[p] • Obtain buy-in with influential individual contributors, managers, and executives.[q] • Acknowledge and learn from mistakes.[r] • Thank others and groups for their contributions.[s] • Share with your direct manager the *Communicating Like Agents* practice and encourage your direct manager to implement the manager tactics (Box 8.5). ***Marquet's Clarity Approach*** • Help others understand completely the organization, organizational goals, and how work aligns to these goals.[t] • Leverage the organization's legacy to clarify organizational purpose.[u]

Figure 8.2 Practice summary: Communicating Like Agents. (*Continued*)

- Consider guiding principles when making decisions.[v]
- Begin thinking with the end in mind.[w]
- Encourage others to question rather than accept blind obedience.[x]

Sinek's Why Concept

- Clarify the *Why*. *Why* is a belief that explains a team's purpose.[y]
- *How* are actions that help you realize your belief.
- *What* are the results of your actions.

Blanchard et al. on Commitment

Commitment is the amount of motivation and self-confidence someone has for accomplishing a specific task. If someone is low on commitment but has the ability, then you provide a supportive role.[z]

Models, Techniques, and Tools	*Grenny et al on Motivation* There are three categories of motivation: personal, social, and structural. - *Personal motivation* involves allowing for authentic choice and making the task meaningful.[aa] - *Social motivation* involves making sacrifices (your time, money, ego, previous priorities, and giving up self-centered values), engaging in opinion leaders, and creating group accountability.[bb] - *Structural motivation* involves using rewards but only after making the task satisfying intrinsically and obtaining social support. Rewards should be small incentives and reward key behaviors rather than results.[cc] *Drexler/Sibbet Team Performance Model®* Use this model to analyze and diagnose needs for your team. Stages in the model include: 1. Orientation 2. Team Building 3. Goal Clarification 4. Commitment 5. Implementation 6. High Performance 7. Renewal

[a] Marquet, 2012, *Turn the Ship Around!*, 59, 207, 213.
[b] Alberts and Hayes, 2011, *Understanding Command and Control*, 2, 8, 39.
[c] Wiseman, 2010, *Multipliers*, 141–151.
[d] Grenny et al., 2013, *Influencer*, 173–175.
[e] Wiseman, 2010, *Multipliers*, 78–79.
[f] Grenny et al., 2013, *Influencer*, 159–161.
[g] Wiseman, 2010, *Multipliers*, 151.
[h] Grenny et al., 2013, *Influencer*, 178.
[i] Ibid., 223, 231–232; Wiseman, 2010, *Multipliers*, 83–84.
[J] Kouzes and Posner, 2012, *The Leadership Challenge*, 280–281.
[k] Wiseman, 2010, *Multipliers*, 118.
[l] Ibid., 108, 111–112, 114–116.
[m] Grenny et al., 2013, *Influencer*, 84, 88, 90–91.
[n] Ibid., 96.

Figure 8.2 (*Continued*) Practice summary: Communicating Like Agents.

[o] Ibid., 159–161.
[p] Wiseman, 2010, *Multipliers*, 149; Marquet, 2012, *Turn the Ship Around!*, 92.
[q] Grenny et al., 2013, *Influencer*, 163.
[r] Wiseman, 2010, *Multipliers*, 84–86.
[s] Kouzes and Posner, 2012, *The Leadership Challenge*, 285-288.
[t] Marquet, 2012, *Turn the Ship Around!*, 161.
[u] Ibid., 176–177.
[v] Ibid., 182.
[w] Ibid., 189.
[x] Ibid., 162.
[y] Sinek, 2009, *Start with Why*, 67.
[z] Blanchard et al., 2001, *The 3 Keys to Empowerment*, 24, 26.
[aa] Grenny et al., 2013, *Influencer*, 111.
[bb] Ibid., 182–183.
[cc] Ibid., 245.

Figure 8.2 (*Continued*) Practice summary: Communicating Like Agents.

What to Do

Table 8.4 lists recommendations for applying this practice immediately, in the short term, and in the long term.

Table 8.4 Recommended Actions for Applying Communicating Like Agents

Immediate
Analyze and Diagnose Your Current Team Examine how your current team leverages concepts in the three areas of the *Communicating Like Agents* practice: building the team, performing the work, and reflecting on the work. Start identifying gaps between your team's current state and the desired state. Consider the gap implications and how you might influence the team to close the gaps. ***Build Your Team*** With your manager, clarify your team's purpose and how your work aligns with organizational goals. With your manager, clarify how your work contributes to the primary or support processes. From the perspective of your formal role, determine how you can support others, build your team, share your story, and get to know your teammates better. ***Performing the Work*** Encourage the team to collaborate on planning the work. Determine or explain how your team's work aligns with organizational goals and supports the primary or supporting processes. When solving problems, involve others.

(*Continued*)

Table 8.4 (*Continued*) Recommended Actions for Applying Communicating Like Agents

Reflecting on the Work Research techniques for reflecting on the work and how you can do this with your team. Begin to acknowledge mistakes and what you learn from them. Thank others for their support and work.
Short Term
Read about IBL Marquet has published two books about IBL and a workbook, which you can find in the bibliography. Even if you don't implement IBL in an organization, you can begin leveraging the methodology with your team, even if you aren't the team's supervisor or manager. *Share with Others* Share with others what you learn about *Communicating Like Agents* practice. Talk with your direct manager about *Communicating Like Agents* and encourage your direct manager to leverage the practice. *Learn More about Clarity, Why, Situational Leadership® II, and the Three Multiplier Disciplines* You can find the following in Appendix IX: Bibliography. In *Turn the Ship Around!*, read how Marquet uses clarity. In *Start with Why*, read how Sinek explains the why concept. Also, view his TED talk: *How Great Leaders Inspire Action*. In *Helping People Win at Work* and *The 3 Keys to Empowerment*, read about Situational Leadership® II. In *Multipliers*, read about the three disciplines: liberator, challenger, and decision maker.
Long Term
Study More about Building Teams Begin leveraging resources that can help you develop your ability to build teams. The Grove (http://www.grove.com) is an excellent resource for learning how a team works together. On their YouTube channel, you can watch videos about the Drexler/Sibbet Team Performance Model, which explains the stages of team development (https://www.youtube.com/channel/UCVfzRnyP_Oth9CmQvPLQ9XA). You can use this model to create and sustain a team's high performance. In *Team Leader Guide*, The Grove provides 86 best practices in which each practice aligns to one of the seven stages in the model.[a] Read Lencioni's *The Five Dysfunctions of a Team*.[b] In this fable, Lencioni addresses the absence of trust, fear of conflict, lack of commitment, avoidance of accountability, and inattention to results. Continue to read about IBL. You also can subscribe to the YouTube channel, Leadership Nudges with David Marquet (https://www.youtube.com/c/LeadershipNudges).

[a] The Grove, 2008, *Team Leader Guide*.
[b] Lencioni, 2002, *The Five Dysfunctions of a Team*.

Word of Caution

The purpose of *Communicating Like Agents* is to influence others to act, but it isn't intended to manipulate or convince others to think what you want them to think. While clarifying your values and thoughts is essential, understanding the values and thoughts of those you work with and building shared values is just as important. As Kouzes and Posner explain, shared values between you and your team are the means to fostering productive working relationships.[40]

Chapter 9

Practice 5: Directing Like Guides

The result of increased technical competence is the ability to delegate increased decision making to the employees. Increased decision making among your employees will naturally result in greater engagement, motivation, and initiative. You will end up with significantly higher productivity, morale, and effectiveness.[1]

Marquet

Multipliers operate from a belief that talent exists everywhere and they can use it at its highest if they can simply identify the genius in people...Diminishers are owners of talent, not developers of talent. Because they don't actively develop talent, people in their organizations languish and can actually regress.[2]

Wiseman

Introduction: Importance and Benefits of Directing Like Guides

If you motivate others effectively and morally so that they want to act but cannot due to limited abilities, then *Directing Like Guides* is for you. *Directing Like Guides* is interlinked with *Communicating Like Agents*. Both

DOI: 10.4324/9781003273448-12

are important for influencing change. *Communicating Like Agents* is about influencing so that others want to act, and *Directing Like Guides* is about improving capabilities so that others are capable of taking action.

Enabling others through developing their capabilities contributes to acting morally and builds their confidence and capabilities for future actions. Moreover, helping them models the importance of supporting teammates. This is true, especially when helping others takes time away from your duties and responsibilities; modeling this type of sacrifice encourages those around you to help others as well.

In this chapter, I discuss the characteristics of *Directing Like Guides*. I then discuss assessing the capability needs of those you work with and how to match your approach to meet their needs. I offer some techniques on how you can help others improve their abilities. I then provide three leading examples and discuss using this practice.

Characteristics of Directing Like Guides

When someone is highly motivated but lacks the necessary ability, change cannot occur. The challenge is to figure out if the person lacks motivation or ability. Patterson et al. note that "Motivation and ability are linked at the hip. They aren't separate entities. More often than not, they blend into one another."[3] Hence, someone might appear unmotivated to act, but the underlying reason for inaction is the lack of ability. You may have difficulty getting someone motivated to take on a challenge when the person doesn't have the ability to accomplish the task (Box 9.1).

Assessing Abilities Using Situational Leadership® II

When helping people build their capabilities, you need to determine the help to provide. Some people may have no related experiences for accomplishing specific tasks and may need substantial guidance. Others may only require feedback that they are completing the task correctly. One model that may clarify how to help others is Situational Leadership® II (SLII®).

SLII® helps others become self-reliant in accomplishing a specific task in an empowered manner.[4] I list the characteristics that describe SLII® (Box 9.2).

Note that leadership style isn't equivalent to traditional leadership styles.

BOX 9.1   CHARACTERISTICS OF DIRECTING LIKE GUIDES

■ While *Communicating Like Agents* inspires others to act (motivation), *Directing Like Guides* enables others to act (ability).

■ Resistance to taking the right action may appear due to a lack of motivation, but the root problem is due to the inability to act. Likewise, some may seem to lack the ability to act, but the root problem is due to a lack of motivation. Sometimes, motivation and ability are interconnected in such a way that both are the cause of inaction. Thus, determining the motivation and ability of others is critical for determining how to help others act.

■ People's abilities and motivation can vary substantially. The challenge to help others to act is determining the best approach to take. In Situational Leadership® II (SLII®), if ability is low in some, then you should provide either directives or coaching. If ability is moderate to high, then you should provide either support or delegation.[5]

BOX 9.2   SITUATIONAL LEADERSHIP® II

Situational Leadership® II is a

■ Powerful way to determine how best to develop ability in relation to a person's current ability and a given task.

■ Tactical and intended for two people: The leadership practitioner and the person who is being helped.

■ Mechanism around a specific task that a person intends to accomplish.

■ Mechanism to help a person be self-reliant in accomplishing a task. To help someone become self-reliant, the person may need to meet distinctive needs before achieving high competence and commitment for the specific task.

■ Way to determine a person's needs for accomplishing a specific task at one of four development levels. Each level represents the typical competence level (ability) and commitment level (motivation) that a person has for a given task. As a person develops for accomplishing the task, the person's development level increases.

■ Model that is used to align the person's development level to the approach needed to help the person: Directing, coaching, supporting, or delegating. Each approach, called *leadership style*, has a certain amount of directive and supportive levels.

> **BOX 9.3 SITUATING DIRECTIVE AND**
> **SUPPORTIVE BEHAVIORS**
>
> Situational Leadership® II teaches us that to get the best performance and to develop people's skills, you match the right combination of directive and supportive behaviors to address the person's current level of competence and commitment.[6]
>
> **Blanchard et al.**

SLII®'s leadership styles are more descriptive of a technique: directing, coaching, supporting, or delegating (Box 9.3). In the following list, I summarize how the development levels align with the leadership styles.

1. When *competence* is low and *commitment* is high, use directing. *Directing* is high directive and low supportive.
2. When *competence* is low to some and *commitment* is low, use coaching. *Coaching* is high directive and high supportive.
3. When *competence* is moderate to high but *commitment* is variable, use supporting. *Supporting* is low directive and high supportive.
4. When *competence* and *commitment* are high, use delegating. *Delegating* is low directive and low supportive.

SLII® Example

Because SLII® is an effective model for helping others develop, I provide the following example and the three leading examples at the end of this chapter. Table 9.1 depicts examples of directive and supportive behaviors.

Table 9.1 Directive and Supportive Behavioral Examples[a]

Directive	Supportive
Tell and show when to do the task. Provide frequent feedback on results.	Praising Listening Encouraging Involving others in problem-solving and Decision-making

[a] Blanchard et al., 2001, *The 3 Keys to Empowerment*, 26.

In this example, I denote the development level that Scott is at while Candice helps him develop his behavioral interviewing capabilities.

Candice, a senior recruiter, has been helping Scott orient to their larger company. Scott is a new recruiter with some experience working at a smaller organization. Scott has never used behavioral interviewing questions to screen candidates, but he is confident that he can use the technique. For this task, Scott is at D1.

To help Scott build his capabilities, Candice offers Scott the opportunity to practice interviewing her as if she were a candidate. She cautions Scott that the technique might be more difficult than it seems. Before starting the practice, Candice models how the technique works and explains the guidelines. Scott then tries interviewing Candice. Even though he has screened candidates before, Scott has some trouble stating the questions in a way that comes across naturally, and he ends up reading the questions more than stating them in his own words. Scott becomes a little frustrated with the awkward phrases of "tell me about a time when...." Scott is at D2.

Candice coaches Scott specifically on how to phrase the questions so that they come across more naturally for him. She models how she would phrase certain questions, and then she has Scott do the same. After the practice, Scott thanks Candice for her help and is grateful that he didn't try screening a candidate using the technique without practicing.

After a few screening sessions with entry-level candidates, Scott feels more competent about behavioral interviewing. Hari, Scott's manager, asks Scott to screen an executive. Scott isn't too comfortable using the behavioral questions with executives and asks Candice for suggestions on how he might approach executives differently than entry-level candidates. Scott is at D3.

Candice understands his concerns and suggests some ways to set up the interview and ask questions. With her suggestions, Scott completes the candidate's interview without any issues. After completing several behavioral interviews, Scott is comfortable using the technique and even helps new teammates improve using it. Scott is now at D4 in asking behavioral interviewing questions.

Techniques for Building Capability

To help you influence someone's ability, I describe two techniques: Bandura's Vicarious Learning and Cognitive Apprenticeship. Both are powerful techniques for helping others learn simple to complex procedures,

BOX 9.4   VICARIOUS LEARNING

The capacity to learn by observation enables people to acquire rules for generating and regulating behavioral patterns without having to form them gradually by tedious trial and error.[7]

Bandura

skills, and behaviors. In addition, I also reintroduce Grenny et al.'s Personal Ability category that I described in Chapter 7.

Bandura's Vicarious Learning

According to Bandura, much of what people can learn from direct experience can also be learned vicariously by observing others performing a procedure or experiencing something. You can observe another person's actions and further observe the results of those actions. When Brad watched little Joey burn himself by touching a hot stovetop, Brad learned not to touch stovetops without having direct experience. When Amy watched how Erika won over a new client in a conversation, Amy learned a new technique for selling the company's services (Box 9.4).

Bandura cautions readers that trial-and-error learning possibly can lead to costly mistakes. When the risks are high in that they could cause loss of life, injury, or emotional distress, instructors will serve the public and learners better by instructing more from observation and using techniques such as Cognitive Apprenticeship. Most people, for example, would probably disagree with a company that allows new technicians to learn the operation of a nuclear reactor by using trial-and-error learning.

Cognitive Apprenticeship

Using Social Cognitive Learning principles, Cognitive Apprenticeship socializes learners to a procedure or a set of behaviors.[8] The technique emphasizes learning types of situations rather than addressing a specific problem. The five phases involve having an instructor model the appropriate behaviors as defined by a set standard for resolving a situation type and then allowing learners to practice the appropriate behaviors in controlled conditions that approximate the actual environment. The intent is to build proficiency safely and in conditions that promote success. Table 9.2 lists the five phases.

Table 9.2 Cognitive Apprenticeship Phases

No.	Phase	Instructor's Role	Learner's Role
1	Observation with articulation	**Instructor's role = model** While demonstrating, the model articulates aloud what he or she is thinking (explaining "why").	**Learner's role = observer** The observer watches and listens to the model perform the entire procedure.
2	Scaffolding	**Instructor's role = coach** The coach observes the performers, asks questions to elicit thinking, and provides feedback and correction as needed.	**Learner's role = performer** Under controlled conditions, the performer completes the desired procedure. While performing, the learner states aloud what he or she is thinking.
3	Fading	**Instructor's role = coach** As the learner improves, the coach decreases coaching and scaffolding.	**Learner's role = performer** The performer continues to approximate the procedure but under more realistic conditions.
4	Self-directed learning	**Instructor's role = consultant** The consultant provides assistance only when requested.	**Learner's role = performer** The performer practices the actual procedure. The performer requests consultations as needed.
5	Generalization	Instructor and learner discuss generalizing the procedure to other procedures. Instructors can use this phase as an advanced organizer for instructing a similar procedure.	

You can apply Cognitive Apprenticeship to various procedures and behaviors, including learning sales steps, interpersonal skills, aviation techniques, and medical procedures. Cognitive Apprenticeship is effective, especially when procedures and behaviors can have harmful consequences if practitioners fail to follow a defined and agreed-on standard.

Grenny et al.'s Tactics for Influencing Personal Ability

In Chapter 7, I discussed Grenny et al.'s Six Sources of Influence™. Their Personal Ability category aligns with *Directing Like Guides*, and their social and structural ability categories align with *Nurturing Like Gardeners*. The tactics that Grenny et al. advocate include deliberate practice, providing immediate feedback against a clear standard, and preparing for setbacks by interpreting them as guidance for improving and refining a technique.[9] Mistakes that people make include believing the following:

- People don't need to study and practice interpersonal skills.[10]
- People cannot resolve certain problems due to flaws in their genetics or character rather than believing that training with practice can help them resolve these problems.[11]
- People don't need to continue developing a skill once it becomes automatic and reach an acceptable level (sometimes referred to as arrested development).[12]

Leading Examples

Individual Contributor Leading Example: Helping an Aircraft Maintainer Build Competence

Kathleen, a new aircraft maintainer, started her first assignment working under Timothy. Timothy recognized that Kathleen was highly motivated to complete her first preflight inspection of a fighter aircraft. However, Timothy also knew that Kathleen didn't have enough experience or ability to accomplish the task effectively. Timothy asked Juliet, an expert aircraft maintainer, to help Kathleen. With Juliet's agreement, Timothy assigned Juliet to model the preflight inspection and coach Kathleen.

Juliet started by explaining to Kathleen the preflight inspection process, discussing the importance of the process, and agreeing on how the process contributed to the success of the team's goals. Kathleen observed Juliet performing the inspection. While doing so, Juliet explained what she was doing and thinking as she completed each process. When ready, Kathleen performed the preflight inspection with Juliet observing. During each step, Juliet had Kathleen talk aloud about what she was doing, why she was doing it, and what she considered or looked for while performing. Juliet provided coaching, assistance when needed, and on-the-spot feedback. Juliet's support helped Kathleen learn quickly what to do and what to look for when inspecting an aircraft. While using all the required materials, Kathleen continued to practice technical orders, personal protective equipment, and the required tools. As Kathleen became more competent, Juliet talked less, provided less oversight, and acted less like a coach and more like a consultant.

With Timothy's approval, Juliet invited John, Craig, and Rebecca, three other technicians, to be peer mentors so that Kathleen could continue developing her technical skills and her ability to collaborate, innovate, communicate, network, and think critically and make decisions. With the appropriate decreased level of support, Kathleen's confidence continued to grow, and she improved her accuracy and speed at preflight inspections safely. Over time, Kathleen excelled in her role, and the maintainer won two quality assurance awards within a year.

Manager Leading Example: Transitioning from Academic to Business Writing

Vivian, an Operations Manager, hired Eric as a Senior Project Manager. Eric had just completed his Ph.D. from a nearby university. While highly motivated and committed, this was Eric's first job in the corporate sector, and he had no experience working on cross-functional teams and communicating with multiple stakeholders.

After Eric completed orientation, Vivian talked with Eric about developing his business writing and taking the corporate training course. Having a Ph.D., Eric wasn't enthusiastic about the idea, but he wanted to please his new boss. The following week, he attended the three-day class.

What impressed Eric was how different writing for business is compared with academic writing. During the first day, he realized that his academic writing style would interfere with his communications with colleagues, stakeholders, and sponsors.

Throughout his career, Eric continued to develop his business writing and started to take courses in technical writing. Eric attributes much of his accomplishments to his training in writing, and he appreciates Vivian's decision to develop his communication capabilities.

Executive Leading Example: Transitioning a Training Department

For years, Seth, Managing Partner of Human Resources (HR), worked with Melinda, Training Department Head. Melinda's department served the organization diligently by producing whatever training the department heads wanted. Often, Seth questioned the value of most of the training and wondered if the training cost the organization more than the value of what employees learned.

About a year ago, Melinda retired, and Seth interviewed several potential replacements. Seth wanted to find someone who could assure him that the training benefited the firm and who could turn down a department head's request for training that had no positive return on investment. Of the candidates interviewed, Marty seemed different. Marty was an assistant vice president (AVP) of training in another industry. Marty explained to Seth that he could provide evidence of the value (or lack of value) of training and eliminate unwarranted training requests. Marty proposed to reposition the training department as a performance consulting department. Marty assured Seth that most of the department's work would be training, but Marty wanted to add consulting and analysis to the department's core competencies. If hired, Marty envisioned that his department would become a better business partner to the other departments by discovering and mitigating root problems rather than training requests that sometimes addressed symptoms but never met real needs. Seth agreed to hire Marty and provided funding to develop his existing trainers. In return, Marty would eliminate programs that didn't add value and manage the firm's operational budget more effectively.

During his first year, Marty met with the training teams and developed a shared vision for what the new department would look like. He then met with department heads and obtained their buy-in to the new concept or, at least, skeptically support his efforts. Marty also contracted with Jackie, Butch, and Hugh to train his employees as performance consultants. After certifying most of the employees, Jackie, Butch, Hugh, and Marty supported the senior managers and managers as they transitioned to their new roles.

While the transition of Marty's department was far from perfect, the department heads started to recognize the value and began to think of the senior managers and managers as trusted business partners.

As the first year progressed, Marty kept Seth informed of their progress and shared reports showing the value of their efforts. By the year-end, Marty shared with Seth and the department heads a return-on-investment report, providing evidence of how the new training department added value to the firm.

Summary: What to Do

Summary

For others to act, they need motivation and ability. While practicing *Communicating Like Agents* helps others want to act, practicing *Directing Like Guides* builds the abilities of others so that they can act. You can leverage SLII® to determine how best to help others build their abilities. Use techniques such as Vicarious Learning, Cognitive Apprenticeship,

	Directing Like Guides Practice
Characteristics	• Resist While *Communicating Like Agents* inspires others to act (motivation), *Directing Like Guides* enables others to act (ability). • At times, resistance to take the right action may appear due to a lack of motivation, but the root problem is due to the inability to act. Likewise, some may seem to lack ability to act, but the root problem is due to a lack of motivation. At other times, motivation and ability are interconnected in such a way that both are the cause of inaction. Thus, determining the motivation and ability of others is critical for determining how to help others act. • People's abilities and motivation can vary substantially. The challenge to help others to act is determining the best approach to take. In SLII®, if ability is low to some, then you should provide either directives or coaching. If ability is moderate to high, then you should provide either support or delegation.[a]
Principles, Guidelines, and Rules of Practice	**Related 21st Century Leadership Principles** • Put Others First • Give Up Control • Encourage Growth • Collaborate with Others
Models, Techniques, and Tools	**SL® II** • Development Level 1: If competence is low and commitment high, be directive. • Development Level 2: If competence is low to some and commitment low, coach. • Development Level 3: If competence is moderate to high and commitment variable, support. • Development Level 4: If competence is high and commitment high, delegate. *Cognitive Apprenticeship* A technique used to help others learn complex tasks in five phases: 1. Observation and articulation 2. Scaffolding 3. Fading 4. Self-directed Learning 5. Generalization *Bandura's Vicarious Learning* Instead of learning from direct experiences, people can learn vicariously by observing others perform procedures or experiencing something. *Grenny et al's Personal Ability* Personal ability is one of the Six Sources of Influence™ for influencing behaviors. Grenny et al advocate tactics such as Deliberate Practice, providing immediate feedback against a clear standard, and preparing for setbacks.[b]

[a] Blanchard et al., 2001, *The 3 Keys to Empowerment*, 23.
[b] Grenny et al., 2013, *Influencer*, 121, 128, 133.

Figure 9.1   Practice summary: Directing Like Guides.

and Grenny et al.'s Personal Ability techniques to build ability in others. Figure 9.1 summarizes this practice.

What to Do

Table 9.3 lists recommendations for applying this practice immediately, in the short term, and in the long term.

Table 9.3 Recommended Actions for Applying Directing Like Guides

Immediate
Adjust Your Approach for Helping Others Improve Their Abilities Explore the Ken Blanchard website for resources, including a summary of SLII®. (https://kenblanchard.com). Reflect on SLII® and the four approaches to helping others improve their abilities: directing, coaching, supporting, and delegating. Start assessing the person's development level and aligning your approach to best match their needs. ***Learn about Vicarious Learning and Cognitive Apprenticeship*** If you conduct a video search on Vicarious Learning and Cognitive Apprenticeship, several potential resources are available. Wikipedia has entries as well. If you are inclined, I discuss both topics in my dissertation as the concepts apply to family practice specialists learning specialty-interest areas.[a]
Short Term
Share with Others Share with others what you learn about *Directing Like Guides* practice. Helping others understand these practices builds buy-in and helps you learn the practice. ***Assessing Abilities*** In *Crucial Accountability*, read Patterson et al.'s discussion on assessing abilities and the interrelationship with motivation.[b] Determining the cause of inaction can be complicated and ambiguous. Patterson et al. explain this effectively. ***Learn More about SLII®*** Read about SLII® in *Helping People Win at Work* and *The 3 Keys to Empowerment*. You can find these in the Bibliography. ***Bandura's Vicarious Learning*** In *Influencer*, Grenny et al. write about Bandura's Vicarious Learning, which they entitle, *vicarious experience* or "the *in between* influence technique."[c] Their story of Bandura's usage of the technique illustrates the power of learning from secondhand experience and is worth reading.
Long Term
Study the Approaches for Helping Others Improve Ability Set a goal to improve how you align your approach to helping others improve their ability. Search for opportunities to improve using the techniques in this chapter and SLII® with coaching and support.

(Continued)

Table 9.3 (*Continued*) Recommended Actions for Applying Directing Like Guides

Using resources that might be available through your organization (such as the Corporate Executive Board), resources from your associations, or free resources (such as from Human Capital Institute and Training Magazine), search for recorded webinars that provide insights into coaching and supporting others.

[a] DePaul, 1998, *Alternative Types of Learning in Clinical Specialty-Interest Areas of Family Practice Medicine*, 18–22, 81–84, 89–91, 94–95, 123–126.
[b] Patterson et al., 2013, *Crucial Accountability*, 138–143.
[c] Grenny et al., 2013, *Influencer*, 99, 101.

Word of Caution

When using SLII® as a way to determine development levels, keep in mind that SLII® is intended to apply to a specific task and not as a way to generalize about a person's abilities. Labeling people as being a D1 or D4, for example, shifts the focus from behavior to character and can overgeneralize someone as incompetent ("Gisa is such a D1, we cannot trust her with anything.") or competent ("Just have Marc do that; he can do anything!"). This type of thinking may hold people labeled as D1 from developmental opportunities or overburden others labeled as D4 with more work than they can handle. Moreover, this characterizes people unfairly and causes resentment on their part.

Chapter 10

Practice 6: Nurturing Like Gardeners

When you add value to people, you lift them up, help them advance, make them a part of something bigger than themselves, and assist them in becoming who they were made to be.[1]

Maxwell

Introduction: Importance and Benefit of Nurturing Like Gardeners

While *Communicating Like Agents* is about influencing people to want to act, and *Directing Like Guides* is about enabling them to act, *Nurturing Like Gardeners* is about making it easier for others to act. If you want teams to produce consistently, reduce errors, and avoid being distracted from having to complete tedious tasks, then *Nurturing Like Gardeners* is for you.

You can learn a great deal about leadership by observing how gardeners work. Gardeners optimize the physical space of their gardens. They change the temperature and humidity using greenhouses, use specific mixtures of soil and nutrients, and manage the amount of water. They encourage certain insects to interact with their gardens and discourage other insects and visitors. They remove weeds, prevent them from interfering with growth, and monitor ways to enhance development. Like gardeners, leadership practitioners change the work environment to remove barriers and promote growth.

DOI: 10.4324/9781003273448-13

When environments are unattended and left on their own, they can cause harm. If you hire a toxic executive, the toxicity poisons the soil and changes how people treat one another for the worse. At a Fortune 100 company, a director told me that he didn't believe that one person could ruin a resilient culture. However, when the SVP hired a toxic executive, he discovered that one person could cause chaos and harm. As a result, some employees quit, others were restricted in their effectiveness, and, as Wiseman describes, several "became one of the walking dead that roam the halls of so many organizations. On the outside, these zombies go through the motions, but on the inside they have given up. They 'quit and stay.'"[2]

At the beginning of Chapter 4, I describe how environments can trigger unethical behaviors that go against our moral code. In a story, Goldsmith describes Karl, an executive with a dictatorial management style. Karl was "obsessive, strict and punitive." Some employees took unethical shortcuts because of the increased pressure and damaging changes to the workplace environment. When the truth came out, the employee behavior cost the company tens of millions in euros.[3] Goldsmith's concluding statement captures how one person's harmful practices caused employees to compromise their ethical standards (Box 10.1).

When it comes to gardening in an organization, Grenny et al. note that people aren't good at doing this (Box 10.2).

When gardens are observed, maintained, they flourish. Sometimes, simple corrections make the difference. Whether rearranging the layout of a restaurant to make stations align better with the work or providing accounting software that automates manual work, changing the environment can contribute to productivity, reduce stress, and improve engagement. Environmental changes can even reduce conflict and influence happiness.

In this chapter, I discuss the characteristics of *Nurturing Like Gardeners*. I reintroduce Grenny et al.'s Structural Ability tactics. I then present ways to make work easier by introducing performance-support solutions such

---

BOX 10.1   KARL'S BEHAVIOR HARMED THE GARDEN

Karl's defense was, "I never asked my people to do anything immoral or illegal." He didn't need to. The environment he created did the work for him.[4]

Goldsmith

> ## BOX 10.2 FAILURE TO RECOGNIZE PHYSICAL SPACE AS A SOURCE OF INFLUENCE
>
> Rarely does the average person conceive of changing the physical world as a way of changing human behavior. We see that others are misbehaving, and we look to change them, not the environment. Caught up in the human side of things, we completely miss the impact of subtle yet powerful sources such as the size of a room or the impact of a chair. Consequently, one of our most powerful sources of influence (our physical space) is often the least used because it's the least noticeable.[5]
>
> **Grenny et al.**

as procedures, templates, tools, and job aids. Next, I provide three leading examples and discuss using this practice.

Characteristics of Nurturing Like Gardeners

Nurturing Like Gardeners involves encouraging and caring for others by creating favorable environments for work and development. Like someone who cultivates a garden, you can provide resources to improve productivity. Resources can be in the form of changes to the physical space. Resources can also include tools, templates, and performance-support solutions to improve quality, promote consistency, save time, and cut costs. Standardizing how teams work together to support processes is another example.

Like gardeners removing weeds that compete for space and harm vegetation, you can remove barriers that interfere with productivity and distract from the work. You can accomplish this by changing the environment or how your team works with people who act like barriers (Box 10.3).

Grenny et al.'s Structural Ability Tactics

As I discussed in Chapter 7, Grenny et al. identify Six Sources of Influence™. One of these, Structural Ability, aligns with *Nurturing Like Gardeners*.

**BOX 10.3   CHARACTERISTICS OF
NURTURING LIKE GARDENERS**

■ *Nurturing Like Gardeners* involves improving the work environment by changing the physical space (or even the electronic virtual workspace) and things such as reconfiguring a room to promote interactions. Grenny et al. caution that people are ineffective at doing this and, quoting Fred Steele, most are "environmentally incompetent."[6] However, the authors note, "The more we watch for silent forces in the space around us, the better prepared we'll be to deal with them."[7]

■ Elements of work environments such as procedures, reporting structures, and the effect of distance often remain invisible; *Nurturing Like Gardeners* involves making the invisible visible.[8]

■ Changing the environment aligns with the Six Boxes® Model's Box 2, Tools and Resources.

■ What makes this practice more challenging is figuring out what to change in the environment; this isn't easy.[9] To improve, you need to cultivate your awareness, study what others do, and practice.

■ You can change the environment either to influence key behaviors or to remove barriers such as undesired key behaviors. For example, to decrease arguments about what to do next in a process, you can introduce documented standard and agreed-on procedures.

■ Make work easy. Introduce templates, tools, and performance aids that can automate tedious or error-prone work.

Table 10.1 provides examples of Structural Ability tactics that the authors recommend using to influence behaviors by changing the environment.

Make It Easy: Handshaw and Performance-Support Solutions

Changing the environment's structure is one way to make it easy for others to perform. Another way is to use performance-support solutions. According to Handshaw, performance support is a mechanism to transfer learning to on-the-job performance.[10] Performance-support solutions include templates,

Table 10.1   Example Structural Ability Tactics

Tactic	Explanation
Change the space	Grenny et al. note: "Distance keeps people from routinely interacting…and often leads to animosity and loss of influence."[a] Changing the space to make it so people have to encounter other people is one solution to influence interactions and decrease animosity.
Make the invisible visible	Provide visual cues for the behaviors that you want to influence.[b] Common examples include labeling doors as enter or exit only, street signs, warning labels, fill lines on liquid containers, and fire exit maps.
Use data to tell a new story	Use data to tell a story about "visible, timely, and accurate information" that others may be unaware of that can provide a new perspective.[c]
Make it unavoidable[d]	Change the space to make the right behaviors easier and the wrong behaviors harder, such as adding safety features to prevent injury, like a grill to prevent anyone from sticking a finger in a fan blade.[e] Another example is mandated checklists such as aviation pre-flight safety operations required by the Federal Aviation Administration (FAA).[f]

[a] Grenny et al., 2013, *Influencer*, 270.
[b] Ibid., 256.
[c] Ibid., 262, 265.
[d] Ibid., 282–283.
[e] Ibid., 276, 283.
[f] Ibid., 283.

job aids, documented standard procedures, applications such as financial systems, and mobile applications used with smartphones.

Unfortunately, some resist performance support, especially job aids. In our arrogance, we believe that simple lists are unnecessary. We go to the grocery store to buy four items but forget one of them. We complete a pre-flight procedure from memory but forgot a crucial step that endangers passengers. Doctors are offended by simple checklists that save lives. In doing so, a doctor makes a mistake, skips a step, and causes a Staphylococcus infection. Goldsmith summarizes how ego (how our brains work) (Box 10.4).

At times, this type of solution can even solve problems without the need for more training.[11] Make it easy, for example, by creating a list of codes with explanations that you can access electronically rather than the old way of

---

BOX 10.4   RESISTING PERFORMANCE SUPPORT CHECKLISTS

One of our most dysfunctional beliefs is our contempt for simplicity and structure. We believe that we are above needing structure to help us on seemingly simple tasks.[12]

In the same way that surgeons reject the simple proven structure of a checklist for washing their hands, many executives are too proud to admit they need structure. They consider repetitious activity as mundane, uncreative, somehow beneath them.[13]

Goldsmith

---

memorizing the most common ones. Want teammates to avoid mathematical errors? Create a spreadsheet template that calculates for you. Do people forget how to write a particular report because of infrequent use? Create a template with built-in instructions along with some sample reports to use as models. Handshaw's point is that we can make performance easier with the proper support solutions, and making performance-support solutions available is a way to take care of your people. Marquet writes about this (Box 10.5).

Leading Examples

Individual Contributor Leading Example: Using Job Aids for Performance Support

Tracey, a Military Equal Opportunity (EO) Specialist, had problems executing the complaint investigation process. Specifically, she had issues remembering

---

BOX 10.5   HELPING OTHERS WITH PERFORMANCE SUPPORT

Taking care of your people does not mean protecting them from the consequences of their own behavior. That's the path to irresponsibility. What it does mean is giving them every available tool and advantage to achieve their aims in life, beyond the specifics of the job.[14]

Marquet

---

the proper steps of the complicated process. Earlier that year, Aaron, another EO Specialist, had the same challenge and had recently created a set of job aids to help him visualize the entire investigation process by using tables and figures to illustrate:

■ Required steps and descriptions.
■ Required time spent on each step.
■ Support contacts' telephone numbers and locations when needed for referrals.

Aaron shared his job aids with Tracey to see if the documents could help. Aaron worked in the same office as Tracey, and Aaron provided support and feedback to Tracey when she met with customers.

Aaron found that the job aids helped in a couple of ways. First, Tracey leveraged them to successfully resolve five cases in eight months and provided expert guidance to several military members. Second, Aaron found that the job aids helped employees learn about the process. They could use the job aids to make rational decisions about complaints by learning the differences between formal and informal complaint investigation processes.

Aaron shared the job aids with other specialists, and the documents became a standard for supporting the EO specialist role.

Manager Leading Example: Establishing Department Standards

Andre recently started working for a Fortune 500 company in a project management office (PMO) as a manager of project managers. The department includes 20 project managers, support staff, two other managers, and a director. One substantial difference between Andre's previous company and this one is that his new company's PMO didn't define their standards. The PMO informally approximated the standards in the Project Management Institute's (PMI) book of knowledge (commonly known as PMBOK). Still, they didn't have a documented process or shared templates and tools.[15] Andre also noticed that the other project managers tended to use similar project management software but varied greatly in their use of templates (or didn't use templates at all); some skipped specific PMI standards, and success varied depending on the project manager in charge of the project.

Andre discussed his concerns with Kendra and Rick, the other PMO managers. They agreed that this was a problem and wanted to address it but hadn't due to their workload. With Andre willing to help, the three managers obtained permission from Philip, the Director, to collaborate with project managers to define their standards and create templates.

The newly formed standards team met with the project managers and defined their standard process, discussed how to modify the process to meet the needs of smaller projects, and identified standard templates needed to support the process. Using a central database filing structure, the team collected templates from project managers and created new templates branded with the company's logo. They then partnered with some of the PMO's internal customers to obtain their buy-in and agreement to support the new process and standards.

After publishing the standards and confirming that the project managers were committed to using the new templates, the PMO managers communicated to their customers that they would officially begin using the new process.

After about nine months, Philip met with the department and shared how successful the PMO operated with the new standards. Philip read a few emails from customers and then expressed his appreciation for how much work everyone had put into changing their operation. Several project managers thanked Andre, Kendra, and Rick for making their jobs easier and more enjoyable.

The PMO continued with the standards team and rotated members annually. The team updated and refined standards as the business changed and coached new PMO employees.

Executive Leading Example: Making Managers More Accessible by Changing the Space

Angel, a general manager at a mid-sized US company, found one result from the last employee opinion survey troubling: Employees perceived management to be inaccessible, especially upper-level managers. Angel knew that employees weren't exactly lining up to talk with people in management, but she noticed that her directors and managers tended to be in their offices with their doors closed. Often, they would be meeting with people, but Angel observed that they tended to keep their doors closed or partially closed.

Angel found that the offices were a barrier and wanted to do more than enforce an open-door policy or talk with directors and managers about being more available, which she didn't think would help. Angel presented the problem to her direct reports and asked what they thought. Her direct reports acknowledged that this was a problem and that the employee survey confirmed that employees perceived this as a problem. Roy, the Vice President (VP) of Sales, jokingly suggested that the Maintenance Department remove the doors to always be open. Angel appreciated the thought, but Kathleen, the VP of Operations, believed Roy was on to something. From the employee survey, several people complained that the company didn't have enough meeting space. Kathleen suggested moving the directors and managers from their offices to large cubicles in the middle of their departments and teams. Directors and managers would have to walk past employees to get to their desks and most likely would interact with employees. With the rooms empty, maintenance could convert the offices to meeting rooms, set some aside for reservations and others for impromptu meetings for anyone to use when discussing sensitive matters such as human resources (HR)-related conversations.

Over the next couple of weeks, Angel met with groups of directors and managers to discuss the potential change, get their reaction, and find out if they could improve the change. To Angel's surprise, most of her management team were receptive to the idea, and others became more open to the plan when they found out that they would have some rooms available for HR-related and short meetings. Angel also talked with employees who were likewise receptive to the change.

As part of the change, Angel arranged for maintenance to set up cubicles in the different buildings for her to use. While not asking her direct reports to move out of their offices, Angel planned to work occasionally from a cubicle in one of the buildings.

After maintenance had completed the conversion, Angel received positive employee comments. Some of the managers thanked her; they had felt distant from the teams they managed. Relocating closer to them made a difference. Privacy didn't become an issue, and morale improved.

Summary: What to Do

Summary

Nurturing Like Gardeners involves encouraging and caring for others by creating favorable environments for work and development. Like someone who cultivates a garden, you can provide resources to improve productivity. This includes changing the space or providing performance-support solutions. Figure 10.1 provides a summary of this practice.

	Nurturing Like Gardeners Practice
Characteristics	• *Nurturing Like Gardeners* involves improving the work environment by changing the physical space (or even electronic virtual work space) and things such as reconfiguring a room to promote interactions. Grenny et al caution that people are ineffective at doing this and, quoting Fred Steele, most are "environmentally incompetent."[a] However, the authors note, "The more we watch for silent forces in the space around us, the better prepared we'll be to deal with them."[b] • Elements of work environments such as procedures, reporting structures, and the effect of distance often remain invisible; *Nurturing Like Gardeners* involves making the invisible visible.[c] • Changing the environment aligns with the Six Boxes® Model in Box 2: Tools and Resources. • What makes this practice more challenging is figuring out what to change in the environment; this isn't easy.[d] To improve, you need to cultivate your awareness, study what others do, and practice. • You can change the environment either to influence key behaviors or to remove barriers such as undesired key behaviors. For example, to decrease arguments about what to do next, you can introduce documented standard and agreed upon procedures. • Make work easy. Introduce templates, tools, and performance aids that can automate tedious or error-prone work.
Principles, Guidelines, and Rules of Practice	**Related 21st Century Leadership Principles** • Believe in Others • Put Others First • Encourage Growth • Collaborate with Others
Models, Techniques, and Tools	**Grenny et al and Structural Ability Tactics** • Change the space. • Make the invisible visible. • Use data to tell a new story. • Make it unavoidable so that the right behaviors are easier and wrong ones harder. **Handshaw and Performance Support Solutions** Use this to transfer learning to on-the-job performance. Types of performance support solutions include the following: • Templates • Job aids • Documented standard procedures • Applications • Mobile aps

[a] Grenny et al., 2013, *Influencer*, 250.
[b] Ibid., 254.
[c] Ibid., 253, 256.
[d] Ibid., 254.

Figure 10.1   Practice summary: Nurturing Like Gardeners.

What to Do

Table 10.2 lists recommendations for applying this practice immediately, in the short term, and in the long term.

Table 10.2   Recommended Actions for Applying Nurturing Like Gardeners[a]

Immediate
Search for Opportunities to Make Work Easier Observe your physical space for potential improvements. This includes how you and your team use virtual space such as shared network drives. Examine existing standards and potential performance support. Discuss with your immediate manager and peers opportunities for improving the environment and ways to make work easier.
Short Term
Share with Others Share with others what you learn about the *Nurturing Like Gardeners* practice. Helping others understand these practices builds buy-in and helps you learn the practice. ***Read More about Structural Ability and Performance Support*** In *Influencer*, read the Structural Ability examples. In *Training that Delivers Results*, read about Handshaw's approach to leveraging performance supports that can complement training or eliminate the need for formal training. In *The Idea-Driven Organization*, in Chapter 3, read the topic entitled, *Creating. Horizontal Linkages*, for Robinson and Schroeder's structural solution ideas.[a]
Long Term
Research More about Structural Ability and Performance Support Using online resources such as academic databases or services such as Books24x7 or LinkedIn Learning, learn more about becoming more environmentally competent. If your organization subscribes to consulting services such as the Corporate Executive Board or Josh Bersin Academy, contact them to help you find best practices in areas such as space management and developing performance-support solutions.

[a] Robinson and Schroeder, 2014, *The Idea-Driven Organization*, 47–67.

Word of Caution

As Grenny et al. explain, when people don't behave the way you want, the tendency is to change the person rather than the environment. Focusing on others' motivation and abilities can be more costly and less sustainable than changing the environment so that the right behaviors are easier than the wrong ones. From the Six Boxes® Model perspective, focus on the boxes in the order of the model. Note that Box 2, Tools and Resources, appears before Consequences and Incentives, Skills and Knowledge (Ability), and even Motives and Preferences (Motivation).

ADDING VALUE

> Like treasures waiting to be discovered, people will teach us all
> kinds of things that make life exciting.[1]
>
> **Freiberg and Freiberg**

In Section III, the last three practices involve adding value through self-discovery, finding resources for your team and organization, and helping others develop. Section IV practices are about adding value from a development perspective. *Facing the Unknown Like Lions* involves listening critically in a meaningful way to improve how you practice leadership and build relationships. *Developing Like Scouts* encompasses searching externally for ideas and talent that can excel your team and organization to work more effectively toward your team's and organization's goals. *Communicating Like Broadcasters* is about stewardship: Sharing your knowledge and skills that you apply successfully to benefit your team, organization, local community, and global community.

Although these chapters are short and the concepts are simple, few practice them regularly or effectively. Those who fail to apply these three practices exhibit one or more of the following:

- Fail to listen to others seriously and critically.
- Shy away from any constructive feedback.
- Downplay or deny their mistakes and fail to learn from mistakes.
- Avoid learning how their behavior negatively affects those around them.
- Don't look externally for better ways to achieve goals.
- Build external networks passively.

DOI: 10.4324/9781003273448-14

- Don't search for talented consultants, contractors, freelancers, and prospective unless directed to do so.
- Don't share their expertise and professional insights with their team, peers, organization, local community, or global community.

If taken seriously, these three practices can enable you to avoid the bad habits listed in this bulleted list and can improve your leadership and relationships substantially. Moreover, they enable teams to achieve their goals. In other words, these practices can provide a return on investment, enabling you and others to work smarter, safer, and efficiently.

Chapter 11

Practice 7: Facing the Unknown Like Lions

I vowed to treat every encounter with every person on the ship as the most important thing at that moment.[1]

Abrashoff

You can't learn very much if you're unwilling to find out more about the impact of your behavior on the performance of those around you.[2]

Kouzes and Posner

When people commit to getting better, they are doing something difficult and heroic.[3]

Goldsmith

Introduction: Importance and Benefits of Facing the Unknown Like Lions

Want to build on how you practice your leadership so that you are more effective and make better moral choices? Want to build your relationships in ways that you cannot even imagine? If so, then *Facing the Unknown Like Lions* is for you. Facing the unknown involves listening and feedback. As Freiberg and Freiberg write, "Listening is powerful because it shows a genuine desire

DOI: 10.4324/9781003273448-15

to understand the unique needs and feelings of others."[4] Feedback is a type of listening that enables you to improve how you practice leadership.

There is a catch, though: You have to be motivated and dedicated to listening and obtaining feedback. This isn't easy for two reasons. First, people don't want to sacrifice their ego and hear from others how they lack motivation, commitment, or ability related to leadership, especially when the feedback comes from direct reports or peers.

At one Fortune 100 organization, some of the company's officers refused to allow the Human Resources (HR) Department to start a 360° feedback program. People who practice leadership, particularly traditional leadership, don't want to face the unknown. They don't want to discover that people think less about their leadership capabilities or find flaws in their behaviors. They have difficulty getting past the opinions and perceiving them as opportunities to improve their leadership practices.

The second reason is that people lack the ability and mechanisms to request genuine feedback, listen critically to feedback, and process feedback. Like leadership and most soft skills, educational institutions typically ignore or teach people to manage feedback poorly.

Here is the good news: You can learn to manage feedback effectively and listen critically. By obtaining some process knowledge and incorporating some practice, you can position yourself to receive, accept, and internalize feedback for future improvement. Over time, listening and receiving feedback becomes easier. Moreover, as you practice this, people who work with you will be more open to you, take you more seriously, and respect you more—all because you demonstrate your desire to do the right thing and better yourself. This leads to better relationships, better work environments, and newly developed levels of trust.

In this chapter, I discuss the characteristics of *Facing the Unknown Like Lions*. I explain what serious listening means and describe Grave's Five Levels of Listening. Next, I describe obtaining feedback, Goldsmith's feedforward technique, Kouzes and Posner's advice on feedback, and 360° feedback. Finally, I provide leading examples and discuss using this practice.

Characteristics of Facing the Unknown Like Lions

Fixing a car is much easier than practicing leadership. With a broken car, a mechanic receives feedback on how well the car works after fixing it. If the car doesn't run after a fix, the mechanic knows to diagnose the problem and try another solution until the car runs. Leadership is different. From the perspective of your role, achieving performance goals or helping teammates achieve performance goals isn't an accurate indicator that you practice leadership effectively. Achieving performance goals and getting others to achieve performance goals isn't what leadership is designed to achieve. Instead, leadership is about building character (or maturing mental and moral qualities, capabilities, and behaviors) by applying the nine leadership practices to your role's processes. Because you can't rely on achievements, you need another mechanism for feedback.

To collect feedback, especially for the first time, you need to be like lions. *Lions* represent bravery and strength. You need to be willing to sacrifice your ego and acknowledge that while you have the best intentions, you more than likely need to continuously improve your own commitment and abilities.

Acting like lions has another meaning: Someone who is a lion is highly influential.[5] By facing the unknown, you further build your influence by modeling the courage and dedication to improve continuously, even at the expense of your ego and hurt feelings (such as when you discover that your good-intentioned behaviors caused unintended harm). As Kouzes and Posner note, seeking feedback is how you show others a way to improve yourself (Box 11.1).

Serious listening and receiving feedback are learned skills and the means to *Facing the Unknown Like Lions*. By learning this practice, you can accelerate your leadership development while improving team safety and relationships (Box 11.2).

Serious Listening

Why Listening Is Undervalued, Underrated, and Challenging

Kouzes and Posner proclaim that those who practice extraordinary leadership are great listeners.[6] Yet, listening isn't easy, and most people aren't effective listeners but believe that they are, as Goldsmith explains (Box 11.3).

BOX 11.1   SEEKING FEEDBACK

Seeking feedback makes a powerful statement about the value of self-improvement and how everyone can be even better than he or she is today.[7]

Kouzes and Posner

BOX 11.2 CHARACTERISTICS OF FACING THE UNKNOWN LIKE LIONS

■ The way to accelerate developing 21st Century Leadership practices is through seeking feedback on how well you practice leadership.

■ Serious listening and 360° feedback are two mechanisms for improving your leadership practices. You need to develop listening and receiving feedback deliberately and with extensive practice.

■ Serious listening means to
  – Shut down internal thinking.
  – Focus intentionally on what the other person is conveying.
  – Attempt to perceive as the other person does.

To do so, you must ask clarifying questions and request examples.

■ Whether from serious listening or 360° feedback, acting on what you learn not only contributes to your development but also gives you a way to respect others.

■ 360° feedback is a way to obtain feedback and encourage honest feedback because of the anonymity of the process.

■ 360° feedback involves summarizing and sharing the results, selecting one to two specific objectives for leadership development, and asking those whom you work with to support you in achieving your objectives.

These are probably the same people who believe that there is nothing insightful with the *Facing the Unknown Like Lions* practice—"nothing new here and just the same old stuff that others have discussed!" Moreover, I have worked with several professionals at all levels of an organization who advocate listening but prefer talking to listening. Abrashoff explains this preference to talking this way: "Like most organizations, the Navy seemed to put managers in a transmitting mode, which minimized their receptivity."[8]

Goldsmith explains that listening is simple but not easy.[9] He writes, "If you [listen], everything will get better. So much of our interpersonal problems at work are formulaic." We easily slip into behavioral patterns that create friction just as easily as slipping into "behavioral patterns that don't create friction. That's why simple disciplines—such as thinking before speaking, listening with respect, and asking, 'Is it worth it?—work. They don't require nuance. We just need to do them."[10]

BOX 11.3   INEFFECTIVE VS GOOD LISTENING

80 percent of our success in learning from other people is based upon how well we listen...The thing about listening that escapes most people is that they think of it as a passive activity. You don't have to do anything. You sit there like a lump and hear someone out. Not true. Good listeners regard what they do as a highly active process—with every muscle engaged, especially the brain. Basically, there are three things that all good listeners do: They think before they speak; they listen with respect; and they're always gauging their response by asking themselves, "Is it worth it?"[11]

Goldsmith

Why is listening, a skill that seems so simple, so difficult? The root problem isn't that people don't want to listen—they may have the best intentions to do so. Jennings writes that the root problem may have more to do with how our brains comprehend the conversation (Box 11.4).

To overcome the 135 words/minute and 400% faster comprehension that Jennings describes, we need to deliberately focus our attention and engage with the person speaking. Goldsmith describes a U.S. President (doesn't matter which one)[12] who mastered engaging with speakers (Box 11.5).

BOX 11.4   WHY YOU LOSE FOCUS WHEN LISTENING

The average speaker talks at a rate of 135 words a minute. But the average listener comprehends at a rate 400 percent faster. This means that when you are listening, your mind unavoidably races ahead of the speaker. You can't help but think other thoughts and sandwich in random observations as the speaker is telling you what she wants, thinks, or is concerned about. Your focus slips enough to routinely miss critical signals (an implication, a look of anxiety, or something subtle that changes the meaning of the word just spoken). That loss of focus causes you to ask the wrong questions at the wrong time and reach the wrong conclusions, making the dialog a lot less productive for you and irritating for the speaker.[13]

Jennings

BOX 11.5 HOW A U.S. PRESIDENT ENGAGED WITH LISTENING

It didn't matter if you were a head of state or a bell clerk, when you were talking with [the President] he acted as if you were the only person in the room. Every fiber of his being, from his eyes to his body language, communicated that he was locked into what you were saying. He conveyed how important you were, not how important *he* was.

If you don't think [listening] is an active practically aerobic piece of mental and muscular exertion, try it sometime in a receiving line of 500 people, all of whom regard this brief transaction with you as part of their lifetime highlight reel.

If you've never done it, listening with respect makes you sweat.[14]

Goldsmith

What you need are techniques to refine how you listen and process information. I call the collection of listening techniques, Serious Listening. These techniques stem from active listening, and Hunter describes active listening as a discipline (Box 11.6).

Active listening is an excellent start to Serious Listening, but Serious Listening involves more than just active listening. Table 11.1 summarizes the Serious Listening techniques. Note that some are the same as Kouzes and Posner's advice on obtaining feedback, which I will summarize later in this chapter.

BOX 11.6 THE DISCIPLINE OF ACTIVE LISTENING

Active listening requires a disciplined effort to silence all that internal conversation while we're attempting to listen to another human being. It requires a sacrifice, an extension of ourselves, to block out the noise and truly enter another person's world…Active listening is attempting to see things as the speaker sees them and attempting to feel things as the speaker feels them.[15]

Hunter

Table 11.1   Summary of the Serious Listening Techniques

No.	Technique	Description
1	Preparation	Before a dialogue or at the beginning of one, consciously remind yourself that you intend to fully practice Serious Listening and self-evaluate afterward.
2	Purpose	Listen for the other person's purpose. People seldom start by explaining this.
3	Seek clarity	Ask questions and ask for examples to clarify the other person's meaning. This could involve having the other person explain acronyms, concepts, or summations. For example, when Jack stated that the staff meeting was helpful, have Jack explain what helpful means in this context; have Jack clarify behaviors so you can understand how he arrived at the conclusion that the staff meeting was helpful. Paraphrase and summarize to confirm that you understand. This helps ensure that you pay attention, enabling the other person to correct and confirm.
4	Observe the nonverbal behaviors	If in person, carefully watch facial expressions and posturing as indicators of emotions, expressions of openness, or signs of defensiveness.
5	Attend to your nonverbal behaviors	Be aware of your own nonverbal behavior. Monitor what you are communicating with your posturing.
6	After comprehending the message, contribute and confirm	After clarifying what the other person is conveying, shift the dialogue to your perspective. As you express your thoughts and feelings, verify that the other person understands what you are communicating. You can accomplish this by asking clarifying questions.
7	Summarize	Summarize the conversations and any tasks you asked for or agreed to do. Summarizing can occur at the end of a conversation and as a follow-up such as in an email. This helps to ensure mutual expectations. Blanchard writes, "…as Stephen Covey says, 'Nearly all conflict comes from differences in expectations.'"[a]

(Continued)

Table 11.1 (*Continued*) **Summary of the Serious Listening Techniques**

No.	Technique	Description
8	Express thanks	Because you value communication, express your appreciation for the other person's time and willingness to convey their thoughts and feelings. This reinforces your belief in how valuable others are to you.
9	Assess how you performed	Reflect on the communication in terms of how well you performed the following: • Understood the dialogue's purpose • Obtained clarity • Observed the other person's and your nonverbal behaviors • Contributed your thoughts and feelings • Confirmed the other person's understanding of your thoughts and feelings • Summarized • Expressed thanks

[a] Blanchard and Ridge, 2009, *Helping People Win at Work*, 24.

Graves' Five Levels of Listening

You need to be aware of the type of listening you do, and Graves describes his Five Levels of Listening with the lowest level called *Pretending* and the highest level called *Empathic*. Table 11.2 summarizes Graves' Five Levels of Listening.[16] Evolved from Covey's Listening Continuum, Graves has refined his Five Levels of Listening to help professionals improve their abilities to connect and collaborate with others.[17]

To develop your listening, refer to the *What to Do* topic at the end of this chapter.

Miscommunication

Too frequently, we think we communicated our messages effectively but later discover we didn't. Misunderstandings occur in too many conversations. In *VisuaLeadership*, Cherches shares six tips to avoid miscommunication. Here's the abbreviated version:[18]

1. People are not mind readers. When people communicate ambiguously, seek clarification. Inquire, and avoid misinterpretations.

Table 11.2 Graves' Five Levels of Listening

Level	Title	Description of Listeners' Actions
1	Pretend	Listeners want to give the speaker the impression that they are listening, but they are not interested in what the speaker wants to communicate. This patronizing practice is often used to minimize conversing with the speaker.
2	Selective	Whether practicing this consciously or unconsciously, listeners filter what they hear. They filter from the conversation what they don't want to hear and focus only on what interests them. Filters may be based on listeners' backgrounds, worldviews, values, and interests.
3	Passive	When engaged in a conversation, listeners mentally prepare a response to what they hear. They are more focused on impressing the speaker with a response than being impressed by what the speaker wants to communicate. By doing so, listeners miss the intent and may not fully understand the meaning behind what the speaker is conveying. Thus, listeners who are more interested in what they want to say wait for an opening to interject and even interrupt the speaker.
4	Attentive	Listeners focus on what the speaker says and hear the words, but listeners do so from their own viewpoint and perspective. Listeners may be affected emotionally by the speaker's words, but these emotions are from the listeners' perspective and may or may not reflect what the speaker is feeling. By not focusing on the communication from the speaker's perspective, listeners may miss a significant meaning and message.
5	Empathic	Many people listen effectively from their viewpoint but never develop the ability to listen with empathy. To achieve Level 5, listeners need to adopt an entirely new mindset. At this level, listeners use attentive listening but view the conversation from the speaker's perspective. Empathic listeners can empathize with what the speaker says and feels. If a speaker relates a life experience, listeners can put themselves in the speaker's place and not just hear what the speaker is saying, but imagine what the speaker experienced and feel what the speaker is feeling.

Source: Adapted from Graves, R., *Creating Space for Performance Improvement.* Copyright 2014 Ronald Graves. With permission.

2. Validate understanding. As stated in Chapter 2 (Box 2.1), when someone advocates a belief, inquire to ensure understanding.
3. Read between the lines. Cherches described it best. He writes, "Peter Drucker said that the most important part of communication is to hear what isn't being said."[19]
4. It's not just your words—but your tone of voice and body language.
5. Use visuals, nonverbal cues, analogies, and metaphors to get your ideas across.
6. Be careful with jargon and acronyms.

Complementing these tips are Cherches eight tips to become a better listener. The first letter of the eight spell LISTENUP![20] Here's the abbreviated version:

1. **Look at the person.** "Make eye contact. Pay attention to facial expressions, body language and tone."[21]
2. **Inquire.** "Ask questions. Ask follow-up questions. Delve deeper."[22]
3. **Show that you're interested.** Revisit Goldsmith's President story (Box 11.5).
4. **Treat the person with respect.**
5. **Encourage the other person.** "Create an environment of dialogue, exchange, interaction, openness, honesty, self-disclosure, vulnerability, and trust."[23]
6. **Never make someone regret that they opened up to you.**
7. **Understanding is your primary objective.**
8. **Put your smartphone down.**

Obtaining Feedback

You cannot develop leadership practices effectively without feedback. Feedback is the gateway to discovering the depth of blind spots of how you behave and think. With more than 150 biases,[24] misguided assumptions, and faulty beliefs, you need an outsider's perspective to reflect what you cannot perceive.

Informal feedback is the simplest. Ask someone for feedback. If concerned about filtered feedback, have a professional administer a 360° feedback survey. If that isn't available, try feedforward.

BOX 11.7 KOUZES AND POSNER ON RECEIVING FEEDBACK

1. **Resist defending or justifying your behaviors.** The intent is to understand how others interpret your behavior and not to correct their perception.
2. **Focus on listening to understand the other person's perspective.** Understanding how others interpret your behavior can provide insight into how you can clarify your behavior's intentions.
3. **Attend to your nonverbal behavior and remain as relaxed as possible.** You may not voice defensiveness, but your body might. For example, avoid folding your arms.
4. **Listen and don't judge.** Judging the value of the feedback could be another way to be defensive and avoid accountability.
5. **Ask questions to clarify.** If they use labels, such as saying that your attitude is abrupt, find out what they mean by *abrupt*.
6. **Ask for examples.** Focus on specific instances in which you can identify particular behaviors.
7. **Thank the other person for the feedback.** You want others to feel safe in giving feedback and in trusting you. Feedback can be as tough to give as it is to receive.[25]

Kouzes and Posner on Receiving Feedback

Kouzes and Posner write extensively about listening and receiving feedback. Not only is *listening deeply* important for discovering what is important and what motivates others, but listening is also a powerful mechanism that enables you to act as their agent.[26] Moreover, listening is critical for using feedback to improve.

Asking for feedback signals your openness for wanting to improve. When receiving feedback about your leadership performance, Kouzes and Posner advise us what to do (Box 11.7).

Goldsmith's Feedforward Technique

Feedback is reflecting on past behaviors, and feedforward is considering future possibilities. Goldsmith's feedforward is a positive technique for learning how to improve (Box 11.8). As Goldsmith notes, many people don't

---

BOX 11.8   11 REASONS FEEDFORWARD IS POSITIVE

1. We can change the future. We can't change the past.
2. It can be more productive to help people learn to be "right," than prove they were "wrong."
3. Feedforward is especially suited to successful people.
4. Feedforward can come from anyone who knows about the task. It does not require personal experience with the individual.
5. People do not take feedforward as personally as feedback.
6. Feedback can reinforce personal stereotyping and negative self-fulfilling prophecies.
7. Face it! Most of us hate getting negative feedback, and we don't like to give it.
8. Feedforward can cover almost all the same "material" as feedback.
9. Feedforward tends to be much faster and more efficient than feedback.
10. Feedforward can be a useful tool to apply with managers, peers, and team members.
11. People tend to listen more attentively to feedforward than feedback.[27]

Goldsmith

---

like to hear negative feedback, but they love getting ideas for improving future behavior. Thus, people are less likely to interpret feedforward as criticism as with feedback.[28]

Goldsmith describes nine feedforward steps (Box 11.9).

Using 360° Feedback

360° feedback is a powerful and safe way to give and receive feedback. According to Heathfield, 360° is a metaphor: Feedback is solicited and given from all directions and levels of the organization.[29] To determine how well you practice leadership, you would solicit feedback from peers, direct reports, superiors, customers and clients, teammates, and anyone else who has had the opportunity to observe you practice leadership.

Anyone who practices leadership can implement a 360° feedback. The challenge is getting others to agree to the feedback and submitting the information anonymously. At one organization, I used the company's Microsoft SharePoint site to administer my own 360° feedback and help a

BOX 11.9   FEEDFORWARD STEPS

1. Pick one behavior that they would like to change. Change in this behavior should make a significant, positive difference in their lives.
2. Describe this behavior to randomly selected fellow participants. This is done in one-on-one dialogues. It can be done quite simply, such as, "I want to be a better listener."
3. Ask for feedforward—for two suggestions for the future that might help them achieve a positive change in their selected behavior. If participants have worked together in the past, they are not allowed to give ANY feedback about the past. They are only allowed to give ideas for the future.
4. Listen attentively to the suggestions and take notes. Participants are not allowed to comment on the suggestions in any way. They are not allowed to critique the suggestions or even to make positive judgmental statements, such as, "That's a good idea."
5. Thank the other participants for their suggestions.
6. Ask the other persons what they would like to change.
7. Provide feedforward—two suggestions aimed at helping the other person change.
8. Say, "You are welcome." when thanked for the suggestions. The entire process of both giving and receiving feedforward usually takes about two minutes.
9. Find another participant and keep repeating the process until the exercise is stopped.[30]

Goldsmith

colleague do so. Alternatively, you may ask someone you trust to collect and compile feedback for you.

In Appendix V, I provide a 360° feedback diagnostic tool that you can use to conduct your own 360° feedback. Note, though, I have not tested the tool for reliability or validity. The tool includes 27 items that represent the nine practices in this book.

Word of Caution

360° feedback programs need to be administered by experts who know how to share the results with recipients. If administered correctly, the

---

BOX 11.10   IMPORTANCE OF GIVING FEEDBACK

"My manager gives me way too much feedback!" said by no employee ever. No matter how much feedback a manager gives, it often feels, to many people, that it's not enough. Leaders need to be aware that in the absence of feedback, it is human nature to fill that void of silence with negativity. So, one of a leader's most important responsibilities— and privileges—is to set their people up for success by letting them know how they are doing and how they can do better.[31]

Cherches

---

feedback can lead to successful behaviors. However, some research has had mixed results.[32] One issue that NoWack and Mashihi identified is variance in how people interpret rating scales. For example, NoWack found that supervisors rate more on performance-related behaviors and direct reports focus more on interpersonal and relationship behaviors.[33]

Giving Feedback

In addition to obtaining feedback, practicing leadership includes giving feedback. Managers are particularly bad at giving feedback because the feedback tends to be infrequent. As noted in Chapter 5, Rummler observed that feedback is a crucial element of the Human Performance System (Figure 5.2). Cherches clarifies why giving feedback is crucial (Box 11.10).

Leading Examples

Individual Contributor Leading Example: Hunter's Leadership Assessment

Recently, Mallori read Hunter's *The World's Most Powerful Leadership Principle*.[34] In an appendix, Mallori found Hunter's Leadership Skills Inventory: 25 items and two open-ended questions designed to help readers assess their strengths and areas for improvement in practicing servant leadership. Mallori decided to use the tool to collect 360° feedback.

Using Survey Monkey, Mallori created a survey by copying the assessment items. She then emailed 20 people in her organization, asking them to complete the survey by the end of the month. In the email, she explained that she had read Hunter's book and wanted to identify her strengths and areas for improvement. Mallori clarified that she had designed the survey to maintain everyone's anonymity, but she would welcome a conversation if anyone would be open to discussing her leadership development. Mallori also acknowledged that she didn't manage anyone but asked people to think of leadership more broadly.

By the end of the month, Mallori had received 15 responses. From the results, she found that most responded the same with one occasional outlier. What stood out was Mallori's ability to listen and be supportive with peers. She also learned that some perceived that she had a negative attitude about the executives and directors within the department and that sometimes Mallori didn't hold people accountable. Some comments about her strengths were flattering, but Mallori felt hurt by some open comments. This was the first time that Mallori had received such open feedback, and she wasn't fully prepared for the comments. After some time, Mallori realized that people were sincere in trying to help her to accomplish her goal, and Mallori became more objective about the results.

A few people who completed the survey confirmed Mallori's belief that survey respondents sincerely wanted to help rather than write hurtful comments. After completing the survey, four of Mallori's colleagues met with her to discuss their feedback. They expressed how impressed they were that Mallori would allow herself to be open to feedback and clarified what they thought about her leadership approach. They also offered their support as Mallori tried to improve, and one asked Mallori to help him conduct his own 360° feedback later in the year.

Manager Leading Example: Identifying Annual Leadership Objectives Using 360° Feedback

As with Mallori, Joanna, a manager, used Hunter's Leadership Skills Inventory to conduct a 360° feedback.[35] Because Joanna only has three direct reports, she wanted to conduct a 360° feedback and use the results to identify some objectives for her annual performance plan.

After summarizing the results, Joanna identified three leadership-related objectives for her annual performance plan:

1. In the morning and when in the office, begin by talking with direct reports and team leads. Ask about them, how they are doing with projects and tasks, and how to help.

2. When mistakes or problems occur, notify those involved to (1) Clarify the mistake or problem, (2) Collaborate on how to resolve it, (3) and Determine how to learn from it.

3. During one-on-one weekly meetings with direct reports, use Blanchard's Situational Leadership® II to assess the direct report's development level with completing specific tasks and what leadership approach to use.[36]

Although she didn't consistently meet these objectives, Joanna's direct reports expressed how productive the team has become. They also experienced a decrease in mistakes and setbacks.

Executive Leading Example: Obtaining Executive Team Feedback for a General Manager

Chip, a general manager at a mid-sized US organization, wanted to better understand how he could work with his direct reports. Chip asked Gene, the Vice President (VP) of Change Management, to help him figure out a way to get his direct reports to talk openly about his strengths and shortcomings. Chip ultimately wanted to improve how well he worked with others but wasn't sure how to get honest feedback.

Gene arranged for Chip and the direct reports to meet off-site, and he explained to Chip and the direct reports the session's purpose and expectations and how to prepare. Gene then met individually with each of Chip's direct reports to ensure that everyone was comfortable with the process and to allow them to express any concerns or suggestions for improving the process.

At the beginning of the session, Chip talked candidly about wanting to serve the company and the direct reports, but he didn't know what he needed to do to improve. Chip knew that he wasn't perfect and asked his direct reports to help him broaden his own perspective about his leadership abilities. Chip explained that his intentions were to do what was right, but he wasn't sure if his behavior reflected his intentions or if he selected the best behaviors to achieve his intent.

Next, Gene reviewed the process again with everyone before starting the first phase. Here are the process steps that Gene described:

1. With Chip out of the room, Gene facilitates a discussion with the direct reports to identify Chip's strengths and areas for improvement. Gene uses Table 11.3 to summarize their findings.

2. The direct reports leave the room, and Gene invites Chip to review the findings. Gene helps Chip understand each item and helps him to process and interpret the overall message.

Table 11.3 Feedback Session Findings

No.	Strength	Examples	Importance to the Team (High, Medium, Low)	Areas for Improvement	Importance to the Team (High, Medium, Low)	Examples
1						
2						
3						

3. The direct reports then reenter the room, and Chip discusses his thoughts about their findings. As a group, the team talks about one or two behaviors that Chip can focus on and how the direct reports can support Chip in implementing the new key behaviors.

The direct reports identified six strength areas and four improvement areas. During Phase 2, Chip was surprised about two strength areas and three improvement areas. Although Chip was a little hurt by the critique, Gene helped Chip position the feedback as an opportunity to improve his behavior and to connect more with his direct reports. Gene also explained that only through dialogue were the direct reports able to articulate the areas for improvement. Chip sincerely appreciated the direct reports for trusting him enough to be honest and for risking how Chip might respond.

With the help of his direct reports, Chip identified two key behaviors to develop. With their support, Chip started applying the behaviors.

The process had two immediate effects on Chip and his direct reports. First, the team became more upfront with their opinions. Secondly, the direct reports had a new respect for Chip because of his courage to receive honest feedback and willingness to change.

Summary: What to Do

Summary

Facing the Unknown Like Lions involves Serious Listening and obtaining feedback. Serious listening involves using specific techniques to remain focused on what others communicate. Obtaining feedback is a way to identify gaps in our leadership performance and find ways to improve how we practice leadership. Figure 11.1 summarizes this practice.

	Facing the Unknown Like Lions Practice

Characteristics	• The way to accelerate developing 21st Century Leadership practices is through seeking feedback about how well you practice leadership.
	
	• Serious listening and 360° feedback are two approaches for learning how you can improve your leadership practices. You need to develop listening and receiving feedback deliberately and with extensive practice.
	
	• Serious listening means to:
	    • Shut down internal thinking
	    • Focus intentionally on what the other person is conveying
	    • Attempt to perceive as the other person does.
	To do so, you must ask clarifying questions and ask for examples.
	
	• Whether from serious listening or 360° feedback, acting on what you learn not only contributes to your development but gives you a way to respect others.
	
	• 360° feedback is a way to obtain feedback and encourage feedback by reducing the risk of the feedback provider.
	
	• 360° feedback involves summarizing and sharing the results, selecting two specific objectives for leadership development, and asking for those whom you work with to support you in achieving your objectives.

Principles, Guidelines, and Rules of Practice	*Related 21st Century Leadership Principles* • Connecting with Others • Put Others First • Give Up Control • Develop Leadership Practices Continuously *Kouzes and Posner Advice on Receiving Feedback*[a] 1. Resist defending or justifying your behaviors. 2. Focus on listening to understand the other person's perspective. 3. Attend to your nonverbal behavior and remain as relaxed as possible. 4. Listen and don't judge. 5. Ask questions to clarify. 6. Ask for examples. 7. Thank the other person for the feedback.
Models, Techniques, and Tools	*Serious Listening Techniques* 1. Preparation 2. Purpose 3. Seek clarity 4. Observed nonverbal behavior (if applicable) 5. Attend to your own nonverbal behavior 6. After comprehending the messaging, contribute and confirm 7. Summarize 8. Express thanks 9. Assess how you performed *Graves' Five Levels of Listening*[b] 1. Pretend 2. Selective

Figure 11.1   Practice summary: Facing the Unknown Like Lions. (*Continued*)

3. Passive

4. Attentive

5. Empathic

Cherches Six Tips to Avoid Miscommunication[c]

1. People are not mind readers.

2. Validate understanding.

3. Read between the lines.

4. It's not just your words—but your tone of voice and body language.

5. Use visuals, nonverbal cues, analogies, and metaphors to get your ideas across.

6. Be careful with jargon and acronyms.

Cherches Eight Tips to Become A Better Listener—LISTENUP![d]

1. Look at the person

2. Inquire.

3. Show that you're interested.

4. Treat the person with respect.

5. Encourage the other person.

6. Never make someone regret that they opened up to you.

7. Understanding is your primary objective.

8. Put your smartphone down.

Appendix V: Nine Practices 360-Feedback Diagnostic Tool

[a] Kouzes and Posner, 2012, *_e Leadership Challenge*, 86.
[b] Graves, 2014, *Creating Space for Performance Improvement.*
[c] Cherches, 2020, *VisuaLeadership*, 234-237.
[d] Ibid., 243-244.

Figure 11.1   (*Continued*) Practice summary: Facing the Unknown Like Lions.

What to Do

Table 11.4 lists recommendations for applying this practice immediately, in the short term, and in the long term.

Word of Caution

Most people who think that they are effective listeners aren't. Our habit is to listen selectively and become defensive about feedback. Serious Listening and receiving feedback require deliberate practice. When practicing, you need to think consciously about how you listen and receive feedback and rate how well you do until these become new habits. Setting periodic

Table 11.4 Recommended Actions for Applying Facing the Unknown Like Lions

Immediate
Practice Serious Listening Before a conversation, plan to use serious listening. Review the practice. During conversations, focus on listening to understand rather than respond. After conversations, assess how you did. Did your mind wander? Were you defensive? Did you focus more on responding than understanding?
Short Term
Share with Others Share with others what you learn about *Facing the Unknown Like Lions* practice. Helping others understand these practices builds buy-in and helps you learn the practice. ***Read and Watch More about Listening*** Research the subject of active listening using any resources in your organization. Ronald Graves recommends two resources: Covey's *The 8th Habit* (Chapter 10) and Goulston's *Just Listen*.[a] Goulston is a psychologist who works with special weapons and tactics (SWAT) teams to improve their negotiation abilities in hostage situations by training them on listening effectively. Consider watching Julian Treasure's TED videos: *5 Ways to Listen Better* and *Shh! Sound Health in 8 Steps*.[b] ***Learn More about Feedback*** Read Wimer and Nowack's article, *13 Common Mistakes Using 360° Degree Feedback*.[c] In *Survival of the Savvy*, the authors discuss two political styles and propose a third style. In Chapter 5, "Map Political Styles," they discuss how to map your political style as well as others. Obtaining feedback from others is a critical way to learn about your political style and what areas you need to improve.[d] Several books and articles on 360° feedback explain the positive aspects of this tool and the challenges. For example, Jackson discusses seven reasons why 360° feedback programs fail, and Heathfield writes about the good, the bad, and the ugly of 360° feedback.[e] Learning more can help prepare you for conducting your own 360° feedback.

(Continued)

Table 11.4   (*Continued*) Recommended Actions for Applying Facing the Unknown Like Lions

Long Term
Conduct Your Own 360° Feedback When ready, try conducting your own 360° feedback. Feel free to use the Nine Practices 360° Feedback Diagnostic Tool in Appendix V. You might consider reviewing these resources as well: • Hunter's Leadership Skills Inventory[f] • Smart et al.'s *Power Score*[g]

[a] Covey, 2004, *The 8th Habit*; Goulston, 2010, *Just Listen*.
[b] TED, 2011, *Julian Treasure: 5 Ways to Listen Better*; TED, 2010, *Julian Treasure: Shh! Sound Health in 8 Steps*.
[c] Wimer & Nowack, 2006, 13 Common Mistakes Using 360-Degree Feedback.
[d] Brandon and Seldman, 2004, *Survival of the Savvy*, 63–72.
[e] Jackson, 2012, *The 7 Reasons Why 360 Degree Feedback Programs Fail*; Heathfield, 2021, *360 Degree Feedback*.
[f] Hunter, 2004, *The World's Most Powerful Leadership Principle*, 216.
[g] Smart, Street, & Foster, 2015, *Power Score*.

reminders for monitoring how well you practice Serious Listening and receiving feedback can be an effective way to ensure that you don't regress to old habits. Also, ask others to hold you accountable as you develop your listening and feedback abilities.

Chapter 12

Practice 8: Developing Like Scouts

You have to constantly be looking outside yourself and your
organization for new and innovative products, processes, and
services.[1]

Kouzes and Posner

I believe—although I cannot prove—that potential Level 5 leaders
are highly prevalent in our society. The problem is not a dearth of
potential Level 5 Leaders. They exist all around us, if we just know
what to look for.[2]

Collins

Introduction: Importance and Benefits of Developing Like Scouts

Want to find better ways to work to make what you do more efficient and
easier? Want to find the next superstar to work at your organization? If so,
then *Developing Like Scouts* is for you. Investing a few hours a week can
substantially improve how you, your team, and your organization produce
products and services.

In this chapter, I discuss the characteristics of *Developing Like Scouts*. I list some of Kouzes and Posner's tactics for finding new ideas. Finally, I provide leading examples and discuss using this practice.

Characteristics of Developing Like Scouts

Developing our mental and moral qualities, capabilities, and behaviors is critical for 21st Century Leadership. Unfortunately, many rely on their organizations to provide developmental opportunities and seldom take the initiative to manage and search for networking opportunities and professional development on their own time. Those who take the initiative act as scouts: They search outside of their organization to learn more about their market area, products and services, best practices, lessons learned, and ways to manage and execute work better. They also act like talent scouts looking for prospective employees, business partners, consultants, and contractors. While they may not be in an authority position to hire anyone, networking with talent enables access when talent is needed.

Developing Like Scouts applies to all aspects of work. This includes technical skills, organizational management, process management, leadership development, project management, change management, career development, and relationship management. You can apply this practice to developing a broad range of competencies; for example, in *FYI*, Lombardo and Eichinger identify 167 professional competencies and describe how to improve them.[3] For a list of qualities that you might want to develop, refer to Appendix VI: *Related Quality Terms*. I summarize the characteristics of *Developing Like Scouts* (Box 12.1).

Robinson and Schroeder's Mechanisms for Innovation: Idea Activators and Idea Mining

Have you ever heard executives or managers tell employees not to talk to them about problems without having solutions? This might be their way to minimize complaining, but it also limits creativity and innovation.

According to Robinson and Schroeder, there are two parts of creativity: finding problems and solving problems. While many organizations focus more on problem-solving, finding problems that have remained unidentified

BOX 12.1   CHARACTERISTICS OF DEVELOPING LIKE SCOUTS

■ Practicing 21st Century Leadership involves future thinking about innovation within the three performance levels: Organization, process, and performer.

■ Anyone can innovate and find the next big idea for an organization.

■ To exceed expectations, you need more than good intentions and business-as-usual activities; you need new ideas and perspective.

■ According to Kouzes and Posner, most professionals find innovative ideas from sources outside their organization.[4]

■ You can find sources of new ideas in professional webinars, books, articles, databases, universities, chapter associations, informal networking meetings, conferences, blogs, professional website resources, contractors, freelancers, and consultants.

■ Those in charge don't always welcome using work time to innovate, and as practitioners, you often feel pressure to focus only on the work due to time constraints. Likewise, people have other obligations after work and prefer not to use their personal time to network or participate in professional events such as evening association chapter programs.

■ Chapters, universities, conferences, and consulting groups are excellent sources for finding talent and ideas. Organizations often purchase enterprise subscriptions to services such as Skillsoft (https://www.skillsoft.com/), Gartner (https://www.gartner.com/en), and the Josh Bersin Academy (https://bersinacademy.com/). These can be valuable resources for innovation.

can lead to several small and large creative opportunities.[5] Robinson and Schroeder identify two components to problem finding:

Idea activators: "…short training or educational modules that teach people new techniques or give them new perspectives on their work that will trigger more ideas."[6]

Idea mining: the process of looking at implemented ideas and solutions and then critically analyzing the solutions to identify implications for the design and management of the three performance levels (organization, process, and perform—discussed in Chapter 6).[7]

With finding problems, professionals also may identify how to solve them. However, not everyone has the answers to solve specific problems. By encouraging problem finding even without solutions, teams could collaborate to resolve the identified problems.

When scouting how other professionals innovate, you may be able to help your organization find opportunities and problems that are worth addressing. Whether learning new mechanisms for finding opportunities and problems or mining ideas that others have implemented, Robinson and Schroeder's creative approach can contribute towards cost savings or revenue generation.

Kouzes and Posner's Tactics for Generating New Ideas

In *The Leadership Challenge*, Kouzes and Posner provide tactics for generating new ideas that could lead to the next innovation for your organization. Three of these tactics are to hone your outsight, make idea gathering a regular routine, and invite guest speakers to the organization for brainstorming (Box 12.2).

These are only a few of Kouzes and Posner's tactics in their Search for Opportunities commitment that is part of their Challenge the Process practice.

**BOX 12.2   KOUZES AND POSNER'S TACTICS
FOR GENERATING NEW IDEAS**

Hone your outsight.[8] *Outsight* is "the capacity to perceive external things."[9] As you listen to the news, learn what others do, and keep in the back of your mind to watch for outsights that can start generating new ways of thinking.

Make idea gathering a regular routine.[10] Talk with several people to generate new ideas. If you work in retail at the corporate office, work in a store, and talk with customers. If you are an executive at a hotel chain, work the front desk. Talk with suppliers, business partners, thought leaders in your profession, and even friends and family members.

Invite guest speakers to the organization for brainstorming.[11] Use discussions as a mechanism to share ideas and to generate innovative thinking. Leverage social media such as internal collaboration systems and wikis to post ideas for online discussions.

Leading Examples

Individual Contributor Leading Example: Vendor Management Process

Rita, Andy's manager, asked him if he could figure out a standard way to evaluate and monitor the quality of the department's vendors. During the previous three years, the department had relied heavily on vendors, and the department's teams hadn't shared how they had leveraged vendors or how effective they were. In one instance, a manager hired a vendor for some work but didn't know that another manager had a terrible experience with the same vendor.

Andy had never developed any vendor standards, so he contacted an external research service for help. The organization had an enterprise contract with the research service, and any employee could contact them for help. Andy explained to Kate, a researcher, what Rita wanted and asked if she had any best practices or examples from other companies. Within a few days, Kate provided vendor management examples from 15 companies that described in detail their processes and tools. From the research and within a week, Andy created an annual evaluation process and a central database to manage information about vendors.

Andy piloted the evaluation process with three vendors. This involved having the vendors self-evaluate, having the primary contacts in Andy's department evaluate the vendors, and comparing the two results. From the experience, the vendors and department contacts found gaps in their perspective, and the department contacts were able to help the vendors rethink and improve their services. The process went so well that Thomas, one of the vendor account managers, asked Andy if he could adopt the process and share it with his other clients to ensure that his company met his other clients' needs.

Manager Leading Example: Starting a New Training Department

At a mid-sized national organization, Monica hired Leslie to start a centralized training organization. Historically, the company had supervisors train employees. The company didn't have any formally trained instructional designers, and in a recent organizational assessment, the company found that this approach placed the organization at risk of losing growth opportunities. While Leslie was knowledgeable about managing training teams, Shelley, the Chief Operations Officer (COO), wanted to ensure that Monica and Leslie effectively governed the new training department. The three agreed to attend a national training conference to identify best practices for managing the training organization and aligning the work to organizational goals.

At the conference, the three attended sessions related to training governance talked with presenters after their sessions and networked with other training department heads. By the end of the conference, Leslie, with help from Shelley and Monica, had designed a strategy and a three-year plan for supporting the organization's business needs.

Executive Leading Example: College Competition Sponsorship

At an international conference, Frank, the Vice President (VP) of the Six Sigma Department, signed up to be a sponsor for a college competition. Frank wanted to find new talent for his team, but he wasn't ready to hire. From the sponsorship, Frank and some of his employees observed the students compete with one another. Before the end of the conference, Frank and his employees attended a social event with the faculty and college students. During the social, Frank talked with most of the students to better understand their talents, interests, and willingness to relocate.

After the conference, Frank periodically followed up with some of the students. He established LinkedIn connections and kept notes about each student. When Frank was ready to hire more employees, he successfully recruited Jeff and Todd, two student competitors, for entry-level positions. Frank also found Julian, a more experienced candidate who Todd had recommended as a referral. The three new employees knew each other from college and supported one another as they transitioned to a corporate environment.

Summary: What to Do

Summary

Developing Like Scouts involves searching for new ideas and talent. You need to plan and consciously organize how to improve your work and contribute to the organization. This involves taking deliberate breaks to reflect on

	Developing Like Scouts Practice
Characteristics	• Practicing 21st Century Leadership involves future thinking about innovation within the three performance levels: organization, process, and performer.
	• Anyone can innovate and find the next big idea for an organization.
	• To exceed expectations, you need more than good intentions and business-as-usual activities; you need new ideas and perspective.
	• According to Kouzes and Posner, most professionals find innovative ideas from sources outside the organization.[a]
	• You can find sources for new ideas come from free professional webinars, books, articles, databases, universities, chapter associations, informal networking meetings, conferences, blogs, professional website resources, contractors, freelancers, and consultants.
	• Executives and management often pressure people to accomplish work rather than taking a small amount of work time to innovate. Likewise, people have other obligations after work and prefer not to take personal time to network or participate in professional events such as evening association chapter programs.
	• Chapters, universities, conferences, and consulting groups are excellent sources for finding talent and ideas. Organizations often purchase enterprise subscriptions to services such as Skillsoft, Corporate Executive Board, and Bersin by Deloitte. These can be valuable resources for innovation.
Principles, Guidelines, and Rules of Practice	**Related 21st Century Leadership Principles** • Connect with Others • Encourage Change • Develop Leadership Practices Continuously **Build your network of talent** • Connect with consultants, contractors, and freelancers. • Search for peers in other organizations and meet with them periodically to exchange ideas. • Identify prospective talent who might fit your organization. • Attend professional association events within your area. **Kouzes and Posner's Tactics for Generating New ideas** • Hone your outsight.[b] • Make idea gathering a regular routine.[c] • Invite guest speakers to the organization for brainstorming.[d]

[a] Kouzes and Posner, 2012, *The Leadership Challenge*, 172.
[b] Ibid.
[c] Ibid., 181.
[d] Ibid., 176.

Figure 12.1 Practice summary: Developing Like Scouts.

our work and seek external resources to improve all aspects of our lives. Figure 12.1 summarizes this practice.

What to Do

Table 12.1 lists recommendations for applying this practice immediately, in the short term, and in the long term.

Table 12.1   Recommended Actions for Applying Developing Like Scouts

Immediate
Learn about Your Business Start searching for professional associations, chapters, and other groups within your area or nationally. Find out if your organization has any enterprise licenses for consulting services. This can be difficult to discover, especially if one silo purchases the service but doesn't communicate to the enterprise. If you have a training department, talk with people there. They may have access to databases such as (https://books24x7.com).
Short Term
Share with Others Share with others what you learn about the *Developing Like Scouts* practice. Helping others understand these practices builds buy-in and helps you learn the practice. ***Read about Mechanisms on Improving Innovation Thinking*** In *The Idea-Driven Organization*, read Chapter 3 entitled, "Ways to Get More and Better Ideas," for Robinson and Schroeder's mechanisms: Idea activators and idea mining.[a] ***Build Your Professional Network*** Using services such as LinkedIn and local chapters, find like-minded professionals in your area. Connect with them over lunch to share ideas and learn what they are doing within their organizations. ***Read More about Searching for Opportunities*** In *The Leadership Challenge*, read more about Kouzes and Posner's *Search for Opportunities* commitment in their *Challenge the Process* practice. The authors provide several examples to illustrate this commitment. ***Search for Talent*** Identify consultants, contractors, freelancers, and other professionals that work in your profession. Leverage professional organizations to meet talent. Before beginning the hiring process for a position, read *Who* by Smart and Street. The authors provide a powerful process for hiring talent successfully.[b]

(Continued)

Table 12.1 *(Continued)* **Recommended Actions for Applying Developing Like Scouts**

Long Term
Attend International and National Conferences Work with your organization to support your attendance at international and national conferences. At these conferences, get to know other attendees. Talk with presenters after concurrent sessions. Often, conferences will have networking events that you can attend. Learn the innovators of your field who attend conferences regularly. Get involved: Find ways to volunteer; this is a great way to meet other professionals and practice stewardship.

[a] Robinson and Schroeder, 2014, *The Idea-Driven Organization*, 47–67.
[b] Smart and Street, 2008, *Who*.

Word of Caution

Earlier in this chapter, I mentioned that organizations may want people to innovate and find the next great idea. Still, organizations often pressure people to focus on accomplishing the work itself. To practice leadership effectively, *Developing Like Scouts* is a critical practice and can ultimately provide your team and organization with a powerful cost-saving and revenue-generating advantage.

Chapter 13

Practice 9: Communicating Like Broadcasters

Too many leaders are like bad travel agents. They send people places they have never been. Instead, they should be more like tour guides, taking people places they have gone and sharing the wisdom of their own experiences.[1]

Maxwell

It's one thing to communicate to people because you believe you have something of value to say. It's another to communicate with people because you believe they have value.… It may sound corny, but it's really true: People don't care how much you know until they know how much you care.[2]

Maxwell

Introduction: Importance and Benefits of Communicating Like Broadcasters

As you practice *Developing Like Scouts*, you'll acquire many knowledge, skills, and insights into your formal role, organization, and profession. Throughout your career and as you deliberately find development opportunities, people come into your life and assist you along your developmental path. Similar to how people have helped you develop

DOI: 10.4324/9781003273448-17

and find career opportunities, you'll discover ways to help others. *Communicating Like Broadcasters* is a type of stewardship in which you give back to your community and profession. Beyond helping your immediate team, this practice involves sharing your insights with your department, local professional community, and global community.

Practicing *Communicating Like Broadcasters* can strengthen your capabilities. As you teach others, you develop a richer comprehension of your knowledge and skills. Thus, you learn while teaching others.

In this chapter, I describe the characteristics of *Communicating Like Broadcasters* and provide some media suggestions for reaching a broader audience than your immediate team. I then present Maxwell's guidelines for connecting with others. Finally, I provide leading examples and discuss using this practice.

Characteristics of Communicating Like Broadcasters

Communicating Like Broadcasters is about conveying to others the knowledge and skills that enable you to accomplish your work and contribute to your success. Like media broadcasters, you share your ideas with a diverse and broader audience than your immediate team.

Maxwell's Eight Guidelines for Connecting with Others

In *The 21 Irrefutable Laws of Leadership*, Maxwell writes that regardless of whether you are addressing a large audience or talking with one person, you need to connect with others.[3] Table 13.1 summarizes Maxwell's Eight Guidelines for Connecting with Others.

Leading Examples

Individual Contributor Leading Example: Sharing Technical Expertise

Erin, a business analyst at an auditing firm, had developed an analysis model that she used in her work. She shared the model with other analysts who leveraged the model with positive results. After using the model

Table 13.1 Summary of Maxwell's Eight Guidelines for Connecting with Others

No.	Guideline	Explanation
1.	Connect with yourself[a]	Build your confidence and competence in yourself. Know why, how, and in what way you want to connect with others to help them develop and grow.
2.	Communicate with openness and sincerity[b]	Be authentic with what you communicate and why.
3.	Know your audience[c]	For individuals, learn their names, history, and aspirations. For groups, learn their history, mission, and goals. Convey what they care about rather than simply what you want to convey.
4.	Live your message[d]	Model your credibility by practicing what you communicate.
5.	Go to where they are[e]	Like the third guideline, connect with those you communicate with by respecting their background, culture, education, and perspective.
6.	Focus on them and not yourself[f]	Inexperienced speakers focus on themselves and not their audience. Focusing on them accelerates connection.
7.	Believe in them[g]	Maxwell states it best: "It's one thing to communicate to people because you believe you have something of value to say. It's another to communicate with people because you believe they have value."[h]
8.	Offer direction and hope[i]	Provide an authentic and feasible path to achieve what you are communicating.

[a] Maxwell, 2007, *The 21 Irrefutable Laws of Leadership*, 117.
[b] Ibid.
[c] Ibid., 118.
[d] Ibid.
[e] Ibid.
[f] Ibid.
[g] Ibid., 118–119.
[h] Ibid.
[i] Ibid., 119.

for about three years, she wanted to share what she had developed with professionals outside of her organization. With support from her manager, she submitted a proposal to present the model at an upcoming conference, and the conference chair accepted her proposal.

**BOX 13.1   CHARACTERISTICS OF
COMMUNICATING LIKE BROADCASTERS**

■ This is a stewardship practice: Helping others benefit from the knowledge and skills that enable you to accomplish your work.
■ Conveying your knowledge and skills might start by presenting within your organization to peers, your department, or even the whole organization.
■ Media for broadcasting includes the following:
  – Informal groups such as professionals from local organizations that periodically gather over breakfast or a similar occasion to discuss professional interests.
  – Presenting at association chapters and conferences.
  – Presenting as a guest lecturer to colleges and universities.
  – Presenting at national and international conferences.
  – Publishing a blog, article, or book either independently or through a formal publisher or association.

This was Erin's first time presenting at a conference. To prepare, she reviewed her presentation with her manager and practiced presenting to some colleagues. At the conference, six participants attended her concurrent session (most attended the well-known presenter sessions), but her manager provided support. The session went well, but Erin thought of ways to improve and wasn't prepared to have only six attendees.

The following year, the chairs invited her to present her session again as an encore event. They had read the evaluations, reviewed the handouts, and believed that the model substantially contributed to the field.

After that first session, Erin presented the model at three more conferences and two chapter events, and she published a short blog in one of the association's online newsletters. Erin later presented other topics, helping others develop their technical expertise.

Manager Leading Example: Leadership Development Breakfast Club

When Jessica and Ben met for breakfast for the first time, they didn't know that their meetings would evolve into a breakfast club. Both were new directors in their organizations and had met at a local chapter meeting. They worked in their organizations' training department specializing in leadership development. They thought it would be good to get together and share what their teams were doing to develop leaders. After the first breakfast, they decided to meet every other month. At some meetings, they brought coworkers from their leadership development team to join them.

Independently, Jessica and Ben met other leadership development directors and managers who lived in the area, and they would invite them to join their breakfast gatherings. Jessica and Ben agreed that the only rule wasn't to invite anyone who the regular attendees would consider a competitor, but that never became a problem.

At these breakfast sessions, the group talked about their initiatives, leadership approaches, and departmental influence on their organizations. Participants offered suggestions, recommended new books and articles, and shared news about upcoming events such as free webinars and conferences.

After a year, the gathering grew to about ten people. Some participated once or twice, while others attended most sessions. At times, neither Jessica nor Ben could attend the breakfast, but the group continued to meet.

Executive Leading Example: Sharing Leadership at the Corporate Office

Roger, a vice president (VP) at a Fortune 50 company, has a successful career working in operations. He is grateful for all the role models who have influenced how he works with his people to accomplish the extraordinary. Roger attributes part of his success to servant leadership. Over the years, the organization has brought leadership authors to speak to executives and upper management, and Roger has spent hours listening to them and reading their books. He has carefully documented how he applies servant leadership to his role and regularly engaged his peers in reflective conversations about leadership and how they could continue improving in leading others.

Because of Roger's growing reputation as a leader, the training department began inviting Roger to talk about leadership to new hires, interns, and visiting groups of managers from satellite locations.

After speaking to a few groups with positive feedback, Roger became inspired to continue speaking about leadership. He refined his message and spoke with more passion. As a result, people thanked him for influencing how they think about leadership and letting Roger know how much his talks help.

Recently, Linda, the Chief Operations Officer (COO), asked Roger to present his personal story about leadership to all operations (more than 200,000 employees) during a special broadcast to offices throughout the United States. The media department managed the broadcast and posted the video on their intranet site for employees who missed it or wanted to view it again.

Since the broadcast, Roger has added volumes of short videos on leadership to the organization's intranet site and has reached many employees with his views on leadership. Many employees have moved to other organizations and most likely have passed on Roger's messages about leadership.

Summary: What to Do

Summary

Throughout your career, people assist you along the way. *Communicating Like Broadcasters* is about stewardship and giving back to those in your organization and those outside your team, profession, and community. Figure 13.1 summarizes this practice.

What to Do

Table 13.2 lists recommendations for applying this practice immediately, in the short term, and in the long term.

Word of Caution

As with some of the other 21st Century Leadership practices, *Communicating Like Broadcasters* can be misused. The emphasis of this practice is sharing critical knowledge and skills with a broader audience. Consequently, this draws more attention to you and can feed your ego. Recall the 21st Century Leadership Belief 9, Leadership Is Action that Focuses on Others and Not the Actor. Leadership isn't about you and drawing attention to yourself but rather about sharing your knowledge and skills and helping others develop their leadership (Belief 26). When practicing *Communicating Like Broadcasters*, you need to carefully manage your intentions and motivation.

	Communicating Like Broadcasters Practice
Characteristics	• This is a stewardship practice: helping others benefit from your knowledge and skills that enable you to accomplish work. • Conveying your knowledge and skills might start by presenting within your organization to peers, your department, or even the whole organization. • Media for broadcasting includes the following. • Informal groups such as professionals from local organizations who gather over breakfast or similar occasion periodically to discuss professional interests • Presenting at association chapters and conferences • Presenting as a guest lecturer to colleges and universities • Presenting at national and international conferences • Publishing a blog, article, or book either independently or through a formal publisher or association
Principles, Guidelines, and Rules of Practice	*Related 21st Century Leadership Principles* • Believe in Others • Connect with Others • Put Others First • Give Up Control • Encourage Change • Develop Leadership Practices Continuously *Maxwell's Eight Guidelines for Connecting with Others[a]* 1. Connect with yourself 2. Communicate with Openness and sincerity 3. Know your audience 4. Live your message 5. Go to where they are 6. Focus on them and not yourself 7. Believe in them 8. Offer direction and hope

[a] Maxwell, 2007, *The 21 Irrefutable Laws of Leadership*, 117-119.

Figure 13.1   Practice summary: Communicating Like Broadcasters.

Table 13.2   Recommended Actions for Applying Communicating Like Broadcasters

Immediate
Identify Media for Communicating If you haven't done so, identify the media you can use to communicate. This could be local association chapters, conferences, or published media. Determine what media you feel comfortable leveraging.
Identify What to Communicate Based on your development, determine what you are interested in communicating.

(*Continued*)

Table 13.2 (*Continued*) **Recommended Actions for Applying Communicating Like Broadcasters**

Short Term
Share with Others Share with others what you learn about the *Communicating Like Broadcasters* practice. Helping others understand these practices builds buy-in and helps you learn the practice. Find out if others are interested in presenting or writing on the topic area with you.
Learn More about Your Topics Research your topic using the Internet, online databases, and any services available through your organization. Find out what others in your profession have written or presented about your topic and incorporate and reference their findings. In *The 21 Irrefutable Laws of Leadership*, read Maxwell's chapter on the law of connection, and consider his section on applying the law of connection to your life.

Long Term
Expand on Topics for Broadcasting As you continue developing your knowledge and skills, incorporate what you learn into the topics you broadcast. Continue to strengthen the depth of your topics and expand to new topics.

CONTINUING TO GROW

The committed leader is dedicated to growing, stretching, and continuously improving.[1]

Hunter

In *The Servant*, Hunter warns that servant leadership seems easy when it isn't.[2] In *The Servant Leadership Training Course*, Hunter emphasizes that only about 10% put leadership into practice and into their lives.[3] This may be true of 21st Century Leadership. To shift from knowing to doing, we need to move the knowledge from our heads to our hearts and then to our hands.[4] In other words, you have to do something like the following:

1. Study leadership principles, beliefs, and practices, and figure out how to apply them to your role.
2. While applying the practices, gather feedback on how well you apply them.
3. Using feedback, refine how you apply the principles, beliefs, and practices.
4. Learn more about leadership and integrate your new knowledge into practice.
5. Gather feedback and refine your leadership practices.
6. And so on…

I designed this book to help you study and apply 21st Century Leadership. Section I defines 21st Century Leadership, principles, and beliefs. Sections II

DOI: 10.4324/9781003273448-18

through IV describe the nine practices. Section V provides guidance for your leadership development.

Chapter 14 explains the 21st Century Leadership Development Roadmap. You can leverage the roadmap to monitor and manage your personal leadership development.

Chapter 15 describes implications for organizations in terms of strategy, diversity, and training. Chapter 15 also explains how organizations can use the nine practices to influence employees to practice 21st Century Leadership.

Chapter 14

Maturing and Sustaining Your Leadership Practices

Getting people to agree with the principles of servant leadership is an easy task. Getting people to change and get the principles into their game is another matter altogether. The greater challenge is how to move the principles from their head to their heart, and from their heart into making it their habit...It can be a long journey from head to habit...The part most fail to grasp is that leadership is a skill, a learned or acquired ability. It is not something you are born with.[1]

Hunter

Introduction

In his training course audiobook, Hunter talks about the challenge of developing and sustaining leadership practices, a concern he repeats in *The Servant*. In both publications, Hunter explains that attending workshops and reading leadership books (like the one you are reading now) aren't enough to join the small percentage of people who practice authentic leadership successfully.[2] While building your leadership knowledge is necessary, you need more.

In addition to building a leadership body of knowledge—what Hunter calls *foundation*—you need two things to practice 21st Century Leadership

DOI: 10.4324/9781003273448-19

successfully.[3] First, you need to become a continuous learner. According to several leadership authors, those who practice leadership successfully are lifelong learners.[4] For Kouzes and Posner, lifelong learners have a passion for becoming fluent and excelling in leadership, are devoted to practicing and learning leadership deliberately, and believe strongly that leadership practices are learnable and teachable.[5] Thus, having a high commitment to continuous learning is necessary; however, you need more than a commitment to learning.

Second, you need to have a mechanism to support your leadership development. As I explained in Chapter 9, *Directing Like Guides*, commitment and motivation aren't enough; you need the ability as well. This chapter helps make it easier to develop your leadership practices.

This chapter is about developing your leadership capability. The first part describes the process, and the second part describes the roadmap.

The Leadership Development Process

Figure 14.1 illustrates that leadership development is cyclical with four steps:

1. Foundation
2. Feedback
3. Friction
4. Follow-up

I adapted the process from Hunter and Goldsmith[6]. To illustrate how the model works, I describe how Yvette, a contact center agent who aspires to be a supervisor, uses the process to develop her listening capability.

Step 1: Foundation

During this step, you gather knowledge about leadership. You become aware of methodologies, principles, beliefs, strategies, and tactics. You also begin trying to adopt new behaviors to lead more effectively.

One tactic that supports foundational work is letting people know that you want to become better at leadership. Ask for their support. As you try new behaviors, let people know what you are doing. People can surprise you with how helpful they can be.

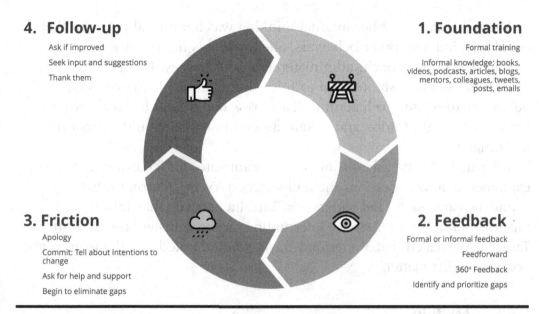

4. Follow-up

Ask if improved

Seek input and suggestions

Thank them

1. Foundation

Formal training

Informal knowledge: books,
videos, podcasts, articles, blogs,
mentors, colleagues, tweets,
posts, emails

3. Friction

Apology

Commit: Tell about intentions to
change

Ask for help and support

Begin to eliminate gaps

2. Feedback

Formal or informal feedback

Feedforward

360° Feedback

Identify and prioritize gaps

Figure 14.1   Goldsmith/Hunter Leadership Development Process.

In our example, Yvette learns about listening by taking an eCourse, watching videos on YouTube, and reading some leadership books. She begins to apply what she learned to strengthen listening to customers, colleagues, and her supervisor.

Step 2: Feedback

Chapter 11 explains the *Facing the Unknown Like Lions* practice in which you leverage feedback to identify behaviors that need development. Feedback is how you identify behavioral gaps. Whether through a 360° survey, informal discussions, or feedforward, determining behaviors to strengthen or expose your harmful behaviors, feedback raises your awareness, enables you to prioritize behavioral changes, and begins the process.

Using feedforward, Yvette learned some ways to improve her listening:

- Before assuming she understood what someone is communicating, inquire to ensure understanding.
- Use empathy to confirm or correct.
- As someone talks, avoid:
  – Internal thinking—letting your mind wander.
  – Working on a response or what to say next.
- If you can see the person talking, note the nonverbal behavior.

Yvette believed that her internal thinking was her critical behavior that could help improve other behaviors. She made this her priority.

Carlos, Yvette's coach, administered a 360° survey. From the results, Yvette learned that she tended to interrupt. She also learned about behaviors unrelated to listening that Carlos could help her improve. For now, though, Carlos and Yvette agreed that she should focus on listening.

Informally, Yvette asked some of her teammates for feedback. Tanisha explained that, on occasion, she had watched Yvette interrupt other teammates and Alton, her supervisor. Tanisha believed that Tanisha did this to defend her position. By interrupting, her teammates seemed hurt; Tanisha speculated that Yvette may have communicated that the teammates' opinions didn't matter.

Step 3: Friction

Friction is how you mitigate behavioral gaps and reconnect with people you may have hurt by your past behaviors. It is when you get serious about changing your behavior and improving how you lead.

Step 3 involves some sub-steps: share results, apologize, get buy-in, and get started. How you execute the sub-steps depends on your situation and career level.

Step 3.A: Share Results

Once you have your feedback and a plan, share your feedback results. You don't have to share everything.

Step 3.B: Apologize

If you intend to connect and build trust, you need to acknowledge wrong behavior, label it as bad behavior, say you're sorry, and explain how you will do better. After your feedback increases self-awareness and self-perception, you need to apologize to those you've wronged with your bad behavior. Goldsmith explains how this is done (Box 14.1).

During a team meeting, Yvette apologized to Alton and her teammates. For those Yvette believed to have wronged more than others, she met with them individually to apologize. Some teammates explained that they hadn't been good listeners and also apologized.

BOX 14.1   APOLOGY

The best thing about apologizing, I tell my clients, is that it forces everyone to let go of the past. In effect, you are saying, "I can't change the past. All I can say is that I'm sorry for what I did wrong. I'm sorry it hurt you. There's no excuse for it and I will try to do better in the future. I would like you to give me any ideas about how I can improve.

That statement–an admission of guilt, an apology, and a plea for help—is tough for even the most cold-hearted among us to resist.[7]

Goldsmith

Step 3.C: Ask for Help

After sharing feedback results and apologizing, explain what you will work to improve. You want them to observe you and notice when you change. After explaining, ask for help. By yourself, you can improve. With the support of your manager and peers, you can accelerate your improvement. You want them to be invested in your development.

If you regress to your bad habits, ask to be confronted. "Hey, you're doing that thing again." If you do better, ask for recognition. "You did a great job at the meeting. I like how you are changing."

When people agree to help, your growth process also builds the team in a contagious way. Everyone grows, trust increases, and team performance improves, as Goldsmith explains (Box 14.2).

After apologizing to her team, Yvette explained how she intends to improve her listening. She asked her teammates to stop her if she didn't

BOX 14.2   TO CHANGE EFFECTIVELY, GET BUY-IN

When you declare your dependence on others, they usually agree to help. And during the course of making you a better person, they inevitably try to become better people themselves. This is how teams improve, how divisions grow, and how companies become world-beaters.[8]

Goldsmith

> ### BOX 14.3 KARL'S BEHAVIOR HARMED THE GARDEN
>
> Our research on behavior change is clear. If leaders get feedback, follow-up and involve their co-workers in the change process, they get better. If they don't follow-up and involve their co-workers, they usually are not seen as improving.[9]
>
> **Morgan, Harkins, and Goldsmith**

seem to be paying close attention to what they said. The teammates who also apologized asked if Yvette would help them improve as well. "We can be in this together!"

Step 3.D: Get Started

After asking for help, it is time to get started and execute your plan.

Step 4: Follow-Up

As you execute your plan, ask people how you are doing. Doing so communicates that you want to get better and value the people you ask. According to Goldsmith, people perceive little or no change when you don't follow up. When follow-up happens, the perceived growth increases dramatically. Morgan, Harkins, and Goldsmith noted this as well (Box 14.3).

Yvette asked Alton, teammates, and others about how she was doing. Most agreed that Yvette was improving, and Yvette could tell a difference; she felt like a better listener! Some offered more advice, and Yvette listened.

The 21st Century Leadership Development Roadmap

In Chapter 10, *Nurturing Like Gardeners*, I discussed making ability development easier with standards, templates, performance aids, and tools. Table 14.1 is a job aid for supporting leadership development. I use the Six Boxes® Model to help you plan and anticipate developing your leadership practices.

In Table 14.1 under Box 2 (Tools and Resources), I mention the 21st Century Leadership Development Roadmap (Figure 14.2). The roadmap

Table 14.1   Opportunities for Supporting Leadership Development by Category

1. Expectations and Feedback	2. Tools and Resources	3. Consequences and Incentives
Ask for specific ways to support your leadership development from: • Your direct manager • Peers • Your team • Other colleagues Find a mentor and successful practitioners for support and feedback Ask others to provide immediate confirmative and corrective feedback on how well you practice leadership; to hold you accountable Ask others to complete upcoming 360° feedback surveys	Use the 21st Century Leadership Development Roadmap as a compass for monitoring your progress In Sections II through IV of this book, use each chapter's What to do table as a guide for learning and developing the nine practices In Sections II through IV, leverage tools such as: • Anatomy of Performance • Six Boxes® Model • Drexler/Sibbet Team Performance Model® Build a social support network within and outside your organization to access its knowledge, personal resources, and support from others	Set professional development goals (one or two) and define measures for meeting the goals successfully; use the data to monitor progress; if you have one, incorporate your goals in your organization's performance management process to add emphasis to accountability Share with others the result of 360° feedback surveys and discuss how you can incorporate the feedback to improve your behavior; when ready, use the feedback to define one to two new goals with measures for future development

4. Skills and Knowledge	5. Selection and Assignment (Capacity)	6. Motives and Preferences (Attitude)
Study the 21st Century Leadership definition, principles, beliefs, and practices Training on practicing leadership practices Discuss leadership practices regularly with others and learn from others' experiences vicariously	Mentally prepare for setbacks in performance and for harsh feedback by interpreting them as guides to help you refine your leadership techniques and to keep learning; avoid thinking of setbacks and harsh feedbacks as roadblocks but as a necessary part of the development process	Continue to make leadership practice a personal choice Build personal experiences by practicing 21st Century Leadership; examine the consequences for how others benefit and develop from your practices Read and hear how others apply 21st Century Leadership successfully

Organizational standard
Train traditional leadership
(executives and managers only)
High risk / low opportunity

Organizational standard
Train 21st Century Leadership
Low risk / high opportunity

Commit to change

Stage IV: I don't know what I don't know
Committed to 21st Century Leadership
High confidence
Unconscious / skilled
Promote shared command and control
Practice stewardship (technical functional and leadership development)

Stage III: I know that I don't know
Begin to integrate 21st Century Leadership principles and beliefs
Confidence building
Conscious / skilled
Share more command and control
Seek leadership development opportunities

Stage II: I don't know
Awareness of traditional leadership limitations
Decreased confidence
Conscious / unskilled
Experiment with sharing command and control
Value leadership development

Stage I: I know
Committed to traditional leadership
False confidence
Unconscious / unskilled
Own command & control
Indifferent to leadership development

Commit to change

Figure 14.2   21st Century Leadership Development Roadmap.

describes the developmental stages for becoming fluent in 21st Century Leadership practices. Consider the roadmap as a guide or a compass for monitoring your leadership development progress and cueing you to which tactics you should be applying, depending on where you are on the roadmap. The remainder of this chapter describes the four stages of the 21st Century Leadership Development Roadmap. I then discuss what you can do to use the roadmap for monitoring and managing your leadership development.

Having a roadmap helps you find your path, recognize pitfalls, and setbacks as a natural part of the journey, and anticipate what to expect before advancing. As depicted in Figure 14.2 and Table 14.2, the 21st Century Leadership Development Roadmap consists of four stages, with traditional leadership as the first stage and 21st Century Leadership as the fourth stage. The stages roughly approximate Blanchard's development levels in Situational Leadership® II (SLII®) as described in Chapter 9, *Directing Like Guides*, although SLII® is meant to be applied to specific tasks and not stages. Therefore, I align these metaphorically. Thus, D1 approximates Stage I, D2 approximates Stage II, D3 approximates Stage III, and D4 approximates Stage IV. I intend to explain what the experience could be like at each stage; however, I'm not implying that someone's leadership practices

Table 14.2   21st Century Leadership Development Roadmap Stages

Stage	Experience Representation
1.	Traditional leadership
2.	The elimination of some traditional leadership assumptions and practices replaced by some 21st Century Leadership principles, beliefs, and practices (assimilation of 21st Century Leadership)
3.	A break from traditional leadership and integration of 21st Century Leadership principles, beliefs, and practices (adaption of 21st Century Leadership)
4.	21st Century Leadership

and actions are only at a specific development level. Alex, for example, is at Stage III on the roadmap. Many of the leadership tasks that Alex practices tend to be at D3, but some are at D1, D2, and D4.

Each stage has a set of characteristics. Table 14.3 summarizes these characteristics and discusses them in the following topics. To advance to the next stage, you'll need to meet a set of criteria, which I also describe in the following topics.

Stage I: I Know

Characteristics

There is a broad continuum of people at Stage I. At one extreme are those who are accidental managers given authority without any formal management training and those who are aware that they know little about leadership and management other than their personal experience of watching others. At the other extreme are those who think of themselves as leadership experts who believe they know what is best for their organization and people. Wiseman labels the second group as *diminishers*. The amount of experience someone has while in this stage varies from newly appointed managers to traditional leaders with a year's worth of experience repeated for several years. You may have met people who claim to have 20 years of technical experience but perform as well as someone who typically has one year's experience (hence, they seem to have had one year of experience repeated 20 times).

Practitioners at Stage I tend to convey an "I know" attitude. They may appear confident in what they are doing, but often their confidence level

Table 14.3 21st Century Leadership Development Roadmap's Characteristic Summary

Category	Stage I	Stage II	Stage III	Stage IV
The continuum between traditional leadership and 21st Century Leadership	Committed to traditional leadership	Aware of traditional leadership limitations	Begin to integrate the 21st Century Leadership principles and beliefs	Committed to 21st Century Leadership
Confidence level	False confidence	Decreased confidence	Confidence building	High confidence
The four stages of competence[a]	Unconscious/unskilled	Conscious/unskilled	Conscious/skilled	Unconscious/skilled
C2 approach	Own command and control	Experiment with sharing command and control	Share more command and control	Promote shared command and control
Leadership development approach	Indifferent to leadership development	Value leadership development	Seek leadership development opportunities	Practice stewardship (technical, functional, and leadership development)

Mistakes	Deny mistakes	Recognize mistakes	Make fewer mistakes	Manage mistakes
Leadership performance	Unaware of leadership gaps	Identify some leadership gaps and strengths	Share leadership gaps with others, address gaps, and confirm strengths	Continue to monitor and address leadership gaps and strengths
Nine practices usage	Unaware of the nine practices	Study, reflect, and begin to apply the nine practices	Continue to study, reflect, apply, refine, and internalize the nine practices	Continue to improve applying and internalizing the nine practices
Short-term vs. long-term focus	Focus more on short-term results	Focus more on short-term results but aware of the need for having a long-term focus	Focus more on long-term results	Focus more on long-term results
Metaphorical alignment to development levels	D1: Low competence and high commitment	D2: Low to some competence and low commitment	D3: Moderate to high competence and variable commitment	D4: High competence and high commitment

[a] Hunter, 2012, *The Servant*, xxvii; Mindtools, n.d., *The Conscious Competence Ladder.*

> ### BOX 14.4   WHY SOME DO NOT DEVELOP
> ### LEADERSHIP PRACTICES
>
> People aren't given feedback and assume what they are doing is working. Sometimes, many times, people don't want to be coached. They don't think they are the problem or that they need to improve.[10]
>
> **Bishop et al**

isn't based on any criteria other than a gut feeling. Stage I practitioners lack the knowledge and skills to practice 21st Century Leadership. Thus, they see little value in leadership development, are unaware of their leadership gaps and the nine practices. They tend to retain and not share the command-and-control tasks in which they must approve the actions of others and determine what others should do and often how to do what to do.

Unfortunately, some become stuck at Stage I. In a University of North Carolina at Charlotte qualitative study, leadership-development experts explained why some clients choose not to develop. In interviews, the experts shared that some resist developing their leadership because of a variety of excuses:

- Don't have enough time to train and have competing priorities
- Resist giving and receiving feedback
- Lack of commitment

Interviewees explained that some are egotistic or have a weak self-awareness (Box 14.4)

In practice, they ignore or deny their own mistakes and often blame others for problems. As I noted in Chapter 5, Rummler frequently encountered such managers and executives in his career and expressed his frustration with how they blame subordinates and others for organizational and process problems.

What You Need to Advance to Stage II

To advance to Stage II, you need to accomplish at least the following actions:

- Become aware of 21st Century Leadership principles, beliefs, and practices. Hunter calls this setting the standard for great leadership or the

Foundation Step.[11] You can accomplish this by reading leadership books or attending workshops.

■ Recognize that traditional leadership is problematic and agree intellectually that 21st Century Leadership is what people should be practicing.
■ Be willing to improve how you practice leadership.

Accomplishing these actions isn't enough to sustain new leadership practices, and attending a workshop won't be enough. These actions enable you to begin the journey from traditional leadership towards 21st Century Leadership practices.

Stage II: I Don't Know

Characteristics

At Stage II, people know that practicing leadership is challenging and that traditional leadership has limitations. The more people study 21st Century Leadership principles, beliefs, and practices, the more realistic their confidence level becomes, and the more they realize that they don't know leadership. They are more conscious of their abilities and recognize that they need to develop how they practice leadership. They identify some of their leadership gaps and areas of strength.

Practitioners at Stage II realize that they don't know everything about leadership. They recognize some mistakes they have made while studying, reflecting, and applying the nine practices. Previously, they focused on short-term results, but now they consider the long-term results for accomplishing work while improving team relations and feelings of safety.

What You Need to Advance to Stage III

To advance to Stage III, you need to accomplish at least the following actions:

■ Continue studying leadership. Keep performance aids such as a list of principles, beliefs, and practices nearby to remind you what you should be holding yourself accountable to and should be practicing.
■ Experiment with applying new leadership practices. Recognize that you will experience some success but also some setbacks.

- Conduct a 360° feedback. Hunter calls this the *Feedback Step.*[12] Obtain quality feedback data on leadership practices to identify gaps to know what to start doing, keep doing, and stop doing. Acknowledge strengths and areas for improvement.
- Identify one to two specific goals to work on and determine measures for success. Talk with your team and others about your goals and how you want to make sustainable changes. Ask the team and others to provide support and to hold you accountable. Make it safe for others to do this. Hunter calls this the *Friction Step.*[13]
- Obtain enough feedback and data to confirm that you achieved your goals for at least one month.
- Once you feel comfortable about the first one or two goals, add another goal to work on.

Accomplishing these actions is enough to demonstrate a commitment to move from traditional leadership practices toward 21st Century Leadership practices. Most flounder within this stage make some improvements but fail to advance. Some experience what Grenny et al. call arrested development.[14] With arrested development, people learn some leadership practices or specific tasks until the practices or tasks become automatic. With their success, they believe that they have reached an acceptable level, but they actually experience a developmental plateau. They fail to develop fully and never realize their limited development.

Stage III: I Know That I Don't Know

Characteristics

People in Stage II know about leadership, but people in Stage III experience leadership, including the immediate and short-term performance results and the long-term business results. Moreover, some make the connection between leadership practices and societal results. Wiseman and McKeown label these people at Stage III as *multipliers.*

Stage III practitioners know that they don't know everything about leadership and how to practice leadership. They are still learning and are building their confidence. They actively seek leadership development opportunities to further their studies and reflect on refining and internalizing 21st Century Leadership practices. They make fewer mistakes and still seek feedback from others to improve. They use 360° feedback surveys to identify one to two leadership goals to develop and ask others to support them to achieve the goal or goals.

In practice, they share more of the command-and-control function. When working with others, they view the shared work systemically and think more about the long-term results that their team can achieve while strengthening working relations. Stage III practitioners apply the first eight practices consistently and have begun practicing *Communicating Like Broadcasters* by sharing their expertise with others beyond their team. They recognize the value of stewardship and giving back to their organization, profession, and community.

What You Need to Advance to Stage IV

To advance to Stage IV, you need to accomplish at least the following actions:

- Continue studying and practicing leadership.
- Continue with 360° feedback surveys. You achieved this action when your last survey results indicated that you progressed in the first eight leadership practices but still have opportunities for improvement.
- Begin practicing stewardship (ninth practice) by sharing with others. This may include technical skills or leadership practices.

Accomplishing these actions demonstrates that you have internalized the first eight practices and begun applying the ninth practice.

Stage IV: I Don't Know What I Don't Know

Characteristics

Stage IV practitioners have fully integrated the 21st Century Leadership principles, beliefs, and practices. They have high confidence but, at the same time, they recognize that they don't know what they don't know. They are still learning and are lifelong learners who continue to develop and grow, including developing how they apply the nine practices. Practicing leadership comes naturally, although this wasn't always the case. They continue to monitor their leadership, make mistakes, ask for feedback, and model how to use a 360° feedback process effectively.

In practice, they share the command-and-control function with others and promote doing the same with their peers. They balance short-term results with long-term results, and they practice stewardship regularly.

What You Need to Maintain Stage IV

To maintain Stage IV, you need to accomplish at least the following actions:

- Continue 360° feedback. This ensures that you maintain your practices and models for others in the *Facing the Unknown Like Lions* practice.
- Find one or two behaviors to focus on exploring and developing.
- Continue to practice stewardship.

What to Do: Using the Roadmap to Sustain Your Journey

As I stated earlier, the roadmap is a way to learn about the journey from practicing traditional leadership to 21st Century Leadership. Use and revisit the roadmap periodically to assess how you are doing, verify if you are working on the most beneficial tasks for your development, and anticipate what you should be doing to transition to your next stage of leadership development.

The roadmap approximates the typical journey. Like any model, the roadmap has limitations and may not accurately represent everyone's experience. For example, you may not be an individual starting your career; traditional leadership doesn't represent you. Given the limitations, determine how you can leverage the roadmap to guide you on your journey. You might find it beneficial to invite like-minded colleagues on a similar journey to review and discuss the roadmap and to offer ways to support one another. Also, leveraging Table 14.1 could help you manage and improve your experience as you move from one stage to another.

Chapter 15

Considering Organizational Implications

People want to make a difference. They want to know how they contribute to the success of an organization. When we know that our work is meaningful, we still have energy at the end of the day because the sanctity of our labor has been affirmed...You may even find a purpose so captivating that it awakens the collective energies of the people with whom you work and inspires them to soar.[1]

Freiberg and Freiberg

If you develop yourself, you can experience personal success. If you develop a team, your organization can experience growth. If you develop leaders, your organization can achieve explosive growth.[2]

Maxwell

Introduction

Organizations that successfully nurture 21st Century Leadership within their teams and departments experience more productivity and a more functional,

DOI: 10.4324/9781003273448-20

positive, and supportive environment. The two organizational challenges for achieving this are influencing teams and departments to

1. Leverage and integrate the nine practices.
2. Sustain the nine practices as employees, teams, and departments experience turnover and orient new employees.

Achieving the first challenge is characterized when the following happens:

■ Managers and executives stop using traditional leadership practices, including:
   – Leverage excessive control.
   – Coercing direct reports to behave as followers.
■ All levels of employees:
   – Have more control than they traditionally had.
   – Practice 21st Century Leadership from the perspective of their formal role.[3]

For the second challenge, the following example illustrates the hallmark of achieving leadership sustainment: Diane, a manager who has successfully practiced leadership within her department for several years, leaves the organization; those who worked with Diane carry on either at the same or at a higher level of positive productivity. Marquet describes this new way of perceiving legacy in *The True Test of Leadership* video (Box 15.1).

As people transition from a team or organization, their legacy is that their peers, direct reports, and superiors continue being productive and practicing leadership after they leave.

BOX 15.1 SHIFTING FROM ONE TO EVERYONE PRACTICING LEADERSHIP: A NEW TYPE OF LEGACY

You want the resilience…, the endurance, the adaptability of the organization not to rely on one single person always making the right judgment calls or making the right decisions. You want it to be embedded in the people and the practices.[4]

Marquet

Leveraging the nine practices is the way to achieve these challenges. For example:

■ Use *Finding Key Behaviors Like Social Psychologists* to set goals, determine measures, and find the one or two key behaviors for integrating 21st Century Leadership within the organization.

■ Use the Six Boxes® Model to identify what influences are needed to help employees adopt the key behaviors needed for practicing 21st Century Leadership.

In addition to organizations influencing employees to adopt the nine practices, there are implications for managing strategy, diversity, and training. I discuss these in the following three topics. I finish the chapter by discussing implications for advancing the leadership body of knowledge.

Managing the Strategy Portfolio

Whether your organization's strategy management is centralized, decentralized, or a hybrid approach, 21st Century Leadership has implications for managing strategy. With leadership, there are two implications:

1. The competitive advantage of having employees at all levels practice leadership.
2. How organizations form, monitor, and refine their strategies.

The Competitive Advantage of Having Employees at All Levels Practice Leadership

In the Preface, I reference Gallup's state of the workplace reports (global and in the United States), which found that employees' immediate managers are responsible primarily for employee engagement.[5] Gallup also found that in 2012, only about 30% of US employees were engaged and that actively disengaged employees cost organizations an estimated $450–$550 billion annually.[6] For organizations to improve employee engagement and decrease productivity losses due to disengaged employees, they need more employees at all career levels practicing 21st Century Leadership.

Executives express the importance of developing leaders in their opinion and operating expenses. In a McKinsey & Company article, Gurdjian et al. cite that most executives surveyed list leadership development as their highest human capital priority, and US organizations invest almost $14 billion in leadership development.[7] According to Marquet, when organizations invest heavily in leadership development, the implication is that employees do not practice leadership. If everyone practiced leadership, the organization wouldn't need expensive leadership development programs.[8] Although Marquet may be correct, some might argue that organizations invest in leadership development programs to help sustain and influence leadership practices, but this could be rationalizing the investment. The reality is that most immediate managers fail to engage, as indicated in the Gallup reports.

While leadership practices are tactical, organizations that promote a leader-leader structure are strategic. Those who own the strategy need to collaborate with several departments, including training and diversity, to influence cultural tendencies from the leader-follower structure toward the leader-leader structure and 21st Century Leadership practices. To do this, you need to apply the nine practices to support this transformation; this includes setting goals and measures, identifying key behaviors, and leveraging the Six Boxes® Model to plan influences for the key behaviors.

The Way Organizations Form, Monitor, and Refine Their Strategies

People who manage organizational strategies should leverage the nine practices to form, monitor, and refine strategies. Instead of top executives determining strategy in isolation, leverage the genius of your employees. Employees at all levels can contribute to all phases of strategy formation:

1. Clarify the challenges and needs of the organization.
2. Formulate strategy design for feasibility.
3. Communicate the plan.
4. Execute the strategy.
5. Monitor the execution.
6. Refine the strategy.

BOX 15.2   FROM HIRING TO LEVERAGING INTELLIGENT PEOPLE

Some corporations have made hiring the most intelligent individuals a core strategy on the basis that smarter people can solve problems more quickly than the competition. But that only works if the organizations can access that intelligence.[9]

Wiseman

Involving all levels of the organization not only produces better strategies, communications, and buy-in, but it also produces better results than if top executives operate in isolation. Marquet states that top executives may be surprised when the least expected employee generates the next great idea and can express the idea through a shared strategic development process.[10] The challenge is finding ways to tap into their intelligence. Wiseman describes the challenge (Box 15.2).

Building Teams with Diversity and Inclusion

There are three implications for building teams with diversity and inclusion. First, what is true with strategy management is true with building teams with diversity. Teams that build diversity within organizations should leverage the nine practices in their work—from setting goals and measures to selecting influence techniques. Second, promoting the nine practices as a mechanism for generating diverse thinking can contribute toward the diversity team's mission and charter. Third, the diversity team should collaborate with those who own the leadership development program. The collaboration would ensure that the programs promote and complement the diversity and inclusion initiatives.

Rethinking Leadership Development

The owners of leadership development for an organization—typically a training department—need to align leadership training to organizational strategy and diversity strategy. Training departments can use leadership development for the following:

- Orient new employees to the cultural practices of leadership.
- Leverage current strategies as a context for practical exercises to apply and rehearse the nine practices.
- Integrate using the nine practices with real work situations; this helps employees learn how to apply the practices from the perspective of their roles.
- Measure leadership program effectiveness with before and after 360-feedback. Measure learners' career development productivity improvements.[11]
- Allow learners to experience some discomfort to enable new levels of leadership development.

In a McKinsey & Company article, Gurdjian et al. explain this last point (Box 15.3).

As Marquet and Grenny et al. might argue, leadership development programs can contribute to the organization by breaking the genetic code (or code of silence). Doing so enables discussions about the culture that have been traditionally discouraged.[12] For Marquet, this involves

---

BOX 15.3   LEADERSHIP DEVELOPMENT SHOULD CAUSE SOME DISCOMFORT

Just as a coach would view an athlete's muscle pain as a proper response to training, leaders who are stretching themselves should also feel some discomfort as they struggle to reach new levels of leadership performance...Identifying some of the deepest, "below the surface" thoughts, feelings, assumptions, and beliefs is usually a precondition of behavioral change—one too often shirked in development programs.[13]

Gurdjian et al.

emancipation or having managers share C2. When C2 is shared, managers enable the employees to express their genius, higher levels of energy, and creativity.[14]

For Grenny et al., breaking the genetic code involves addressing unhealthy norms, such as when executives and managers punish employees who confront harmful norms. Management needs to publicly discourage unhealthy norms to extinguish them.[15]

Another example is 360-feedback. Some HR departments avoid 360-feedback and argue that the executives and managers are too uncomfortable to receive corrective feedback. Thus, Gurdjian et al. advocate for leadership development programs to accept their role of causing some discomfort to help others grow.

Training departments also tend to mix executive and management training with leadership development—maybe training departments confuse this type of training with leadership development. Maybe executives and managers are more open to leadership development than executive or management training, or maybe there is another reason for this blend. Regardless of the reason, training departments tend to offer executives and managers formal training on leadership development but fail to provide leadership development for the remaining employees. When those responsible for leadership development separate leadership practices from executive and managerial processes, they have an opportunity to strategize how to handle executive development, management development, and leadership development. For 21st Century Leadership, this involves strategizing with other departments on influencing more of a leader-leader structure and less of a leader-follower structure. Using the nine practices and related tools and resources to influence 21st Century leadership practices is an effective way to accomplish this.

Advancing 21st Century Leadership

Based on themes and patterns that I have identified in my analysis of 21st Century Leadership authors, this book summarizes my findings, and much could be improved. Table 15.1 suggests areas for further research on the evolving 21st Century Leadership.

Table 15.1   Summary of Further Research about 21st Century Leadership

Area	Explanation	Opportunity
Confusion about leadership	I identify six reasons why leadership is confusing.	Most likely, additional reasons could address the elusiveness of leadership.
21st Century Leadership definition	To create a definition, I removed leadership actions (such as influencing), performance results (such as removing barriers), business results, and societal results. I classify this as a performance-improvement discipline and explain how it differs from other disciplines by building character. Because building character might be misunderstood, I define building character as maturing an individual's mental and moral qualities, capabilities, and behaviors. I further state that it is bidirectional.	After examining 21st Century Leadership elements such as the principles, beliefs, practices, and results, there are opportunities to refine the definition to make it more memorable and easier to grasp without losing the importance of improving mental and moral thinking.
21st Century Leadership principles and beliefs	I identify the principles and beliefs of the authors in my analysis. I identify some from multiple sources, such as the concept of sacrifice. I identify others from one source only. For example, from Wiseman, I sourced Belief 16, Encouraging People to Grow and Leave Their Role Contributes to Organizational Growth.	The list of principles and beliefs could be refined and detailed. Some may be too specific to one source and removed, while others could be combined. There may be more principles and beliefs that I haven't discovered that would be worth adding.
Traditional leadership and assumptions	As with 21st Century Leadership principles and beliefs, I identify the traditional leadership assumptions from my analysis findings. Before publication, I removed some that I felt were uninformative.	As with the principles and beliefs, the assumptions could be refined and detailed.

(Continued)

Table 15.1 (*Continued*) **Summary of Further Research about 21st Century Leadership**

Area	*Explanation*	*Opportunity*
Nine practices	As with the principles, beliefs, and assumptions, I derived the practices from my analysis. Some are more universal than others, such as *Communicating Like Agents* and *Directing Like Guides.* Others seem to be evolving and not discussed frequently, such as *Communicating Like Broadcasters.*	The practices could be refined and detailed. Some might serve better as a subset of another practice or be eliminated. Also, I haven't tried aligning qualities to the nine practices, which may be an opportunity worth exploring.
21st Century Leadership Development Roadmap	Years ago, I was influenced by the concept of maturity models. I developed maturity models for performance, knowledge management, and leadership development. As I worked on this book, the model evolved into a roadmap that illustrates a typical journey from traditional leadership to 21st Century Leadership.	There are opportunities to refine or even rebuild the roadmap. Each stage could be detailed more.
Nine Practices 360-Feedback Diagnostic Tool	In Appendix V, I provide a 360-feedback diagnostic tool based on the nine practices with three questions for each practice.	The 360-feedback tool could be tested, refined, and improved. There may be opportunities to combine this tool based on leadership qualities.

Afterword: The Fundamental Attribution Error

> Whenever others cause us inconvenience or pain, we have a natural tendency to suspect they have selfish motives coupled with malicious intentions.[1]
>
> **Grenny et al.**

As I study the nine practices, I frequently encounter a theme about the need for people to make ambiguous observations clear, mainly related to behavior. Accepting ambiguity without interpretation is difficult to do. When observing someone's behavior, you tend to act on a habit—consciously or unconsciously—of interpreting what you observe. Patterson et al. describe this process as (1) seeing and hearing, (2) telling a story, (3) feeling, and (4) acting[2] (Box A.1).

For example, at an office, Alex sees that Mandy uses company time to shop for a car on websites. Alex thinks that Mandy just doesn't want to do that on her own time and is taking advantage of the company's work time. This—really bothers Alex. Alex starts complaining to coworkers about how Mandy takes advantage of the company.

Making up stories can be harmful. The problem isn't that people don't know the whole story, such as Alex not knowing Mandy's intent or situation. The problem is that people have a habit of replacing ambiguity with a story that is often inaccurate and less than flattering of another person's character. Worse, people generalize about a person's character based not on facts but on made-up stories, so people conclude that others are lazy, dishonest, stupid, incompetent, crazy, deceitful, or even vindictive. Grenny et al. describe *labeling* as assuming the moral defect of others.[3] When you

BOX A.1   ELIMINATE AMBIGUITY BY TELLING A STORY

1. *Seeing and Hearing*: Observe someone's behavior.
2. *Telling a Story*: Because you cannot know what someone is thinking, make up a story and assume the person's intent.
3. *Feeling*: React to the story that you made up, which might include:
   a. Reacting emotionally such as being upset about the assumed intent.
   b. Arriving at a generalization such as the person is lazy or is incompetent.
4. *Acting*: Take action based on your reaction and made-up story.[4]

Patterson et al.

label someone by generalizing from questionable stories, you set the person up so that you and others perceive the person negatively and task the labeled person with the monumental challenge of proving the label to be false or inaccurate. People can change their behaviors, but they have a more challenging time changing labels forced on them—fairly or unfairly.

There is a substantial difference between how people judge themselves and how they judge others. Inside your head, you know your intent, thinking, and rationale. You are moderately aware of external forces influencing your actions and understand your rationale and behavior. As Muzio writes, you cannot know the thinking and intent of others in the way that you know your own thinking and intent (Box A.2).

**BOX A.2   FALLACY OF THINKING OTHERS
ACT FROM PERSONAL CHOICE ONLY**

As it turns out, despite our best intentions, we systematically discount the power of context to drive our actions. Even in seemingly obvious scenarios, we tend to overestimate the role of the individual and underestimate the role of the situation....The people around you are strongly influenced by their peers, their authority figures, and their role sets. But when you observe their actions, you tend to think that they are acting from personal choice alone, and you respond accordingly.[5]

Muzio

BOX A.3   FUNDAMENTAL ATTRIBUTION ERROR

Assuming that others do contrary things because it's in their makeup or they actually enjoy doing them and then ignoring any other potential motivational forces is a mistake. Psychologists classify this mistake as an attribution error. And because it happens so consistently across people, times, and places, it gets a name all its own. It's called the fundamental attribution error.[6]

Patterson et al.

When people make up stories based on guesswork, they make an attribution error by attributing behavioral intent to come more from within the person than the environment. When people make generalizations based on made-up stories, they commit the fundamental attribution error. Patterson et al. describe this error (Box A.3).

The fundamental attribution error and attribution errors are understated and often misunderstood. As habits, people commit these errors regularly, automatically, and often unconsciously. Moreover, people can commit these errors when observing any behavior. As Grenny et al. note, "All behaviors are ambiguous," and people interpret behaviors negatively within environments full of mistrust.[7]

Several of the nine practices are designed to promote the withholding of judgment about behaviors that may be symptoms and promote a curiosity to discover root causes. Also, the nine practices help people discipline themselves to replace making up stories with investigative thinking or acceptance of the unknown. Some practices help others engage in dialogue to learn about others' intent and feelings—humanizing who they are instead of dehumanizing while distancing themselves in isolation.

With so many lousy work environments consisting of people who detach themselves and unfairly interpret actions negatively, you can easily understand how people placed in those harmful environments would change for the worse and assume the worst in others. The tragedy, of course, is that work environments don't have to be like this.

Bruce Alexander wrote a series of fictional books that took place in London, England, around the late 18th century. The stories are about Sir John Fielding, magistrate of Bow Street Court and investigator of crimes, and Jeremy, his young protégé. Along with Mr. Donnelly, the medico and coroner's assistant, they encounter villainous characters who leave horrific crime scenes in their wake. As they investigate, they interact with various citizens, some who are honest and hardworking and others who are down on their luck. After Jeremy puts his trust in one person with unfavorable results, Mr. Donnelly shares some advice with Jeremy about his misfortune that has left him sad and disappointed.

> There is so much misery in this world, Jeremy, and so little charity, that I would not have you harden your heart to anyone. As you grow to be a man, you will hear many tales of misfortune and injustice from individuals, and some may prove to be false, told simply to gain a shilling or some favor. But the next tale you hear may be true, and the innocence you perceive in the teller may be as real as real can be. So let us help as we can, and not look too deeply into motives.[8]

> **Alexander**

After having several bad experiences in which people take advantage of you, you might overcompensate and assume the worst in others. At times, society can be a harmful environment full of mistrust and defensiveness. The truth is that you may never fully understand why people behave the way they do, and you may never have the opportunity to learn more about another's intent. As much as possible, try avoiding the natural tendency to make up stories that explain behaviors. Instead, as Marquet suggests, maintain a sense of curiosity and try not to rush to judgment. Allow yourself to be surprised when you learn the rest of the story, as Paul Harvey might say. Maybe by doing so, all of us could make the world a little better for others. At the very least, even at the risk of failure, we should try.

Appendix I
21st Century Leadership Definition, Principles, Practices, and Results

Definition	A bidirectional set of practices founded on guiding principles and beliefs	Designed to mature mental and moral: • Qualities • Capabilities • Behaviors
Principles	Believe in others Connect with others Put others first Give up control	Encourage growth Collaborate with others Develop leadership practices continuously
Practices	Analyzing Like Detectives Diagnosing and Treating Like Doctors Finding Key Behaviors Like Social Psychologists Communicating Like Agents	Directing Like Guides Nurturing Like Gardeners Facing the Unknown Like Lions Developing Like Scouts Communicating Like Broadcasters
Immediate Results	Fulfilled needs rather than wants	Removed or reduced barriers Improved performance
Short and Long-Term Results	Improved work environment Increased feelings of safety among teammates Increased collaboration	Strengthened relationships Increased mental and moral capabilities, especially creativity, innovation, and learning
Business Results	Increased employee engagement Increased profitability Decreased operational costs Improved customer experience	Decreased absenteeism and turnover Reduced product theft, defects, and damages Decreased safety incidents (amount and severity)
Societal Results	Improved local and larger communities Improved leadership communities of practice	Increased volunteering activities Increased stewardship practices

Appendix II
21st Century Leadership Principles, Beliefs, and Practices Alignment

21st Century Leadership Definition: Bidirectional practices designed to mature mental and moral qualities, capabilities, and behaviors

No.	Underlying Principles		Primarily Related Beliefs	Related Practices (Primary, Secondary, and Tertiary)
1	Believe in others	1	Intelligence is not static and can be developed continuously	Directing Like Guides Nurturing Like Gardeners Communicating Like Broadcasters
		2	Everyone can practice leadership regardless of role	Communicating Like Agents Directing Like Guides Nurturing Like Gardeners
2	Connect with others	3	Being vulnerable and getting to know others builds trust and relationships	Communicating Like Agents Directing Like Guides Facing the Unknown Like Lions

(Continued)

No.	Underlying Principles		Primarily Related Beliefs	Related Practices (Primary, Secondary, and Tertiary)
		4	Sharing your mistakes builds credibility	Communicating Like Agents Directing Like Guides Facing the Unknown Like Lions
		5	Celebrations build community, connect events to values, renew commitment, promote social support, and improve everyone's well-being	Communicating Like Agents Directing Like Guides Nurturing Like Gardeners
3	Put others first	6	Giving credit for accomplishments to others is more important than taking credit	Communicating Like Agents Directing Like Guides Nurturing Like Gardeners
		7	Employees serve customers before serving management	Analyzing Like Detectives Diagnosing and Treating Like Doctors Finding Key Behaviors Like Social Psychologists
		8	When outcomes are disappointing, accepting responsibility but never blaming (others or bad luck) is critical for personal accountability	Communicating Like Agents Directing Like Guides Facing the Unknown Like Lions
		9	Leadership is action that focuses on others and not the actor	All
		10	Sacrificing or volunteering time, energy, resources, ego, and previous priorities to help others inspires loyalty and commitment	Communicating Like Agents Directing Like Guides Communicating Like Broadcasters

No.	*Underlying Principles*		*Primarily Related Beliefs*	*Related Practices (Primary, Secondary, and Tertiary)*
4	Give up control	11	Control erodes relationships	Communicating Like Agents Directing Like Guides Facing the Unknown Like Lions
		12	Leading well is about empowering others	Communicating Like Agents Directing Like Guides Nurturing Like Gardeners
		13	By making yourself dispensable, you make yourself indispensable	Communicating Like Agents Directing Like Guides Nurturing Like Gardeners
		14	Command and control is a shared responsibility	Communicating Like Agents Directing Like Guides Nurturing Like Gardeners
5	Encourage growth	15	Helping others figure out their development enhances their ability to contribute	Analyzing Like Detectives Diagnosing and Treating Like Doctors Directing Like Guides
		16	Encouraging people to grow and leave their role contributes to organizational growth	Diagnosing and Treating Like Doctors Communicating Like Agents Directing Like Guides
		17	Allowing teams to make mistakes enables them to be open with their mistakes and learn from the experience	Analyzing Like Detectives Communicating Like Agents Directing Like Guides

(Continued)

No.	*Underlying Principles*		*Primarily Related Beliefs*	*Related Practices (Primary, Secondary, and Tertiary)*
		18	If you change the conditions in which others operate, you can change their behaviors	Communicating Like Agents Directing Like Guides Nurturing Like Gardeners
6	Collaborate with others	19	Organizational charts limit thinking	Finding Key Behaviors Like Social Psychologists Communicating Like Agents Nurturing Like Gardeners
		20	Considering problems from a systemic perspective minimizes using blame	Analyzing Like Detectives Diagnosing and Treating Like Doctors Finding Key Behaviors Like Social Psychologists
		21	Leadership doesn't reside with one person	Communicating Like Agents Directing Like Guides Communicating Like Broadcasters
		22	Influence comes from all directions	Analyzing Like Detectives Diagnosing and Treating Like Doctors Finding Key Behaviors Like Social Psychologists
		23	Leadership practices work the same with all populations, including peers, customers, supervisors, and subordinates	All

No.	*Underlying Principles*		*Primarily Related Beliefs*	*Related Practices (Primary, Secondary, and Tertiary)*
7	Develop leadership practices continuously	24	To become fluent in leadership, practice leadership regularly, and monitor your effectiveness	Facing the Unknown Like Lions Developing Like Scouts Communicating Like Broadcasters
		25	Knowing everything about leadership is not enough	Finding Key Behaviors Like Social Psychologists Facing the Unknown Like Lions Developing Like Scouts
		26	Leadership involves helping others practice leadership	Communicating Like Agents Directing Like Guides Communicating Like Broadcasters

Appendix III
Traditional Leadership Assumptions and Related Consequences

Category	No.	Assumption	Why Assume This?	Example Leaders' Behaviors	Short-Term Results on Team
Characterizing leadership	1	Leaders need authority	Teams only follow leaders with authority Leaders need authority to control teams	Make decisions without team input Emphasize the disciplinary consequences for poor performance	Compliant Worry about negative consequences if you do not perform well Unwilling to voice concerns
	2	Leaders are heroes who leave a legacy	Teams are incapable of solving problems or helping themselves without a leader Leadership is about rescuing teams from problems and incidents Leaders are smarter than team members	Make all team decisions Require team members to obtain approval from the leader before doing anything	Compliant Discouraged from making decisions or owning problems
	3	Intimacy weakens leadership	Teams may take advantage of leaders who are intimate and vulnerable Leaders need to avoid having a manager–friendship conflict Leaders do not trust teams	Avoid sharing personal life with the team Discuss only work with the team while minimizing interactions	Believe that the leader doesn't know the team well or how the leader affects their feelings Worries that the leader does not personally like the team Do not feel valued
	4	Giving away power weakens leadership	Leaders who empower teams weaken their authority and appear to have less value and are therefore dispensable Organizations trust and assign power to leaders but not team members Team members are not smart enough to handle power effectively	Make all decisions for the team Become too involved in day-to-day work Limit what team members can do and say to other teams and customers	Compliant Wait for the leader to approve work or respond to requests Frustrated with delays

(Continued)

Category	No.	Assumption	Why Assume This?	Example Leaders' Behaviors	Short-Term Results on Team
	5	Only one person—typically a manager—functions as the leader	Teams with more than one leader have too many conflicts and productivity problems Organizations assign leadership roles only to executive and middle-manager positions Leaders feel threatened if team members try to lead (taking away authority from the leader) Teams are incapable of leading	Dominate team discussions Discipline team members who try to lead Discourage teams from being too vocal	Discourage collaboration with the leader Believe the leader will not consider opposing views Unsure of the boundaries between following and leading
	6	The leader is the smartest	Leaders believe that intelligence is rare and that they are intelligent Over time, leaders assume that teams cannot figure out any solutions or make sound decisions without help from leadership	Limit what team members can do to contribute to projects Criticize team members when they make mistakes Frequently remind the team of past mistakes	Rely on the leader to make all decisions Withhold suggestions Fear being criticized by the leader
Characterizing team members	7	Team members are the cause of unproductivity	Because teams do the work, team members cause productivity problems Leaders do not consider (or know how to consider) root causes Leaders distrust team members	Monitor work too closely Discipline teams unfairly Blame the team when deliverables are late, not to quality, or too costly	Compliant after being disciplined Distrust the leader when the team unfairly blamed for problems
	8	Team members cannot be trusted	Teams are dishonest and lazy Without leaders constantly monitoring, teams fail to accomplish work on time and to quality Teams are not accountable	Frequently monitor teams Prevent teams from working from home Question team members' loyalty to the organization	Only feel obligated to work Distrust the leader
	9	Team members are less important than revenue, profits, operational expenses, and leaders	Without revenue and profits, organizations cannot pay teams Unproductive team members should be terminated during financial difficulties Leaders are more difficult to replace than team members	When profits are low, terminate team members Terminate unproductive team members rather than helping them improve	Distrust the leader Fear losing their jobs
Working in teams	10	Talking is more important than listening	Leaders know best Leaders do not value team members' thoughts and input Leaders do not know how to listen and may not be aware of this	Interrupt team members when they are talking Focus on responding to team member comments without trying to understand the perspective Argue with team members	Withhold ideas and suggestions Avoid talking with the leader

Category	No.	Assumption	Why Assume This?	Example Leaders' Behaviors	Short-Term Results on Team
	11	Recognition is a formal process	Leaders do not believe recognition is necessary except when the organization requires recognition Leaders believe teams already know their value Leaders believe that too much recognition is counter-effective	Complain about having to recognize the team Display nonverbal behavior that implies a dislike for formal recognition	Perceive recognition to be artificial and a waste of time Feel undervalued
Becoming a leader	12	Leadership requires little or no training	Because of initial accomplishments, leaders believe that they have mastered leadership Because leadership is a simple concept, leaders require no ongoing training Leaders perceive problems with teams and the organization to be caused by team members but not leadership	Avoid any optional leadership training Collect leadership books but do not read them	Distrust the leader Believe that the leader does not value training or want to improve
	13	Leaders know how effective their leadership is	Leaders believe that their leadership is self-apparent and effective Leaders assume that their behavior has a positive impact on team members Leaders are afraid of feedback and prefer to think that they are effective leaders	Never request 360-feedback or ask the team for feedback Cause team members to be uncomfortable when they try to provide feedback Punish team members who offer constructive feedback	Withhold feedback from the leader Complain to each other about the leader

Appendix IV
Nine Practices

No.	Practice	Description	Principles, Guidelines, and Rules of Practice	Models, Techniques, and Tools	Book and Web Resources
1	Analyzing Like Detectives	Use systemic thinking to investigate problems and opportunities Discover data to aid decision-makers Promote critical thinking and improve how teams and others collaborate	Six fundamental laws of organizational systems Three levels of performance Four common mistakes when designing and managing performance levels	Anatomy of Performance (AOP) Human Performance System (HPS) Troubleshooting the HPS Performance Chain Six Boxes® Model	*Human Competence* *Improving Performance* ispi.org *Organizational Intelligence* *Performance Architecture* *Serious Performance Consulting* sixboxes.com *The Ten-Day MBA*
2	Diagnosing and Treating Like Doctors	Discover root problems Minimize reacting to symptoms and treating symptoms as if they are the root problem Use diagnostics to compare and contrast the desired or normal state with the current state and then determine the differences Avoid the mistake of prescribing a single treatment to complex problems and situations	Results Improvement Process (RIP)	Seven Key AOP Alignment Points Data-gathering techniques	*Baldrige Award Winning Quality* *Baldrige Performance Excellence Program* *Handbook of Human Performance Technology* *Handbook of Task Analysis Procedures* ispi.org *Performance-Based Evaluation* *Performance Consulting* *Serious Performance Consulting* *Strategic Business Partner*
3	Finding Key Behaviors Like Social Psychologists	Find and influence others to adopt the right key behaviors while avoiding the wrong behaviors Set goals and measures; find key behaviors; use multiple influences to support the new key behaviors	Pareto principle The golden rule of habit change Three keys to influence change	Six Sources of Influence™	Aberdeen Group *All Washed Up!* (video) APQC Behaviour Change (video) Josh Bersin Academy *Change Habits* (video) Corporate Executive Board *Crucial Accountability* Human Capital Institute Human Capital Media *Influencer* Process Excellence Network Skillsoft Books Strategy+Business *The Power of Habit*

(Continued)

No.	Practice	Description	Principles, Guidelines, and Rules of Practice	Models, Techniques, and Tools	Book and Web Resources
4	Communicating Like Agents	Use communication to influence others to want to act effectively and morally Avoid using coercion and verbal persuasion techniques such as threatening (explicitly or implicitly), complaining, or begging Act as agents on behalf of stakeholders not present when conveying thoughts and feelings Share command and control with others Collaborate with others to clarify purpose	Influence tactics for those assigned to manage individual contributors and teams Tactics for all formal roles to influence others to act Marquet's clarity approach Sinek's Why concept Blanchard, Zigarmi, and Zigarmi on commitment	Grenny et al. on motivation Drexler/Sibbet Team Performance Model"	*Helping People Win at Work* *How Great Leaders Inspire Action* (video) *Multipliers* *Start with Why* *The 3 Keys to Empowerment* *The Five Dysfunctions of a Team* *Turn the Ship Around!* www.grove.com
5	Directing Like Guides	Help others improve their capabilities to enable them to act When others choose not to act, determine if the source is due to motivation, inability, or a mixture of the two; motivation and ability are often interrelated and inseparable	–	Situational Leadership® II Cognitive apprenticeship Bandura's vicarious learning Grenny et al.'s personal ability	*Crucial Accountability* *Helping People Win at Work* *Influencer* *The 3 Keys to Empowerment*
6	Nurturing Like Gardeners	Make it easier for others to act by changing the environment and providing performance support Change the space and environment to make the right choices easier and the wrong choices more difficult	–	Grenny et al. and structural ability tactics Handshaw and performance-support solutions	*Influencer* kenblanchard.com *Training that Delivers Results*
7	Facing the Unknown Like Lions	Listen critically to others in a way that the majority of people fail to do so Avoid losing focus when listening to others Have the courage to leverage direct and indirect feedback to improve your leadership practices	Kouzes and Posner's advice on receiving feedback	Serious listening techniques Graves' Five Levels of Listening Nine Practices 360-Feedback Diagnostic Tool	*360 Degree Feedback: The Good, the Bad, and the Ugly* (webpage) *5 ways to listen better* *Just Listen* *Power Score* *Shh! Sound health in 8 steps* *The 7 Reasons Why 360 Degree Feedback Programs Fail* (webpage) *The 8th Habit* *The World's Most Powerful Leadership Principle*
8	Developing Like Scouts	Search outside the organization for the next great idea and network connection As discovered by many CEOs, connecting with others outside the organization and putting yourself in new situations lead to innovation and creativity	Build your network of talent Kouzes and Posner's tactics for generating new ideas	–	*The Leadership Challenge* *Who*

No.	Practice	Description	Principles, Guidelines, and Rules of Practice	Models, Techniques, and Tools	Book and Web Resources
9	Communicating Like Broadcasters	Give back to your organization, profession, and community through stewardship Continue to learn through teaching others Convey your years of learning through a variety of media	–	Maxwell's eight guidelines for connecting with others	*The 21 Irrefutable Laws of Leadership*

Appendix V
Nine Practices 360° Feedback Diagnostic Tool

One technique for identifying areas for developing leadership practices is 360° feedback. Use the following table to have others evaluate your leadership practices. There are 27 items, 3 for each of the nine practices, in the table. Refer to Chapter 11, *Facing the Unknown Like Lions*, for more details about 360° feedback.

To increase the success of this diagnostic tool, follow these high-level steps:

1. Use the tool to self-assess.
2. Invite respondents to participate.
3. Prepare the assessment. Use a survey application such as Survey Monkey or Zoomerang. Ensure that the respondents' responses are anonymous.
4. Email your respondents either a link to your survey or attach a document version. Include a deadline.
5. Compile the results.
6. Compare your self-assessment to the compiled respondents' assessments. Identify areas for improvement and prioritize the top one (or at most two) to address.
7. For each area, create an objective, a measure to know when the objective is achieved, and a deadline to complete the objective(s).
8. If you have a team, meet with them to summarize what you discovered. Share your objectives and seek their support. Based on any feedback, revise your objectives as needed.
9. Thank your respondents and let them know your objectives.

Instructions: With each item, circle the response number or letter to rate how you believe the statement accurately describes the person you are evaluating. Use the comment field to provide any insight into your selection.

No.	Statement	Response 4 = Strongly Agree 3 = Agree 2 = Disagree 1 = Strongly Disagree U = Unknown	Comment
1	Withholds judgment until the person can examine facts, seek clarification, and uncover what is actually happening	4 3 2 1 U	
2	Knows not only how business in general works but also how the organization where the person works is structured to provide for customers	4 3 2 1 U	
3	Collaborates with others to solve problems and find opportunities	4 3 2 1 U	
4	Diagnoses problems effectively and responsibly to find solutions	4 3 2 1 U	
5	Uses measurements effectively to determine if solutions are achieved	4 3 2 1 U	
6	Helps others avoid rushing to solutions without diagnosing the problem	4 3 2 1 U	
7	Influences the behaviors of others effectively while maintaining positive relationships with them	4 3 2 1 U	
8	Avoids using verbal persuasion such as threats (expressed or implied), complaining, nagging, or begging	4 3 2 1 U	
9	Influences others to work effectively and collaboratively	4 3 2 1 U	

#	Item	4	3	2	1	U	
10	Clarifies expectations when working with others	4	3	2	1	U	
11	Acknowledges and learns from mistakes	4	3	2	1	U	
12	Involves others with problem-solving and decision making	4	3	2	1	U	
13	Coaches others to build their capabilities	4	3	2	1	U	
14	Supports others who may need help accomplishing tasks	4	3	2	1	U	
15	Provides feedback to help others learn	4	3	2	1	U	
16	Encourages and cares for others by making the environment more favorable for work and development	4	3	2	1	U	
17	Finds creative solutions that make work easier for everyone (such as making job aids, templates, and other support documents)	4	3	2	1	U	
18	Uses data to provide others with insight	4	3	2	1	U	
19	Listens carefully to what others say with the intent to understand their perspective rather than listening to respond	4	3	2	1	U	
20	Seeks feedback from others to improve leadership practices	4	3	2	1	U	
21	Shares leadership goals and asks for support in achieving them	4	3	2	1	U	
22	Beyond what the organization requires, invests time in professional development opportunities such as attending webinars, chapter association events, and conferences	4	3	2	1	U	
23	Maintains a strong professional network outside the organization	4	3	2	1	U	
24	Regularly searches for new ideas and ways of practicing and shares these with others in the organization	4	3	2	1	U	

(Continued)

No.	Statement	Response 4 = Strongly Agree 3 = Agree 2 = Disagree 1 = Strongly Disagree U = Unknown	Comment
25	Practices stewardship by sharing technical expertise and leadership knowledge with others outside the person's immediate team	4 3 2 1 U	
26	Actively participates in the professional community such as through an association or professional network	4 3 2 1 U	
27	Communicates with other professionals through email exchanges, blogs, networking events, chapter events, or conferences	4 3 2 1 U	

For more about this tool, an FAQ, and additional free resources, go to garyadepaul.com.

Open-Ended Questions

- What three strengths related to leadership do you perceive the person to have?
- What are three ways that the person could improve in practicing leadership?

Item No.	Related Practice
1–3	Analyzing Like Detectives
4–6	Diagnosing and Treating Like Doctors
7–9	Finding Key Behaviors Like Social Psychologists
10–12	Communicating Like Agents
13–15	Directing Like Guides
16–18	Nurturing Like Gardeners
19–21	Facing the Unknown Like Lions
22–24	Developing Like Scouts
25–27	Communicating Like Broadcasters

Appendix VI
Related Quality Terms

From three LinkedIn discussions, moderators asked group members to identify leadership qualities. The following table summarizes the leadership qualities that members identified.

1.	Ability to learn and grow	17.	Big-picture thinking
2.	Access knowledge	18.	Broad perspective
3.	Accountable	19.	Build capacity
4.	Adaptability	20.	Building teams
5.	Advocacy	21.	Business acumen
6.	Advocate diversity	22.	Business development
7.	Agility	23.	Business literacy
8.	Aligning to culture	24.	Business systems thinking
9.	Analytical	25.	Business focused
10.	Anticipate	26.	Calm under pressure
11.	Articulate	27.	Cares for others
12.	Assertiveness	28.	Catalyst
13.	Assimilating	29.	Celebrating success
14.	Authenticity	30.	Champion others
15.	Be human	31.	Champion ideas
16.	Behavioral knowledge	32.	Change agent

(*Continued*)

33.	Change management	61.	Current
34.	Close gaps	62.	Customer centricity
35.	Coaching	63.	Customer impact
36.	Collaboration	64.	Decision making
37.	Comfortable with conflict	65.	Decisive
38.	Command	66.	Debate
39.	Committed	67.	Dedicated
40.	Communication	68.	Define purpose
41.	Compassion	69.	Dealing with uncertainty
42.	Compel others to contribute their best	70.	Delegate
43.	Concern	71.	Determination
44.	Confidence	72.	Develop alliances
45.	Connect with others	73.	Developing strengths
46.	Consistency	74.	Diagnostic
47.	Continuous improvement	75.	Difficult conversations
48.	Contributor	76.	Diplomacy
49.	Corporate citizenship and responsibility	77.	Directing others
50.	Courage	78.	Diversity
51.	Create culture	79.	Divergent thinking
52.	Create more leaders	80.	Ego management
53.	Create opportunities	81.	Embrace change
54.	Creative	82.	Embrace planning
55.	Credible	83.	Embrace strategy
56.	Critical thinking	84.	Emotional awareness (others)
57.	Cultural ethics	85.	Emotional awareness (self)
58.	Cultural savvy	86.	Emotional intelligence
59.	Curation	87.	Empathy
60.	Curiosity	88.	Empowerment

89.	Encourage cooperation	118.	Good
90.	Encourage others to continuously improve	119.	Grow organizations
91.	Endure	120.	Grow teams
92.	Energetic	121.	Handle criticism
93.	Engagement	122.	Handling feedback
94.	Enhances people productivity	123.	Help others
95.	Enthusiastic	124.	Honesty
96.	Entrepreneurship	125.	HR professional
97.	Ethics	126.	Human skills
98.	Example setting	127.	Humble
99.	Execute	128.	Humility
100.	Facilitation	129.	Inclusive
101.	Fail fast	130.	Influence
102.	Failure ownership	131.	Information mining
103.	Fair	132.	Innovation
104.	Faithful	133.	Inquisitive
105.	Firm	134.	Insightful
106.	Flexibility	135.	Inspirational
107.	Forecasting	136.	Integrity
108.	Foresight	137.	Interpersonal
109.	Friend	138.	Involve others
110.	Friendly	139.	Joy
111.	Generosity	140.	Joyful
112.	Gentle	141.	Just
113.	Genuine care for others	142.	Know the work
114.	Get things done through others	143.	Know your people
115.	Global	144.	Know yourself
116.	Goal establishment	145.	Knowledge management
117.	Goal-oriented	146.	Knowledge sharing

(*Continued*)

147.	Lead in the right direction	176.	Nobility
148.	Lead self	177.	Nurturing
149.	Leading by example	178.	Observer
150.	Leading under pressure	179.	Obtain commitment
151.	Leads to leave	180.	One with the heart
152.	Learning agility	181.	Openness
153.	Leaves a legacy	182.	Organizing
154.	Letting go	183.	Organizational development
155.	Link goals to tasks	184.	Overcome obstacles
156.	Listening	185.	Own performance
157.	Loving	186.	Partnering
158.	Manage failures	187.	Passion
159.	Manage greed	188.	Patient
160.	Manage priorities	189.	Pathfinder
161.	Manage resources	190.	Peacemaker
162.	Manage success	191.	Peaceful
163.	Manage team performance	192.	People skills
164.	Manage the means	193.	Perceptive
165.	Market insights	194.	Performance coaching
166.	Measure results	195.	Performance-oriented
167.	Mediator	196.	Personal values
168.	Mentoring	197.	Planning
169.	Message effectively	198.	Political savvy
170.	Mission-oriented	199.	Positive
171.	Moral	200.	Presentation skills
172.	Motivate	201.	Priority management
173.	Negotiation	202.	Proactive
174.	Networking	203.	Problem-solving
175.	Nimble	204.	Promoting others

205.	Proposal writing	234.	Social literacy
206.	Questioning effectively	235.	Social responsibilities
207.	Realistic	236.	Social skills
208.	Reasoning	237.	Socially responsible
209.	Recognition	238.	Speed to decision
210.	Recover quickly	239.	Stay focused
211.	Reflective thinking	240.	Strategic
212.	Relationship building	241.	Strategic thinking
213.	Relationship management	242.	Support others
214.	Reliable	243.	Sustain commitment
215.	Reputation focused	244.	Sustain relationships
216.	Resource protector	245.	Systems approach
217.	Resource-based	246.	Systems thinking
218.	Respect others	247.	Taking charge
219.	Responsible	248.	Talent liberator
220.	Results-focused	249.	Team leadership
221.	Right attitude	250.	Team player
222.	Risk-taking	251.	Teacher
223.	Role model	252.	Tech-savvy
224.	Sacrifice	253.	Technical/functional
225.	Scalability	254.	Tenacity
226.	See beyond scope of profits	255.	Time management
227.	Self-assess	256.	Think differently
228.	Self-aware	257.	Thought leader
229.	Self-controlled	258.	Translating vision
230.	Self-improvement	259.	Transparency
231.	Self-regulation	260.	Trustworthy
232.	Sense of humor	261.	Truthful
233.	Set standards	262.	Understand leader/manager differences

(Continued)

263.	Visionary	267.	Willingness to ask questions
264.	Vulnerable	268.	Wise
265.	Watchful	269.	Withstanding pressure
266.	Walk the talk	270.	Workaholic

LinkedIn, 2014, *What are the most important skills and behaviors of modern leadership in your opinion?*; LinkedIn, 2014, *What traits should leadership development programs focus on?*; LinkedIn, 2014, *What competencies do you find are missing in action?*

Appendix VII
Intent-Based Leadership (IBL) Manifesto

We live by these principles…

- We view people as our purpose, not as a means.
- We commit to leading in a way that invites people to think, not in a way that gets people to do.
- We commit to creating environments where people can be great, just the way they are, instead of trying to "fix" people.
- We recognize that we don't see everything and commit to being curious about what others see and think.
- We commit to leadership that creates additional leaders and reject the idea that leaders attract followers.
- We commit to pushing authority to information, instead of pushing information to authority.
- We understand that we will fail to live up to our commitments and appreciate our own fallibility, resolving to try again.
- We will frequently evaluate what we do and how we do it. Anything not awesome will be improved. We will strive to get better, never protecting a reputation for being good.

Marquet, 2018, *The Turn the Ship Around! Workbook*, 217.

Endnotes

Preface, Second Edition

1. Masters, 2022, *Third-Costliest Year on Record for Weather Disasters in 2021*.
2. Chugh, 2021, *What is 'The Great Resignation'? An Expert Explains*.
3. Ahearn, 2022, *"Great Resignation" Goes On as 4.2 Million Quit Jobs in January 2022*.
4. Resume Builder, 2022, *1 in 4 workers plan on quitting in 2022, as Great Resignation continues*.
5. Rosalsky, 2021, *Why Are So Many Americans Quitting Their Jobs?*
6. DePaul, 2022, 126: Peri Chickering Talks about the Mind-Body Disconnect.
7. Hunter, 2012, *The Servant*, xxiii.
8. Doshi & McGregor, 2015, *Primed to Perform*, 12.
9. Ibid., 6–13.
10. TED, *The Surprising Science of Happiness*.

Preface, First Edition

1. Gallup, 2014, *State of the American Workplace*, 25.
2. Ibid., 13.
3. Ibid., 13.
4. Ibid., 28.
5. Ibid., 9.
6. Gallup, 2014, *State of the Global Workplace*, 40.
7. Maxwell, 1993, *Developing the Leader Within You*, x.
8. Hunter, 2006, *The Servant Leadership Training Course*.

Section I

1. Maxwell, 2007, *The 21 Irrefutable Laws of Leadership*, xix.
2. Kouzes & Posner, 2012, *The Leadership Challenge*, 332.
3. Petrie, 2015, *Future trends in leadership development*, 6.

Chapter 1

1. Wiseman, 2010, *Multipliers*, 216.
2. Maxwell, 1993, *Developing the Leader Within You*, 1.
3. Asghar, 2014, *Ranking the 9 Toughest Leadership Roles*.
4. Encyclopaedia Britannica, n.d., *Role*.
5. Ibid.
6. Maxwell, 2007, *The 21 Irrefutable Laws of Leadership*, 13; Kouzes & Posner, 2012, *The Leadership Challenge*, 329.
7. Maxwell, 2007, *The 21 Irrefutable Laws of Leadership*, 25.
8. Kouzes & Posner, 2012, *The Leadership Challenge*, 336.
9. Hunter, 2012, *The Servant*, xxiv.
10. Binder et al., 2002, *Fluency*, 1.
11. Ibid., 4.
12. Ibid., 5.
13. Cherry, 2021, *The Major Leadership Theories*; Nandan, 2014, *Theories of Leadership*; Zigarelli, 2013, *Ten Leadership Styles in Five Minutes*; Leadership-Central.com, 2020, *Leadership Theories*.
14. To learn more details about each theory, view Leadership-Central.com, 2020, *Leadership Theories*.
15. Bogardus, 2003, *PHR/SPHR*.
16. Ideas on Management, 2020, *Mary Parker Follett (1868–1933)*.
17. Educationleaves, 2021, *Leadership vs Management | Difference between Leadership and Management*.
18. ProjectManager, 2018, *Leadership vs Management, What's the Difference?— Project Management Training*.
19. Sinek, 2018, *Management vs. Leadership*.
20. In *Improving Performance*, 1995, Rummer and Brache describe organization, process, and job/performer level as the Three Levels of Performance, 18–25. I added managers of projects.
21. Adapted from Rummler & Brache, *Improving Performance*, 1995, 20–21.
22. TED, 2014, Simon Sinek: *Why Good Leaders Make You Feel Safe*.
23. Lexico, n.d., *Literal*.
24. Mirror.co.uk, 2014, *From Abandon to Nice*.
25. Ibid.
26. Fun Games Kids Play, 2014, *Follow the Leader Game*.

Chapter 2

1. Kouzes & Posner, 2012, *The Leadership Challenge*, 342–343.
2. Miller, 2004, *QBQ!*, 95–96.
3. Hunter, 2012, *The Servant*.

4. Gallup, 2014, *State of the American Workplace*; Gallup, 2014, *State of the Global Workplace*.
5. Hunter, 2006, *The Servant Leadership Training Course*.
6. Crisp, 2021, *Ep. 62 — John Maxwell — Leadership is a Verb, Not a Noun*.
7. Kouzes & Posner, 2012, *The Leadership Challenge*, 15.
8. Lencioni describes the exchange as advocacy-inquiry exchange in Lencioni, 2012, *The Advantage*, 22.
9. Hunter, 2012, *The Servant*, 67.
10. Ibid., xix, 44.
11. Blanchard & Ridge, 2009, *Helping People Win at Work*, 59.
12. Hunter, 2012, *The Servant*, 67.
13. West et al., 1991, *Instructional Design*, 230.
14. Hunter, 2012, *The Servant*, 67.
15. Freiberg & Freiberg, 1996, *Nuts!*, 319; Hunter, 2012, *The Servant*, xix.
16. Wiseman, 2010, *Multipliers*, 34, 62.
17. Ibid., 78–79.
18. Sinek, 2014, *Leaders Eat Last*, 61.
19. Ibid., 78.
20. Rummler & Brache, 1995, *Improving Performance*, 13.
21. Sinek, 2014, *Leaders Eat Last*, 203.
22. Ibid., 58.
23. Freiberg & Freiberg, 1996, *Nuts!*, 316–317.
24. Sinek, 2014, *Leaders Eat Last*, 153.
25. Examples can be found in: Hunter, 2012, *The Servant*, 41; Sinek, 2014, *Leaders Eat Last*, 205; Maxwell, 2007, *The 21 Irrefutable Laws of Leadership*, 17, 138.
26. Hunter, 2012, *The Servant*, 41.
27. Hunter, 2012, *The Servant*, xxv–xxvi.
28. Collins, 2001, *Good to Great*.
29. Wiseman, 2010, *Multipliers*.
30. Kouzes & Posner, 2012, *The Leadership Challenge*.
31. Sinek, 2009, *Start with Why* and *Leaders Eat Last*.
32. Gallup, 2014, *State of the American Workplace*, 25.
33. Ibid., 13.
34. Ibid., 9.
35. Ibid., 5.
36. Ibid., 11.
37. Ibid., 4.
38. Ibid., 5.
39. Ibid., 9.
40. Kaufman, 2009, "Becoming your own leader," 32.
41. Hunter, 2006, *The Servant Leadership Training Course*.
42. Maxwell, 2007, *The 21 Irrefutable Laws of Leadership*, 26.
43. Kouzes & Posner, 2012, *The Leadership Challenge*, 336.
44. Ibid., 201; Wiseman, 2010, *Multipliers*, 77.

45. Blanchard & Ridge, 2009, *Helping People Win at Work*, 45.
46. Hunter, 2012, *The Servant*, 88.
47. Bill Daniels, personal conversation, April 16, 2014. Used with permission.
48. Marquet, 2012, *Turn the Ship Around!*, 191.
49. Maxwell, 2007, *The 21 Irrefutable Laws of Leadership*, 151.
50. Freiberg & Freiberg, 1996, *Nuts!*, 303–304.

Chapter 3

1. Sinek, 2009, *Start with Why*, 11.
2. Kouzes & Posner, 2012, *The Leadership Challenge*, 332.
3. Marquet, 2012, *Turn the Ship Around!*, xxvi.
4. Lexico, n.d., *Assumption*.
5. Wikipedia, n.d., *Rational Emotive Behavior Therapy*.
6. Maxwell, 2007, *The 21 Irrefutable Laws of Leadership*, 15.
7. Freiberg & Freiberg, 1996, *Nuts!*, 301, 303; Kouzes & Posner, 2012, *The Leadership Challenge*, 332; Hunter, 2012, *The Servant*, 32, 59; Wiseman, 2010, *Multipliers*, 66.
8. Maxwell, 2007, *The 21 Irrefutable Laws of Leadership*, 18.
9. Sinek, 2009, *Start with Why*, 5–6.
10. Ibid., 134–135.
11. Sinek, 2014, *Leaders Eat Last*, 119.
12. Freiberg & Freiberg, 1996, *Nuts!*, 301–302.
13. Maxwell, 2007, *The 21 Irrefutable Laws of Leadership*, 130.
14. IMBD, 2017, *Star Wars Films (1977–2015)*.
15. Campbell, 1973, *The Hero with a Thousand Faces*, vii.
16. Kouzes & Posner, 2012, *The Leadership Challenge*, 329.
17. Ibid., 69.
18. Lexico, n.d., *Intimacy*.
19. Ibid., *Weakness*.
20. Kouzes & Posner, 2012, *The Leadership Challenge*, 289.
21. Ibid., 289.
22. Maxwell, 2007, *The 21 Irrefutable Laws of Leadership*, 115.
23. Freiberg & Freiberg, 1996, *Nuts!*, 302.
24. TubeCoach1, 2013, *John Cleese on Creativity*.
25. Maxwell, 2007, *The 21 Irrefutable Laws of Leadership*, 146–147.
26. Sinek, 2014, *Leaders Eat Last*, 169.
27. Maxwell, 2007, *The 21 Irrefutable Laws of Leadership*, 147.
28. Ibid., 147.
29. Marquet, 2012, *Turn the Ship Around!*, xxi.
30. Wiseman, 2010, *Multipliers*, 5.
31. Ibid., 18.

32. Ibid., 5.
33. Jennings, 2012, *Reinventors*, 41.
34. Kouzes & Posner, 2012, *The Leadership Challenge*, 22.
35. Wiseman, 2010, *Multipliers*, 39–40.
36. Kouzes & Posner, 2012, *The Leadership Challenge*, 276–277.
37. Sinek, 2014, *Leaders Eat Last*, 30–31.
38. Ibid., 30–31.
39. Abrashoff, 2002, *It's Your Ship*, 158.
40. Sinek, 2014, *Leaders Eat Last*, 78.
41. Collins, 2001, *Good to Great*, 35.
42. Wiseman, 2010, *Multipliers*, 186.
43. Cohen, 1997, *The Way of Qigong*, 347.
44. Sinek, 2014, *Leaders Eat Last*, 10.
45. Kouzes & Posner, 2012, *The Leadership Challenge*, 219.
46. Sinek, 2014, *Leaders Eat Last*, 146.
47. Jennings, 2012, *Reinventors*, 115.
48. Ibid., 142.
49. Abrashoff, 2002, *It's Your Ship*, 44.
50. Hunter, 2012, *The Servant*, 104.
51. Kouzes & Posner, 2012, *The Leadership Challenge*, Chapters 10 and 11.
52. Gallup, 2014, *State of the American Workplace*, 13.
53. Ibid., 11.
54. Kouzes & Posner, 2012, *The Leadership Challenge*, 84.

Chapter 4

1. Freiberg & Freiberg, 1996, *Nuts!*, 309–310.
2. Goldsmith, 2015, *Triggers*, 84.
3. Ibid., 29.
4. Lexico, n.d., *Perilous*.
5. Ibid., *Life*.
6. Ibid., *Environment*.
7. Scarlett, 2016, *Neuroscience for Organizational Change*, 116.
8. Ibid., 115.
9. Quinn & Quinn, 2015, *Lift*, 84-84.
10. Ibid., 2-3.
11. Freiberg & Freiberg, 1996, *Nuts!*, 314.
12. Dweck, 2016, *Mindset*.
13. Scarlett, 2016, *Neuroscience for Organizational Change*, 45.
14. The content comes from one of my blogs, DePaul, 2021, *A Short Explanation about Fixed and Growth Mindsets*.
15. Scarlett, 2016, *Neuroscience for Organizational Change*, 52.

16. Ibid.

17. Wiseman, 2010, *Multipliers*, 1–4.

18. Ibid., 4.

19. Freiberg & Freiberg, 1996, *Nuts!*, 322–323.

20. Kouzes & Posner, 2012, *The Leadership Challenge*, 14; Blanchard & Ridge, 2009, *Helping People Win at Work*, 146; Miller, 2004, *QBQ!*, 95–96.

21. Kouzes & Posner, 2012, *The Leadership Challenge*, 30; Maxwell, 2007, *The 21 Irrefutable Laws of Leadership*, 25.

22. Maxwell, 2007, *The 21 Irrefutable Laws of Leadership*, 17.

23. InfoQ, 2019, *Author Q&A*.

24. TED, 2017, *Amy Edmondson How to Turn a Group of Strangers into a Team*.

25. Scarlett, 2016, *Neuroscience for Organizational Change*, 121–122.

26. Giles & Giles, *Ingroups and Outgroups*, 142.

27. DePaul, 2021, *Judy Hale and the Brown Suit*.

28. Ibid., 192–193.

29. Sinek, 2014, *Leaders Eat Last*, 154.

30. Kouzes & Posner, 2012, *The Leadership Challenge*, 222.

31. Ibid.

32. Ibid., 290–291.

33. Ibid., 290; Hunter, 2012, *The Servant*, 45.

34. Sinek, 2014, *Leaders Eat Last*, 101.

35. Ibid., 36.

36. Kouzes & Posner, 2012, *The Leadership Challenge*, 227–228.

37. Maxwell, 2007, *The 21 Irrefutable Laws of Leadership*, 63–64.

38. Sinek, 2014, *Leaders Eat Last*, 146.

39. Kouzes & Posner, 2012, *The Leadership Challenge*, 301–302.

40. Ibid., 320–321.

41. Ibid., 310.

42. Ibid., 314.

43. Ibid., 305–306.

44. Ibid., 312.

45. Freiberg & Freiberg, 1996, *Nuts!*, 315.

46. Collins, 2001, *Good to Great*, 21.

47. Maxwell, 2007, *The 21 Irrefutable Laws of Leadership*, 223.

48. Grenny et al., 2013, *Influencer*, 231–232.

49. Hunter, 2012, *The Servant*, 62; Blanchard & Ridge, 2009, *Helping People Win at Work*, 145.

50. Collins, 2001, *Good to Great*, 35.

51. Collins, 2001, *Good to Great*, 35.

52. Miller, 2004, *QBQ!*, 18.

53. Ibid., 107, 23, 56, 83, 23, 41.

54. Maxwell, 2007, *The 21 Irrefutable Laws of Leadership*, 51.

55. Lexico, n.d., *Sacrifice*.

56. Ibid.

57. Ibid.
58. Freiberg & Freiberg, 1996, *Nuts!*, 308; Maxwell, 2007, *The 21 Irrefutable Laws of Leadership*, 222–223; Grenny et al., 2013, *Influencer*, 158–162.
59. Sinek, 2014, *Leaders Eat Last*, 66.
60. Ibid., 119–120.
61. Ibid.
62. Ibid, 147.
63. Grenny et al., 2013, *Influencer*, 84.
64. Ibid., 84–85.
65. Grenny et al., 2013, *Influencer*, 77–111.
66. Wiseman, 2010, *Multipliers*, 39.
67. Hunter, 2012, *The Servant*, 32.
68. Grenny et al., 2013, *Influencer*, 88.
69. Ibid., 90.
70. Hill, 2013, *Giving Away Power*, 36.
71. Kouzes & Posner, 2012, *The Leadership Challenge*, 202.
72. Sinek, 2014, *Leaders Eat Last*, 169.
73. Sinek, 2014, *Leaders Eat Last*, 48.
74. Alberts & Hayes, 2011, *Understanding Command and Control*, 2.
75. Ibid., 8.
76. Kouzes & Posner, 2012, *The Leadership Challenge*, 186.
77. Hill, 2013, *Giving Away Power*, 35.
78. Freiberg & Freiberg, 1996, *Nuts!*, 322–323.
79. Wiseman, 2010, *Multipliers*, 63.
80. Ibid., 48.
81. Grenny et al., 2013, *Influencer*, 235.
82. Ibid., 26.
83. Kouzes & Posner, 2012, *The Leadership Challenge*, 218–219; Sinek, 2014, *Leaders Eat Last*, 135–136; Freiberg & Freiberg, 1996, *Nuts!*, 299.
84. Rummler & Brache, 1995, *Improving Performance*, 9.
85. Ibid.
86. Ibid.
87. Wiseman, 2010, *Multipliers*, 66.
88. Rummler & Brache, 1995, *Improving Performance*, 9.
89. Ibid.
90. Wiseman, 2010, *Multipliers*, 170.
91. Freiberg & Freiberg, 1996, *Nuts!*, 299.
92. Ibid., 304
93. Ibid.
94. Ibid., 299.
95. Hunter, 2012, *The Servant*, 42.
96. Blanchard & Ridge, 2009, *Helping People Win at Work*, 137.
97. Kouzes & Posner, 2012, *The Leadership Challenge*, 202.
98. Wiseman, 2010, *Multipliers*, 20–21.

99. Hunter, 2012, *The Servant*, xxii.
100. Grenny et al., 2013, *Influencer*, 208.
101. Ibid., 208.
102. Hunter, 2012, *The Servant*, xxiii.
103. Ibid., xxiv.
104. Marquet, 2012, *Turn the Ship Around!*, 204.
105. Maxwell, 2007, *The 21 Irrefutable Laws of Leadership*, 249.

Section II

1. Maxwell, 2007, *The 21 Irrefutable Laws of Leadership*, 145.
2. Rummler & Brache, 1995, *Improving Performance*, 13–14.
3. SkillSoft Books, 2014, *David Marquet: Turn the Ship Around!*
4. Feser, Mayol, & Srinivasan, 2015, *Decoding Leadership*.
5. Rummler, 2007, *Serious Performance Consulting*, xiii–xiv.
6. Sinek, 2014, *Leaders Eat Last*, 78.

Chapter 5

1. Abrashoff, 2002, *It's Your Ship*, 15.
2. Maxwell, 1993, *Developing the Leader within You*, 86.
3. SkillSoft Books, 2014, *David Marquet: Turn the Ship Around!*
4. Sinek, 2009, *Start with Why*, 11.
5. Rummler & Brache, 1995, *Improving Performance*, 13–14.
6. Ibid.
7. Ibid., 9.
8. Ibid., 13.
9. Wiseman, 2010, *Multipliers*, 170–171.
10. Rummler & Brache, 1995, *Improving Performance*, 9.
11. Ibid., 8–9.
12. Rummler, 2007, *Serious Performance Consulting*, 16.
13. Silber & Kearny, 2010, *Organizational Intelligence*, 4.
14. Rummler, 2007, *Serious Performance Consulting*, 119–120.
15. Silber & Kearny, 2010, *Organizational Intelligence*, 4.
16. Ibid., 120.
17. Ibid., 24.
18. Ibid., 24–25.
19. Ibid., 24.
20. Ibid.
21. Ibid.
22. Ibid., 24–25.

23. Binder, personal email exchange, January 11, 2015. Used with permission.

24. Binder, 2009, *What's So New about the Six Boxes® Model?*, 4.

25. Grenny et al., 2013, *Influencer*, 6.

26. Binder, 2009, *A View from the Top*, 8.

27. Binder, 2009, *What's So New about the Six Boxes® Model?*, 5.

28. Ibid., 2.

29. Binder, email exchange, January 17, 2015. Used with permission.

30. Binder, 2009, *A View from the Top*, 2.

31. Ibid., 4.

32. Ibid., 5.

33. While I have no evidence for this, I suspect that Gilbert's anonymous "coach" used in this example is Paul "Bear" Bryant. Some of the details remind me of stories I heard about Bryant's coaching methods.

34. Gilbert, 2007, *Human Competence*, 90.

35. Ibid., 87.

36. Ibid., 90.

37. Ibid., 86.

38. Binder, 2009, *A View from the Top*, 5.

39. Binder, 2009, *A View from the Top*, 2.

40. Ibid.

41. Grenny et al., 2013, *Influencer*, 292.

42. Binder, 2009, *What's So New about the Six Boxes® Model?*, 4.

43. Binder, 2009, *A View from the Top*, 4.

44. Gilbert, 2007, *Human Competence*, 91.

45. Lexico, n.d., *Shrinkage*.

46. Thanks to Art Stadlin for permitting me to share his experience. Some years ago, Art shared his story with me and later presented his experience as a case study during a conference: Stadlin et al., *Skip-Level Communications with Six Boxes® Model*, THE Performance Improvement Conference, ISPI, 2009.

Chapter 6

1. Sinek, 2009, *Start with Why*, 14–15.

2. Rummler, 2007, *Serious Performance Consulting*, 33.

3. Refer to Chapter 5, *Analyzing Like Detectives*.

4. For an in-depth example, refer to Rummler, 2007, *Serious Performance Consulting*, 39–75.

5. Rummler, 2007, *Serious Performance Consulting*, 5.

6. Ibid., 33.

7. Ibid., 41.

8. Rummler, 2007, *Serious Performance Consulting*, 35; Brooks, 1986, *No Silver Bullet: Essence and Accidents of Software Engineering*.

9. Jonassen et al., 1989, *Handbook of Task Analysis Procedures*, 371–401.
10. Ibid., 35–36.
11. National Institute of Standards and Technology, n.d., *Baldrige Performance Excellence Program*.
12. National Institute of Standards and Technology, n.d., *Baldrige Criteria for Performance Excellence*, 9.
13. Foster, n.d., *Leadership is A Collective Process*.

Chapter 7

1. Sinek, 2014, *Leaders Eat Last*, 146.
2. Marquet, 2012, *Turn the Ship Around!*, 206.
3. Grenny et al., 2013, *Influencer*, 9.
4. Donald L. Kirkey, personal conversation, November 22, 2014. Used with permission.
5. Grenny et al., 2013, *Influencer*, 9.
6. Duhigg, 2014, *The Power of Habit*, 100.
7. Grenny et al., 2013, *Influencer*, 40.
8. Duhigg, 2014, *The Power of Habit*, 176–177, 180.
9. Cherry, 2020, *An Overview of Social Psychology*.
10. Grenny et al., 2013, *Influencer*, 13–14.
11. Ibid., 44.
12. Ibid., 6; Duhigg, 2014, *The Power of Habit*, 100.
13. Grenny et al., 2013, *Influencer*, 67–68.
14. Ibid.
15. Ibid., 28, 14; Grenny et al., 2008, *How to 10x Your Influence*, 2.
16. Duhigg, 2014, *The Power of Habit*, 109.
17. Ibid., 20.
18. Ibid., 47–50.
19. Ibid., 25–27.
20. Ibid., 62.
21. Grenny et al., 2013, *Influencer*, 13.
22. Ibid., 18.
23. Ibid., 25–26.
24. Ibid., 26.
25. Ibid., 234–235.
26. Duhigg, 2014, *The Power of Habit*, 100.
27. Ibid., 146–147.
28. Ibid., 47–50, 59.
29. Grenny et al., 2013, *Influencer*, 69.
30. Duhigg, 2014, *The Power of Habit*, 62.
31. Ibid., 151.

32. Ibid., 78.
33. Ibid., 180.

Section III

1. Goldsmith, 2015, *Triggers*, 4.
2. Ibid., 187.
3. "Helping others to want to take action" comes from Patterson et al., 2013, *Crucial Accountability*, 105.
4. "Making it easier for others to keep commitments" comes from the same source: Ibid., 137.
5. Adapted from Goldsmith's definitions for self-discipline and self-control, 2015, *Triggers*, 138.

Chapter 8

1. Blanchard & Ridge, 2009, *Helping People Win at Work*, 54.
2. Patterson et al., 2013, *Crucial Accountability*, 237.
3. Goldsmith, 2015, *Triggers*, 5.
4. Lencioni, 2012, *The Advantage*, 21.
5. The Grove, 2008, *Team Leader Guide*, 10.
6. Ibid.
7. Ibid.
8. The Grove, 2008, *Team Leader Guide*, 10.
9. Marquet, 2012, *Turn the Ship Around!*, 59, 207, 213.
10. Alberts & Hayes, 2011, *Understanding Command and Control*, 2, 8, 39.
11. Wiseman, 2010, *Multipliers*, 141–151.
12. Grenny et al., 2013, *Influencer*, 173–175.
13. Wiseman, 2010, *Multipliers*, 78–79.
14. Grenny et al., 2013, *Influencer*, 159–161.
15. Wiseman, 2010, *Multipliers*, 151.
16. Grenny et al., 2013, *Influencer*, 178.
17. Ibid., 223, 231–232; Wiseman, 2010, *Multipliers*, 83–84.
18. Kouzes & Posner, 2012, *The Leadership Challenge*, 280–281.
19. Wiseman, 2010, *Multipliers*, 118.
20. Ibid., 108, 111–112, 114–116.
21. Grenny et al., 2013, *Influencer*, 84, 88, 90–91.
22. Ibid., 96.
23. Ibid., 159–161.
24. Wiseman, 2010, *Multipliers*, 149; Marquet, 2012, *Turn the Ship Around!*, 92.
25. Grenny et al., 2013, *Influencer*, 163.

26. Wiseman, 2010, *Multipliers*, 84–86.
27. Kouzes & Posner, 2012, *The Leadership Challenge*, 285–288.
28. Marquet, 2018, *The Turn the Ship Around! Workbook*, 1.
29. Marquet, 2020, *Leadership Is Language*, 55.
30. Ibid.
31. Marquet, 2018, *The Turn the Ship Around! Workbook*, 25.
32. Marquet, 2020, *Leadership Is Language*, 318.
33. Ibid., 48.
34. Ibid., 97.
35. Marquet, 2018, *The Turn the Ship Around! Workbook*, 25.
36. Ibid., 209–210.
37. Ibid., 163.
38. Ibid., 120.
39. Ibid.
40. Kouzes & Posner, 2012, *The Leadership Challenge*, 57.

Chapter 9

1. Marquet, 2012, *Turn the Ship Around!*, 132.
2. Wiseman, 2010, *Multipliers*, 56.
3. Patterson et al., 2013, *Crucial Accountability*, 138.
4. Originally developed by Paul Hersey and Ken Blanchard and updated by Blanchard, Don Carew, Enice Parisi-Carew, Fred Finch, Laurie Hawkins, Drea Zigarmi and Patricia Zigarmi as noted in Blanchard et al., 2001, *The 3 Keys to Empowerment*, 257; Blanchard et al., 2001, *The 3 Keys to Empowerment*, 19, 25.
5. Blanchard et al., 2001, *The 3 Keys to Empowerment*, 23.
6. Ibid., 25.
7. Bandura, 1986, *Social Foundations of Thought and Action*, 19.
8. Brandt et al., 1993, "Cognitive apprenticeship approach to helping adults learn," 69–78.
9. Grenny et al., 2013, *Influencer*, 121, 128, 133.
10. Ibid., 122.
11. Ibid., 124.
12. Ibid., 126.

Chapter 10

1. Maxwell, 2007, *The 21 Irrefutable Laws of Leadership*, 53.
2. Wiseman, 2010, *Multipliers*, 39.
3. Goldsmith, 2015, *Triggers*, 29.
4. Goldsmith, 2015, *Triggers*, 30.
5. Grenny et al., 2013, *Influencer*, 250.

6. Ibid., 250.
7. Ibid., 254.
8. Ibid., 253, 256.
9. Ibid., 254.
10. Handshaw, 2014, *Training that Delivers Results*, 196.
11. Handshaw, 2014, *Training that Delivers Results*, 154.
12. Goldsmith, 2015, *Triggers*, 17.
13. Ibid., 172.
14. Marquet, 2012, *Turn the Ship Around!*, 172.
15. Project Management Institute, 2013, *A Guide to the Project Management Book of Knowledge*.

Section IV

1. Freiberg & Freiberg, 1996, *Nuts!*, 321–322.

Chapter 11

1. Abrashoff, 2002, *It's Your Ship*, 44.
2. Kouzes & Posner, 2012, *The Leadership Challenge*, 85.
3. Goldsmith, 2007, *What Got You Here Won't Get You There*, 186.
4. Freiberg & Freiberg, 1996, *Nuts!*, 308.
5. Lexico, n.d., *Lion*.
6. Kouzes & Posner, 2012, *The Leadership Challenge*, 84.
7. Ibid., 118.
8. Abrashoff, 2002, *It's Your Ship*, 44.
9. Ibid., 151.
10. Ibid., 151–152,
11. Goldsmith, 2007, *What Got You Here Won't Get You There*, 149.
12. To avoid cognitive dissonance, I do not mention the US President's name. Politics in the US has become so polarized that those who dislike the other party's President tend to discount the lessons that could be learned. Likewise, those that like the described President would use the knowledge as confirmation bias. If you really want to know which President Goldsmith describes, refer to the next endnote for the reference.
13. Jennings, 2012, *Reinventors*, 143.
14. Goldsmith, 2007, *What Got You Here Won't Get You There*, 151.
15. Hunter, 2012, *The Servant*, 105.
16. Ronald Graves, personal conversation, January 1, 2015; Graves, 2014, *Creating Space for Performance Improvement*.
17. Covey, 2004, *The 8th Habit*.
18. Cherches, 2020, *VisuaLeadership*, 234–237.

19. Ibid., 235.
20. Ibid., 243–244.
21. Ibid., 243.
22. Ibid., 243.
23. Ibid., 244.
24. Scarlett, 2016, *Neuroscience for Organizational Change*, 119.
25. Ibid., 84–87.
26. Kouzes & Posner, 2012, *The Leadership Challenge*, 117–118.
27. Goldsmith, 2015, *Try Feedforward Instead of Feedback*, 2–4.
28. Goldsmith, 2007, *What Got You Here Won't Get You There*, 174.
29. Heathfield, 2021, *360 Degree Feedback*.
30. Ibid., 1–2.
31. Cherches, 2020, *VisuaLeadership*, 66.
32. NoWack & Mashihi, 2012, *Evidence-based Answers to 15 Questions about Leveraging 360-Degree Feedback*.
33. Ibid., 164.
34. Hunter, 2004, *The World's Most Powerful Leadership Principle*, 216.
35. Ibid.
36. Blanchard & Ridge, 2009, *Helping People Win at Work*, 101–116.

Chapter 12

1. Kouzes & Posner, 2012, *The Leadership Challenge*, 20.
2. Collins, 2001, *Good to Great*, 37.
3. Lombardo & Eichinger, 2009, *FYI*.
4. Kouzes & Posner, 2012, *The Leadership Challenge*, 172.
5. Ibid., 136.
6. Ibid., 137.
7. Ibid., 142.
8. Kouzes & Posner, 2012, *The Leadership Challenge*, 172.
9. Ibid., 172.
10. Ibid., 181.
11. Ibid., 176.

Chapter 13

1. Maxwell, 2007, *The 21 Irrefutable Laws of Leadership*, 162.
2. Ibid., 119, 121.
3. Ibid., 117.

Section V

1. Hunter, 2012, *The Servant*, 119–120.
2. Ibid.
3. Hunter, 2006, *The Servant Leadership Training Course*.
4. Ibid.

Chapter 14

1. Hunter, 2012, *The Servant*, xxii–xxiv.
2. Hunter, 2006, *The Servant Leadership Training Course*; Hunter, 2012, *The Servant*, xxiv.
3. Hunter, 2006, *The Servant Leadership Training Course*.
4. Ibid.; Freiberg & Freiberg, 1996, *Nuts!*, 318; Blanchard & Ridge, 2009, *Helping People Win at Work*, 137; Kouzes & Posner, 2012, *The Leadership Challenge*, 335; Maxwell, 2007, *The 21 Irrefutable Laws of Leadership*, 26.
5. Kouzes & Posner, 2012, *The Leadership Challenge*, 335.
6. Hunter, 2012, *The Servant*; Goldsmith, 2007, *What Got You Here Won't Get You There*; Goldsmith, 2015, *Triggers*.
7. Goldsmith, 2007, *What Got You Here Won't Get You There*, 85.
8. Ibid., 86
9. Goldsmith, 2005, *Applying the Behavioral Coaching Model Organization-Wide*, 227.
10. Bishop et al., 2020, *Reflections on Leadership Development*, 12.
11. Hunter, 2012, *The Servant*, xxviii.
12. Ibid., xxix.
13. Ibid., xxix–xxxi.
14. Grenny et al., 2013, *Influencer*, 126.

Chapter 15

1. Freiberg & Freiberg, 1996, *Nuts!*, 321.
2. Maxwell, 2007, *The 21 Irrefutable Laws of Leadership*, 249.
3. Skillsoft Books, 2014, *David Marquet: The Most Important Role of a Leader*.
4. Skillsoft Books, 2014, *David Marquet: The True Test of Leadership*.
5. Gallup, 2014, *State of the Global Workplace*, 40.
6. Gallup, 2014, *State of the American Workplace*, 13, 9.
7. Gurdjian et al., 2014, *Why Leadership-Development Programs Fail*.
8. Skillsoft Books, 2014, *David Marquet: Create an Environment for Leadership Development—Not a Program*.
9. Wiseman, 2010, *Multipliers*, x.

10. Skillsoft Books, 2014, *David Marquet: Create an Environment for Leadership Development—Not a Program.*
11. Gurdjian et al., 2014, *Why Leadership-Development Programs Fail.*
12. Marquet, 2012, *Turn the Ship Around!*, 59; Grenny et al., 2013, *Influencer*, 173–175.
13. Gurdjian et al., 2014, *Why Leadership-Development Programs Fail.*
14. Marquet, 2012, *Turn the Ship Around!*, 213.
15. Grenny et al., 2013, *Influencer*, 173–175.

Afterword

1. Grenny et al., 2013, *Influencer*, 83.
2. Patterson et al., 2013, *Crucial Accountability*, 50.
3. Grenny et al., 2013, *Influencer*, 82.
4. Patterson et al., 2013, *Crucial Accountability*, 50.
5. Muzio, 2010, *Make Work Great*, 5–6.
6. Patterson et al., 2013, *Crucial Accountability*, 52.
7. Grenny et al., 2013, *Influencer*, 156.
8. Alexander, 2005, *Rules of Engagement*, 273.

Bibliography

All of the endnotes and table notes are sourced in this bibliography. I categorize the bibliography into three headings:

21st Century Leadership Bibliography: These are the primary sources for synthesizing the 21st Century Leadership principles, beliefs, and practices as well as for defining traditional leadership. The books that I list represent the primary sources of my meta-analysis and are only a sample of books that describe this leadership approach.

Bibliography: These references enabled me to detail the leadership concept, traditional leadership, and the 21st Century Leadership definition, principles, beliefs, and practices.

Recommended Reading: To gain further depth about leadership and 21st Century Leadership, I recommend several sources listed under this heading.

21st Century Leadership Bibliography

Abrashoff, Captain D. M. (2002). *It's Your Ship: Management Techniques from the Best Damn Ship in the Navy.* Business Plus.

Alberts, D. S., & Hayes, R. E. (2011). *Understanding Command and Control: The Future of Command and Control.* CCRP.

Blanchard, K., & Ridge, G. (2009). *Helping People Win at Work: A Business Philosophy Called "Don't Mark My Paper, Help Me Get an A."* FT Press.

Collins, J. (2001). *Good to Great: Why Some Companies Make the Leap and Others Don't.* HarperCollins.

Freiberg, K., & Freiberg, J. (1996). *Nuts! Southwest Airlines' Crazy Recipe for Business and Personal Success.* Bard Press.

Grenny, J., Patterson, K., Maxfield, D., McMillan, R., & Switzer, A. (2013). *Influencer: The New Science of Leading Change* (2nd ed.). McGraw Hill Education.

Hunter, J. C. (2006). *The Servant Leadership Training Course: Achieving Success through Character, Bravery, and Influence.* Sounds True.

Hunter, J. C. (2012). *The Servant: A Simple Story about the True Essence of Leadership.* Crown Business.

Kouzes, J. M., & Posner, B. Z. (2012). *The Leadership Challenge: How to Make Extraordinary Things Happen in Organizations* (5th ed.). Jossey-Bass.

Marquet, D. L. (2012). *Turn the Ship Around! A True Story Turning Followers into Leaders.* Penguin Group.

Maxwell, J. C. (2007). *The 21 Irrefutable Laws of Leadership: Follow Them and People Will Follow You.* Thomas Nelson.

Sinek, S. (2009). *Start with Why: How Great Leaders Inspire Everyone to Take Action.* Penguin Group.

Sinek, S. (2014). *Leaders Eat Last: Why Some Teams Pull Together and Others Don't.* Penguin Group.

Wiseman, L. (2010). *Multipliers: How the Best Leaders Make Everyone Smarter.* Harper Business.

Bibliography

Addison, R. (2010). *How Can I Use HPT: Let's Build a Performance System Together* (Workshop).

Ahearn, T. (2022, March 11). *"Great Resignation" Goes on as 4.2 Million Quit Jobs in January 2022.* Employee Screening Resources. https://www.esrcheck. com/2022/03/11/great-resignation-4-2-million-quit-jobs-january-2022/#:~:text= The%20%E2%80%9CGreat%20Resignation%E2%80%9D%20in%20the,Labor's %20Bureau%20of%20Labor%20Statistics

Alexander, B. (2005). *Rules of Engagement: A Sir John Fielding Mystery.* Penguin Group.

Asghar, R. (2014, February 25). Ranking the 9 Toughest Leadership Roles. Forbes. https://www.forbes.com/sites/robasghar/2014/02/25/ranking-the-9-toughest-leadership-roles

Binder, C. (2003). Doesn't everybody need fluency? Performance Improvement, 42(3), 14–20. https://onlinelibrary.wiley.com/doi/10.1002/pfi.4930420304

Binder, C. (2009). A View from The Top: Human Performance in Organizations. The Performance Thinking Network. https://www.sixboxes.com/_customelements/uploadedResources/155921_SixBoxesViewfromTop.pdf

Binder, C. (2009). What's so New About the Six Boxes® Model? [Whitepaper]. The Performance Thinking Network. https://www.sixboxes.com/_customelements/uploadedResources/160039_SixBoxesWhatsSoNew.pdf

Binder, C., Haughton, E., & Bateman, B. (2002). Fluency: Achieving True Mastery in the Learning Process. The Fluency Project. http://binde1.verio.com/wb_fluency.org/Publications/BinderHaughtonBateman2002.pdf

Bishop, J., Green, K., Ingram, K., Laney, K., Morse, J., Ramsey, H., Rhodes, J., Schaefer, D.M., She, L., Bosworth, J., Caviness, V., Foster, D., Hess, L., Jensen, P., King, W., Miller, C., Popoff, B., Rosequist, L., Taylor, J., Tieber, B., Vogel, N., & Wood, A. (2020, December 3). *Reflections on Leadership Development* [Whitepaper]. University of North Carolina at Charlotte via HPT Treasures. https://hpttreasures.files.wordpress.com/2021/12/20211203leadership developmnetexpertswhitepaperuncc-1.pdf

Blanchard, K., Carlos, J. P., & Randolph, A. (2001). The 3 Keys to Empowerment. Berrett-Koehler.

Bogardus, A. M. (2003). PHR/SPHR: Professional in Human Resources Certification Study Guide. Sybex.

Brandt, B. L., Farmer, J. A., & Buckmaster, A. (1993). Cognitive apprenticeship approach to helping adults learn. New Directions for Adult and Continuing Education, 59, 69–78. https://onlinelibrary.wiley.com/doi/10.1002/ace.36719935909

Brooks, Jr., F. P. (1986). No Silver Bullet: Essence and Accidents of Software Engineering [Whitepaper]. http://worrydream.com/refs/Brooks-NoSilverBullet.pdf

Brown, M. G. (2013). Baldrige Award Winning Quality: How to Interpret the Baldrige Criteria for Performance Excellence (18th Ed.). Productivity Press.

Campbell, J. (1973). The Hero with a Thousand Faces (3rd. Ed.). Princeton University Press.

Cherches, T. (2020). *VisuaLeadership: Leveraging the Power of Visual Thinking in Leadership and in Life*. Post Hill Press.

Cherry, K. (2020, July 05). An Overview of Social Psychology. Very Well Mind. https://www.verywellmind.com/social-psychology-4157177

Cherry, K. (2021, November 18). The Major Leadership Theories. Very Well Mind. https://www.verywellmind.com/leadership-theories-2795323

Chugh, A. (2021, November 29). What is 'The Great Resignation'? An Expert Explains. World Economic Forum. https://www.weforum.org/agenda/2021/11/what-is-the-great-resignation-and-what-can-we-learn-from-it

Cohen, K. S. (1997). The Way of Qigong: The Art and Science of Chinese Energy Healing. Ballantine Books.

Crisp (2021, June 28). Ep. 62 — John Maxwell — Leadership is a Verb, Not a Noun || Crisp Video [Video]. YouTube. https://www.youtube.com/watch?v=84x0Vv-qT58

Dent, S. (2012, October) What Is the Strangest Change in Meaning that Any Word Has Undergone. http://blog.oxforddictionaries.com/2012/10/change-in-wordmeanings

DePaul, G. A. (1998). Alternative Types of Learning in Clinical Specialty-Interest Areas of Family-Practice Medicine. [Unpublished doctoral dissertation]. University of Illinois at Urbana-Champaign.

DePaul, G. A. (Host). (2021, January 12). 004: Judy Hale and the Brown Suit [Audio Podcast Episode]. In *Unlabeled Leadership*. https://anchor.fm/unlabeled-leadership/episodes/004-Judy-Hale-and-the-Brown-Suit-eogpbc

DePaul, G. A. (2021, May 30). A Short Explanation about Fixed and Growth Mindsets. Medium. https://medium.com/an-idea/a-short-explanation-about-fixed-and-growth-mindsets-b03e6f24c5b6

DePaul, G. A. (Host). (2022, January 21). 126: Peri Chickering Talks about the Mind-Body Disconnect (Bonus Episode) [Audio Podcast Episode]. In *Unlabeled Leadership*. https://anchor.fm/unlabeled-leadership/episodes/126-Peri-Chickering-Talks-about-the-Mind-Body-Disconnect-bonus-e1d887e

Doshi, N. & McGregor, L. (2015). *Primed to Perform: How to Build the Highest Performing Cultures through the Science of Total Motivation*. Harper Business.

Duhigg, C. (2014). The Power of Habit: Why We Do What We Do in Life and Business. Random House Trade Paperbacks.

Dweck, C. S. (2016). *Mindset: The New Psychology of Success*. Ballantine Books.

Educationleaves. (2021, May 29). *Leadership vs Management | Difference between Leadership and Management* [Video]. YouTube. https://www.youtube.com/watch?v=mhkLc0HEtR0

Encyclopaedia Britannica. (n.d.). Role. http://www.britannica.com/EBchecked/topic/507038/role

Feser, C., Mayol, F., & Srinivasan, R. (2015, January 1). Decoding Leadership: What Really Matters. *McKinsey Quarterly*. https://www.mckinsey.com/featured-insights/leadership/decoding-leadership-what-really-matters

Foster, J. (2011) Leadership Is a Collective Process [Video]. [Video: URL no longer exists]

Fun Games Kids Play. (2014). *Follow the Leader Game*. https://fungameskidsplay.com/followtheleadergame.htm

Gallup. (2013). *Engagement at Work: Its Effect on Performance Continues in Tough Economic Times*. http://www.gallup.com/services/176657/engagement-work-effect-performance-continues-tough-economic-times.aspx

Gallup. (2014). *Great Jobs and Great Lives: The 2014 Gallop-Purdue Index Report*. http://www.gallup.com/services/178496/gallup-purdue-index-inaugural-national-report.aspx

Gallup. (2014). *State of the Global Workplace*. http://www.gallup.com/services/178517/ state-global-workplace.aspx

Gallup. (2014, September 22). *State of the American Workplace*. https://www.gallup.com/services/176708/state-american-workplace.aspx

Gilbert, T. F. (2007). *Human Competence: Engineering Worthy Performance* (Tribute ed.). Pfeiffer.

Giles, H., & Giles, J. (2012). Ingroups and Outgroups. In A. Kurylo (Ed.), *Inter/Cultural Communication: Representation and Construction of Culture* (pp. 141–162). SAGE Publications, Inc. https://www.sagepub.com/sites/default/files/upm-binaries/48648_ch_7.pdf

Gini, A. (2013). *Ten Virtues of Outstanding Leaders: Leadership and Character*. Wiley-Blackwell.

Goldsmith, M. (2005). Applying the Behavioral Coaching Model Organization-Wide. In Morgan, H., Harkins, P., & Goldsmith, M. (Eds.), *The Art and Practice of Leadership Coaching: 50 Top Executive Coaches reveal Their Secrets* (pp. 225–231). John Wiley & Sons, Inc.

Goldsmith, M. (2007). What Got You Here Won't Get You There: How Successful People Become Even More Successful. Profile Books.

Goldsmith, M. (2015). *Triggers: Creating Behavior that Lasts – Becoming the Person You Want to Be.* Crown Business.

Goldsmith, M. (2015, October 29). *Try Feedforward Instead of Feedback.* http://marshallgoldsmith.com/articles/try-feedforward-instead-feedback

Gonzalez, M. (2012). *Mindful Leadership: The 9 Ways to Self-Awareness, Transforming Yourself, and Inspiring Others.* Jossey-Bass.

Graves, R. (2014, November 13). *Creating Space for Performance Improvement* [Event presentation]. Charlotte Chapter, Charlotte, NC, United States.

Grenny, J., Maxfield, D., & Shimberg, A. (2008). *How to 10x Your Influence.* https://www.vitalsmarts.com/influ-encerreport

Gurdjian, P., Halbeisen, T., & Lane, K. (2014, January 1). Why Leadership-Development Programs Fail. *McKinsey Quarterly.* https://www.mckinsey.com/featured-insights/leadership/why-leadership-development-programs-fail

Handshaw, D. (2014). *Training that Delivers Results: Instructional Design that Aligns with Business Results.* AMACOM.

Heathfield, S. M. (2021, January 4). 360 Degree Feedback: The Good, the Bad, and the Ugly. The Balance Careers. https://www.thebalancecareers.com/360-degree-feedback-information-1917537

Hill, J. (2013). *Giving Away Power: Sharing Power and Building Confidence Inside Organizations.* Proofpoint Systems.

Hunter, J. C. (2004). *The World's Most Powerful Leadership Principle: How to Become a Servant Leader.* Crown Business.

Ideas on Management. (2020). *Mary Parker Follett (1868–1933).* http://ideasonmanagement.blogspot.com/p/mary-parker-follett-1868-1933.html

IMBD. (2017, April 16). *Star Wars Films (1977–2015).* https://www.imdb.com/title/tt0076759/?ref_=nv_sr_srsg_5

InfoQ. (2019, December 4). *Author Q&A: The 4 Stages of Psychological Safety.* https://www.infoq.com/articles/book-stages-psychological-safety

Jackson, E. (2012, August 17). The 7 Reasons Why 360 Degree Feedback Programs Fail. Forbes. https://www.forbes.com/sites/ericjackson/2012/08/17/the-7-reasons-why-360-degree-feedback-programs-fail

Jennings, J. (2012). *The Reinventors: How Extraordinary Companies Pursue Radical Continuous Change.* The Penguin Group.

Jonassen, D. H., Hannum, W. H., & Tessmer M. (1998). *Handbook of Task Analysis Procedures.* Praeger.

Kaufman, R. (2009). Becoming Your Own Leader: From Leader to Possible Failure and Back Again—A Pragmatic Approach. *Performance Improvement,* 48(4), 29–34. https://onlinelibrary.wiley.com/doi/10.1002/pfi.20068

Leadership. (2015, August 31). *John Maxwell The Five Levels of Leadership* [Video]. YouTube. https://www.youtube.com/watch?v=2jy8TPYVcK8

Leadership-Central.com. (2020). *Leadership Theories.* https://www.leadership-central.com/leadership-theories.html

Lencioni, P. (2012). *The Advantage: Why Organizational Health Trumps Everything Else in Business.* Jossey-Bass.

Lexico. (n.d.). *Ability.* https://www.lexico.com/en/definition/ability

Lexico. (n.d.). *Assumption.* https://www.lexico.com/en/definition/assumption

Lexico. (n.d.). *Behavior.* https://www.lexico.com/en/definition/behavior

Lexico. (n.d.). *Build.* https://www.lexico.com/en/definition/build

Lexico. (n.d.). *Capability.* https://www.lexico.com/en/definition/capability

Lexico. (n.d.). *Character.* https://www.lexico.com/en/definition/character

Lexico. (n.d.). *Competency.* https://www.lexico.com/en/definition/competence

Lexico. (n.d.). *Develop.* https://www.lexico.com/en/definition/develop

Lexico. (n.d.). *Environment.* https://www.lexico.com/en/definition/environment

Lexico. (n.d.). *Influence.* https://www.lexico.com/en/definition/influence

Lexico. (n.d.). *Intimacy.* https://www.lexico.com/en/definition/intimacy

Lexico. (n.d.). *Life.* https://www.lexico.com/en/definition/life

Lexico. (n.d.). *Lion.* https://www.lexico.com/en/definition/lion

Lexico. (n.d.). *Literal.* https://www.lexico.com/en/definition/literal

Lexico. (n.d.). *Mature.* https://www.lexico.com/en/definition/mature

Lexico. (n.d.). *Moral.* https://www.lexico.com/en/definition/moral

Lexico. (n.d.). *Perilous.* https://www.lexico.com/en/definition/perilous

Lexico. (n.d.). *Quality.* https://www.lexico.com/en/definition/quality

Lexico. (n.d.). *Result.* https://www.lexico.com/en/definition/result

Lexico. (n.d.). *Sacrifice.* https://www.lexico.com/en/definition/sacrifice

Lexico. (n.d.). *Shrinkage.* https://www.lexico.com/en/definition/shrinkage

Lexico. (n.d.). *Skill.* https://www.lexico.com/en/definition/skill

Lexico. (n.d.). *Trait.* https://www.lexico.com/en/definition/trait

Lexico. (n.d.). *Weakness.* https://www.lexico.com/en/definition/weakness

LinkedIn. (2014) *What Traits Should Leadership Development Programs Focus on?* https://www. linkedin.com/grp/post/718907-5870584588169928708

LinkedIn. (2014). *What Are the Most Important Skills and Behaviors of Modern Leadership in Your Opinion?* https://www.linkedin.com/grp/post/98001-273055216

LinkedIn. (2014). *What Competencies Do You Find Are Missing in Action?* https://www.linkedin.com/grp/post/718907-5851739761982586880

Lombardo, M. M., & Eichinger R.W. (2009). *FYI For Your Improvement*™ (5th ed.). Lominger International.

Marquet, D. (2018). *The Turn the Ship around Workbook: Implement Intent-Based Leadership in Your Organization.* Portfolio/Penguin.

Marquet, D. (2020). *Leadership Is Language: The Hidden Power of What You Say, and What You Don't.* Portfolio/Penguin.

Masters, J. (2022, January 25). Third-Costliest Year on Record for Weather Disasters in 2021: $343 Billion in Damages. Yale Climate Connections. https://yaleclimateconnections.org/2022/01/third-costliest-year-on-record-for-weather-disasters-in-2021-343-billion-in-damages

Maxwell, J. C. (1993). *Developing the Leader within You*. Thomas Nelson.

Miller, J. G. (2004). *QBQ! The Question Behind the Question: Practicing Personal Accountability at Work and in Life*. The Penguin Group.

Mindtools. (n.d.). *The Conscious Competence Ladder*. https://www.mindtools.com/pages/article/newISS_96.htm

Mirror.co.uk. (2014). *From Abandon to Nice...Words that Have Literally Changed Meaning through the Years*. https://www.mirror.co.uk/news/uk-news/words-literally-changed-meaning-through-2173079

Molinaro, V. (2013). *The Leadership Contract: The Fine Print to Becoming a Great Leader*. Wiley.

Muzio, E. G. (2008). *Four Secrets to Liking Your Work: You May Not Need to Quit to Get the Job You Want*. FT Press.

Muzio, E. G. (2010). *Make Work Great: Super Charge Your Team, Reinvent the Culture, and Gain Influence One Person at a Time*. The McGrawHill Companies, Inc.

Nandan, Kesari. (2014). Theories of Leadership. Slideshare. http://www.slideshare.net/kesarinandan96/ theories-of-leadership-13415459

National Institute of Standards and Technology. (n.d.). *Baldrige for Performance Excellence*. http://www.nist.gov/baldrige/publications/criteria.cfm

National Institute of Standards and Technology. (n.d.). *Baldrige Performance Excellence Program*. http://www.nist.gov/baldrige/publications/education_criteria.cfm

NoWack, K. M., & Mashihi, S. (2012). Evidence-based Answers to 15 Questions about Leveraging 360-Degree Feedback. *Consulting Psychology Journal Practice and Research*, 64(3), 157–182. https://www.apa.org/pubs/journals/features/cpb-64-3-157.pdf

Patterson, K., Grenny, J., Maxfield, D., McMillan, R, & Switzer, A. (2013). *Crucial Accountability: Tools for Resolving Violated Expectations, Broken Commitments, and Bad Behavior* (2nd ed.). McGraw Hill Education.

Petrie, N. (2015, April). Future Trends in Leadership Development [Whitepaper]. Center for Creative Leadership. http://www.ccl.org/wp-content/uploads/2015/04/futureTrends.pdf

Project Management Institute. (2013). *A Guide to the Project Management Book of Knowledge* (5th ed.). Project Management Institute.

ProjectManager. (2018, October 8). *Leadership vs Management, What's the Difference?—Project Management Training* [Video]. YouTube. https://www.youtube.com/watch?v=to6dPqKQan0

Quinn, R. W., & Quinn, R. E. (2015). *Lift: The Fundamental State of Leadership* (2nd ed). Berrett-Koehler Publishers, Inc.

Resume Builder. (2022, January 3). *1 in 4 Workers Plan on Quitting in 2022, as Great Resignation Continues*. https://www.resumebuilder.com/1-in-4-workers-plan-on-quitting-in-2022-as-great-resignation-continues

Robinson, A. G., & Schroeder, D. M. (2014). *The Idea-Driven Organization: Unlocking the Power in Bottom-up Ideas*. Berrett-Koehler.

Rosalsky, G. (2021, October 19). *Why Are So Many Americans Quitting Their Jobs?* NPR. https://www.npr.org/sections/money/2021/10/19/1047032996/why-are-so-many-americans-quitting-their-jobs

Rummler, G. A. (2007). *Serious Performance Consulting: According to Rummler*. Wiley.

Rummler, G. A., & Brache, A. P. (1995). *Improving Performance: How to Manage the White Space on the Organization Chart* (2nd ed.). Jossey-Bass.

Scarlett, H. (2016). *Neuroscience for Organizational Change: An Evidence-based Practical Guide to Managing Change*. Kogan Page Limited.

Silber, K. H., & Kearny L. (2010). *Organizational Intelligence: A Guide to Understanding the Business of Your Organization for HR, Training, and Performance Consulting*. Pfeiffer.

Simon S. (2018, April 3). *Management vs. Leadership* [Video]. https://www.youtube.com/watch?v=sr0d_HbbbcQ

Skillsoft Books. (2014). *David Marquet: The Most Important Role of a Leader: Give Control and Create Leaders* [Video]. [Video: URL no longer exists].

Skillsoft Books. (2014). *David Marquet: The True Test of Leadership* [Video]. [Video: URL no longer exists].

Skillsoft Books. (2014). *Marquet, D. Create an Environment for Leadership Development—Not a Program* [Video]. [Video: URL no longer exists].

SkillSoft Books. (2014). *David Marquet: Turn the Ship Around! How to Create Leadership at Every Level* [Video]. [Video: URL no longer exists].

Smart, G., & Street, R. (2008). *Who*. Ballantine Books.

Sorenson, S., & Garman, K. (2013, June 11). How to Tackle US Employees' Stagnating Engagement. Gallup Business Journal. https://news.gallup.com/businessjournal/162953/tackle-employees-stagnating-engagement.aspx

Talks at Google. (2015, July 16). *The Growth Mindset | | Carol Dweck | Talks at Google* [Video]. YouTube. https://www.youtube.com/watch?v=-71zdXCMU6A

TED. (2010, May 4). *Simon Sinek: How Great Leaders Inspire Action* [Video]. YouTube. https://www.youtube.com/watch?v=qp0HIF3SfI4

TED. (2010, September 24). *Julian Treasure: Shh! Sound Health in 8 Steps* [Video]. YouTube. https://www.youtube.com/watch?v=ELgvDMTKyBE

TED. (2011, July 29). *Julian Treasure: 5 Ways to Listen Better* [Video]. YouTube. https://www.youtube.com/watch?v=cSohjlYQI2A

TED. (2012, April 26). *The Surprising Science of Happiness | Dan Gilbert* [Video]. YouTube. https://www.youtube.com/watch?v=4q1dgn_C0AU

TED. (2014, May 19). *Simon Sinek: Why Good Leaders Make You Feel Safe* [Video]. YouTube. https://www.youtube.com/watch?v=lmyZMtPVodo

TED. (2017, October). *Amy Edmondson How to Turn a Group of Strangers into a Team* [Video]. YouTube. https://www.ted.com/talks/amy_edmondson_how_to_turn_a_group_of_strangers_into_a_team

The Grove. (2008). *Team Leader Guide*. The Grove. https://grovetools-inc.com/products/team-leader-guide

THINK BIG. (2014, December 16). BDI Behaviour Change Behavioural Dynamics Institute [Video]. YouTube. https://www.youtube.com/watch?v=Bh9Bi_adLA0

TubeCoach1. (2013, March 18). *John Cleese on Creativity (Video from a Training)* [Video]. YouTube. https://www.youtube.com/watch?v=y70nbDJI5Uk

UniversalDesign.com. (n.d.). ADA Wall Guard. Product Reviews. http://www.universaldesign.com/index.php?Itemid=1814

West, C. K., Farmer, J. A., & Wolff, P. M. (1991). *Instructional Design: Implications from Cognitive Science*. Prentice Hall.

Wikipedia. (n.d.). *Rational Emotive Behavior Therapy*. https://en.wikipedia.org/wiki/Rational_emotive_behavior_therapy

Wimer, S., & Nowack, K. M. (2006). 13 Common Mistakes Using 360-Degree Feedback. Optima360. https://www.360degreefeedback.net/media/13CommonMistakes.pdf

Zigarelli, M. (2013, August 17). *Ten Leadership Styles in Five Minutes* [Video]. YouTube. https://www.youtube.com/watch?v=XKUPDUDOBVo

Recommended Reading

Brandon, R., & Seldman, M. (2004). *Survival of the Savvy*. Free Press.

Brown, M. G. (2014). *Baldrige Award Winning Quality: How to Interpret the Baldrige Criteria for Performance Excellence* (18th ed.). CRC Press.

Chabris, C., & Simons, D. (2009). *The Invisible Gorilla: And Other Ways Out Intuitions Deceive Us*. Broadway Paperbacks.

Connors, R., Smith, T., & Hickman, C. (2004). *The Oz Principle: Getting Results through Individual and Organizational Accountability*. Portfolio.

Covey, S. R. (2004). *The 8th Habit: From Effectiveness to Greatness*. Free Press.

Crucial Learning. (2009, September 21). *All Washed Up!* [Video]. YouTube. https://www.youtube.com/watch?v=osUwukXSd0k

Fitzpatrick, O. (2013, December 4). *Change Habits: Breaking Bad Behaviours* [Video]. YouTube. https://www.youtube.com/watch?v=CojSlsMwDOg

Goulston, M. (2010). *Just Listen: Discover the Secret to Getting through to Absolutely Anyone*. AMACOM.

Hale, J. (2002) *Performance-Based Evaluation: Tools and Techniques to Measure the Impact of Training*. Jossey-Bass/Pfeiffer.

Hirsch, W. (2017, October 9). Five Questions about Psychological Safety, Answered. Science for Work. https://scienceforwork.com/blog/psychological-safety

Krames, J. (2015). *A Lead with Humility: 12 Leadership Lessons from Pope Francis*. AMACOM.

Kusy, M. E., & Hollowya, E. L. (2009) *Toxic Workplace! Managing Toxic Personalities and Their Systems of Power*. Jossey-Bass.

Lencioni, P. (2002). *The Five Dysfunctions of a Team: A Leadership Fable*. Jossey-Bass.

Love, A. (2018, July 23). How Leaders Can Foster a Growth Mindset. Smartbrief. http://smartbrief.com/original/2018/07/how-leaders-can-foster-growth-mindset

McRaney, D. (2011). *You Are Not So Smart*. Avery.

Pershing, J. A. (Ed.). (2006). *Handbook of Human Performance Technology: Principles, Practices, and Potential* (3rd ed.). Pfeiffer.

Robinson, D. G., & Robinson, J. C. (2005). *Strategic Business Partner: Aligning People Strategies with Business Goals*. Berrett-Koehler.

Robinson, D. G., Robinson, J. C., Phillips, J. J., Phillips, P. P., & Handshaw, D. (2015). *Performance Consulting: A Strategic Process to Improve, Measure, and Sustain Organizational Results*. Berrett-Koehler.

Silbiger, S. A. (2012). *The Ten-Day MBA* (4th ed.). HarperCollins Publishers.

Smart, G., Street, R., & Foster, A. (2015). *Power Score: Your Formula for Leadership Success*. Ballantine Books.

Tavris, C., & Elliot, A. (2007). *Mistakes Were Made (but Not by Me): Why We Justify Foolish Beliefs, Bad Decisions, and Hurtful Acts*. Harcourt, Inc.

Index

A

Ability, 5
Abrashoff, D. Michael, 33, 50, 95, 223, 226
Accountability, 183
Active listening, 228
Addison, Roger, 9
Alberts, D. S., 79
Alexander, Bruce, 293–294
Ambiguity, elimination, 292
Analyzing Like Detectives, 108–109, 110–116
    characteristics of, 97–98
    human performance system, 101–108
    importance and benefits of, 95–97
    influencing behaviors, common mistakes with, 111–115
    leading examples, 116
        investigating inventory losses, 116, 118–119
        mapping primary and support processes, 125–126
        skip-level dialogues, investigating opportunities through, 120–124
    organizational systems, laws of, 98–101
    Performance Chain Model, 108–110
        examples, 109
        overview, 109–110
    practice summary, 126–127
    recommended actions for applying, 128–129

Six Boxes® Model
    overview, 110–111
    troubleshooting with, 116, 117
    usage of, 111
    as valuable practice, 96
    word of caution, 129–130
Anatomy of performance (AOP), 101, 133
    alignment points, 134
    human performance system and, 101–108
    of organizations, 102–105
Anticipated needs, 28
Apologizing, 268–269
Asghar, Rob, 4
Ask for help, 269–270
Assumptions, traditional leadership, 43–55, 303–305
    by category, 44
    giving away power weakens leadership, 48
    intimacy weakens leadership, 47–48
    leader as smartest, 49–50
    leaders are heroes leaving legacy, 45–47
    leadership requires little or no training, 54–55
    leaders know how effective their leadership, 55
    leaders need authority, 43–45
    long-term results of, 44
    manager functions as leaders, 48–49
    recognition as formal process, 54
    talking is important than listening, 53–54

team members are less important than revenue, profit, operational costs, and leaders, 52–53

team members as cause of unproductivity, 50–51

Attentive (levels of listening), 230

B

Baldrige National Quality Program, 145

Bandura, A., 199–200

"Becoming Your Own Leader" (Kaufman), 35

Behavioral or skill theory, 13

Behaviors, 82, 93

  change, 270

  common mistakes with influencing, 111–115

  Key, Finding Like Social Psychologists, *see* Key Behaviors, Finding Like Social Psychologists

  leadership theories explain leadership, 12

  maturing, 37

  vital, 82, 155

Beliefs of 21st Century Leadership, 38–39, 297–301

  being vulnerable and building trust, 68–70

  celebrations build community, 70–71

  claiming responsibility when things go wrong, 73

  command and control, 79–80

  control erodes relationship, 76–77

  developing those around you, 80

  employees serve customers before serving management, 72–73

  empowering others makes you indispensable, 78–79

  everyone practice leadership regardless of role, 65

  helping others learn leadership, 89

  influence comes from all directions, 85–86

  intelligence isn't static, 64–65

  knowing everything about leadership isn't enough, 88–89

  leadership doesn't reside with one person, 85

  leadership works with all populations, 86

  leading well is about empowering others, 77–78

  leaving current role contributes to organizational growth, 80–81

  making mistakes and learning from experience, 81

  organizational charts limit thinking, 82–84

  practicing leadership and monitor effectiveness, 87–88

  problems from systemic perspective minimizes using blame, 84–85

  recognizing others for accomplishments, 71–72

  sacrificing to help others, 75

  serving others and not oneself, 74

  sharing mistakes builds credibility, 70

  vital behaviors, 82

Bidirectional, leadership, 37–38

Binder, Carl, 11, 97, 109, 110, 113

Blanchard, K., 86, 173, 272

Blockers, 29

Brache, Alan P., 82, 83, 93, 98, 99

Brain, 58–59

Brethower, Dale, 134

Business

  defined, 103

  writing, transitioning from academic to, 203

Business results, 25, 26, 33–35, 285

C

Cable shrinkage, example findings for, 118, 119

Capabilities, 33, 37, 65, 152, 196

Celebrations

  importance of, 71

  as way to build community, 70–71

Cherches, T., 230

Chess analogy, 52

Cleese, John, 48

Clegg, Nick, 19

Clifton, Jim, 33, 34

Cognitive Apprenticeship, 199, 200–201

Cohen, Kenneth S., 51

Collins, Jim, 33, 34, 50, 71, 72, 73, 245

Command and control
functions of, 79
as shared responsibility, 79–80

Communicating Like Agents, 171, 173–194
characteristics of, 174–175
Drexler/Sibbet Team Performance Model, 184–186
groups and teams differ, 179
importance and benefits of, 173–174
influence tactics, 180
leading examples
blaming the Vice President, 188–189
knowledge sharing across teams, 186–187
transitioning from traditional C2 to a shared C2, 187–188
Marquet's Intent-Based Leadership, 181–184
point of clarification between teams and groups, 179
practice summary, 189–192
recommended actions for applying, 192–193
tactics for influencing others to take action, 176
word of caution, 194

Communicating Like Broadcasters, 221, 255–264
characteristics of, 256, 258
Guidelines for Connecting with Other (Maxwell), 256, 257
importance and benefits of , 255–256
leading examples
leadership development breakfast club, 258–259
sharing leadership at the corporate office, 259–260
sharing technical expertise, 256–258
practice summary, 260, 261
recommended actions for applying, 260, 261–262
word of caution, 260

Comparative need, 28

Competency, 5

Contingency theory, 13

Control
benefits of giving, 76
command and, 79–80
erodes relationship, 76–77

Creativity, leadership ego and, 48

Cultural results, 30–32

D

Daniels, Bill, 37

Decision-makers reacting to symptoms, 132

Desired results, 26–35
business results, 33–35
immediate results, 27–30
introduction, 26
short and long-term results, 30–33
societal results, 35

Developing Like Scouts, 221
characteristics of, 246
idea activators, 246–248
idea mining, 246–248
importance and benefits of, 245–246
leading examples
college competition sponsorship, 250
starting new training department, 249–250
vendor management process, 249
practice summary, 250–251
recommended actions for applying, 251–253
tactics for generating new ideas, 248
word of caution, 253

Development process, leadership
feedback, 267
follow-up, 270
foundation, 267
friction, 268–270

Diagnosing and Treating Like Doctors
balanced scorecard matrix, 139–141
characteristics of, 133, 135
importance and benefits of, 131–133
knowledge-management hypothesis example, 146

leading examples
fighting fires, diagnosing, 145–146
ineffective performers, diagnosing,
143–145
project management, diagnosing and
treating, 142–143
practice summary, 146–147
recommended actions for applying, 146,
148–149
Rummler's RIP, *see* Results Improvement
Process
word of caution, 147, 149
Diminishers, 49
Directing Like Guides, 171, 195–207
building capability, techniques for, 199–202
Bandura's Vicarious Learning, 199–200
Cognitive Apprenticeship, 199,
200–201
personal ability, tactics for influencing,
201–202
characteristics of, 196, 197
directive and supportive behaviors, 198
importance and benefits of, 195–196
leading examples
helping an aircraft maintainer build
competence, 202–203
transitioning a training department,
203–205
transitioning from academic to
business writing, 203
practice summary, 204–205
recommended actions for applying,
205–207
Situational Leadership® II
assessing abilities using, 196–198
defined, 197
examples, 198–199
leadership styles, 198
word of caution, 207
Doyle, Arthur Conan, 101
Drexler/Sibbet Team Performance Model,
184–186
Duhigg, Charles, 155–156
on finding key behaviors, 158
influencing key behaviors and,
159–161
Dweck, C. S., 62

E

Ego, leadership, 48
Eichinger R.W., 246
Emancipation, 183
Empathic (levels of listening), 230, 231
Empowerment, 48, 77–78, 183
Energy destroyers, 49
Expressed need, 28

F

Facing the Unknown Like Lions, 221
characteristics of, 224–225, 226
feedback
giving, 236
obtaining, 232–234
360°, 234–236
Goldsmith's feedforward technique,
233–234, 235
importance and benefits of, 223–224
Kouzes and Posner on receiving
feedback, 233
leading examples
Hunter's leadership assessment,
236–237
identifying annual leadership
objectives, 237–238
obtaining executive team feedback for
a general manager, 238–240
listening, serious, 225–232
discipline of active, 228
Graves' five levels of listening, 230,
231
miscommunication, 230, 232
techniques, summary of, 229–230
as undervalued, underrated and
challenging, 225–228
practice summary, 239–241
recommended actions for applying, 241,
242–243
seeking feedback, 225
360° feedback, 234–236
word of caution, 241, 243
Feedback, 87–88, 224
giving, 236
informal, 232

leadership development process, 267
   obtaining, 232–234
   receiving, 233
   results, sharing, 268
   seeking, 225
   360°, 224, 226, 234–236, 237–238
Feedback Step, 277
Feedforward technique, 233–234, 235
Felt, category of need, 28
Fixed mindset, 62–63, 64
Follett, Mary Parker, 14
Follow-up, leadership development process, 270
Forbes.com, 4
Formal roles, 6, 43–44, 181
Fortune 500, 125, 215
Foundation, leadership development process, 267
Foundation Step, 277
Freiberg, Jackie, 29, 38, 45, 46, 47, 57, 62, 65, 71, 80, 85, 221, 223, 281
Freiberg, Kevin, 29, 38, 45, 46, 47, 57, 62, 65, 71, 80, 85, 221, 223, 281
Friction, leadership development process, 268–270
Friction Step, 277
Fulfilled needs, 27–29
Fundamental attribution error, 291–294
Fundamental state, of leadership, 60
Future needs, 28
FYI (Lombardo and Eichinger), 246

G

Gallup, 23, 33–34, 54–55, 283, 284
Gibb, Jack, 184
Gilbert, Tom, 112, 116, 134
Giving Away Power (Hill), 78
Goldsmith, M., 57, 171, 210, 213, 214, 223, 226, 227, 228, 233–234, 235, 266, 267, 269, 270
Good to Great (Collins), 71
Great man theory, 13
The Grove, 179
Growth mindsets, 63, 64
Guidelines for Connecting with Other (Maxwell), 256, 257

H

Habit loop, 156
   components, 158
Hale, Judith, 67
Handshaw, Dick, 212, 214
Harkins, P., 270
Hayes, R. E., 79
Helping People Win at Work (Blanchard and Ridge), 86
The Hero with a Thousand Faces (Campbell), 46
Hill, J., 78, 80
Human performance system (HPS), 105–106, 133
   blaming performers for trouble, 106
   organizational problems, triggers for, 104
   root problems at performance levels, 108
   troubleshooting, 107
   trouble spots in, 105, 106–108
Hunter, James C., 23, 24, 27, 29, 32, 33, 45, 86, 87, 88, 89, 263, 265, 278
   on active listening, 228
   on building relationships, 32
   on building trust, 69
   leadership as knowledge and skill, 10–11
   leadership assessment, 236–237
   leadership development process, 266–270
   on selective listening, 53

I

Idea activators, 246–248
Idea killers, 49
Idea mining, 246–248
I don't know (Stage II, 21st Century Leadership Development Roadmap), 272, 277–278
   advancing to next stage, needs for, 277–278
   characteristics, 277
I don't know what I don't know (Stage IV, 21st Century Leadership Development Roadmap), 272
   advancing to next stage, needs for, 280
   characteristics, 279–280

I know (Stage I, 21st Century Leadership
    Development Roadmap), 272,
    273–277
    advancing to next stage, needs for,
        276–277
    characteristics, 273, 276
I know that I don't know (Stage III, 21st
    Century Leadership Development
    Roadmap), 272, 278–279
    advancing to next stage, needs for, 279
    characteristics, 278
Immediate results, 23, 25, 295
    fulfilled needs, 27–29
    improved performance, 30
    removed or reduced performance
        barriers, 29–30
Improving Performance (Rummler and
    Brache), 98
Individual growth results, 32–33
Influencer (Grenny et al.), 77, 82, 154, 157,
    159
Influences
    attempt to
        with one category, 115
        without collaborating other
            departments, 114–115
        without focusing on valuable
            accomplishments, 111, 113–114
    by category, 112
        action items and follow-up, 124
        creating incompetence applied to,
            114
        example themes, 122–123
        skip-level questions, 121
        troubleshooting questions, 117
    defined, 110
    usage, to optimize subsystem, 115
Informal feedback, 232
Ingroups, 66–68
Intent-Based Leadership (IBL), 181–184,
    323
Intimacy weakens leadership, 47–48
It's Your Ship (Abrashoff), 33

J

Jennings, Jason, 49, 53, 227

K

Kaizen principles, 81
Key Behaviors, Finding Like Social
    Psychologists, 151–170
    characteristics of, 153–154, 155–156
    Duhigg on, 158
        influencing key behaviors and,
            159–161
    goal statement comparison, 156
    Grenny et al. on, 157–158
        six sources of influence for influencing
            key behaviors, 159
    importance and benefits of, 151–153
    influencing and adopting new, 159–161
    leading examples, 161–167
        changing the selling process,
            163–164
        eliminating tribal knowledge, 164–167
        inspiring multidirectional
            collaboration, 161–163
    mistakes that occur when not using,
        152–153
    practice summary, 167, 168–169
    recommended actions for applying, 167,
        169–170
    setting goals and measures, 154–157
    systemic approach for, 157–158
    tactics for, 157
    word of caution, 167–168
Kirkey, Don, 152
Kouzes, James M., 1, 7, 10, 24, 33, 37, 42, 45,
    46, 79, 223, 245, 246
    on building trust, 68, 69
    on celebrations, 70–71
    on intimacy weakens leadership, 47
    on receiving feedback, 231
    on seeking feedback, 225
    on self-fulfilling prophecies, 50
    tactics for generating new ideas, 248

L

Lateral prefrontal cortex (LPFC), 59
Leader–leader structure, 20, 49, 89, 284
Leader-member exchange theory, 13
Leaders, 72, 75, 151

accidental, traditional leadership
  includes, 41–42
effectiveness of, 55
as heroes leaving legacy, 45–47
as hero myth, 46
humility and crediting others, 72
managers functioning as, 48–49
need for authority
  rationale, 43–44
  as wrong assumption, 45
as smartest, 49–50
talking is important than listening, 53–54
Leaders Eat Last (Sinek), 31, 74
Leadership, 3–4
  bidirectional, 37–38
  books on, 8
  defined, 4
  development process, 266–270
    feedback, 267–268
    follow-up, 270
    foundation, 267
    friction, 268–270
  ego, and creativity, 48
  ego discourages creativity, 48
  elusiveness of, 20–21
  giving away power weakens, 48
  intimacy weakens, 47–48
  management *vs.*, 13–19
  meaning of, 19–20
  normal state *vs.* fundamental state, 60
  practices, 86–89
    conformational and corrective
      feedback, 87–88
    developing and sustaining, 265
    knowledge, 87
    shifting from one to everyone
      practicing, 282
  quality related terms, 317–322
  reasons for confusing, 4–20
  rethinking development, 285–287
  role and, 4–7
  role *vs.*, 6–7
  as set of qualities, 7
  skill and, 10–11
  styles, theories overlap with, 12–13
  teams, 179
  in terms of qualities, 8

terms related to, 36
theories
  explaining leadership behaviors, 12
  overlap with leadership styles, 12–13
  referenced as leadership styles, 12
traditional, *see* Traditional leadership
training and, 54–55
The Leadership Challenge (Kouzes and
  Posner), 47, 248
The Leadership Contract (Molinaro), 8
Lift (Quinn and Quinn), 59
Listening, 223–224
  ineffective *vs.* good, 227
  losing focus while, 227
  serious, 225–232
    discipline of active, 228
    Graves' five levels of listening, 230,
      231
    miscommunication, 230, 232
    techniques, summary of, 229–230
    as undervalued, underrated and
      challenging, 225–228
  U.S. President engaged with, 228
Literal, meaning of, 19
Lombardo, M. M., 246
Lone Ranger, as model for leadership,
  46

M

Management
  categories of, 14–16
  defined, 14
  employees serve customers before
    serving, 72–73
  knowledge, hypothesis example, 146
  leadership *vs.*, 13–19
  vendor management process, 249
Manager
  functions as leader, 48–49
  primary role of, 83
Manager's Fallacy, 16
Managers of people, 15–16
Marquet, David L., 20, 89, 95–96, 151,
  181–184, 195, 214, 282, 284,
  285, 294; *see also* Intent-Based
  Leadership (IBL)

Maxwell, John C., 1, 3, 7, 10, 24, 32, 37, 45, 46, 48, 70, 71, 74, 89, 91, 95, 209, 255, 256, 257, 281
McKinsey & Company, 93, 284, 286
Mental qualities, maturing, 36
Mindful Leadership (Gonzalez), 8
Mindset (Dweck), 62
Mindsets, 62
    fixed, 62–63, 64
    growth, 63, 64
    shifting, 64
Miscommunication, 230, 232
Mistakes
    allowing teams to make, and learn from experience, 81
    with influencing behaviors, 111–115
    sharing, builds credibility, 70
Moral qualities, maturing, 36–37
Morgan, H., 270
Multipliers (Wiseman and McKeown), 30, 49, 64, 101

N

Needs
    categories of, 28–29
    fulfilled, 27–29
Neuroscience for Organizational Change (Scarlett), 58
Normal state, of leadership, 60
Normative need, 28
Nurturing Like Gardeners, 171, 209–219
    characteristics of, 211, 212
    Handshaw and performance-support solutions, 212–214
    importance and benefit of, 209–211
    leading examples
        establishing department standards, 215–216
        making managers more accessible by changing the space, 216–217
        performance support, using job aids for, 214–215
    physical space as source of influence, 211
    practice summary, 217–218
    recommended actions for applying, 218–219

    structural ability tactics, 211–212
    word of caution, 219
Nuts! (Freiberg and Freiberg), 38

O

Organization
    building teams with diversity and inclusion, 285
    challenges, for influencing teams, 282
    clint analyzing, 125–126
    problems, triggers for, 104
    rethinking leadership development, 285–287
    strategy portfolio, managing, 283
        competitive advantage of employees practice leadership, 283–284
        form, monitor and refine strategies, 284–285
    systems, laws of, 98–101
Organizational charts, 99
    limit thinking, 82–84
    purposes of, 82
    simplified, 83
Organization managers, 15
Outgroups, 66–68

P

Pareto principle, 155
Participative theory, 13
Partnership results, 32
Passive (levels of listening), 230
Performance
    anatomy, human performance system and, 101–108
    extraordinary, requirements for, 177–178
    improving, with systemic thinking, 93–94
Performance Chain Model, 108–110
    examples, 109
    overview, 109–110
Performance Design Lab, 97
Performance Improvement Journal, 35
Performance needs, 16
Performance results, 26
    immediate results, 27–30
    short and long-term results, 30–33

Performance-support solutions, 212–214
  defined, 212
  Handshaw and, 212–214
  helping others with, 214
Performance Thinking Network, 109, 110
Personal ability, tactics for influencing,
    201–202
Personal accountability, questions
    promoting, 73
Physical space, as source of influence, 211
Posner, Barry Z., 1, 7, 10, 24, 33, 37, 42, 45,
    46, 79, 223, 245, 246
  on building trust, 68, 69
  on celebrations, 70–71
  on intimacy weakens leadership, 47
  on receiving feedback, 231
  on seeking feedback, 225
  on self-fulfilling prophecies, 50
  tactics for generating new ideas, 248
Practices, 25, 295
  defined, 9
  illustration of term, 9–10
  of 21st Century Leadership, 297–301,
    307–309
    Analyzing Like Detectives, *see*
      Analyzing Like Detectives
    Communicating Like Agents, *see*
      Communicating Like Agents
    Communicating Like Broadcasters, *see*
      Communicating Like Broadcasters
    Developing Like Scouts, *see*
      Developing Like Scouts
    Diagnosing and Treating Like Doctors,
      see Diagnosing and Treating Like
      Doctors
    Directing Like Guides, *see* Directing
      Like Guides
    Facing the Unknown Like Lions, *see*
      Facing the Unknown Like Lions
    Finding Key Behaviors Like Social
      Psychologists, *see* Key Behaviors,
      Finding Like Social Psychologists
    Nurturing Like Gardeners, *see*
      Nurturing Like Gardeners
Pretending (levels of listening), 230, 231
Primary and support processes, mapping,
    125–126

Principles of 21st Century Leadership, 25,
    38–39, 295, 297–301
  believing in others, 60–65
    everyone practice leadership
      regardless of role, 65
    intelligence isn't static, 64–65
  collaborate with others, 82–86
    influence comes from all directions,
      85–86
    leadership doesn't reside with one
      person, 85
    leadership works with all populations,
      86
    organizational charts limit thinking,
      82–84
    problems from systemic perspective
      minimizes using blame, 84–85
  connect with others, 65–71
    being vulnerable and building trust,
      68–70
    celebrations build community, 70–71
    psychological safety, 66
    sharing mistakes builds credibility,
      70
  developing leadership practices
    continuously, 86–89
    helping others learn leadership, 89
    knowing everything about leadership
      isn't enough, 88–89
    practicing leadership and monitor
      effectiveness, 87–88
  encourage growth, 80–82
    developing those around you, 80
    leaving current role contributes to
      organizational growth, 80–81
    making mistakes and learning from
      experience, 81
  give up control, 76–80
    command and control, 79–80
    control erodes relationship, 76–77
    empowering others makes you
      indispensable, 78–79
    leading well is about empowering
      others, 77–78
  put others first, 71–75
    claiming responsibility when things go
      wrong, 73

employees serve customers before
serving management, 72–73
recognizing others for
accomplishments, 71–72
sacrificing to help others, 75
serving others and not oneself, 74
Process
defined, 9
illustration of term, 9–10
recognition as formal, 54
Process managers, 15
Psychological safety, 66

Q

Quality(ies)
defined, 5
leadership as set of, 7
moral, maturing, 36–37
related terms, 317–322
Quinn, R. E., 59
Quinn, R. W., 59

R

Recognition
as formal process, 54
others for their accomplishments, 71–72
Redknapp, Jamie, 19
Reinventors (Jennings), 53
Relationships
control erodes, 76–77
difficult to maintain without trust, 69
Results
business, 25, 26, 33–35
cultural, 30–32
defined, 26
desired, 26–35
individual growth, 32–33
partnership, 32
performance, 26–35
immediate results, 27–30
short and long-term results, 30–33
short- and long-term, 25, 30–33
societal, 25, 26, 35
Results Improvement Process (RIP),
132–133, 154

barriers determined and changes
specified, 136–138
example activities, 137
changes designed, developed, and
implemented, 138–141
balanced scorecard matrix, 139–141
example treatments, 138
desired results determined and project
defined, 134–136
data-gathering techniques and
function, 136, 137
result gaps at the three performance
levels, 136
introduction of, 133–134
result evaluated and maintained or
improved, 142
Ridge, G., 86, 173
Robinson, Alan G., 246, 247
Role
actions and, 5
formal, 6, 43–44, 181
leadership *vs.*, 6–7
practicing leadership regardless of, 65
qualities and, 5, 7
in sociological terms, 4–5
teacher's, 5
Rummler, Geary A., 31, 82, 83, 93–94, 97,
98, 99, 106, 132; *see also* Results
Improvement Process (RIP)

S

Sacrifice
examples, from different career levels, 75
to help others, 74–75
Scarlett, Hilary, 58, 59, 62, 67, 68
Schroeder, Dean M., 246, 247
Selective listening, 53, 231
Self-fulfilling prophecies, 50
Serious Performance Consulting (Rummler),
93–94, 133–134
The Servant (Hunter), 10–11, 27, 86, 263, 265
Servant leadership theory, 13
Short and long-term results, 25, 30–33, 295
cultural results, 30–32
individual growth results, 32–33
partnership results, 32

Sinek, Simon, 14, 16, 17, 31, 32, 33, 45, 49–50, 69, 79, 96, 151
Situational Leadership® II (SLII®), 272
  assessing abilities using, 196–198
  defined, 197
  directive and supportive behaviors, 198
  examples, 198–199
  leadership styles, 198
Situational theory, 13
Six Boxes® Model, 97, 108–109, 110–116, 120, 133, 283
  alignment between the influence sources and, 159
  nine examples of 26 influence tactics align to, 160
  overview, 110–111
  troubleshooting with, 116, 117
  usage of, 111
Six Sources of Influence™, 94, 159, 201, 211
Skill
  defined, 5
  development levels, 11
  leadership and, 10–11
Skip-level dialogues, opportunities through, 120–124
Societal results, 25, 26, 35, 285
Southwest Airlines, 31, 38, 47, 85
Stadlin, Art, 120
Star Wars movie, 46
Storytelling, 69–70
Structural ability tactics, 211–212, 213
System barrier, 29
Systemic thinking, 93–94, 97

T

Team members
  cannot be trusted, 51–52
  as cause of unproductivity, 50–51
  less important than revenue, profit, operational costs, and leaders, 52–53
Teams, 70
  allowing, to make mistakes and learn from experience, 81
  building with diversity and inclusion, 285

knowledge sharing across, 186–187
  leadership, 179
  point of clarification between groups and, 179
Technology, Entertainment, Design (TED) talk, 16, 17
Ten Virtues of Outstanding Leaders (Gini and Green), 8
The 21 Irrefutable Laws of Leadership (Maxwell), 10
360° feedback, 224, 226, 234–236, 237–238, 287, 311–315
Tichy, Noel, 86
Traditional leadership
  assumptions, *see* Assumptions, traditional leadership
  defined, 41
  extreme case of, 42
  includes accidental leaders, 41–42
  reasons for practice, 42
Trait, defined, 5
Trait theory, 13
Transactional or managerial theory, 13
Transformational theory, 13
The True Test of Leadership, 282
Trust
  building, 66, 68–70
  getting to know others builds, 69–70
  without, difficult to maintain relationships, 69
Turn the Ship Around! (Marquet), 184
21st Century Leadership, 263, 283
  advancing, 287–289
  behaviors, maturing, 37
  bidirectional, 37–38
  capabilities, maturing, 37
  defined, 24–25, 285
  desired results, 26–35
    business results, 33–35
    immediate results, 27–30
    introduction, 26
    short and long-term results, 30–33
    societal results, 35
  development roadmap, 270, 272–273
    I don't know (Stage II), 272, 277–278

I don't know what I don't know
(Stage IV), 272, 279–280
I know (Stage I), 272, 273–277
I know that I don't know (Stage III),
272, 278–279
to sustain your journey, 280
immediate results, 25, 27–30, 285
introduction, 23–24
mental qualities, maturing, 36
moral qualities, maturing, 36–37
opportunities for supporting, 271
practices, *see* Practices
terms related to, 36

U

Understanding Command and Control
(Alberts and Hayes), 79
Unlabeled Leadership, 67

V

Vicarious Learning, 199–200
VisuaLeadership (Cherches), 230
Vital behaviors, 82, 155
Vulnerability, 66

W

Wants, 29
Wiseman, Liz, 1, 30, 33, 45, 49, 50, 65, 81,
84, 99, 101, 195, 285
Work-life imbalance, 31
*The World's Most Powerful Leadership
Principle* (Hunter), 236

Y

Young, Arthur M., 184

Acknowledgments

I am grateful for my parents, Donald and Betsy, family, friends, and colleagues who supported my decision to write this book. In April 2014, I had lunch with Jim Hill, who encouraged me to think big. At the time, he referred to starting a consulting practice, and I don't think that he realized how our talk would inspire me to write this book. Several conversations and email exchanges with colleagues nudged me forward: Roger Addison, Guy Wallace, Judith Hale, Rhea Norwood, Lynn Kearny, Jennifer Eichenberg, Carl Binder, Joel Rodriguez, and of course, Edwin Muzio.

I'm particularly thankful to Dick Handshaw and the Handshaw™ Team for providing me with enough contract work to make ends meet while writing this book. The Handshaw Team, Brent Jennings, Beth Hughs CPT, Kim Caldwell, Chris Adams, and Peter Engels, gracefully allowed me to use their offices to finalize the book. Dick Handshaw is not only a colleague and a friend, but he has also made substantial contributions to the performance-improvement field by writing about the integration of instructional systems design with performance consulting.

Like Dick, Donald L. Kirkey, EdD, is a colleague and a friend and has spent numerous hours discussing with me the concepts in the book. Don helped me refine the definitions, principles, beliefs, and assumptions. Also, like Dick, he allowed me to work in his personal office to write part of this book. Don's pursuits of scholarly research, practical applications, and love of reading books serve him well, and I have benefited likewise.

Tami X. McNally has been extremely helpful with technical editing. She helped improve my writing capability, coached me on how to improve my writing style, and improved the flow of several chapters.

Tara McGarity with Skillsoft has been supportive as well. Tara helped me obtain access to Books24×7 so that I could validate some references.

Through the Books24×7 website, I learned about L. David Marquet's book and watched several of his short videos referenced in this book.

Over the years, I have found Books24×7 to be an excellent source for research and professional development.

In June 2014, I presented to the Hampton Roads ISPI Chapter on maturity models and the 21st Century Leadership Development Roadmap. Bill Piersol attended the talk. Not only did Bill introduce me to the evolving C2 concept, but he also mailed me a copy of Alberts and Hayes' book, which I included in my meta-analysis. I sincerely appreciate what Bill did for me, and I appreciate his stewardship.

While at the University of Alabama at Birmingham, I completed several linguistic courses taught by Edwin Battistella. Some of what he taught stuck with me and helped shape Chapter 1. I wasn't confident with what I wrote, and I am grateful to Edwin for providing feedback on improving the chapter and some general aspects of the book.

Some time ago, I had the privilege to act as an interim manager for a small team of professionals: Brooke Leslie, Erin Finke Ridolfo, Jessica Checca, Jessica M. Baker, Lindsay Butler, and Shardae Brown. Maybe without realizing it, the team modeled how Marquet's leader-leader structure worked in the business world and inspired me to advocate for that structure.

Thanks again to all these people for their support, stewardship, and kindness. I couldn't have written this book without their leadership.

Author

Gary A. DePaul helps individuals, teams, business units, and organizations build leadership capabilities through consulting, keynotes, podcasts, and publications. With more than 20 years of practitioner and academic experience in the fields of Performance Improvement, Human Resources, and Talent Development, Gary shares what he has learned with thousands of practitioners.

Practitioner Experience

Gary has served executives and teams in international and national organizations, including Lowe's Companies Inc., Ceridian Benefits Services, Fidelity Information Services, Johnson Controls Inc., and Arthur Andersen LLP. He has held several formal roles, including senior manager of training and knowledge management, senior instructional designer, Performance-improvement director, and workforce readiness manager.

Academic and Credential Experiences

At the University of Illinois at Urbana-Champaign, Gary completed his PhD and EdM through the Department of Educational Organization and Leadership. He completed his bachelor's degree in history and philosophy from the University of Alabama at Birmingham. The International Society for Performance Improvement designated him a certified performance technologist (CPT).

Speaker and Publication Experience

Gary has curated and shared leadership and performance-improvement insights through keynotes and workshops for companies and at conferences.

He has guest lectured at Notre Dame's Mendoza College of Business and presented to association chapters, including:

- International Coach Federation (ICF)
- Project Management Institute (PMI)
- The Association for Talent Development (ATD)
- The International Society for Performance Improvement (ISPI)
- The Society for Human Resource Management (SHRM)
- The Society for Technical Communication (STC)

Gary has written performance-improvement articles for *PerformanceXpress.com* and *Performance Improvement Journal*. In *The Trainer's Portable Mentor*, he co-authored an article with Donald L. Kirkey on formative evaluation. While in graduate school at the University of Illinois at Urbana-Champaign, Gary was one of many co-authors of two evaluation articles published under the mentorship of Robert Stake. Gary has self-published two books: *The Most Effective and Responsible Clinical Training Techniques in Medicine* and *What the Heck Is Leadership and Why Should I Care?* He is also the author of *The HRBP Report Series*.

In addition, Gary is the host of Unlabeled Leadership, a podcast series designed to demystify *leadership* through the stories and insights from his guests.

Academic Work

Gary is an Adjunct Professor at the University of North Carolina at Charlotte. As part of the Learning, Design and Technology Program in the Department of Educational Leadership, Gary teaches graduate students about leadership and management.

Contact Information

If you are interested in contacting Gary about speaking or consulting, you can contact him through his website or by email:

www.garyadepaul.com
unlabeledleadership.com
gary@garyadepaul.com

Printed in the United States
by Baker & Taylor Publisher Services